JEWISH COUNTRY HOUSES

EDITED BY JULIET CAREY
AND ABIGAIL GREEN

PHOTOGRAPHY BY HELENE BINET

JEWISH COUNTRY HOUSES

Brandeis University Press
Waltham, Massachusetts

Published with generous support from
the Martin J. Gross Family Foundation

Published in association with the National Trust

Contents

Acknowledgements. 6

A Jewish and a European story 8
Abigail Green, Tom Stammers and Juliet Carey
with Silvia Davoli and Jaclyn Granick

A combination of many visions 38
Hélène Binet

CHAPTER 1
The stories we tell: Salomons Estate. 42
Tom Stammers and Abigail Green

CHAPTER 2
Hughenden Manor: a home for a prime minister 58
Robert Bandy

CHAPTER 3
The Château de Ferrières: a European powerhouse. 80
Pauline Prevost-Marcilhacy

CHAPTER 4
In Walpole's footsteps: Lady Waldegrave at Strawberry Hill 96
Nino Strachey

CHAPTER 5
Playing with the past at Waddesdon Manor 118
Juliet Carey

CHAPTER 6
Two houses, two countries, one cosmopolitan family:
Torre Alfina and Champs-sur-Marne 144
Alice S. Legé

CHAPTER 7
Agriculture et ars: Villa 'La Montesca' in Città di Castello. 160
Luisa Levi D'Ancona Modena

CHAPTER 8
Kérylos: 'the Greek Villa' 184
Henri Lavagne (translated by Abigail Green)

CHAPTER 9
Schloss Freienwalde:
the Jewish restoration of a Prussian legacy. 206
Martin Sabrow (translated by Abigail Green)

CHAPTER 10
Nymans: an English house and garden 228
John Hilary

CHAPTER 11
Max Liebermann's villa at Lake Wannsee: a public retreat 248
Lucy Wasensteiner

CHAPTER 12
From the palatial to the modern:
industry and luxury in Habsburg Europe .270
Petr Svoboda

CHAPTER 13
Trent Park: a house under German occupation 298
Helen Fry

CHAPTER 14
An American postscript 312
Juliet Carey and Abigail Green

Exploring the traces 324
Abigail Green
with Juliet Carey, Silvia Davoli, Jaclyn Granick and Tom Stammers

Endnotes 332
Biographies 346
Index 347
Picture credits 350

Acknowledgements

This book owes everything to the vision and commitment of three extraordinary people: James Pullen, our heroic agent, without whom it would never have got past first base; Ruth Ur, whose brilliant idea it was to bring us together with Hélène Binet, and who worked so hard to set things up for all of us; and Briony Truscott, our fantastic project administrator, whose tireless efforts have supported us throughout and enabled us to pull everything together at the end.

The Jewish Country Houses project is a very special intellectual partnership, and it has come to mean a great deal to everyone involved. It was Juliet who initiated the project when she started thinking about Waddesdon as a Jewish country house and realised that it could only be understood in relation to other such houses. Since then, this project has grown beyond anything we could have imagined, and this book would not have been possible without the involvement of us all: the other members of the core team, Silvia Davoli, Jaclyn Granick and Tom Stammers, who have all assisted with the editorial process; Marcus Roberts, co-curator of the *Country Houses, Jewish Homes* exhibition; Luisa Levi D'Ancona Modena, whose deep knowledge of the Italian context feeds into every aspect of the project; and Oliver Cox, who first thought to introduce the two of us, when – at Juliet's request – he organised an exploratory workshop at Waddesdon. Above all, we would like to thank Hélène Binet and her assistant Jasmine Bruno, for making this a book of beauty as well as learning.

Like all books, this one also owes everything to our publishers: Andrew Franklin at Profile and Sue Ramin at Brandeis, both of whom have taken this project to their hearts, and Christopher Tinker at the National Trust, which has embraced the Jewish Country Houses project so warmly. More specifically, we would like to thank Eleanor Ridsdale, who designed the book so beautifully; Angela Koo for her extraordinary efforts readying the book for publication; Peter Jones and Caroline Clark for their endless flexibility and willingness to go the extra mile; and Sylvia Fuks Fried for thinking through what this book means on the other side of the Atlantic. The National Trust also gratefully acknowledges a generous bequest from the late Mr and Mrs Kenneth Levy, which has supported the cost of preparing this book through its Cultural Heritage Publishing programme.

Books like this depend on many people who support them behind the scenes. We would like to thank the late Lord Rothschild, Pippa Shirley and the Rothschild Foundation at Waddesdon, where we held part of the conference that underpins this book, for their support of both it and the Jewish Country Houses project in general, as well as a number of Juliet's colleagues at Waddesdon who have helped in various ways. We would also like to thank Barbara Zweifel for organising the first of many JCH conferences; Jenny Lebard and Bernard Le Magoarou at the Centre des Monuments Nationaux for making it possible for us to hold a conference at

Kérylos, from which we have also drawn a chapter; Jana Hunter, for her work on the manuscript; James Stevenson and Ken Jackson at Cultural Heritage Digitisation for the new photography in the Salomons chapter; Gillian Chandler and Philip Parker at Brasenose, and Jane Smith in the Oxford History Faculty, for always going the extra mile. In addition, we would like to thank all our colleagues at Brasenose and Waddesdon for helping us to free up the time and mental space it took to make this book. We are particularly sad that Lord Rothschild did not live to see it.

This is merely the tip of the iceberg. Besides those who have written for this volume (and often contributed in other ways to the project), we would like to thank all those who presented at our conferences, as well as Rebecca Abrams, Natalie Attwood, Fabrizio Boldrini, Philippe Bélaval, John Bowers, Boaz Brosh, Caroline Carey, Justin Cavernelis-Frost, Heather Dawson-Mains, Amanda-Jane Doran, Adam Eaker, Heather Ewing, Ewald Frie, Sasha Goldstein-Sabbah, Rebecca Graham, Cyril Grange, Charlotte Green, Christopher Green, Justin Gunter, Rebecca Hagen, Assumpció Hosta, Celia Hughes, Chris Jones, Michele Klein, Rebecca Kobrin, Jarosław Kurski, Michelle Leake, Laura Leibman, Philippe Malgouyres, Peter Mandler, Chris McKenna, Florian Medici, Olga Medvedkova, John Montiel, Llewelyn Morgan, Alan Perkin, Scott Perkins, Aubrey Pomerance, Lucy Porten, Alice Purkiss, Derek Purnell, David Rechter, Chris Rowlin, Reinhard Schmook, Justina Sebag-Montefiore, Michael Shrive, Mark Sladen, Victor Sorenssen, Catherine Taylor, Katrien Timmers and Antide Viand.

The research behind this project has been enabled by many different kinds of funding and practical support: the Jeffrey Fund at Brasenose College, which supported the initial scoping project and final photography work; Abigail's AHRC Leadership Fellowship, 'Liberalism and the Jews: an International History' (AH/N00631/1), the John Fell Fund at the University of Oxford, and the Paul Mellon Centre for British Art, which provided initial seed-funding for the first conference that underpins this book; TORCH at the University of Oxford, which helped us develop the project through two Knowledge-Exchange Partnerships, and also helped to finance our work with Hélène Binet through the Creative Industries and Business Engagement and Partnerships Seed Funds, as did the Brasenose College Research Fund and the Montefiore Endowment, while the Czech National Heritage Institute and the Museum of the City of Brno – Villa Tugendhat supported it in other ways; the Leverhulme Foundation, which awarded Abigail a Senior Research Fellowship that has made it easier for her to bring this project to completion; and of course the AHRC Research Grant, 'Jewish Country Houses – Objects, Networks, People' (AH/S006656/1), which has enabled us to take the Jewish Country Houses project to a whole new level, in partnership with the AEPJ, the National Trust, Strawberry Hill House and Waddesdon Manor. Our thanks to all for this invaluable support.

Throughout this period, a series of other conferences – organised in partnership with, and supported by, the Centre des Monuments Nationaux, the Musée Nissim de Camondo, the Domaine de Seneffe, the Czech National Heritage Institute with its branch Methodological Centre of Modern Architecture in Brno, the Wiener–Anspach Foundation and Brasenose College – have further enriched our thinking. In particular, we should mention the conference at Brno, funded by the Claims Against Germany Conference (G-2301-37264 and G-2006-27260), which brought the Holocaust dimensions of this story into sharp relief.

Finally, we would like to thank Marty Gross, whose passion for books, learning and culture has inspired him to support this book and many others. Scholarship needs more such benefactors.

Juliet Carey and Abigail Green

A Jewish and a European story

Abigail Green, Tom Stammers and Juliet Carey
with Silvia Davoli and Jaclyn Granick

Little remains of East Cliff Lodge, a country house overlooking the English Channel that was, for over fifty years, one of the undisputed centres of the Jewish world.[1] For that elegant Gothic Revival mansion, with its Regency spires, Italianate glasshouse and romantic chalk tunnels descending to the sea, was home to Sir Moses Montefiore: the pre-eminent Jewish leader of his age, whose quasi-diplomatic missions in the cause of international Jewish relief rendered him one of the first global celebrities.[2] In his lifetime, Montefiore was honoured for combining strict Jewish observance with all the attributes of the English gentleman. Here, on the outskirts of Ramsgate, he and his wife Judith created a home in which the different cultures that

Leisured aristocracy

and Dissenters, should be granted political rights. In London, Montefiore attended Bevis Marks Synagogue, tucked away in a private courtyard because, when it opened in 1701,

Jews had only recently been readmitted to Britain and were forbidden from building on the high street. Today, the little synagogue near East Cliff (shown opposite and on the following pages) is hidden between suburban housing estates, accessible via a narrow footpath marked by ivy-covered gateposts (see p. 331). Back then, it was out and proud: built like a Regency townhouse and, in due course, adorned with a chiming clock. As Paul Goodman, one of Montefiore's earliest biographers, noted, the 'typically English connexion between manor-house and parish church – which has no parallel in modern Jewry – has found at Ramsgate a Jewish setting'.[4]

Sticklers might beg to differ, or read into Goodman's assertion the typical inability of an Estonian-born Jew to understand English society. In architectural terms, East Cliff seems perhaps to resemble a seaside villa more than a country house, freighted with the associations that term has acquired over centuries, whether as a feudal 'manor' at the heart of an agricultural estate, a seat of dynastic power anchoring a family over generations in a specific landscape and community, or an emblem of taste and gentlemanly virtue in an arcadian setting. Yet despite its modest proportions, with only 24 acres of arable land, East Cliff Lodge (see p. 14) was deemed sufficiently prestigious to figure as the 'Seat of Lord Keith' in an 1805 volume of the *Beauties of England*.[5] Proximity to business, parliament and high society rendered a London townhouse an indispensable asset both for members of the aristocracy and new money, where alternative tastes, aspirations and

never the essential accoutrement of political or social status they remained in Europe.[14] Ultimately, however, the Jewishness of all such houses inhered not in matters of style but in how they were used and perceived, and ultimately how they and their proprietors were remembered. To interpret such houses properly, we need to read them side by side.

Existing scholarship dwells on particular properties, on particular families, or on particular national case studies.[15] In this introduction we survey the whole of Europe to explore the story of such houses: the people who bought, built or renovated them; their architectural and artistic features; their estates and hinterlands; their connection to Jewish politics and philanthropy; and their ambiguous place in European culture and society. If our examples are biased towards Britain, then that reflects the fact that nowhere else did the country house become so invested with ideas of national character and continuity, and nowhere else does it retain the same symbolic importance today.[16] The rest of the book is constructed as a series of case studies, drawn from houses open to the public, each of which tells a very specific story about a family or a place. That means this is not simply a book about country houses; it is also a book about Jewish memory in post-Holocaust Europe: something we elaborate in a little more detail at the end.

Homes, but rarely principal residences, the houses in this book always had both private and public dimensions – even in the United States, where most country homes appeared to be more overtly family spaces. No house existed in isolation, and the owner's aesthetic choices acquire meaning in relation to other houses, and how they too were inhabited: sometimes in the same county, sometimes on another continent. Individually, these buildings and their stories are fascinating. Collectively, they reveal a hidden thread running through the history of modern Europe that amounts to more than the sum of their parts.

Emancipation, land and power

'Jewish' country houses have escaped systematic study because they do not fit existing paradigms of the aristocratic landowner and the metropolitan Jew.[17] Such houses were, in fact, to be found in many parts of late nineteenth- and early twentieth-century Europe, often clustered within easy reach of capital cities or near exclusive seaside and spa resorts: prodigy houses and private retreats, houses at the heart of agricultural estates and waterside villas, houses for hunting, and houses created to show off art collections or to stage lavish entertaining. In a society that had historically barred Jews from landownership and often confined them to urban ghettos, all such properties had a transgressive quality. They reveal not just the aspirations of their owners but the extent to which Jewish emancipation recast established hierarchies and reshaped European society and culture as it did so. In short, these houses cannot simply be understood as symbols of wealth, power and exploitation because, uniquely, they also served as a vehicle for the emancipation of a historically persecuted and disadvantaged minority.

Historians of class often forget that religion was hardwired into the European *ancien régime*: a world in which the landed aristocracy remained an essential pillar of the social and political order. All religious minorities experienced inequality, and often persecution, but the position of Jews as a pan-European, non-Christian minority was exceptional.[18] Only limited comparisons can be drawn with, for example, British Catholics, so long shut out from the Anglican establishment, whose nineteenth-century houses celebrated Magna Carta and a lost 'gothic' liberty.[19] Not only were there Catholics in the House of Lords, but Catholic houses also laid claim to deep roots within the national past in a way that Jewish houses could not.

With the exception of the Netherlands, Jewish residence had been regulated across pre-revolutionary Europe, where Jews were excluded both from the nobility and from owning real estate. Like Doornburgh, a property on the Vecht River, the first Jewish country houses were consequently to be found in Holland, the

Anonymous, *Publish'd for Mr Foreskin at the great pair of breeches in the Parish of Westmter*, 1753, etching and engraving. This satire on the Jewish Naturalisation Act ('Jew Bill') suggests that the Duke of Cumberland (who supported the bill) is to be circumcised or castrated. Drawing on antisemitic stereotypes, a Jew kneels in front of a chest of money, two Jews behind him conversing. One says, 'We can buy Estates now'; the other adds 'Ah, & have places, too.'

property of seventeenth-century Sephardic merchants.[20] The Dutch financiers who settled in late seventeenth- and eighteenth-century Britain were also among the first Jews to acquire country houses, but considerable legal ambiguity remained over whether Jews could own freehold land without converting, and hence transmit these houses to their heirs.

The Jewish Naturalisation Act (1753; see satire above) represented an attempt to remove this uncertainty: it prompted riots on the streets of London and had to be repealed. The Jewish financier Samson Gideon was a key figure in this episode; his purchase of Belvedere House in Kent apparently motivated his support for the Act. Its failure led him to cut formal ties with the Jewish community. He returned his Jewish brokers' licence, never again publicly attended synagogue, and had his son baptised when he discovered that as a Jew he was barred from acquiring a title. Nevertheless, a few prosperous Jews did risk the legal uncertainty and acquired estates stretching westward along the Thames, notably Isleworth (Moses Hart), Mortlake (Naphtali Franks), Merton (Asher Goldsmid) and Roehampton (Benjamin

Goldsmid).[21] Tellingly, Goldsmid registered this property in the name of a Christian employee.[22] When his nephew Isaac Lyon Goldsmid bought East Tytherley Manor, he too registered it in the name of his steward. After the law changed in 1831, this grasping man refused to give up the property, and eventually kept half.[23] Locals remembered these struggles. Nearly 200 years later, a plaque in Connaught Gardens, Sidmouth, described Emanuel Baruh Lousada of nearby Peak House as 'a wealthy retired Jew, and the first of his race to risk owning land in England'.[24] That was inaccurate, but there was truth in the memory all the same.

This very specific chronology helps to explain why Jewish country houses are so little implicated in histories of slave ownership.[25] The situation in the colonies was different, but the uncertainty around Jewish landownership in Britain meant that Jewish families whose fortunes were strongly linked to slavery could not simply follow the example of merchants like the Lascelles and Hibberts by buying into the landed gentry. For West Indian Jews like Manasseh Masseh Lopes of Maristow House, country-house ownership was a stepping stone not just to politics but, inevitably, to conversion.[26] Only at Peak House, which belonged to his relatives the Lousadas, did the histories of Jewish and slave emancipation really intersect, when the second Emanuel Lousada inherited several hundred enslaved people around the time of the Slavery Abolition Act (1833). For this he was generously compensated while the enslaved people themselves received nothing. Ten years later, he would become the second English Jew to serve as a High Sheriff, but his heirs had already turned away from Judaism. In this sense, Peak House looks back to the economy of the Sephardic Atlantic, rather than forward to a future in which dynasties like the Rothschilds were able to integrate into the landed world of the British aristocracy without either assimilating or marrying out.[27]

Except in France, European Jews fought for emancipation not into a society of more or less equal citizens but into a society that remained in part a society of orders. Everywhere, noble estates had a specific legal status, which usually brought specific political rights. In Austria, the ability of Jews to own land remained uncertain long after the 1781 Edict of Toleration (*Toleranzpatent*). In 1789, Emperor Joseph II had clarified the law in the Jews' favour, but these changes met with such stiff opposition from the Lower Austrian nobility that within twenty years they were comprehensively revoked.[28] Throughout the German-speaking lands of Central Europe, resistance to Jewish liberties turned on the question of landownership, and the ability of Jews to join the corporate bodies of the provincial nobility, known as 'estates'. Writing in the mid-1860s, Fanny Lewald recounts how the Westphalian knights (*Ritterschaft*) failed to prevent Jakob Löb, a practising Jew, from admittance to the Provincial Estates (*Kreistag*) after he acquired Schloss Caldenhof, near Hamm in the Ruhr.[29] Meanwhile, the Moravian Estates rejected a 40,000-*Gulden* sweetener and refused Salomon von Rothschild's request to purchase land in the area, prompting him to acquire Schillersdorf in Prussian Silesia instead (see Chapter 12).[30]

Ultimately, Jewish country houses only became viable once issues around Jews owning real estate were resolved. This process began earlier in revolutionary France and its sister republics, continuing, for example, in Napoleonic Italy. In Central Europe, Jews were barred from holding land until the revolutions of 1848, or the emancipation legislation of the 1860s. Thereafter things changed rapidly. Jews had been legally barred from settling in Lower Austria before the constitution of 1867 asserted freedom of residence as a universal civil right. Within eight years, Albert von Rothschild had become the largest landowner in that area; eventually Emperor Franz Josef was forced to receive him at court: an honour he never accorded other Habsburg Jews with noble titles, of whom there were now quite a few.[31] This reminds us that the emancipation process was never linear, but marked instead by contingency, partial gains and sudden reversals.[32] Jewish estates were smaller in other parts of Austria, but the transfer of land was significant. By 1876, Jews owned no fewer than 289 estates in Habsburg Galicia, rising to 561 by World War One, when they represented 22 per cent of all Galician landowners.[33] In Russia, however, Jews were still classed as a group apart. Families like the Poliakovs and Efrons may have been ennobled after years devoted to working with the government; formally, they remained unemancipated Jews into the early twentieth century.

Politics lay at the heart of this transformation because land was intimately linked to the exercise of political power. Throughout the nineteenth century, many parliamentary deputies continued to rely on the local influence that came with landownership for election. Jews understood this perfectly. In 1841, for example, Anselm von Rothschild wrote to his brother-in-law Lionel to say that, with the brothers now established as Buckinghamshire squires, he hoped 'in a year or two to be able to congratulate you on a seat in Parliament & to admire your eloquent speeches'.[34] Several Rothschilds would indeed represent Buckinghamshire constituencies over the years. In Italy and France too, Jews like Leopoldo Franchetti (Chapter 7) and Théodore Reinach (Chapter 8) were elected to their respective national parliaments by the communities where their country seats were located. To own an estate was a way of acquiring an 'interest' in the country; with ownership came a new set of social relations and responsibilities.

Large houses with large lands entailed a large workforce, whose management and conditions became part of the landowners' concern. There were plenty of Yiddish-speaking farmworkers and officials on the manorial estates in eastern Galicia where the historian Lewis Namier (né Ludwik Bernstein) spent his childhood, but this was exceptional.[35] Throughout rural Europe, the local population was overwhelmingly non-Jewish. Take Schenkendorf in Brandenburg, acquired in the 1890s by the Jewish press baron Rudolf Mosse.[36] Mosse's grandson George, another famous historian, later recalled that local villagers regarded his parents as 'lords of the manor'. The Mosses donated a pair of bells to the Lutheran church in 1928, incised with two of their children's names, and arranged for a village band to assemble on the terrace to serenade a complacent young George on his birthday. In a rural society still structured by Christianity, it was unusual, indeed unnerving, to see Jews presiding over the rituals of deference that still remained ubiquitous in the countryside.[37]

The localised philanthropy that was incumbent upon country-house owners went beyond inspecting the tenantry. Some Jewish landowners took a profound interest in the structural problems of the countryside. In Sweden, in 1872, wholesaler August Abrahamson created a *slöjd* (craft) school for local boys who had finished their compulsory schooling at his lakeside Nääs estate; in due course it would become an internationally renowned teacher training college, thanks to the progressive educational ideas of his nephew Otto Salomon.[38] Several decades later, Emma Zorn would support similar causes in Mora, where her husband Anders painted (see p. 20).[39] Deep in rural Umbria, the Franchettis worked energetically to modernise agriculture, stimulate handicrafts and promote education (Chapter 7). No less passionate about her tenants was Lady Desart (née Bischoffsheim), the first Jew to serve as a senator in the Irish Free State, who set up home three miles from Kilkenny, and established an entire model village at Talbot's Inch.[40]

The more established landed classes had diversified their economic interests long ago, but land remained the foundation of

Henry Barraud, *Lionel Nathan de Rothschild introduced in the House of Commons on 26 July 1858 by Lord John Russell and Mr Abel Smith*, 1872, oil on canvas. Rothschild was first elected as an MP for the City of London in 1847 but, as a Jew, refused to take an oath 'upon the true faith of a Christian' to enter the House of Commons. His seat remained empty until 1858, when the law changed so that MPs could choose between swearing on the Old or New Testament and Rothschild could take his place in parliament.

their wealth and class identity; by contrast, these Jewish houses, like those of other *nouveaux riches*, were acquired and built with city money. They carried fewer dynastic associations and could be bought and sold as easily as other commodities. Most Jewish landowners led peripatetic lifestyles, moving between several houses for different seasons for social, commercial, sporting and even medical reasons, just as non-Jews did. The richest families and individuals typically owned a townhouse and several rural retreats: a hunting box in Warwickshire and a villa on the Riviera, in the case of Lord and Lady Bearsted (see p. 22). All engaged them in new kinds of social relationship, whether as country landlords or as members of an international jet set.

Most Jewish country houses were located near capital cities and other major centres of Jewish residence, so that parliamentary or business interests could be combined with rural living. Sometimes, a house was even chosen for its relation to a specific industry. In 1890s Hungary, the Hatvany-Deutsch family built a summer house at Sárvár next to their sugar factory, the largest of its kind in Europe. Ludwig Mond, too, chose to live in Winnington Hall, directly adjoining the chemical works he had founded in Cheshire.[41] Yet often, Jews clustered together: from the first Dutch-Jewish country houses, within easy walking distance of the Portuguese synagogue in Maarssen, through the well-known grouping of British Rothschild properties in Buckinghamshire (opposite) and its Lower Austrian counterpart in the Ybbs and Erlauf valleys, to the fashionable attractions of the French Riviera, and lakeside resorts like Wannsee (Germany), Bad Ischl (Austria) and Svanemøllen (Denmark).[42] These enclaves served many functions: they offered a promise of integration and access to social and cultural worlds from which Jews had long been excluded, while protecting them from the threat of prejudice and isolation.[43] Acknowledging both his singularity and the comparative freedom he found in the Norwegian countryside, retail magnate and anti-Nazi activist Moritz Rabinowitz (see p. 23), the only Jew in Haugesund, gave his rural retreat the literal name Jødeland (Jewland).[44]

Distance from the city brought respite from work and crowds, not just for the owners, but also for their guests. The country setting was an attractive venue for hosting intimate salons or entertaining artistic friends. Hans Christian Andersen regarded the Melchiors' house Rolighed, with its stunning views out to the Swedish

Francis Grant, *'Full Cry' (The Four Sons of Baron Nathan Mayer de Rothschild Following Hounds)*, 1841, oil on canvas; hunting in the Vale of Aylesbury, Buckinghamshire, the heart of 'Rothschildshire'.

Øresund, as a 'home from home', which '[g]ave sunshine to my life and made my harp ring'.[45] Places of relaxation and recreation, such houses also provided the space needed to write, think and create. German-Jewish painter Max Liebermann installed a studio upstairs in his lakeside villa in Wannsee, where the garden was a source of constant inspiration (Chapter 11). And at Broomhill in Kent, David Lionel Salomons turned the estate into a giant laboratory, fitted out with the latest technologies (Chapter 1). Renewing the ancient connection between creativity and rural seclusion, these country houses could also foster new experiments in living, whether in terms of artistic colonies, or automobiles and electricity.

The decades after Jewish emancipation coincided with the climax of European imperialism; Jews were just as involved in global trade and the growth of empire as their non-Jewish rivals and business partners. This involved the exploitation of people and resources all over the world. In the Île-de-France, the diamond entrepreneur Jules Porgès commissioned a new Louis XVI-style château on a colossal scale, while Auguste Dreyfus (a convert to Catholicism) ploughed the money he made from Peruvian guano into the beautiful estate of Pontchartrain. In London, meanwhile, Marcus Samuel, 1st Viscount Bearsted, turned his father's business importing curios from the Far East into a giant global shipping and oil enterprise – the Shell Transport and Trading Company. The profits enabled him to buy The Mote in Kent, just as his son Walter would later acquire Upton House in Warwickshire.[46] But the world of the Jewish country house was shaped by traffic moving in both directions. There were several Jews among the so-called Randlords, capitalists who made their fortunes in South Africa. Like British-born Sir Lionel Phillips, who started out as a diamond sorter in the mines at Kimberley, they built vast mansions in the exclusive suburbs of Johannesburg before acquiring estates in Britain, allowing us to trace the evolution of imperial luxury from colony to metropole and back again.[47]

Perhaps most fascinating in this context are the repeated reinventions of the Sassoon dynasty, from their origins in Baghdad to their relocation, via Persia, to Mumbai in 1832. Here, in the suburb of Byculla, David Sassoon created Sans Souci: a classicising house that invoked the spirit of Frederick the Great's palace in Potsdam and hosted glittering receptions for the Hindu, British and Parsee elites, with a resident *schochet* (ritual slaughterer), and a *mikveh* (ritual bath) for the women of the household.[48] The country houses that his children and grandchildren subsequently acquired and restored in Britain, like sixteenth-century Ashley Park in Surrey, testify to their genius for cultural adaptation.[49] The acceptance of these Jewish 'Indians' by the British establishment

contrasts with the fate of German-Jewish families like the Monds who, despite political and commercial success, encountered virulent antisemitism and anti-German feeling, and eventually turned to Zionism. In the late 1920s, Alfred Mond built Villa Melchett on the shores of Lake Galilee in Mandate Palestine, combining neo-Ottoman with Art Deco elements (opposite top). Of all his houses, it was here that Alfred reportedly felt most at peace.[50]

The journey of the Sassoons from the Tigris to the Thames speaks to a bigger trend of westward migration. Many of the German-Jewish financiers who joined the international *haute banque* chose to settle and spend their money in Paris, acquiring houses in the French countryside.[51] The same was true of Russian Jews like the Ephrussis and the Gunzburgs, and of the Ottoman Camondos.[52]

Such trajectories serve as an important supplement to recent scholarship, which has recast the European country house as a dynamic component of increasingly globalised networks of commerce and kinship, with particular emphasis on its imperial and colonial histories.[53] For while the Jewish families whose fortunes built and transformed these houses often had global dimensions, the meaning of these houses, both for their owners and for others, continued to be dictated by their place on the old continent, at the pinnacle of quintessentially European social hierarchies. If the simultaneous possession of a townhouse remained central to Jews' professional and cultural lives, the country house bestowed upon these families a special claim to gentlemanly leisure and largesse.

Historicising houses

As homes, sites of self-fashioning and stages for different kinds of sociability, each of these houses embodied a certain vision of the world and the place of Jews within it; this vision was expressed through architecture, interiors and art collections. Differing considerably in scale and style, all these houses nonetheless articulated notions of civilisation, cultural identity and nationhood through material culture. Even new houses were often demonstrations of how well the owner understood, and could speak, the languages of various artistic traditions. At Villa Montesca (Chapter 7) that meant Florence and Venice, and a bringing together of styles representative of the triumph of Italian art; when it came to Ascott in Buckinghamshire, this meant using the architect George Devey's Arts and Crafts style to create a sense of organic continuity with the half-timbered Jacobean farmhouse at its core. As the wealth of the landed aristocracy waned, they looked to marriage with members of the industrial and financial elite, including Jews, as a means by which dilapidated estates could be returned to their former glory. In France, the fortune of Samuel Haber bankrolled renovations at the seventeenth-century Château de Courances, where the architect Gabriel-

The property portfolio of Sir Walter Samuel, 2nd Viscount Bearsted, chairman of Shell Oil, comprised: 1 Carlton Gardens in London; Phones, a grouse-shooting estate near Newtonmore in the Cairngorms, Scotland; Upton House; and the Villa 'La Serena', a modern retreat on the French Riviera.

Top left
Upton House, set high on Edge Hill, near Banbury, Warwickshire.

Bottom left
Noel Sampson, *The Garden of the Villa 'La Serena', Saint-Jean-Cap-Ferrat*, 1931, watercolour on paper.

Hippolyte Destailleur was set to work, fitting a staircase salvaged from Fontainebleau; in Britain, Sybil Sassoon's marriage in 1913 to the Earl of Rocksavage rendered her the châtelaine of Houghton Hall, which she restored to the magnificence intended by its eighteenth-century architect, William Kent.[54]

Close reading of these buildings suggests how the owners sought not just to reconstruct the historic fabric, in an archaeological sense, but also to situate themselves within it and claim it as their own. At stake in these acts of restoration were claims upon a privileged, or foundational, past, which distilled core elements of the national character, or represented a high point in European cultural achievement. For much of the nineteenth century, that high point was the Renaissance, a loosely defined period of cultural flowering in the fifteenth and sixteenth centuries with multiple Italian, French, German, Polish and English iterations. Self-consciously eclectic modern houses like Ferrières (Chapter 3) aimed to bring these different variants into conversation. Around 1900, that foundational past became the eighteenth century – primarily but not exclusively French – and once again interpreted in relation to local conditions. In this way, Jewish patrons drew upon, and customised, the fashionable lexicon of period styles; few were innovators, or desired to be. One of the chief attractions of such styles came from their flexibility, since they could be deployed in a cosmopolitan and universalising, or national and specific, manner.

Take the parallel restoration of houses in France and Belgium at the dawn of the twentieth century. The Château de Champs-sur-Marne outside Paris (Chapter 6) is a splendid example of a French eighteenth-century *maison de plaisance*, complete with Rococo and chinoiserie details, and an association with Madame de Pompadour. Its purchase by Louis Cahen d'Anvers led to an ambitious programme of restoration by Walter Destailleur.[55] The story parallels that of the Château de Seneffe in Belgium, built in a severe neoclassical style in the 1760s for the Depestre family of ennobled merchants. Acquired by the banker Franz Philippson in 1909, this château too was renovated, with a tennis court, swimming pool and English garden added to the grounds (below).[56] Intriguingly, both Philippson and Louis Cahen d'Anvers' son Charles wrote short histories of their respective estates, placing themselves at the end of a long line of previous occupants – just as the Philippson children wrote and performed plays set in the eighteenth century, in an imaginative appropriation and re-animation of the property.[57]

Opposite
Villa Kérylos

Below
Villa 'La Montesca'

Restoration projects were an implicit commentary on the past by the present, often involving reuse of original materials. At Näsby, Swedish industrialist Carl Robert Lamm was determined in 1902 to build his modernised new castle on exactly the same foundations as the original seventeenth-century mansion, ignoring architectural advice to the contrary.[58] This desire for 'authenticity' could backfire: Walther Rathenau's diligent restoration of Schloss Freienwalde (Chapter 9) attracted ridicule before World War One and antisemitic vitriol after it. Gardens raised similar questions of style and national identity, whether in their formal design – resolutely French at Champs – or the origin of their plants and trees. The garden at Nymans (Chapter 10) illustrates how successfully the exotic could be domesticated.

In these houses we can trace how Jews – so long treated as outsiders in Christian Europe – chose to lay claim to, and play with, cultural symbols hallowed by tradition, putting their own spin on what it meant to belong. The vogue for masquerade and fancy-dress balls was a manifestation of this phenomenon, as were the histories, sentimental novels and amateur theatricals that took inspiration from these spaces. Hélène de Rothschild, châtelaine of the Kasteel de Haar (below), outside Utrecht, reflected on the experience of restoring a historic estate (with the help of Rijksmuseum architect Pierre Cuypers) in her 1907 novel *Le chemin du souvenir*.[59] Relevant here too is the self-conscious, sometimes humorous way in which historic references were invoked and slyly inverted, including Christian iconography. At medieval Mottisfont Abbey, Maud Russell, daughter of German-Jewish stockbroker Paul Nelke, commissioned a set of murals from Rex Whistler: 'a kind of modern Gothic,' she specified, 'in other words 1938 Gothic decoration'. He fulfilled the brief admirably, crossing the eighteenth-century idiom of Strawberry Hill with contemporary flourishes, like a black evening glove, to create a form of heraldry packed with symbolism and modern mischief.[60]

The love of history, palpable in many of these houses, went beyond the ludic since it viewed the past in the mirror of modern preoccupations. The historical periods typically chosen for revival were all characterised by social change. Fourteenth-century Venice, fifteenth-century Florence, seventeenth-century Holland, eighteenth-century France: these were moments tied to the development of new ideas and the rise of new money. In this sense, the modern financial aristocracy was celebrating its origins, both within the nation and beyond it. Considering the international currency in historical revivals, it would be naïve to attribute any consistent political meaning to the choice of style: if some houses were oriented towards the nation in which they were found, others invoked more distant historic cultures. Patrons worked closely with architects, decorators, craftsmen, gardeners, art dealers and advisors to create the desired look, often mixing local and international expertise. The dissonance with local surroundings could be startling, at

least for contemporaries, from a Loire-style château in the middle of Buckinghamshire (Chapter 5) to the Erreras' Château du Vivier d'Oie, an eclectic spin on an Italian Renaissance palazzo outside Brussels.[61] This trend reached its acme in the orientalising flourishes at Port Lympne in Kent. The stark contrast between this house and the self-conscious Englishness of Trent Park, another of Philip Sassoon's properties (Chapter 13), illuminates the different cultural poses open to new elites at the dawn of the twentieth century.

Whatever the pull exerted by their different nations, these houses are perhaps best understood by situating them in a transnational context. We know this from studies of the Rothschild houses, which consciously recalled, conversed and competed with each other, and provided inspiration to the wealthy on both sides of the Atlantic (Chapter 14).[62] Waddesdon was the model for many Jewish and non-Jewish millionaires (think of George Vanderbilt's Biltmore), while Gutergötz in Prussia was conceived as Bleichröder's Ferrières, and Schossberger-Kastély in Hungary took inspiration from Halton Hall, Alfred de Rothschild's Buckinghamshire pile. However, when the American banker James Loeb, who was of German-Jewish descent, built Hochried in Bavaria, he opted for an architectural fusion of the Deutscher Werkbund with New England country homes from along the East Coast, like those built by McKim, Mead and White, and even echoes of Frank Lloyd Wright.[63] In short, these borrowings indicated different things in different contexts. In Central and Eastern Europe, they reinforced the pretentions of the wealthiest Jews as ennobled modernisers, demonstrating their fluency not just in vernacular styles (as true patriots), but also in western European fashions: the converted banker Leopold Kronenberg opted for a French Renaissance-style château at Brzezie in Russian Poland, whereas the complex he created at Wieniec Zdrój incorporated both an Italian Renaissance palazzo and a manor house in the English Gothic style. An increasingly mobile network of 'taste professionals',

like the Jewish architects and decorators Mewès and Davis, boasted clients in several countries, accelerating the dissemination of ideas across borders and even oceans.[64] This web of connections shows the benefits of thinking about such houses in a supra-national way.

How their Jewish owners negotiated personal and collective identities varied enormously. Yet the questions and challenges they faced were often similar, giving rise to subtle strategies to manage visibility, from the reclamation of negative tropes (as at Ferrières) to changing patterns of self-concealment and exposure.[65] In this context, even the emergence of modernism appears less of a total break. Early twentieth-century Jews were strongly associated with the European avant-gardes, including by critics determined to resist modernism as an alien import.[66] The dramatic victory of the International Style in the 1920s, though, was propelled by wartime collapse and specific national causes. With the collapse of the Habsburg empire in 1918, the language of historical styles, so closely tied to ideas of the imperial and monarchical past, lost its eloquence; elites in successor states like Czechoslovakia found in modernism an architectural declaration of independence. Looking inward to the nation and outward to a wider community, this new aesthetic – exhibited with supreme elegance at Brno (Chapter 12) but also found in Poland and in Croatia – was another solution to the challenge of Jewish self-fashioning.[67]

Exclusion and belonging

Jewishness is an elusive category and many of those who owned and lived in country houses resisted being defined by it. Some, like the Russian Lazar Poliakov and the Austrian Salomon von Rothschild, were as observant as the very English Montefiores. Others, like Walter Samuel, 2nd Viscount Bearsted, lived superficially less 'Jewish' lives in the countryside than in the metropolis. Some, like the Monds, initially moved away from Judaism, which they re-embraced against the backdrop of Nazism, but retained an interest in international Jewish causes; others, like

Rathenau and Sir Herbert Leon of Bletchley Park, sought to transcend Judaism and the stigma of their Jewish birth through atheism and liberal, rationalist politics. 'Jewish' women often faced particular choices. Some, like Frances Braham of Strawberry Hill (Chapter 4), were the Christian daughters of Jewish fathers who celebrated this Jewish heritage; others, like Sybil Sassoon, hid their Jewishness even from their children.

These pressures were particularly intense in Eastern Europe, where many families embarked on a headlong pursuit of assimilation. Within four years of converting to Catholicism in 1910, Józef Niemirowski (né Bernstein) was making plans for a neo-Gothic chapel on his estate at Koszyłowce in Galicia (see p. 15) with the painter Kazimierz Sichulski (below). Had war not broken out, he would likely have built it. As his great-grandson, Jarosław Kurski, commented in a moving family memoir, 'Józef would even have funded a cathedral, if only it would have ensured sincere, not feigned favour, or even just acceptance by the local landed gentry'.[68] Béatrice Reinach (née Camondo) showed more conviction when she embraced Catholicism in France in 1942, just over two years before she was murdered in Auschwitz, perhaps still cherishing the belief that this new faith left her 'miraculously protected'.[69]

Even in less charged circumstances, the specific difficulties faced by this group can sometimes be discerned in the material fabric of the houses themselves. Many chose to be buried in the new metropolitan cemeteries, but this was not always straightforward. In Berlin, the Rathenau family went so far as to establish a non-denominational variant in Oberschöneweide on the outskirts of Berlin, where they commissioned a mausoleum (see pp. 30–31) designed by Alfred Messel, architect of the 1890s extension to Nymans. A few, like the observant Montefiores and the secularised Cahen d'Anvers, adapted the aristocratic tradition of building a tomb on the estate (Chapter 6), a practice reinvented in a radically different context by the Kaufmanns of Fallingwater in Western Pennsylvania (Chapter 14). Other solutions were more

surprising. Isaac D'Israeli and his wife, the parents of Benjamin, were buried at Bradenham church, despite never having converted to Christianity (Chapter 2). When the only daughter of the d'Avigdor-Goldsmid family drowned in 1963, her parents buried her at All Saints' Tudeley, the parish closest to their country estate, commissioning the great Russian-Jewish artist Marc Chagall to design all twelve of its windows (opposite).[70] This beautiful space, with its hybrid religious traditions, expresses the Jewish patrons' anomalous social position.

Ultimately, the ambivalence these individuals and their families often felt towards their Jewishness reflected a harsh social reality, because the wealth that was the source of their power and privilege was also a source of peculiar vulnerability. The heyday of the 'Jewish country house' was an age of rising political antisemitism, which culminated in genocide, and this was a group for whom the myths about Jewish wealth, solidarity and power that fed antisemitic conspiracy theories had a particular salience. Contemporaries who believed they were living in a time of social decay found the emergence of this new Jewish elite deeply disturbing. In Britain,

Kazimierz Sichulski's unrealised design for the chapel at Koszyłowce in Habsburg Galicia (now Ukraine), May 1914, watercolour and gouache on paper.

the growing visibility of Jewish peers and financiers, whether in the House of Lords, from 1885 onwards, or as members of Edward VII's so-called 'Jewish court', seemed to contrast with the enfeeblement of the old, landed families, struggling to adjust to the new era of democratic politics, rocked by the collapse in rental values and an evaporating labour force in a period of agricultural depression. Taking advantage of relaxed laws on entail, many began selling off their cultural heirlooms, tracts of land and even the houses themselves. This context made the Jewish acquisition of such property especially contentious.

Fiction from the 1880s and 1890s vividly captures the fear and loathing attached to this new class of consumers. Most so-called plutocrats were not Jews, but Jews were particular targets. *The Splendid Paupers: A Tale of the Coming Plutocracy* (1894; see p. 32), by the radical journalist W. T. Stead, has as its chief protagonist a German-Jewish banker and chemist likely modelled on Ludwig Mond. Described in strongly racialised terms, 'the soul of a Jew behind the mask of a Teuton', Faulmann is presented as invading the English countryside with his lead-manufacturing business and literally poisoning inhabitants in a modern version of the medieval calumny. Later, he turns his attention to the landed aristocracy, already 'practically on the verge of liquidation', and hatches a plan to buy up their assets with his international, Jewish co-conspirators: 'whenever there is an ancient castle, or modern treasure house, or charming estate in difficulties, anywhere in the three kingdoms, they are the first to hear of it, and it is very seldom it escapes their clutches.'[71] Fifteen years later, H. G. Wells evoked similar tropes in *Tono-Bungay* (1909), when he sneered at the rise of the 'pseudomorphous' Sir Reuben Lichtenstein. Here, the difference between such Jewish parvenus and the real gentry was measured by the little changes that crept into one country house, Bladesover, 'as though everything had shivered and shrivelled a little at the Lichtenstein touch'.[72]

Continentals, too, harped on the theme of Jewish capitalists invading (and

perverting) the national heritage. In reality, French 'plutocrats' remained overwhelmingly Christian, but Édouard Drumont, author of the bestselling antisemitic diatribe *La France juive* (1886), singled out Ferrières (Chapter 3), a site now saddled with the memory of French military capitulation in 1870, as proof of the Rothschilds' illegitimate usurpation and simulation of the arts of the *ancien régime*.[73] The newspaper he founded, *La libre parole*, ran a column from the late 1890s entitled 'Châteaux d'Israel', documenting the infiltration of wealthy Jewish families into country seats around Paris associated with the monarchy or the aristocracy. In Italy around 1900, Jewish collectors were likewise accused of 'desecrating the national culture', despite the role of Jewish liberal Tullo Massarani in proposing the laws for protecting Italian national patrimony in the first place.[74]

Such discourses reached a horrific climax in the 1930s and 1940s, when the rights of Jewish owners were brutally revoked, and their houses forcibly 'returned' to Aryan ownership. In Holland, in January 1940, the estates of several English and Dutch Jews featured in the Dutch newspaper *Het Nationale Dagblad*. Among them was the

Opposite and below
The Rathenau family
tomb, Oberschöneweide,
Berlin; commissioned
by Emil Rathenau and
designed by Alfred
Messel (see Chapter
10), with sculptures by
Hermann Hahn, 1902–4.

As the founder of AEG
(see p. 207), Rathenau
acquired the land and
created the cemetery
and chapel, donating
it to the community as
part of his transformation
of the area around the
firm's headquarters.

home of art dealer Jacques Goudstikker, Nyenrode Castle: 'This now, is the democratic "blood and soil",' the article ran, 'the soil Dutch or English, the blood Jewish.' Goudstikker escaped four months later but met his death crossing the English Channel; his art collections and Nyenrode were acquired by a German banker.[75]

World War Two marked a devastating rupture in the history of Jewish country houses. On 8 September 1943, little Viviano Levi D'Ancona left Florence for San Piero in Frassino in the province of Arezzo, Casentino. The family had owned a country estate there since the 1880s. In December 1943, when the situation became too dangerous, Viviano, his grandfather and his brothers were hidden in several peasant houses on their estate. Five-year-old Viviano was placed with a former governess, whose forebears had for generations worked as peasants for the family. But as a Jewish child well known in the area, Viviano was noted and denounced by a local resident; the brothers fled, finding refuge in Switzerland at the end of January 1944. Like their home in Florence, Villa D'Ancona was deployed as a German commando base.[76]

In Italy, this story was not uncommon, and all over Europe, such houses were destroyed, seized or repurposed by Nazi perpetrators. Some survived precisely because they were appropriated by Nazi high command while their Jewish owners fled or were murdered in the camps. Seneffe, the former home of the Philippsons (see p. 23 and opposite), became the summer residence of General Alexander von Falkenhausen: from here he oversaw the Nazi occupation of Belgium. On the Grundlsee in Austria, Goebbels and his family moved into an Alpine-style villa and hunting lodge built fifty years earlier by a Jewish industrialist. In Moravia, the fifteenth-century castle at Tovačov/Tobitschau (Chapter 12) so lovingly restored by David Guttmann became the engine for the Germanisation of the entire Haná region even as its owners took refuge in Switzerland.

Contemplating the fate of the European Jewish elite during these terrible years reminds us of the ways antisemitism complicated conventional class structures.[77]

As Hannah Arendt perceptively noted, Jews were no longer a distinct corporation, 'a class of their own', but 'they did not belong to any of the classes in their countries' either.[78] German scholars have no difficulty understanding the specificity of a group they tend to describe as the 'German-Jewish bourgeoisie' (a term that does not do justice to the aristocratic dimensions of families like the Mosses).[79] By contrast, British scholars have tended to treat rich Jews as interchangeable with other so-called plutocrats, eliding the antisemitism that coloured their daily lives with the snobbery encountered by rich Americans.[80] Reading *The Splendid Paupers* reminds us how much more loaded the word 'plutocrat' was when applied to Jews; historians should take greater care when deploying terms that replicate rather than interrogate the prejudices of the landed classes.

The parodic frontispiece to W. T. Stead's *The Splendid Paupers: A Tale of the Coming Plutocracy* (1894) looks a decade ahead to a 'liquidation' of the British aristocracy. The names of the agents selling the old castles and estates – Glogoul and Faulmann – invoke the foreign Jews who were a particular target for the author's loathing.

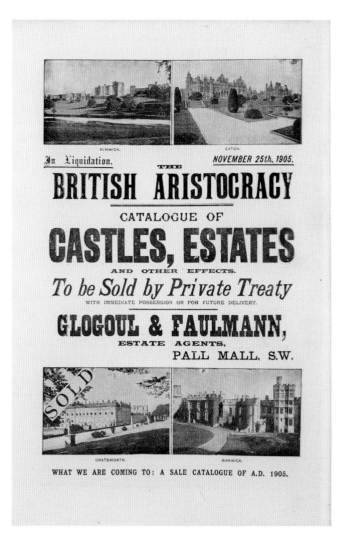

32

General Alexander von Falkenhausen, Military Governor of Belgium, with Princess Marie-José of Belgium at the Château de Seneffe, photographed c.1941–4. After Germany invaded Belgium in 1940, Seneffe was confiscated from the Philippsons; Falkenhausen used it as a local headquarters and as his summer residence.

There is, moreover, another side to this story. To non-Jews, families like the Rothschilds, the Gunzburgs and the Philippsons seemed like interlopers in aristocratic society, but by virtue of their wealth, connections and social status they assumed key positions of political leadership in the Jewish world, not so different perhaps to the leadership positions wealthy Jews had historically occupied in Jewish society, as Court Jews, *shtadlans* (intercessors) and *tujjar al-sultan* (the sultan's Jew).[81] When the eminent British historian David Cannadine opined that it was 'probably more useful to regard the 19th-century Rothschilds as bankers, plutocrats and social climbers than as the self-appointed spokesmen of "the Jewish community"', he demonstrated his ignorance of this deeper past.[82] ChaeRan Freeze, a historian of Russian Jews, saw more clearly when writing instead of the Poliakovs' 'dual habitus', at ease in both the Jewish world and Russian high society.[83]

Not all members of this Jewish elite took pride in both aspects of their heritage or embraced Jewish causes; some rejected them completely. Unquestionably, however, families like the Rothschilds and the Gunzburgs, the Warburgs and the Philippsons formed the backbone of the modern structure of national and international Jewish diplomatic and philanthropic networks and institutions. The cataclysm of the Holocaust threw these connections into sharp relief as some properties, which had been sites of acculturation and integration – often a focus for educational and social charitable projects targeting the local Christian population – became sites of Jewish philanthropy and vehicles for an explicitly Jewish, sometimes national, project.

As early as 1933, the German-Jewish educator Anna Esslinger set to work transplanting the progressive school she had established in Herrlingen in southern Germany to Bunce Court in the Kent countryside, where it became a haven for children fleeing the Nazis.[84] A year afterwards, Herbert Leon's niece Hilde Lion made Stoatley Rough available as a school for refugees.[85] Later, foreign-born Jewish women like Yvonne de Rothschild and Lola Hahn-Warburg worked with British-born Jewish aristocrats like Walter Samuel, 2nd Viscount Bearsted, to coordinate and fund the 1938 *Kindertransport*.[86] Having spent the late 1930s writing and fundraising in support of German Jews, Miriam Rothschild overruled all obstructions to welcome child refugees at Ashton Wold, taking 'first come, no discussion'.[87] In France, Baroness Germaine de Rothschild, one of the main organisers of a parallel initiative, housed 130 *Kindertransport* children at the Château de la Guette before she escaped to the United States, agonising over what she knew would be the children's terrible fate.[88]

The war years therefore witnessed a democratisation of the Jewish stories found at such houses, no longer restricted to a privileged Jewish elite but now encompassing migrants, soldiers and stateless persons from many different social backgrounds – something that applied in different ways to other kinds of country houses. Displaced things, not just persons, also found shelter in the countryside; much of the contents of the London Jewish Museum was housed away from the Blitz on Robert Waley Cohen's Exmoor estate.[89]

This pattern continued after the Holocaust. In 1946, the transatlantic Warburgs recovered the White House, their family villa in Blankenese on the Elbe, and gave it over to Jewish children liberated from concentration camps.[90] In Abbiate Guazzone, the Milanese businessman Astorre Mayer made his villa a sanctuary for Jewish refugees passing through on their way to Palestine.[91] The furniture retailer Sir Benjamin Drage likewise put his more

modest Surrey home at the service of child survivors: it was here that the 'Lingfield children' worked through their traumatic experiences under the supervision of émigré nurse Alice Goldberger.[92] In Sussex, meanwhile, office-equipment manufacturer Sigmund Gestetner and his wife Henny established a Zionist training farm on their estate in Bosham (above).[93] In the Vale of Aylesbury too, James and Dorothy de Rothschild were passionate Zionists who administered their charitable projects from Waddesdon Manor. Few places seem more peripheral to Jewish history than rural Buckinghamshire. Yet, like Ramsgate in the age of Sir Moses Montefiore, the village of Waddesdon is a place where 'the centre and periphery meet'.[94]

Remembering and forgetting

The Holocaust destroyed Jewish life in Europe, while World War Two appeared to herald the demise of the comfortable, aristocratic world of the country house. Only since the 1970s has the country house re-emerged as a symbol of British identity, a central actor in the construction of the idea of a national heritage.[95] Elsewhere too, historic houses evoke the lost world of ancient lineages and landed society, although memories of that world in continental Europe are more conflicted. The place of rich Jews in these histories is problematic.

In Britain, organisations like the National Trust struggled to appreciate their houses because they seemed insufficiently 'English'. When James de Rothschild bequeathed Waddesdon Manor to the Trust in 1957, some of those involved regarded this neo-Renaissance French château in the Vale of Aylesbury with distaste. 'I hate French furniture,' the Trust's Lord Esher informed James's grieving widow Dorothy, while chairman Lord Crawford found 'little interest in anything that is so artificially planted on a pristine English landscape. All the same, in all its horror, it is something: & the contents should be a lot.'[96] The quality of this French furniture, not to mention the paintings, the porcelain, the textiles and the books, was indeed exceptional. Aware of its value as an ensemble, the National Trust eventually agreed to take Waddesdon in its entirety.

In 1973, Lord Rosebery's executors offered the Rothschild treasure house of Mentmore to the nation at the knock-down price of £2 million (see p. 36). Designed by Joseph Paxton of Crystal Palace fame, Mentmore was then the most perfectly preserved of early Victorian houses: its fabulous collection rivalled that of the British royal family, and its decoration, fittings and furniture were completely intact. The terms in which Viscount Norwich attempted to persuade the House of Lords to 'Save Mentmore for the Nation' are telling:

it is not in any way characteristic; it is not typical. It represents ... the international bankers' Jewish taste of the Rothschilds.... But surely, my Lords, it is no worse for that ... what we are really discussing is the fact that here we have superb works of art which infinitely transcend the narrow bounds of Englishness, or of any other country. Great art belongs to the world.[97]

Money and the widespread backlash against excessive Victorian houses in the cash-strapped 1970s ultimately sealed the fate of Mentmore and its contents. Yet Viscount Norwich's intervention reminds us that Jews remained excluded from popular ideas of 'Englishness' and that the antisemitic trope of 'Jewish taste' lived on.[98]

Today, Mentmore is inaccessible to the public, its future uncertain and its fabric in disrepair. In continental Europe too, the post-war neglect of once-opulent residences like the Château de Beauregard (former home of philanthropist Maurice de Hirsch), Mosse's Schenkendorf (now classed as a 'lost place'), and the haunting Villa Antonini-Brunner in Udine, has many different causes, but their collective fate underlines the lack of value attached to even the most spectacular Jewish country houses within nationally constructed heritage cultures.[99] When such houses do open to the public, visitors often encounter a striking failure

to engage with their Jewish context. It is tempting to think this has something to do with the Nazi period. Yet in both France and Belgium, foregrounding Jewishness could also seem to violate the principles of state secularism, and the idea of heritage (*patrimoine*) as a universal category, like citizenship itself. Certainly, in Germany, the politics of Holocaust memory plays out differently. In Wannsee, just outside Berlin, where Max Liebermann's lakeside villa (Chapter 11) was restored by a group of enthusiasts after reunification, the fate of the Liebermanns under the Nazis is central to the story. In the Czech city of Brno, too, where the Tugendhats and Stiassnis built icons of modernist architecture, their tales of flight and expropriation are very much part of the narrative.

Here, and further east, these difficult histories are overlain by an equally difficult history of communism, ethnic cleansing and violent revolution. Houses ravaged by the war years were either pulled down or nationalised and converted to serve new purposes linked to the socialist project. Their original inhabitants, like the Guttmans of Moravia, petitioned in vain for restitution. Lewis Namier's relatives had survived the war by cultivating a new identity as Catholics and as Poles, although his niece was denounced when she returned briefly to their home in Koszyłowce (see p. 15), and his mother was forced into hiding. Long after

The house built for the brewery owner Leiba Strugach in the village of Budenovka/Svyatoi Dukh, near the city of Oshmyany/Ashmiany/ Oshmana in Belarus, photographed in the 1960s. Strugach's son Abraham and all his family were shot by the Nazis in the Oshmana ghetto in 1942. Published in *Sefer zikaron le-kehilat Oshminah* (Tel Aviv, 1969), a *Yizkhor* book – a type of book commemorating Jewish communities destroyed in the *Shoah*.

חצרו של אברהם סטרוגץ

their property had been razed to the ground, they continued to hide all trace of their Jewishness – afraid of what antisemitism might do to them in Poland.[100] In a Europe haunted by the memory of extremism and still awash with perpetrators, it seemed better, for so many reasons, to forget the Jewish country house.

In Britain, meanwhile, many country houses were flattened, and their specific histories forgotten. Farming was modernised, domestic service dried up, and unprofitable old piles were demolished.[101] Worth Park, for example – the late-Victorian home of the Sussex Montefiores – was detonated to make way for modern housing. These transformations may not have been driven by communist ideology, but the modification of country houses to serve new objectives – as airbases (Halton), schools (Somerhill and Townhill Park), luxury hotels (Tylney Hall) and even a safari park (Port Lympne) – has achieved a similar erasure. When houses like Strawberry Hill (Chapter 4) and Bletchley Park re-emerged as museums, they tended to honour only a single element in a more complex history: if you can do the birth of the Gothic Revival or World War Two intelligence, why tell the story of a Jewish country house?

It is easy to find pragmatic reasons for the neglect of these houses and the stories they tell, from a distaste for Victorian or Second Empire aesthetics, to the excess of heritage sites demanding conservation in Italy. After all, it has taken until the start of the twenty-first century to restore a fuller range of stories connected to country houses, from the experience of servants and women to that of enslaved and colonised peoples.[102] This book is one of several related projects to emerge from a partnership now ten years old, between academics, the National Trust and European heritage professionals.[103] The history of rich Jews remains deeply connected with the history of antisemitism; given how many properties have Jewish stories, it is striking how long it has taken for Jews to find their place among a plethora of inclusive heritage initiatives.

And yet. These houses speak to an important moment in European history:

SAVE

MENTMORE FOR THE NATION

A great house and collection for the first time in print

the dream of belonging that preceded the *Shoah*. Contemporaries knew this and wrote about it. In Marcel Proust's great sequence of novels, the distinction between houses bought with new Jewish money and the estates of the old aristocracy figures as the defining cultural fracture of *fin de siècle* France, an idea reflected in the titles of the first and third volumes in the series (*Swann's Way* and *The Guermantes Way* respectively). In the final volume, *Time Regained*, we learn, however, that the paths to the two houses are unexpectedly connected, just like their marital fortunes.

In Albert Cohen's novels too, the Jewish country house came to symbolise the modern European Jewish condition. The eponymous protagonist in his 1930 novel *Solal* is, like Cohen, a socially and culturally mobile Greek Jew in interwar Geneva. He marries into the European elite but cannot escape the ties that bind him to the chaotic world of poverty, tradition and Jewishness

Opposite
The cover of a booklet
published in January 1977
as part of the campaign
by SAVE (Save Britain's
Heritage) to preserve
Mentmore and its
contents for the nation.
In the end the collection
and the mansion were
sold; the building is
now in poor condition.

Below
La règle du jeu,
1939, film poster.

he left behind. Eventually he transports the Jewish population of his Greek island to the grounds of the château he now inhabits, secreting them in a cellar. In this way, the château becomes a place of refuge; it is also where he hides his other self. After the Holocaust, the Italian-Jewish novelist Giorgio Bassani deployed a similar motif, presenting the *Garden of the Finzi-Continis* as a lost Eden, not unlike the Jews' lost fatherland of liberal Italy, where the protagonists could turn their face from the new reality of Mussolini's racial laws. Adapted for the screen by Vittorio de Sica in 1970, the book has become a seminal representation of Italian-Jewish life in the 1930s, drawing crowds of tourists to Ferrara in search of a place that never was.

In this way, the Jewish country house survives as a *lieu de mémoire*; the backdrop for Jean Renoir's darkly satirical 1939 film *La règle du jeu* (below) and the original idyll of István Sazbó's *Sunshine* (1999). It resurfaces periodically in popular consciousness even as the social and political reality it represented has vanished from public memory. *Downton Abbey* (2010–22), which shaped ideas of the Edwardian country house for a new generation, was filmed in Highclere Castle: a property lived in and renovated by Alfred de Rothschild's illegitimate daughter, Almina.[104] Rich Jews and

antisemitism were integral to the aristocratic lifestyle of that time and place, but they are almost never mentioned at Downton, whose châtelaine is one Cora Levinson, Christian daughter of a Jewish father. When they finally make it into the story, the details are wrong in every particular.[105] That gulf between fiction and reality speaks volumes about social forgetting, about what, how and who 'we' choose to remember.

Public memory is one thing; private memories are a different matter. Namier's niece, Anna Kurska (née Modzelewska), loved Poland with a passion but, as her son Jarosław writes, 'her first steps after the fall of the USSR were to the independent Ukraine, to Podolia, where – apart from the family tomb, the remains of her beloved father, and the good memory of the people there – she found almost nothing'.[106] She would return almost every year to the family estate at Koszyłowce (see p. 15), the arcadia of her childhood, which she had left in October 1939, on a peasant cart bound for Lwów so many years earlier. It was here that she chose to be buried.

This book is the first to write Jewish country houses back into European history and to establish their importance as sites of European memory. It is not a book that tries apologetically to fit Jews into tried and tested ways of looking at country houses. Instead, it offers a new way of understanding country houses and a new way of looking at Jewish history. That vision applies not just to the text, but also to the images. In the words of Daniel Libeskind, 'Every time Hélène Binet takes a photograph, she exposes architecture's achievements, strength, pathos and fragility.'[107] As an artist, responding to a newly identified category of houses, Binet recaptures something of a world now distant from our own. She undercuts the familiar formula of the country house, gracious and assertive, with blue sky above and expansive lawn below, to tease out their individual identities and material nature in searching and beautiful ways. It is in this spirit of openness, exploration and enquiry that we invite you to enter the world of the Jewish country house.

A combination of many visions

Hélène Binet

As I was working on the photographic essay for this book, I wondered how I could capture the early dream or vision of each owner, before their house was even under construction. I was intrigued by that very early stage of creation, where the owner's emotions and aspirations for the house were present but not yet defined or distinct. While photographing the houses, however, I started to reflect on the experience of those owners now dwelling in their finished homes. What did they observe, gaze at and rest their eyes upon in their daily lives? My photographs thus began to explore the meeting point between those two different visions: the early dream for the house, and the literal vision of that house shaped by inhabiting it. Through photography, I worked to combine these two visions and to communicate this to an audience.

Photography is a simple and very direct medium of communication – it captures, reduces and frames the world through the intention of the photographer. But this is a world that exists before being photographed. Through the act of framing, we create an area of interest, we exclude other aspects, and we make a field where elements interact to allow new thoughts to be released. We never perceive a photograph in isolation; instead, as we observe it, we immediately associate the image with many other visual past experiences. Rather than describing areas of interest, intimating what lies beyond the frame is an important part of my work. In this case, I had to remain conscious of the fact that these houses are well known and very much part of a large bank of images that shape the way we think about such properties. I felt the need to move away from traditionally static depictions, which have shaped our perceptions of the country house.

Usually, photographs are displayed in exhibitions or in books, presented in pairs and other configurations. How photographs are brought together results in links and juxtapositions that create a sense of dialogue between them. This is a very beautiful and powerful moment. The formulation of this dialogue occurs through perception, and thus belongs only to the observer. Through this intimate perception, a personal story has now emerged. And perhaps it is in this very moment that something from those house owners' early dreams and experiences rises to the surface. An impalpable world made of hope and dreams.

I like to think, then, of this essay as a combination of many visions: a dream and a daily observation, now seen by both photographer and observer.

Note: Except in a few instances, Hélène Binet's photographs appear without captions.

A. SOLOMON.
Doubtful Fortune.

1 The stories we tell: Salomons Estate

Tom Stammers and Abigail Green

Abraham Solomon, *Doubtful Fortune, or Her Future in the Cards*, 1856, oil on canvas. Exhibited at the Royal Academy the year that it was painted, this narrative scene of genteel fortune-telling portrays Jeannette Salomons (wife of Sir David), Emma Salomons (wife of Philip) and their relative Clara Philips in the drawing room at Broomhill.

In 1937, Vera Salomons (1888–1969) formally bequeathed Broomhill outside Tunbridge Wells, where her family had lived for over 100 years, to Kent County Council.[1] Reporting on the official ceremony held the following summer, the *Courier* noted that Vera stressed her family had 'always wished to help others' and was proud that through her bequest 'the good her ancestors had done for nearly a century might continue, although they were no longer there'. It was, she said, 'a pleasure to hand over such a gift to the Council of a free country where her people had always been well treated'.[2] Nowhere in the article did it mention that Vera's people were Jews. It may be that this information seemed otiose; it is equally possible that the author was not immune to contemporary prejudice, or considered Jewishness an embarrassment. Vera herself felt none of these things. She had spent considerable time in Palestine and was drawn to Zionism. She was, in short, acutely aware of what it meant to be a Jew in 1938.

These sensitivities shaped the arrangements Vera made at Broomhill. The deed of trust specified that the house should be used as a college, museum, scientific institute or convalescent home; that 'David Salomons' should form part of its name; and that two rooms be 'used exclusively as a memorial hall containing the mementos now there relating to her father the late Sir David Lionel Salomons and his family', with additional pictures displayed elsewhere, and public access given to all these spaces. Responsibility for the objects and documents Vera chose as 'mementos' was vested in the Jewish Board of Guardians (now Jewish Care). A final clause, reflecting the climate of the late 1930s, instructed the new owners: 'Not to allow any instruction, speeches or entertainment of an anti-Semitic or political tendency or trend to take place or be broadcast in any of the buildings or on any part of the said property.'[3]

By gifting her childhood home to the local community, Vera ensured its survival as a family shrine. Above all she wanted to celebrate the public service and ultimate sacrifice of three close relatives: her great uncle Sir David Salomons (1797–1873), a key figure in the struggle for Jewish political rights, the first Jew to speak in parliament, and the first Jewish Lord Mayor of London; his nephew, her father David Lionel Salomons (1851–1925), a gentleman scientist, inventor and bibliophile who became a pillar of Tunbridge Wells society; and her brother David Reginald Salomons (1885–1915), who died a heroic death on board HMS *Hythe* in World War One.

When selecting the mementos, however, Vera remembered other members of her extended family. Hidden in cupboards beneath the façade of duty and public achievement lies a quantity of more intimate material, much of it completely unsuited

Broomhill, photographed around 1868 by David Lionel Salomons, who was about 17 years old at the time and was experimenting with photography.

to display. The Salomons had been prominent members of 'the Cousinhood', that network of interrelated City of London dynasties that dominated British Jewish life from the early nineteenth into the mid-twentieth century.[4] Their personalities and preoccupations are captured in voluminous photographic albums and myriad cherished domestic possessions. These were things the family treasured; perhaps Vera could not bear to let them go. She herself was no curator, but in her loving choice of objects and documents we can still discern something of the story she wanted to tell.

Since 1937, the house has undergone several changes of ownership. It has been a convalescent home, an administrative training college, a university, and is now a hotel and events venue. The memorial rooms too have experienced different phases: benign neglect under the National Health Service, a substantial curatorial intervention led by Canterbury Christ Church University, and currently a more domestic moment as an overflow tea-room. All this has obscured the ways in which, long before Vera, Sir David Salomons and his nephew David Lionel once sought to narrate their very different achievements here. We can still read Broomhill through its collections – present and absent – but we cannot read it as a house in any straightforwardly linear way.

The photographic record

Nothing remains of the original Broomhill beyond a primitive oil painting of the pretty but unassuming Regency villa purchased on a leasehold basis by the first David Salomons in 1829. Each subsequent iteration has been preserved through photographs. His nephew, David Lionel, was a keen amateur photographer from his teenage years; a reporter for the *Photographic Journal* once noticed him at a talk given by a well-known French photographer, washing one of the prints with a sponge to see if it had been touched up.[5] In 1868, a year after he had moved to Broomhill on the death of his father, Philip, David Lionel captured the south front of the house in a wonderfully atmospheric photograph, complete with two gardeners carefully scything the lawn (above).

Living at Broomhill allowed David Lionel to give full rein to his photographic enthusiasms. He eventually built himself a perfectly equipped studio with three dark rooms, experimented with photographic optics and chemistry in his laboratory, and documented domestic life there through an array of landscapes, portraits and photographic albums. In 1873, about the time he inherited the property from Sir David, who had no children, David Lionel submitted a folio of thirty photographs he had taken of his uncle's art collection to the Annual International Exhibition at the Royal Albert Hall: he wanted to test how far photography could surpass engraving as a medium for reproducing works of art. Other albums at Broomhill document David Lionel's transformation from a young man who enjoyed larking about in fancy dress, to a substantial family man who liked to take pictures of his daughters, dogs and house.

In 1898, David Lionel produced *A Souvenir of Broomhill, Kent*, an album of the estate.[6] A few years earlier, he had commissioned photographs of each phase of the construction of his stables, built between 1890 and 1894 in red brick and Portland stone to the highest contemporary standards.[7] Now he attempted something more comprehensive (see opposite and p. 53).

After a portrait of the author, the opening three photographs document the exterior of the house and grounds, complete with stables and hothouses. Visitors entered the estate past a timber-framed gatehouse, constructed in Arts and Crafts style in 1894. From the imposing stables, a path led the visitor past the Gothic tower David Lionel had constructed in 1876, mounted with a telescope to observe astronomical phenomena and conduct electrical experiments. Built in a medley of different styles, these additions are in marked contrast to the relative sobriety of the house his uncle had built. A close-up of the front entrance gives the misleading impression that the main house remained relatively unaltered, but an electric light bulb dangling in the porch hints at substantial changes behind, beside and within. The album proceeds to document the interiors and collections, including the picture gallery and library, but the bulk of it is devoted to David Lionel's scientific passions: room after room of workshops, electrical power installations, laboratories and switchboards. All this had been built in the 1880s and 1890s, 'almost entirely by local labour', with David Lionel 'his own engineer and architect'.[8]

Looking at these photographs reminds us not only of continuity in central elements of the story of the house, but also of change – many of the objects that once filled Broomhill were pruned and removed before it passed to Kent County Council. To that extent, the house today gives an incomplete sense of who the Salomons were and what they cared about. Sidelined within the collections, Vera's mother, Laura de Stern, was the daughter of Frankfurt-born banker Hermann de Stern, and had received piano lessons from Clara Schumann as a girl. After their marriage, David and Laura enjoyed many contacts on the continent, and owned an apartment in Paris. Vera, too, is surprisingly absent from the displays, allocating herself a supporting role in the family story, although she features repeatedly in David Lionel's more informal photographic shots. For Vera was very close to her father, sharing his passions for photography and the French eighteenth century.

Nor are the family's Jewish connections readily apparent. Yet they were integral to the life of the first David Salomons, who fought for decades against civil disabilities that prevented Jews from holding public office or sitting in parliament. Meanwhile, his brother Philip, David Lionel's father, assembled a pioneering array of Judaica and silverware in the prayer room of his Hove townhouse.[9] Most of these high-quality pieces were acquired by Reuben Sassoon, who exhibited them in 1887 at the landmark Anglo-Jewish Historical Exhibition at the Royal Albert Hall. The Salomons family, however, retained the dark red silk velvet curtains used to

cover the reading desk in Philip's prayer room. This pair of embroideries, with Hebrew verse from Exodus 17:12 ('and his hands were steady') picked out in silver thread above the crown (opposite), are now among the few explicitly Jewish articles at Broomhill.[10]

The life David Lionel led was self-consciously modern and secular. Yet his father was a learned and observant Jew, while his grandfather had been sufficiently embedded in Jewish tradition to leave a substantial legacy to poor Jews in Jerusalem.[11] In keeping with these values, David Lionel received part of his education in a private Jewish school run by Sir Moses Montefiore's secretary, Louis Loewe, a fact he omitted from an autobiographical fragment about his early years.[12] Nevertheless, David Lionel imparted to Vera a pride in her heritage, and a deep sense of connection with Jerusalem.

In her youth, Vera became a subscriber to the Jewish Historical Society of England. It was to Vera that David Lionel entrusted a stone from the Temple in Jerusalem (see p. 56), 'broken off by David Roberts R.A. when painting in the Holy Land, at the risk of his life'.[13] In Judaism this act was blasphemy, but Philip accepted the gift and transmitted it to his son. On the second anniversary of David Reginald's death, when, perhaps, the family lit a candle in his memory, the stone formally passed to his sister Vera. In October 1917, a week before the Balfour Declaration, it was a timely gift.[14] Its presence at Broomhill today reminds us that not all the things David Lionel valued were reflected in the *Souvenir* album or his photographic experiments. For this is a house composed of many layers, as different personalities tried to inscribe their story upon the property, while also working to conserve or elaborate upon materials inherited from the past.

A tradition of public service

Let us turn, then, to the first David Salomons, whose public career still lies at the heart of the house. To own a place like Broomhill was a natural ambition for a successful financier, but it was probably no coincidence that the year in which Salomons acquired it was also the year of Catholic emancipation – a moment when the prospect of Jewish emancipation shifted more clearly into view. By 1831 he had bought another estate nearby, where he constructed a house designed in loosely neo-Elizabethan style by Decimus Burton. Here, Salomons enjoyed playing the rural paternalist.[15] Only after 1851 did he establish Broomhill as his principal residence, demolishing what had previously stood on the site. This was a gesture of self-confidence for a man who was proud that he had made, rather than inherited, his fortune, and wanted a house that conformed to his practical needs and aspirations. In the interim, parliament had indeed passed legislation affirming, after more than a century of uncertainty, the right of Jews to own freehold land. Thus, the secure acquisition of Broomhill was one of the fruits of the struggle for emancipation, a struggle that Salomons waged from his base in the City of London.

The key milestones of Salomons' career can be sketched quickly.[16] In 1831 he became a liveryman in the Worshipful Comany of Coopers; in 1835 he was elected the first Jewish Sheriff of London and Middlesex, after the government dropped the Christian oath that had been a prerequisite to taking office. In 1839 he became High Sheriff of Kent, a role carrying great prestige, and in 1847, he was successfully voted in as Alderman to the Ward of Cordwainers (having been barred from taking up municipal office twice before; see caricature below). In the same year, Lionel de Rothschild was elected as one of four MPs for the City of London, but the Commons' efforts to pass legislation allowing Jews to sit in parliament were continually frustrated by members of the Upper House, for whom this represented a violation of the idea of Christian government (see p. 19). In 1851, Salomons too was elected as a Liberal candidate at Greenwich. Unlike Rothschild, who merely refused to take the Christian oath, he took his seat on the ministerial bench and became the first Jew to

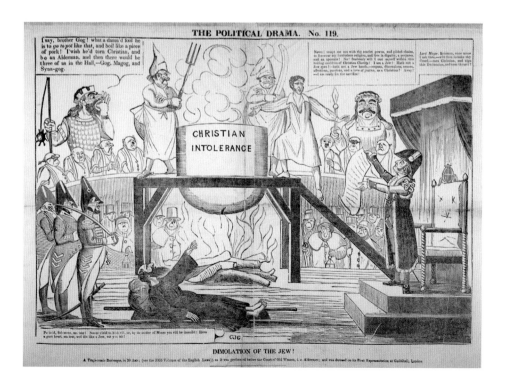

Charles Jameson Grant, *Immolation of the Jew*, c.1836. This political caricature, published after David Salomons was rejected by the Court of the Aldermen, shows him stepping into the cauldron of 'Christian Intolerance' as he refuses the Lord Mayor's entreaty to renounce Judaism in order to assume office. Salomons was eventually elected as an Alderman in 1847.

Solomon Alexander Hart, *Sir David Salomons (1797–1873), Lord Mayor of London*, 1855, oil on canvas. Hart was the first Jewish member of the Royal Academy and David Salomons acquired several of his works on subjects taken from the Middle Ages, Tudor England and Jewish religious life. Salomons presented this portrait of himself to the Guildhall; he is wearing the robes and chain of Lord Mayor.

speak in parliament before being forcibly ejected. That October, a representative of the Office of Works granted him permission to buy the bench in question, adding, 'I wish I could secure you one in the new house on such easy terms.'[17] David Lionel's *Souvenir* album reveals that the contested bench, placed on one side of the entrance hall, was one of the first things encountered by visitors to Broomhill – a bittersweet reminder of barriers overcome.

In many ways, the climax of Salomons' public career came with his election as Lord Mayor of London in 1855 (left). Jewish communities across Britain sent letters of congratulation and took pride in his elevation to the 'chief magistracy of the greatest city in the world'.[18] The position of Lord Mayor was not merely symbolic, but also mediated between the interests of the City, the government and the Crown, providing an important diplomatic platform; a display case in the museum today, for example, recalls his pride on playing host to the future king of Italy during the Crimean War. David Salomons' tenure was commemorated in the sculpture hall at the heart of the house, where the combination of classical and contemporary figures provided a bourgeois twist on the galleries found in great aristocratic houses. Its centrepiece was a white marble sculpture of Dick Whittington by John Edward Carew (see p. 46, middle left), a folkloric version of the real-life merchant and Lord Mayor of London (of whom Carew also produced a statue for the façade of the Royal Exchange).[19] In this way, Broomhill transplanted an icon of the City into the Kentish countryside. The story of Dick Whittington was obviously an allegory for David Salomons' own metropolitan ascent, a point emphasised by the addition of a second canopy above this statue and its central placement next to a bust of Salomons, produced in 1857 by the Hungarian Jewish émigré Joseph Engel.

If Salomons' career showed that the City was essential for Jews, he also affirmed that Jews were essential to the City through his donations to the Guildhall, the City's ceremonial and administrative heart. To the latter he gave a massive silver sculpture presented to him in 1836 by members of the Jewish community 'as an acknowledgement of his exertions in the cause of religious liberty'.[20] In 1846, his brother Philip donated 400 volumes of Hebraica to the Guildhall Library, and this corpus was enlarged in 1873, thanks to £1,000 from David Salomons' will to enable further purchases.[21] As this bequest suggests, the Salomons' mayoralty was in some ways a family achievement. Sir David had no children and his wife Jeannette's health was fragile. Her duties as Lady Mayoress were often taken by her sister Harriet or her sister-in-law Emma, David Lionel's mother. David Lionel tried twice to follow his uncle into parliament, but ultimately became a well-known figure in Tunbridge Wells instead, serving eventually as a county councillor and mayor (1894–5). He left a considerable mark during his tenure, supporting the installation of electricity in the town and holding the world's first motor show there (properly known as the Horseless Carriage Exhibition).

All members of the Salomons family were hence acquainted with the idea of public service; this is reflected by the fact that in many portraits the men appear in some kind of uniform. Certificates at Broomhill record that David Reginald followed family tradition and was inducted into the Coopers' livery company in 1906. Two years before the outbreak of World War One, he had enlisted in the Cadet Company of the Kent Royal Fusiliers. His selfless conduct during the *Hythe* disaster, which won him a posthumous medal, needs to be placed within a longer tradition. This was the example his sister Vera sought to honour in creating a permanent memorial.

Right

David Lionel Salomons, *Reflections for 1911*, sent as a New Year greeting. David Lionel sent little collections of thoughts and observations to friends at the secular New Year; the cover of this one reflects the 18th-century book illustrations that he loved. The past, represented by Phaeton in his chariot, is answered by the future, which belongs to the aeroplane. David Lionel was passionate about aviation; he was one of the eight founder members of the Aéro-Club de France in 1898, and elected Honorary President in 1914.

Below right

Souvenir of Jerusalem, *c*.1863, lithograph on paper. This is an example of the first item produced by the Hebrew printing press set up in Jerusalem by Yoel Moshe Salomon and Michal HaCohen, with the support of Sir Moses Montefiore (see pp. 9–14). Known as the *shoshonata* (from the Hebrew word *shoshana*, meaning 'rose'), and based on earlier European travel-souvenir designs, it is printed on both sides, with views of Jerusalem shown here.

The scientific story

Running alongside the political story there is a parallel insistence upon science and technology. Here too family precedents loomed large. David Lionel was proud to count as a great-grandfather Benjamin Gompertz, an astronomer, Fellow of the Royal Society and mathematician whose calculations underpinned the creation of the insurance business Allied Assurance.[22] His uncle, Sir David, was a member of the Society of Engineers, who had opened the railway line between Reading, Guildford and Reigate (the spade he used to cut the turf is still preserved at Broomhill),[23] and David Lionel himself eventually became director of the South Eastern and Chatham Railway. His fascination with the history of transport, from carriage driving to hot-air ballooning, arose out of this milieu. Appropriately enough, he began his long career as an inventor with a patent for the first automatic signalling system for trains in 1874.

David Lionel's passion for science transformed the house he inherited, for he was among the first to seize on the potential of Victorian technology to revolutionise the country-house interior. In the preface to the *Souvenir* album, he advertised his contribution to 'the adaptation of electric energy to domestic purposes', ranging from lighting to more niche applications like the electric butter churn, iron and sewing machine.[24] These novelties earned Broomhill an illustrated feature on 'Electricity in the Home' in the Edwardian society periodical *The House Beautiful*.[25] The expansion of the house itself, with another storey added by 1910, providing bedrooms for the family and the staff, was matched in the proliferation of machinery, switchboards and dynamos, including the largest electrical magnet in the world and Britain's first architecturally significant garages.[26]

Completed in 1896, the Science Theatre (below left) – the purpose-built venue in which Salomons exhibited his discoveries to invited guests – remains a marvel. Here he could control the shutters and lighting levels at the push of a button, one minute projecting coloured photographs and 'cinematic tableaux', the next filling the space with the sounds of a forty-piece orchestra, an aria sung by Nellie Melba or a Shakespeare speech declaimed by Ellen Terry. Mounted high on the stage is a mechanical Welte organ that, when built, was the largest and most expensive in Britain, costing £4,050 in 1914. The upper galleries of the theatre are supported by cast-iron columns and decorated with shields bearing the names both of titans of science (Kelvin, Faraday, David Lionel himself) and of literature (Shakespeare, Spenser, Milton), stressing the union of science and art.

Below left
'The Science Theatre at Broomhill', photograph from *A Souvenir*, 1898. The largest private construction of its kind in Britain, the theatre had a photographic studio, three dark rooms and a chemical laboratory attached. From 1895, films were shown here and, in 1914, the Welte organ was installed.

Below right
'Electric Power Installation at Broomhill', photograph from *A Souvenir*, 1898. Broomhill was one of the first houses in Britain to use electricity for cooking and other domestic purposes. Salomons also devised perhaps the first automatic electric burglar alarm. One contemporary described his home as 'a modern magician's cave, with electricity to play the part of the good genie'.

David Lionel Salomons in a motor car, photographer and date unknown. Salomons loved automobiles and claimed to have constructed one 'propelled electrically and made out of a tricycle with an electro motor of 2 h. p. attached, worked by a large Bunsen battery' as early as 1874, though the lack of available technology made it unviable. In 1895 he co-founded the Self-Propelled Traffic Association, to fight restrictions against its development.

This mix of qualities characterised the productions of Abraham-Louis Breguet, clockmaker to Marie-Antoinette, whose works David Lionel began to collect in earnest around 1917. 'To carry a fine Breguet watch,' David Lionel wrote in the biography he penned of his hero, 'is to feel that you have the brains of a genius in your pocket.'[27] Breguet's intricate craft appealed strongly to a man who from childhood, he claimed, was a 'born "mechanic"', and who amassed a substantial corpus of iconography related to omnibuses, locomotives, balloons and automobiles. Today, the Salomons Museum retains a small display of Ballooniana, but David Lionel left over 5,000 drawings, prints and lithographs chronicling the history of transport to the Bibliothèque Nationale de France, 'in memory of the kindness and courtesy I have always received in that country'. Across the Channel, Salomons found many friends who shared his passion for new technologies, whether in the Touring Club de France or the Aéro-Club de France. Having corresponded with President Poincaré on their shared love of Breguet, he donated the exceptional 1785 timepiece named for the duc de Praslin to the Musée des Arts Décoratifs in 1924, where the curators threw a dinner to celebrate.[28]

David Lionel Salomons' career testifies to the vitality of the culture of gentlemanly science that infiltrated the country house in the early twentieth century. The grounds of Broomhill contain a mast given to David Lionel by German-born Charles William Siemens, the first president of the Society of Telegraph Engineers, who lived at nearby Sherwood, where electricity was harnessed for farm work.[29] While he gave to his Cambridge alma mater, David Lionel was happiest in professional and learned societies, such as the Institution of Electrical Engineers, and the homosocial haunts of St James's.[30] Yet his view of science was not narrowly restrictive. In his 1876 *Address to the Ladies of England*, he argued that although women should not receive the vote, they should receive a full technical education, including training in photography.[31] His wife Laura became a keen driver, and his daughter Vera was inducted into his photographic experiments. No less than in politics, scientific discussion and experiment in the Salomons' home was a family affair.

Loose ends and missing pieces

Broomhill today remains an evocative monument to a remarkable family. The women of the family are more elusive than the men, but their traces remain in the portraits and portrait miniatures, the abundant family photograph albums, and more intimate possessions like mourning jewellery mounted with hair.[32] Often these objects raise more questions than they answer. David Salomons' wife Jeannette spent over ten years in a mental institution, yet she is remembered here through a trinket box, an embroidered vesper chair and a panel given her by Queen Adelaide, based on their shared love of needlework.[33] Another relic in one of the scrapbooks testifies to Jeannette's sense of humour. On an ornate, but hand-drawn, frontispiece, she has added inscriptions that parody the certificates presented to her husband for his public service: the 'Salomons' Tea-Makers', assembled at 'Tee-total hall, the Polyputthekettleonicon at Bohea-mian Tunbridge Wells', congratulate Alderman Salomons for 'his amenitea and urbanitea at the Breakfast table'.[34] Philip Salomons' wife Emma is remembered through a 'little, worn, manuscript book' bound in black leather, containing handwritten English versions of common Hebrew prayers. Its preservation in the library suggests that the Jewishness of the family was a constant preoccupation, even if it was recorded in ephemeral and subtle ways.[35]

Intriguingly, nothing remains at Broomhill of the most prestigious collections once housed here. This is true for the fine pictures assembled by David Salomons, which he instructed his heirs to keep together.[36] These included numerous works painted on Old Testament themes (such as W. J. Grant's *Accusation of Haman*, from the story of Esther) or by Jewish artists, such as Solomon Alexander Hart (who in 1840 became the first Jewish member of the Royal Academy), and Rebecca Solomon and her brothers Abraham (who painted David Salomons in his Alderman's robes) and the tragic visionary Simeon. (The Solomons, like the Salomons, had Dutch mercantile origins).[37] In *Doubtful Fortune, or Her Future in the Cards* (1856; see p. 42), which now hangs over the library fireplace, Abraham Solomon depicted Jeannette, Emma and their relative Clara Philips in the picture room at Broomhill, looking out towards Rusthall Common; painted at a time when David Salomons was Lord Mayor of London, the frame of the picture was decorated with intricate Star of David motifs.[38] 'I feel much pleasure that it should make one of your valuable collection,' Solomon told his patron, 'not only from my having painted it under much expectation, but that I believe it to be my most finished work.'[39] Decorated in the Louis XVI style, David Salomons' picture gallery was designed to let in natural light from above, allowing works to be carefully inspected. Its subsequent dispersal has stripped the house of one of its chief assets, a record of Salomons' close relationship to the artists and exhibitions of the Royal Academy.[40]

Another aspect of the Salomons' story has been lost with the break-up of the library, filled with French eighteenth-century authors, especially in rare editions, with illustrations and fine bindings. In the preface to his self-authored library catalogue, David Lionel joked that his bibliophilia was an all-consuming pathology ('The microbe of the disease to collect cannot be eradicated from the party so afflicted').[41] The catalogue underscores his discernment, aided by leading booksellers in London and Paris. Émile Bertaux, then director of the Jacquemart-André Museum, hailed the Broomhill library as 'one of the richest collections in England of the French 18ᵗʰ century – a Wallace Collection of the Book'.[42] It was a source of inspiration to Vera, too, who published short studies on the leading illustrators of the French Rococo, containing superb photogravure reproductions.[43] After his death, however, she sold her father's library through auction houses in the United States, permanently diminishing Broomhill's French character.[44]

Piece of stone from the West Wall of Solomon's Temple

A selection of personal items displayed at the Salomons Museum today. These include a fragment of the Western Wall in Jerusalem brought back by the artist David Roberts and a postcard of the site (both presented to Vera by David Lionel in 1917). There is a gold-and-enamel mourning bracelet in memory of the merchant and communal leader Aaron Asher Goldsmid, a brother-in-law of David Salomons, and intimate keepsakes of family members, including framed photographs of Philip and David Salomons, and a memento of Laura Stern Salomons that includes locks of hair from her five children.

Here and elsewhere, tracing the movement of collections beyond Broomhill opens up alternative perspectives on the family's commitments and cultural legacy. David Lionel Salomons' exceptional Breguet watches now form the nucleus of the L. A. Mayer Institute for Islamic Art that Vera founded in Jerusalem. Opening its doors in 1974, this museum was intended to foster closer dialogue between Jews and Arabs, in recognition of her admiration for the archaeologist Leo Ary Mayer, a professor at the Hebrew University of Jerusalem. While French eighteenth-century watches might seem incongruous in this location, the creation of a room named for her father, containing some of his cherished timepieces, fitted with Vera's concern to memorialise her ancestors, as well as her ongoing support for the new Jewish state. Vera had initially created the David Salomons Charitable Trust in 1946 with the aim of promoting 'Art or culture or art associated or derived in some manner (but not necessarily exclusively) with or from the Jewish Race'.[45] Even if the resulting museum ultimately adopted a broader remit, it still distilled her family's long-standing interests in technological ingenuity, craftsmanship, art, public education, Jewish politics and philanthropy.

Posterity

Let us return to the beginning. By leaving Broomhill to Kent County Council, Vera pre-empted both the great wave of country-house sales of the post-war era and the possibility that the National Trust would snap up the property. Almost certainly, it would have done no such thing. Broomhill did not figure in the National Heritage List for England before 1973, and most of the listed elements were added in the twenty-first century. Yet back in the 1970s the fate of the Salomons Estate was a matter of national importance, worth discussing in the House of Lords. By then, the property was an administrative training centre for the South East Thames Regional Health Authority. Luminaries like Sir Hugh Casson recognised that the Science Theatre in particular was of 'outstanding interest', containing an 'extraordinary collection of fixtures – a fine organ, complete period scenery and theatrical machinery, and not least a virtually untouched electrical power and light system that must be one of the earliest known of this country'. Rather than allow this paragon to lie abandoned, or converted into a lecture hall, several peers proposed turning it into a museum.

Among them was Lord Janner, who spoke, self-consciously, 'as a Jew'. Janner argued that Broomhill mattered above all for its association with the first Sir David Salomons, without whom 'it is quite possible that neither I nor any other Jewish person would have been able to come into either House'. He proceeded to make an early plea for what we now term 'inclusive heritage'. It would, he believed 'be a very great attraction for a large number of Jewish people, not only from this country, to go to a place which had this background'; the same would no doubt apply to 'Parliamentarians throughout the world'.[46]

Here, then, were two competing narratives, the scientific and the political, neither of which, in the cash-strapped 1970s, could compel public support. Crafted at different moments, by different actors, and in relation to different spaces, they nonetheless illuminate each other. The Salomons Estate is more than a palimpsest. Instead, through its complex layering of stories and objects, it is a place where opposites meet: the City of London and the countryside, Englishness and cosmopolitanism, technology and tradition, at once a public museum and a private family shrine. The dispersal of the Salomons' collections has made some stories harder to recover. What survives at Broomhill is intimate and poignant, a space that feels homely, even though it is no longer a family house.

2 Hughenden Manor: a home for a prime minister

Robert Bandy

Robe of office worn by Disraeli as Chancellor of the Exchequer.

For a man like Benjamin Disraeli (1804–81), to own a house like Hughenden was not a luxury but a necessity. A member of parliament, who went on to become Chancellor of the Exchequer, leader of the Conservative (Tory) Party, Earl of Beaconsfield and (twice) prime minister, Disraeli was a pillar of the political establishment in an era when that establishment was predominately aristocratic and landed. Yet he was not born into the traditional ruling class, nor did he inherit acres of rolling English countryside. He was, instead, an outsider: a man whose origins and life story captured the European imagination precisely because, to cite his earliest authoritative biographer, Disraeli never denied 'that the fundamental fact [about him] was that he was a Jew.'[1] In his youth, Disraeli identified politics as the best route to social advancement, opining that 'to enter high society, a man must either have blood, a million or a genius'.[2] In later life, he became a thoroughly substantial figure, forever associated with that honourable political tradition called 'One Nation Conservatism' because it emphasises the bonds of responsibility between the social classes. As an individual, however, he remains an enigma. There was something self-consciously performative about Disraeli's brilliance, and something so brilliant about his social performance, that it is hard to disentangle the man from the aphorisms and witty asides that punctuated his conversation and literary production. Hannah Arendt recognised as much when she identified Disraeli as the only educated and assimilated Jew of his generation to transcend the categories of 'pariah' and 'parvenu': a man who succeeded by turning his Jewish otherness into a social advantage.[3] This she attributed to his distance from Jews and Jewish tradition.

Thinking about Disraeli's country estate and his life at Hughenden provides a different perspective. Hughenden was many things: a country base, a source of income, and an essential prop as Disraeli aspired to high office – both a stage and

A statesman's house

These novels established Disraeli as a leader among a certain kind of young Tory gentleman, just as the party he had improbably embraced was beginning to fall apart. The split that followed the repeal of the Corn Laws in 1846 provided him with an opening, heralding his triumphant return to his father's county the following year as MP for Buckinghamshire. This was an era of transition in British politics, but county seats still attracted a particular prestige among the 'backwoodsmen' (peers who rarely attended the House of Lords) who formed a growing bulk of the rump Tory Party to which Disraeli attached himself. A rising star in a grouping largely devoid of talent, he needed a house and lands to match this elevated station. He found a solution in Hughenden Manor. Purchased as a stepping stone to public greatness, it was also a private retreat in which the contradictory elements of his evolving personal and professional identity found permanent expression.

The Hughenden estate, sold by John Norris to Disraeli in 1848, consisted of around 750 acres and contained a modest gentleman's residence. Still, the Disraelis could hardly afford it. Benjamin had married an older woman – Mary Anne – for her money ten years earlier and had been lucky enough to fall in love with her. He now borrowed a further £25,000 from his allies the Bentincks to bridge the gap between their means and his potential. Lord George Bentinck had been Disraeli's close political ally since their joint opposition to the repeal of the Corn Laws. He had undertaken to support Disrael's purchase of a country seat which, despite his sudden death in September 1848, his brothers, Lord Henry Bentinck and Lord Titchfield, concluded. Hughenden was only five miles from Disraeli's father's home at Bradenham, but in the world of Tory politics there was all the difference between renting and landownership: he had joined the landed gentry at last.

The dining room at Hughenden.

When the Disraelis took possession, the house was a white stuccoed building with a splendid hilltop situation. Norris had already begun to gothicise the interior. Disraeli continued and largely finished the work. For the exterior he commissioned Edward Buckton Lamb. It was an unusual choice because Lamb was essentially an ecclesiastical architect and rarely worked on private houses. Contemporaries knew him as a theatrical designer, operating slightly outside accepted conventions, who had been criticised by the *Ecclesiologist* for his failure to adhere to accepted forms.[5]

Gothic was fashionable in the 1840s, and its romantic and historical overtones appealed to Disraeli. Lamb added crenellations and ornate window surrounds to the house, removing the white colouring and transforming it into his idea of an ancient and stately pile. The result was slightly unusual, with ornate 'D's set into the brickwork and Disraeli's new coat of arms above the front door. In a nod to his Sephardic heritage, these featured heraldic staples of lions rampant and an eagle rising, topped by a tower with three ramparts, or crenellations. They suggest Disraeli's pride in his Jewish origins, refracted through the pleasure any arriviste would take in this symbol of status and belonging. Also on display was a bunch of grapes, acknowledging Mary Anne's maiden name of Viney. Disraeli did not just incorporate these arms into the house's frontage, he also set them within the ceilings of the entrance and inner halls: small, low-ceilinged rooms that allow visitors an excellent view. As with so many of his alterations, the ribbing in these rooms was done on the cheap. Not stonework, but plaster and stretched linen provide the perfect setting for the Beaconsfield arms.

The interior of this house is heavy with portraits, each having been chosen for its relationship to Disraeli. The simple family likenesses that occupy much of the ground floor were among the relatively few things he brought with him to Hughenden. Paintings of his father and the paternal grandfather whose name he shared hang proudly in the dining room, gesturing towards different aspects of his own identity (opposite). For Disraeli's grandfather provided a link with the family's grand continental origins, while Isaac had moved in a literary world to which Benjamin, too, felt he belonged. He relegated his terrifying paternal grandmother, Sarah Shiprut de Gabay Villa Real, to the infrequently used State Bedroom. Instead, on the ground floor, a group of delicate drawings of his uncle Ephraim, and of his cousins Emily and Cecilia Lindo (by the Irish painter Daniel Maclise), are tokens of his respect for the maternal line, offering a gentle homage to his Jewish background in a house that otherwise seems to project a rather conventional message. Like many of the family pictures, they are small, intimate images, whispering of Disraeli's loved ones, and of the intellectual milieu centred on Lady Blessington's salon, in which both Disraeli and Maclise moved. Only a few paintings, like those of Mary Anne and his brother James, by James Middleton, are larger and bolder. These articulate Disraeli's role as head of the family, now actively curating their image.

Close to his family hangs dashing, dastardly Lord Byron: the celebrated poet, lover, soldier and exile who provided Disraeli with a model of sorts. Returning from Jerusalem, the future owner of Hughenden had posed in Byronic dress for Maclise as 'the Author of Vivien Grey', complete with divan-style cushions and a hookah pipe (see p. 68). Disraeli's Byronic styling remains unmistakable in the 1851 portrait by Sir Francis Grant that now hangs in the library. Personal ties reinforced Disraeli's sense of kinship to the literary superstar, who had shared a publisher with his father Isaac. Surprisingly perhaps, Byron even described Isaac as one of his favourite authors. Both Isaac and Benjamin treasured a copy of Isaac's *The Literary Character* (1818) that had once belonged to Byron's brother-in-law and contained some marginalia by the great man, said to have inspired some revisions to the second edition. Such was Benjamin's passion for all things Byronic that he even sought

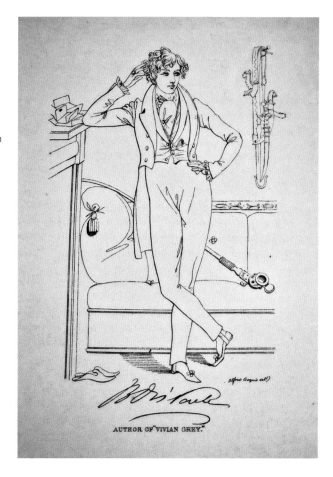

After Daniel Maclise, *Author of "Vivian Grey"* (Benjamin Disraeli), lithograph, published in *Fraser's Magazine for Town and Country*, May 1833. The nonchalant pose and studiedly fashionable dress in this image encapsulate Disraeli's dandyism. The Turkish slippers, cushioned divan, long pipe and sheath of Asian daggers hanging on the wall underline the orientalism in the famous author's self-fashioning.

AUTHOR OF "VIVIAN GREY."

Daniel Maclise, *Giovanni Battista Falcieri (known as Tita)*, 1836 watercolour on paper. Falcieri, portrayed here in Greek costume, was Lord Byron's gondolier in Venice and he held Byron as he died at Missolonghi in Greece. Falcieri accompanied Disraeli to Greece, Turkey and Egypt between 1830 and 1831 and became valet to Disraeli's father at Bradenham.

out Byron's former personal servant, Tita Falcieri, who accompanied him to Jerusalem in 1830 before settling at Bradenham as his father's valet. Here, in 1836, Falcieri posed for a particularly fine chalk portrait by Maclise, also displayed at Hughenden (below left). This, like the painting of his idol Disraeli purchased in 1876, underlines his fascination with a man who was both the archetypal romantic hero and a social pariah.

Here, and elsewhere, Disraeli created an environment subtly different from the properties of more established members of the landed elite, who often lacked the impetus and the freedom to remodel their houses in this way. Not a dynastic house, but a home in which he narrated his own life to himself, his social circle and posterity. Take the portraits of Disraeli's friends and political supporters, hung in loosely chronological order: this 'Gallery of Friendship' honours the men who promoted his unprecedented career in a deliberate echo of the picture galleries of great men often found in country houses. Deeper into the house, a quantity of royal gifts trumpets its owner's intimacy with Queen Victoria. Almost every room testifies to her affection through a painting, an object or a book – most strikingly, perhaps, the royal portraits on the first floor, readily identified by the cushioned crown set grandly atop their frames. These visible signs of royal approval understandably brought great pleasure to a man with uncertain credentials. Disraeli's unequal friendship with Victoria was to form the core of his personal myth-making in later life, central to both his image and his identity.

At first the queen had thought Disraeli 'most singular, – thoroughly Jewish looking, a livid complexion, dark eyes, & eyebrows, & black ringlets', fearing '[t]he country can have no confidence in men like Disraeli'.[6] Things changed after the Conservatives returned to power in 1866 and Disraeli became Chancellor of the

Exchequer, later serving two terms as prime minister. His lively reports amused her, and his attentions after the death of her husband overcame her prejudices. There was flattery here in abundance, but charm, wit and sensitivity too. The gallantry this loyal courtier extended to his monarch, and vice versa, had a self-consciously literary quality. When Victoria visited Hughenden in 1877, she gave Disraeli a painting of herself copied from the portrait by Heinrich von Angeli that was her favourite, and another of her host that she had insisted he sit for. Disraeli, in turn, shortened the legs of one of the dining chairs so that the feet of his diminutive 'Faery Queen' might touch the floor. There it remains to this day, recalling a never-to-be-forgotten moment in the history of the house.[7]

An outsider now stood at the pinnacle of the British establishment. Before his death, Disraeli specified a list of items to remain always at Hughenden. Tellingly, he kept back little of religious significance apart from a few prayer chairs and a precious medieval crucifix from mother-of-pearl that he had acquired in the Holy Land. Nor did he retain many landscapes, or paintings of subjects other than people. What mattered instead were the books he inherited, the portraits of friends and family assembled during his lifetime, gifts from Victoria and other well-wishers, and mementoes of his triumphs and early failures. The latter included a chair that had been optimistically commissioned by Disraeli when he first stood for parliament, to carry him through the streets of High Wycombe after his victory. He did not win, but the 'spare chair' remained in his household. Childless, and uninterested in passing on a title to his undistinguished brother or nephew, Disraeli understood the house and its contents less as the germ of a new dynasty than a monument to his life and achievements as a great man.

A bookish home

The library tells a different story. Historians have focused on Disraeli's written output, and his papers at Oxford provide rich pickings for the biographer. Yet his library — the distillation of his inheritance, thoughts and interests — may provide a truer window onto his soul. With its handsome collection and precious inlaid fireplace by Pietro Bossi, this is the grandest room at Hughenden; the place we come closest to encountering the man behind the glittering persona.

Isaac D'Israeli had been known for the size and quality of his book collection: he reputedly amassed some 25,000 volumes. The 3,373 books now at Hughenden represent just a small fraction of this collection — certainly not the most valuable, but, significantly, the ones his son chose to retain. Benjamin was deeply invested in this literary inheritance. As a ten-year-old boy, he wrote his name under that of his father in a 1774 copy of *Aesop's Fables*: 'Benj Disraeli, Jany 3 1814, his Book.' He kept that volume with its childish drawings (whether by father or son is hard to say). Many other books are rich with annotations and marginalia, well loved and well used. Collectively, they reflect their owner's interests, the kinds of knowledge he valued and what fired his self-regard. Here, for once, he was free to express his thoughts without consideration for audience or public image.

The organisation of Disraeli's library is believed to be faithful to the original, despite the fact that it was originally located in what is now the drawing room. It underlines the fascination felt by both Isaac and Benjamin for Jewish and Christian history, and their interest in the impact of religious ideas (both Jewish and Christian) on historical events. Thus 'Jewish' and 'Christian' texts are jumbled together on the same shelf, perhaps reflecting Disraeli's sense of the close relationship between the two faiths: a view that was not uncommon at the time. These books form an extensive, very visible element to the collection. There are Bibles, works of biblical and Christian history, commentaries on the Old and New Testaments, and a Qur'an.

Isaac Cardoso, *Las Excelencias de los Hebreos*, Amsterdam, 1679. This volume – a defence of Judaism by a Portuguese doctor (and forebear of Disraeli) – was owned by Isaac D'Israeli, whose notes are inserted between the pages. Isaac drew upon it for his own 1833 publication *The Genius of Judaism* and Benjamin gave it a prominent place in his library at Hughenden.[8]

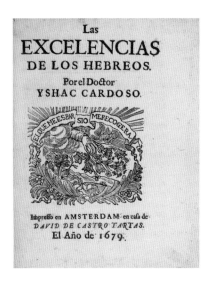

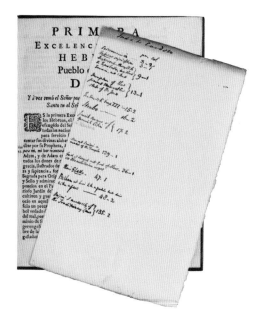

Benjamin Disraeli's study, photographed by J. P. Starling, 1881. This is one of a set of photographs commissioned by Queen Victoria and taken during her visit to Hughenden after Disraeli's funeral.

Queen Victoria, *Leaves from the Journal of Our Life in the Highlands, from 1841 to 1861, to which are prefixed and added extracts from the same journal giving an account of earlier visits to Scotland and tours in England and Ireland and yachting excursions*, edited by Arthur Helps, London (Smith, Elder and Co.), 1868. This gift from Queen Victoria prompted Disraeli to describe the Queen and himself as 'we authors, Ma'am'.

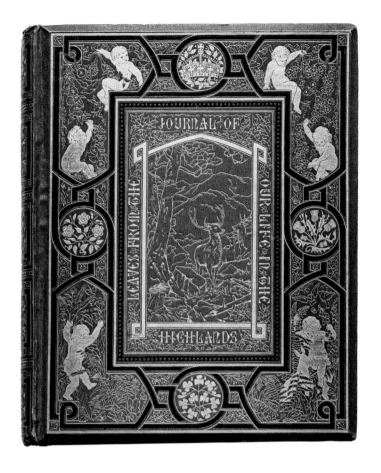

Johann Wolfgang von Goethe, *Faust*, London, Frederick Brukmann, 1877 (with an inscription by Queen Victoria, 1876, pasted in). This new translation into English of a masterpiece of German literature was a Christmas gift to Disraeli from Victoria. The specially commissioned binding is decorated with silver medallions depicting the main characters.

These sit alongside Abraham Kuenen's *The Prophets and Prophesy in Israel* (1877), Salomon Munk's *Palestine* (1845), William Drummond's *The Oedipus Judaicus* (1811) and E. H. Lindo's *The History of the Jews of Spain and Portugal* (1848), to name but a few. Nearby we can see Isaac's three-volume set of *The History of the Jews*, annotated and with Temple plans intact. A few shelves away, there is a copy of William Whiston's translation of the works of Josephus (1737), a widely disseminated text with particular significance for the Disraelis, since it is now supposed Isaac was the author of *A Sequel to the History of the Jews; continued to the present time*, which was appended to Josephus in the Victorian reprinting of Whiston. That edition appeared after Isaac's death, having been completed and published by Benjamin and Sarah in a touching gesture of filial devotion.[9] It was perhaps in this context that father and son engaged with a 1684 copy of the works of John Lightfoot, which still contains an extensive sheet of notes discussing 'The Land of Israel', 'Tradition' and 'Jerusalem a Holy City'. These notes were mostly written by Isaac, although a few are apparently in Benjamin's hand.[10] With their references to Rabbis Akiva, Tarphon and Yohanan ben Zaccai, they suggest an interest in Talmudic sources hampered by an inability to access them, except through the work of earlier Christian scholars.

Here and elsewhere, the library reveals the humanity of a man who loved his Jewish father and took pride in their shared past. Tellingly, it was in a preface to a new, posthumous edition of Isaac's *Curiosities of Literature* that Benjamin most fully articulated his account of the Disraelis and their origins. He dwelt on their 'rich estates' in Spain, their time in Venice, their arrival in England and their notable relatives; he wrote too of Isaac's affection for Buckinghamshire and burial at Bradenham, noting that he had 'repaid England for the protection and the hospitality which this country accorded to his father a century ago'.[11]

Just as Benjamin selectively reinvented his family history, so he enriched the family library with carefully chosen embellishments. 'My library is my weak point,' he once wrote to the wealthy Jewish widow Mrs Brydges Willyams, his friend and admirer. 'It is that, of wh:, of all material possessions I am most proud / & fond. I inherited, & I enriched, it.'[12] A receipt issued in early 1874 suggests he could spend as much as £31 4*s* on a single occasion. Disraeli knew these books and loved them. Writing to Lady Bradford in the 1870s, he described his favourite as 'a thin folio of the sacred time'.[13] That volume was Pietro Bembo's *Prose della volgar lingua* (1525), stamped with the mark of the Medici. Disraeli valued it because of 'the subject, the author, the beautiful printing, the pages, 400 years old but without a stain', and enjoyed its illustrious provenance, noting that this special book had once belonged to Pope Clement VII.[14] Interestingly, Disraeli also purchased the oldest book in the library at about this time: the *Enea Silvio epistole* (1477), a collection of the letters of Pope Pius II. Perhaps he found these papal associations amusing, appreciating the gravitas they brought to his book collection.

Most important, in this regard, were further gifts from Her Majesty. The library houses an inscribed copy of Queen Victoria's *Leaves from the Journal of Our Life in the Highlands*, a publication that prompted Disraeli to describe the pair, teasingly, as 'we authors, Ma'am' (see p. 71, top). Nearby sits a unique copy of *Faust*: a huge volume, with a specially designed embossed cover and a dedication from the queen wishing her friend a merry Christmas (p. 71, bottom). In this way the library testifies not just to Disraeli's origins, but also to his dazzling social ascent.

The monument to Isaac D'Israeli stands on Tinkers Hill, opposite Hughenden. It was commissioned by Mary Anne Disraeli in 1862 and designed by the architect Edward Buckton Lamb, who subsequently remodelled Hughenden. The inscription praises Isaac for 'diffusing among the multitude that elevating taste for literature, which, before his time, was the privilege only of the learned'.

A gentleman's country estate

At Bradenham, Disraeli's father had lived as a certain kind of English gentleman; now Disraeli reinterpreted that lifestyle in his own idiosyncratic key. This was an eighteenth- and nineteenth-century property, but he had a quasi-medieval understanding of his role as 'lord of the manor' and sometimes referred to local workmen as 'the peasants'.[15] His health was fragile, he had little interest in country sports, and his chaotic finances meant he could seldom afford the notoriously expensive local hunts. Yet Disraeli embraced his role as squire of this microcosm, abandoning the dandyish clothes of his youth for country wear and a stick, and chatting freely with local 'bodgers' as they prepared chair legs in the surrounding woods. Supported by Mary Anne, he learned to love this life as a member of the local squirearchy. 'Our rural fete, on Wednesday was very successful', he wrote to Mrs Brydges Willyams in September 1860; 'there were 100 school children, as many farmers & peasants with their wives & all the county families for ten miles round'.[16]

In other ways, Disraeli's country estate served as a backdrop for his eclectic personal mythology. As he asserted to Mrs Brydges Willyams, with blatant disregard for historical accuracy, 'we have restored the house to what it was before the civil wars, & we have made a garden of terraces, in which cavaliers might roam and saunter with their layde-loves'.[17] In fact, he left the design of the Italianate gardens to Mary Anne but gave more thought to the statuary, which references classical antiquity – ancient Greece in particular. He was especially drawn to the story of Hero and Leander: there is a statue of Hero in the drawing room, and he even created a lake in the parkland to represent the Hellespont, naming the swans living on the island Hero and Leander. Byron once swam the Hellespont in honour of Leander, and we may read this feature of Hughenden not just as an affirmation of the power of romantic love but as a reference to this modern hero.

At the bottom of the park, the ground rises gently from the stream and, as it begins to level, there is a shift in emphasis to the legends of the European North. This is not a theme we often associate with Disraeli, who grafted a manna ash to a base of common ash with his own hands to create Hughenden's own Yggdrasil: the Norse tree of life. This grafting of exotic stock onto a sturdy local base was surely intended to echo his own place in society; the manna ash is a deciduous tree native to southern Europe, and we may imagine that Disraeli liked the Old Testament connotations of its name. Elsewhere, he planted cedars of Lebanon from seeds that he had brought back from the Holy Land, and sought to give the woods a Germanic feel with the addition of specimen fir trees.

Disraeli found great pleasure 'in the renovated glories of the woods, which were splendid with sunshine, & deep, perfumed, shade', but the confidence he displayed shaping his home and parkland were limited to the areas surrounding the house.[18] His agent oversaw farm and estate management, leaving Disraeli to boast of the 'magnificent' crops, which included sainfoin, a sileage crop that flowered bright pink.[19] A landowner but never really a farmer, these forays into agriculture were more aesthetic than practical. Although Benjamin's touch was sometimes unsure, the Disraelis did make one significant alteration to the landscape: on the hill opposite Hughenden stands a monumental obelisk, designed by Edward Buckton Lamb, and erected in honour of Isaac (above). Prominently situated and clearly visible from afar, this ostentatious gesture of filial admiration is an unmistakable assertion of the family's status in the area.

3 The Château de Ferrières: a European powerhouse

Pauline Prevost-Marcilhacy

Eugène Lami, *The Smoking Room at the Château de Ferrières*, c.1860, watercolour on paper.

Built for Baron James de Rothschild between 1853 and 1862, the Château de Ferrières is arguably the most important example of French domestic architecture and taste of its time, proof that its owner could create a monument as significant as those the Second Empire was raising in Paris.[1] A symbol of the baron's quest for prestige, Ferrières signalled a new paradigm: technological modernity (represented by the choice of Crystal Palace architect Joseph Paxton) combined with tradition (reflected in interiors by the painter Eugène Lami; 1800–90).[2] Here, Lami appropriated not only royal models, but also those of Emperor Napoléon III's Louvre. These innovations would broaden the boundaries of art and serve as the model for the Beaux-Arts mansions of the United States.

'Rothschild I, King of the Jews'

James Mayer de Rothschild (1792–1868; see p. 82) was the youngest of the Rothschild brothers who settled in five European capitals during the first decades of the nineteenth century, establishing a transnational business dynasty that would dominate European finance. Arriving in France during the last years of Napoléon I, James proved quite as brilliant as his elder brother Nathan, married his niece Betty (p. 82) and integrated quickly into Parisian society. These successes predated the 1830 July Revolution, which heralded the birth of a new regime headed by the deposed king's cousin Louis Philippe, the duc d'Orléans, who ruled as king not of France but the French. In the 1820s, the Bourbons had struggled to reconcile some of the profound innovations unleashed by the original French Revolution with the decision to indemnify the emigré aristocracy and promote a militant, authoritarian vision of Catholic monarchy. In contrast, the Orléanist regime positioned itself as the defender of the principles of the revolution, including state secularism and constitutional freedoms, while strengthening the power of the new capitalist elites.

This was an economic and political moment in which Jews, financiers and industrialists flourished. James rapidly asserted himself as France's leading state banker, laying the foundations of the French rail network in 1835 and investing in major industrial enterprises.[3] A growing property portfolio testified to his social success.[4] In 1818, James had acquired his first Parisian townhouse at 19 rue Lafitte: a distinguished eighteenth-century *hôtel particulier* whose previous owners included the prominent Bonapartist politician and former Jacobin Joseph Fouché, and Empress Joséphine's daughter Hortense, mother of the future Napoléon III.[5] A year earlier, James had bought the Château Boulogne-Billancourt from the banker Jean Charles Davillier, later employing the architect Armand Berthelin to refurbish it in the style of Louis XIV. In 1829, James acquired his second rural estate. This was the Domaine de Ferrières in Seine-et-Marne, a property recently redesigned by Joseph Fouché, when he served as the Minister of Police under Napoléon. In 1838, James complemented the purchase by acquiring the Hôtel de Talleyrand at 2 rue Saint-Florentin in Paris, which had belonged to the legendary French diplomat of the same name. So it was that within the space of two decades, James assumed ownership of 'the houses of the two cleverest politicians of his time' (to cite one near contemporary).[6]

In 1830, Catholicism ceased to be the state religion and the situation of French Jews improved accordingly. Yet the association of Jewish bankers with the traumatic social changes unleashed by industrialisation created a different vulnerability: the new king's favour enabled the Rothschilds to handle all the major financial affairs of his reign. The 1840s consequently saw the emergence of a distinctively socialist antisemitism, with the name Rothschild evoking particular vitriol. In 1846, for example, a fatal crash on the newly built (Rothschild-owned) Chemins de Fer du Nord (Northern Railway Company) prompted the journalist Mathieu Georges Dairnvaell to publish his scathing pamphlet *Histoire édifiante et curieuse de Rothschild Ier, roi des Juifs* ('The Edifying and Curious History of Rothschild I, King of the Jews'; below), attracting praise from none other than Friedrich Engels. The socialist Alphonse Toussenel developed much the same theme in his substantial two-volume work *Les Juifs, rois de l'époque: histoire de la féodalité financière* ('The Jews, Kings of the Age: A History of Financial Feudalism'). Once again, James was the chief target.[7]

Then, in February 1848, the people of Paris overthrew Louis Philippe, ushering in a chaotic period of revolutionary instability that would enable Louis-Napoléon Bonaparte to take power and, after the coup of 2 December 1851, style himself emperor. In his youth, Napoléon III had flirted with revolutionary nationalism in Italy, and his radical past continued to influence some aspects of his political and economic thinking. At the outset, however, the Second Empire was an authoritarian regime that traded on the memory of past glories, and on the promise of peace, order, prosperity and stability. Baron James maintained distant relations with the new government, while his wife was too openly Orléanist to reopen her salon. It was in this context that the (Jewish) Minister of Finance, Achille Fould, implored Napoléon III to endorse the creation of France's first joint-stock bank and 'free himself from the tutelage of the Rothschilds, who reign in spite of you'.[8] Led by Benoît Fould and the Sephardic Pereire brothers, the Crédit Mobilier reflected social theorist Henri de Saint-Simon's radical ideas regarding state and society, and it represented a direct challenge to the Rothschilds.[9]

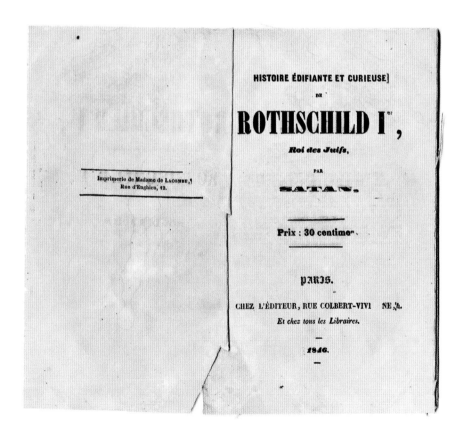

Mathieu Georges Dairnvaell, *Histoire édifiante et curieuse de Rothschild Ier, roi des Juifs*, Paris, 1846, title page. The journalist and pamphleteer Dairnvaell, who used the pen name Satan, was behind some of the most influential antisemitic attacks on the Rothschilds.

HISTOIRE ÉDIFIANTE ET CURIEUSE

DE

ROTHSCHILD Ier,

Roi des Juifs,

PAR

SATAN.

Prix : 30 centimes.

PARIS.

CHEZ L'ÉDITEUR, RUE COLBERT-VIVI NE. 4.

Et chez tous les Libraires.

1846.

Imprimerie de Madame de LACOMBE, Rue d'Enghien, 42.

All this prompted James to find other ways of asserting his status and authority.[10] In 1852 he financed the rebuilding of the synagogue on the rue Notre Dame de Nazareth, in what *L'Illustration* described as 'a spicy mixture of oriental and Byzantine style'.[11] Then came the opening of the Rothschild Hospital on rue de Picpus,[12] followed in due course by the Great Synagogue on the rue de la Victoire – a building of powerful integrity and a worthy companion not just to Ferrières but also to other secular architectural wonders of the time, such as the new opera house (1861–75) built for the emperor by Charles Garnier, and the Gare du Nord (1861–5), whose German architect Jakob Hittorff had been selected under James's personal supervision.[13]

Acquiring the Fouché property at Ferrières had been a strategic decision. It reflected James's desire for a country residence easily accessible from Paris, the attraction of owning land in an area once home to a flourishing medieval Jewish community, and the importance of hunting in aristocratic society (see p. 91). Similar considerations prompted the Pereire brothers to acquire a property at Armainvilliers, just a few kilometres away, transposing the rivalry between these two Jewish business dynasties to this provincial French setting. Yet James de Rothschild did not build his château on the foundations of the Fouché house, but on high ground 300 metres away from it, set apart from the village to which the original seigneurial château house had been bound by ties of mutual obligation. It was a hugely ambitious undertaking that reflected a desire to outdo his British nephew Mayer (who in 1850 had commissioned Joseph Paxton to build his country house at Mentmore), and the more pressing need to gain Napoléon III's favour.[14] What James could not obtain politically, he now sought to achieve artistically. In this sense, Ferrières was a riposte to the emperor's own *grands projets*: the Exposition Universelle of 1855, inspired by the Great Exhibition of 1851 with which Paxton was so closely associated, and the new Louvre, both of which he entrusted to the Pereires, the Rothschilds' staunchest adversaries.[15]

A cosmopolitan house

The Château de Ferrières was one of the most substantial private commissions of its kind at the time. Construction took nine years and called for enormous financial and human resources. The choice of gardener-turned-architect Joseph Paxton (1801–65) was not anodyne: employing an Englishman whose fame had spread beyond his own country distinguished James from his rivals and rendered him assertively modern. Paxton, indeed, had been invited to serve as Universal Advisor to the 1855 Exposition Universelle, for which the emperor apparently hoped he might create a 'Diamond Palace', bigger, better and more permanent than the Crystal Palace original.[16] The construction team at Ferrières, led by John Nuttall, was similarly international, comprising 200 French and English labourers, with the main structure entrusted to the George Myers company, who handled all the Rothschild projects in England.[17] The upshot was not a French house but a self-consciously European château.

Ferrières's massive, square plan with its four-square corner towers, abundance of openings and enormous double-height, glass-roofed central hall, recalls the English Renaissance power houses Paxton had evoked at Mentmore, but the façades speak in Italian and French too (although interestingly, not the German of James's birth). Among the most prominent references to the high-water marks of different national traditions, we find Palladio on the west front (Palazzo Chiericati in Vicenza) representing Renaissance Italy, and Le Vau's Cour Carrée at the Louvre on the south front, recalling *grand siècle* France.[18] In this way, James underlined his family's status as Europe's premier banking dynasty.

The Château de Ferrières, photographed c.1937–8.

The French writer, critic and publisher Edmond de Goncourt would describe Ferrières as 'a hodge-podge of all styles, the foolish ambition to amalgamate all monuments into one', but its owner understood the house as a symbol: a totally modern monument testifying to his status as a prince of international finance and industry.[19] It was in this spirit that the château's triumphal porch explicitly referenced architect Jean-Marie Victor Viel's massive entrance to the Palace of Industry at the Exposition Universelle of 1855. The message was reinforced by sculptures of *Abundance* and *Prosperity* on either side of the clock, and by the family motto, *Concordia, Integritas, Industria*, with its proud embrace of bourgeois virtues. For this was a historicising interior with every modern convenience: central heating throughout, and the kitchen located outside the château, but linked to the dining room by a small train.

Ferrières also gratified James's artistic leanings. The old nobility used their châteaux for a few weeks each year, but Ferrières was conceived as a palace to be inhabited for months on end, with eighteen different apartment suites.[20] Here, for the first time, a country house presented a universal and eclectic collection, itself embodying an international cultural synthesis, in a manner that consciously recalled recent museological schemes. So it was that the main hall became the baron's 'personal museum', organised by Paxton to set off James's collection according to modern museum practice.[21] Here, Paxton followed the French architect Félix Duban who, in 1851, had covered the Louvre's Salon Carré with a vast, generously arched glass ceiling. The role of Eugéne Lami here was fundamental. Lami had close ties to the house of Orléans, having decorated the Tuileries Palace for the duc de Nemours (Louis Philippe's second son), and the apartments of the *petit château* at Chantilly for the duc d'Aumale, his younger brother. Lami also worked as James's decorator and art agent at the Château de Boulogne-Billancourt and at Ferrières. Although Paxton conceived the great hall, Lami was responsible for the staging of James's art collection. More concerned with theatrical effect than historical accuracy, his new decor drew on both Italian and French styles.

Below and opposite top
Eugène Lami, *The Great Hall at the Château de Ferrières*, c.1860, watercolour on paper.

Opposite bottom
Eugène Lami, *The Louis XVI Salon at the Château de Ferrières*, c.1865, watercolour on paper. As well as designing the interiors at Ferrières,

Lami made a series of watercolours that records its interiors – filled with works of art and layered with historical styles – inhabited by the Rothschilds and their friends.

Eugène Lami, *The Salon des Familles*, *c*.1865, watercolour on paper. This room was sometimes known as the Salon des Cuirs, after the painted leather panels depicting the triumph of David over Goliath (see pp. 94–5).

James, who focused on painting and, especially, the decorative arts, saw his collection as an instrument of representation. Sumptuousness ruled supreme. The great hall emulates both the Louvre and the more ephemeral Musée Napoléon III, which opened between May and October 1862 in the Palais de l'Industrie to display the prestigious Campana Collection.[22] But James's ostentatious eclecticism also expressed a certain cosmopolitanism: his fondness for furniture and French *objets d'art* of royal origin is well known, but the quality and abundance of his collection was distinctive. For example, he displayed Chinese objects from the 1860 sack of Beijing in the large sitting room alongside modern pieces. The overall impression was a spectacular alliance of the Renaissance (for instance, the French designer of ornament and spectacle, Jean Bérain) with Louis XIV (Lami's designs frequently paid homage to the Ambassadors' Staircase at Versailles). This became a central characteristic of the so-called Rothschild style, of which Ferrières was an early, and seminal, manifestation. Not for nothing did Édouard Drumont, the prominent French antisemite, write of the great hall in his bestselling *La France juive* ('Jewish France'): 'It is the place's triumphal room: everything here speaks of triumphs.'[23]

The underlying theme of this château is regal power, wielded not by a conventional monarch but by James himself, defiantly subverting antisemitic attacks on his influence and position. His pretensions to royalty found diverse forms of expression. The principal and most explicit was the lavish use of his initials, his monogram and the family emblem topped with a crown, clearly proclaiming the reign of the Rothschilds. The second was the appropriation of French royal emblems like the crescent of Henri II and the sun of Louis XIV, and of imagery borrowed from the Venetian doges of the Renaissance, with whose banker princes and collector merchants the Rothschilds identified. Thus the model for the end wall of the galleried great hall, in which the caryatids representing the *Four Continents* allude overtly to the Rothschilds, was the tomb of Doge Giovanni Pesaro in the church of Santa Maria Gloriosa dei Frari in Venice, while the tomb of Doge Girolamo Venier in the same building is the starting point for the staging of a sculpture of *Hercules and the Nemean Lion* by Ignazio and Filippo Collino in a niche flanked by columns at the top of the main staircase.[24] This identification with the Italian Renaissance, and specifically Venice, was surely intended as a reference to the Jewish merchants who contributed so much to the prosperity of La Serenissima. Visitors would have understood this symbolism on multiple levels. The French sculptor Charles Cordier (1827–1905) had received several commissions from the imperial couple, but Ferrières was his most prestigious. Here, and elsewhere, Cordier's work explored ethnographic themes in a way that reflected nineteenth-century ideas about race, civilisation and empire.[25] Yet this commission also transposed widely disseminated (inherently antisemitic) ideas about Jewish power and the global reach of the Rothschilds into a different cultural register, rendering them instead in a triumphalist mode that recast conventional hierarchies by assimilating the Oriental Jew into the dominant idea of whiteness.

Certainly, Ferrières asserts its place within the history of a cosmopolitan Europe. Yet two spectacular works with biblical themes suggest that James did not neglect his Jewish heritage altogether. The first is the monumental vase he commissioned from Henri de Triqueti in 1856, entitled *The Israelites During Their Captivity in Babylon*, an event deeply etched in Jewish memory. Its significance is hard to read. Did the commission signify James's interest in Jewish history, or does it indicate a taste for the Orléans' favourite sculptor: a Protestant who specialised in large vases bearing an allegorical message? Or was it simply a question of opportunity? (The same scene had been proposed for the choir of St Paul's Cathedral in London, but not executed.)[26] The second is a historic cordovan hanging that James purchased in 1855 at the Schloss Weissenstein sale in Pommersfelden, Bavaria (see pp. 94–5). Unusual both in its 3-metre-high leather support and for the symbolism of its content, it depicts David holding the head of Goliath. Such works had been very fashionable in wealthy homes in the Middle East and North Africa in the sixteenth and seventeenth centuries, but they were extremely rare in nineteenth-century France.[27] Once again, it is unclear whether James was attracted by the biblical subject matter – presented here in spectacular fashion – or if he simply enjoyed acquiring works that were disinctive, exceptional and unfashionable. A more 'Jewish' reading of these acquisitions is complicated by the third of the Gobelins tapestries in the great hall (*The Victory at Tolbiac*), which depicts the triumph of Christianity over pagan barbarism: not an obvious subject for a Jewish home, even if we can understand it as one in a series of secular triumphs (alongside *The Victory of Neptune*, *The Victory of Alexander* and *The Victory of Peace*).

James seems to have been the least observant of the five original Rothschild brothers. His urge towards ostentation and official acceptance was counterbalanced by religious discretion. In contrast to the neighbouring smoking room, decorated by Lami with a fresco that evokes Tiepolo and the carnival of Venice (and depicted by him with figures representing the Rothschild family smoking hubble-bubble pipes *à la turque*; see p. 80), the oratory at Ferrières is a modest space. Inaugurated in October 1863 in the presence of the Chief Rabbi and other leading Jewish figures, the *Archives israélites* described it as 'a simple room which has just four ornaments, the Torah rolls, the seven-branched candlestick … a piano, and several straw chairs'.[28] The piano suggests a less than strictly orthodox observance, while the absence of photographs or any other description of this space underlines the desire of the Rothschilds to treat their domestic worship as a private matter: an approach very much in keeping with French state-secularism, which treated religion as a matter for the individual conscience. Integration and affirmation of identity, a blend of the Christian and non-Christian, of modernity and the distant past – these were perhaps the most characteristic features of the *ésprit Rothschild*.

The splendour and misery of a Rothschild property

Upon completion in 1862, Ferrières became first a centre of Rothschild power, and then a *lieu de mémoire*.[29] Napoléon III's visit on 16 December of that year set an official seal on the rapprochement between James and the emperor: a grand diplomatic event that drew the British ambassador and the French Minister of Foreign Affairs, together with representatives of the British, French, Italian and Austrian branches of the Rothschild family.[30] The imperial flag was raised above one of the towers to mark the emperor's arrival and the day abounded with symbolism.[31] Evelina (daughter of Lionel and Charlotte de Rothschild) reported:

> Uncle James do [sic] the honours, he introduced every body to the Emperor, even Mamie, and of course Mr Lami, who was decorated on the spot and is now officer.… You were quite right in supposing that the Emperor would wish to see every thing, for before breakfast he went with uncle James to view the stables, the gardens, and all the farms.[32]

After the hunt, singers from the Paris Opéra performed works by Giaochino Rossini and Émilien Pacini, conducted by Victor Massé.[33] It was a defining moment in the history of the house: the silver service used at lunch had been made from moulds that were immediately destroyed to avoid duplication, and the emperor planted a cedar tree in the park to commemorate the occasion.

Édouard Riou, 'Hunting at Ferrières', lithograph, from the *Album de chasse illustrée* (Paris, Firmin Didot, 1870). Ferrières is depicted as the backdrop for country sports: from top to bottom, a pheasant shoot; men and women ready for the hunt; the aviary and hunting lodge.

This very public triumph served to establish Ferrières both as a place for diplomacy and a destination in its own right. Shortly afterwards came the Minister of Public Instruction [Education], accompanied by the bishop of Meaux and other leading functionaries of Seine-et-Marne.[34] A special train was arranged for Princess Mathilde's visit in November 1866, and a year later Ferrières proved as much an attraction as the second Exposition Universelle in Paris, when James's guests included the king and queen of Belgium, the grand duchess of Russia and the crown prince of Sweden.[35] The new Prussian chancellor, Otto von Bismarck, also became a regular visitor – a relationship mediated by his private banker, Gerson von Bleichröder, who was the Rothschild agent in Berlin.[36]

Nevertheless, the Franco-Prussian War of 1870–71 proved disastrous for the Rothschilds, who found themselves on opposing sides. The occupation of Ferrières by the Prussian military command marked the dawn of a new era. It was here, on 19 September 1870, after the French army had been routed and the Second Empire overthrown, that Bismarck famously humiliated French Minister of Foreign Affairs Jules Favre, offering peace on terms so unacceptable that the provisional government saw no option but to fight on.[37] His choice of venue was no doubt as deliberate as Bismarck's decision to found the new German Empire in the Hall of Mirrors at Versailles. For, as the Iron Chancellor noted, Ferrières was '[t]oo beautiful for a king, it can belong only to a Rothschild'.[38] This aphorism reflected the raucous antisemitism Ferrières inspired among the conquerors, who marvelled at the luxurious estate of the *Juden-könig* and joked that the heraldic 'J. R.' signified not James de Rothschild, but *Judeaorum Rex*.

There was, of course, another side to this story. Ownership of a château in the nineteenth century required large landholdings to ensure its survival. In 1895, the grounds comprised 400 hectares, to which were subsequently added (by Alphonse and Édouard de Rothschild) 1,500 hectares of farmland and 8,000 hectares of woodland. Like many landowning aristocrats, James indulged in all sorts of scientific experiments and introduced modern farming techniques here, long before he set about constructing his grand Second Empire château. As early as 1842, James's British sister-in-law Hannah wrote to her son Mayer:

> We have been passing a few days at Ferrieres, the shooting place and estate of uncle James. They are doing a great deal to it … 10,000 acres of land are a great many. It's very productive, more so than land is in general in France on account of the soil being moist and rich, and brings in a good revenue.[39]

Ferrières, in fact, became the beating heart of a vast economic system, keeping the Paris townhouses and the Château de Boulogne supplied with food, firewood and forage. The construction of spectacular outbuildings, farmhouses, an orangery, laundry, greenhouses, stables and a dairy underpinned the family's lavish lifestyle, as did the labour of 125 local workers.[40] As the local schoolteacher put it early in the twentieth century, 'At Ferrières there are a château and a magnificent property that keep almost the entire village alive.'[41]

The family were certainly aware of their obligations as landowning local notables. Study of the account books shows a transition away from traditional charity – the creation of a charity bureau in 1854, the appointment of a schoolteacher and doctor for employees, the distribution of money, bread, wheat and so on – to a more modern philanthropic approach.[42] Keen to increase his influence locally, James became actively involved. His social and financial standing enabled him to negotiate substantial state aid for repairs to the local church, and its classification, in 1862, as a historical monument.[43] The local population quadrupled during the first twenty years of Rothschild ownership. When the village hall and schoolroom became too small, James personally appointed an architect, overseeing plans, building work and decoration to ensure a plainness in keeping with the community's rural status.[44] He and Betty also assumed sponsorship of the private, non-confessional primary school at Ferrières, opening it to both boys and girls. They supplemented these traditional philanthropies by building a private theatre and dance hall for the château's staff – an exceptional development in rural France, although one with parallels in the history of other Jewish (and Rothschild) country houses.[45]

The Rothschilds saw Ferrières, too, as a unique entity: 'a symbol of a man and a family, and the expression of a veritable empire'. For James's son Alphonse it was all 'more fit for an Emperor than for beloved papa'.[46] Alphonse's wife Leonora thought it at odds with the Jewish spirit – 'much too fine for people who pray to return to the Promised Land'. Even so, as James's niece Charlotte appreciated, 'the parties James gave for crowned heads … [were] good for the family and for Israelites in general'.[47] But perhaps the most moving account of its place in his family's life comes from its last owner.

Stripped of their French nationality in September 1940, the Rothschilds had seen their belongings confiscated, their châteaux in Ferrières and Armainvilliers occupied by German troops from 20 June 1940 to 1 April 1941, and all their works of art seized and sent to Bavaria.[48] After the war, Ferrières was restored by Guy de Rothschild and his wife Marie-Hélène; for twenty years it was the scene of memorable parties. Then, in 1976, it acquired Historical Monument status and passed to the University of Paris, whose rector envisaged a museum to Napoléon III and a grand setting for seminars. This was a period in which the Second Empire was deeply unfashionable. As Guy lamented only a few years later, 'the dream of renewed life that Marie-Hélène and I held for it when we gave it to the University of Paris did not come true, and today the chateau has fallen into sad, dreamless sleep'.[49]

For Guy, it remained, the 'castle of my childhood'. Here, as a boy, he had hidden under the staircase while listening to Big Bertha shells exploding outside, played hide-and-seek in the cellars, enjoyed shooting parties on Sundays, and observed the Sabbath with his father. He remembered too the 'separate world' of their servants, and the family's charitable duties in the village. For him, Ferrières had been 'a world unto itself ... like an ocean liner in the forest, immobile, but nevertheless an invitation to adventure'. He had relished the grandeur of the main hall as 'a truly magical place', recalling that its 'vast dimensions and the soft light falling from the roof suggested the nave of a cathedral'. It also exemplified the so-called Rothschild style – 'a Napoleon III décor, personalised not only by art objects of all sorts, but above all by a sense of comfort and intimacy which intermingles furs, flowers, plants, family photographs, precious miniatures and rare books'.[50]

Furious with the French state for its administrative incompetence and disregard of the stipulations he had attached to the bequest, Guy regarded the gradual abandonment of Ferrières as 'a fate worse than its complete destruction'.[51] Today, the best known nineteenth-century château in France survives as a cookery school and conference venue. Celebrated and unloved, much like the family who owned it, it symbolises both the extraordinary achievement of the Rothschilds and their ambivalent place in French history.

Dutch School, *The Triumph of David*, *c.*1650, painted and embossed leather panels, laid down on canvas; acquired by James de Rothschild from the Schönborn Collection, Schloss Weissenstein, Pommersfelden, Germany.

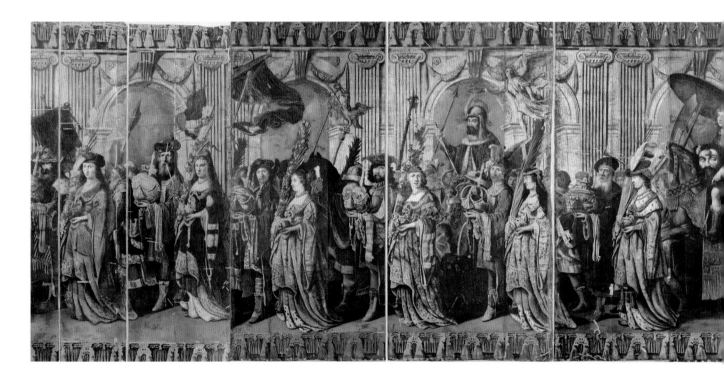

4 In Walpole's footsteps: Lady Waldegrave at Strawberry Hill

Nino Strachey

Few people forget their first glimpse of Strawberry Hill House. A fantasy Gothic castle in miniature, with turrets and pinnacles reaching for the sky, it tempts the eye from every angle. Built between 1747 and 1797 for the antiquarian Horace Walpole (1717–97), Strawberry Hill became famous for its curious architecture, the extraordinary collection formed by Walpole, and its role in inspiring Walpole's *The Castle of Otranto,* the first Gothic novel. Visitors flocked to see the fairy-tale confection he designed with the help of his 'Committee of Taste', the amateur architect John Chute (1701–76) and the artist Richard Bentley (1662–1742), described as '[a] little play-thing-house … the prettiest bauble you ever saw'.[1]

Armed with a printed guidebook, ticket holders admired the intricate decoration, and ever-growing collection of paintings, miniatures, prints and drawings, sculpture, furniture, ceramics and historic relics. Small in scale, but perfect in detail, the house established a new paradigm for the Gothic Revival in England. Walpole delighted in the interplay of real and fanciful, colour and light, fashioning Gothic tracery from papier-mâché, creating three-dimensional effects with *trompe l'oeil.*

Celebrated today as an example of 'outsider architecture', Walpole's vision was playfully subversive, expressing the queer aesthetic shared within his homosocial inner circle.[2] Public opinion was largely favourable during the eighteenth century, but in the nineteenth century, views differed. Reviewing an edition of Walpole's letters, the historian Thomas Babington Macaulay derided Strawberry Hill as a 'grotesque house with pie-crust battlements', the product of 'an unhealthy and disorganised mind'.[3] Although even Macaulay had to admit to the force of Walpole's charm, apparent in everything he did, whether in his building, his writing or his collecting.

One young outsider was seduced by Strawberry Hill from the moment she crossed the threshold. Frances Braham (1821–79; below), daughter of the Jewish opera singer John Braham (1774–1856; opposite), connected instinctively with the performative spirit of the house. As Frances, Countess Waldegrave she went on to inherit Strawberry Hill in 1846, to restore Walpole's original building in 1856, and transform it in her own image in 1862. A Braham by birth, Frances was seen by contemporaries as the daughter of her Jewish father. Regardless of her mother's ancestry, or the faith in which she and her four successive husbands had been raised, Frances figured as the Jewish Lady Waldegrave, her good reputation held perpetually in balance against the weight of hostile prejudice.

Waldegraves and Brahams

After Walpole's death, house and collection passed to the sculptress Anne Damer, and then to the Waldegrave family, descendants of Walpole's niece Maria. Strawberry Hill was no longer open to visitors, but its fame lingered. The collection was a source of prestige for the Waldegraves, who honoured Walpole's memory, both as an individual and as the son of Britain's first prime minister. By the time of Frances's first visit in August 1838, the family finances were in decline. Her hosts were the widowed 6th Countess Waldegrave, her illegitimate eldest child John Waldegrave, and her legitimate second son, George, 7th Earl Waldegrave. Frances married first one brother, then the other – inheriting the entire Waldegrave estate after both died young.

With creditors pressing on every side, George Waldegrave had been forced to settle his debts by selling the Walpole treasures. The Strawberry Hill sale began on 25 April 1842, lasted twenty-four days, and raised £33,468. Casting about for

Alphonse Léon Noël after James Rannie Swinton, *Frances, Countess Waldegrave*, 1851, hand-coloured lithograph, published by Lemercier, Paris, after a pastel of 1850.

Robert Dighton, *Lady Waldegrave's father, the opera singer John Braham (1774–1856) in the character of Orlando from Thomas Dibdin's comic opera 'The Cabinet'*, published 22 March 1802, hand-coloured etching.

someone to blame, George's uncle, Admiral William Waldegrave, decided Frances was responsible: 'So the trinkets of Strawberry Hill are to be sold. O perpetuity! O fame! And family pride! Those acquisitions of Horace Walpole fall into the hands of a Jewess and are sold.'[4]

In reality, it was Frances who arranged for key items to be 'bought in'. Harbouring, like Walpole, a passion for heraldry and genealogy, Frances preserved what she could. Writing in the *Quarterly Review,* Abraham Hayward noted her intention was to retain the most important Walpole and Waldegrave pictures; alas, 'some were sold by mistake, and she was unable to recover them'.[5] A total of eighty-two lots were rescued: paintings, stained glass from the windows, and small quantities of furniture, books and china. Five family portraits by Joshua Reynolds were secured, including *The Ladies Waldegrave* (faintly visible in the background of the image on. p. 116), which is now in the Scottish National Gallery.

Fascinated by Walpole's legacy, Frances was equally proud of her Braham heritage. According to the music historian David Conway, 'John Braham was the first English male singer to command a European reputation', performing for Napoléon in Paris and Nelson in Livorno.[6] His Jewish background set him apart. The *Times* concluded that Braham was 'one of the many instances of the aptitude of the Jewish race for music which can scarcely have escaped the notice of any age'.[7] The *Bath Chronicle* praised him as 'A sweet singer of Israel',[8] while Charles Lamb described him as 'a rare composition of the Jew, the gentleman and the angel'.[9]

John Braham was an only child whose parents were Jewish immigrants from the German lands. Orphaned young, he was taken in by Myer Lyon, *hazzan* (cantor) of the Great Synagogue in Duke's Place. Rumoured to have earned his living selling pencils in the street as a child, Braham's fortunes changed when Lyon recruited him as a *meshorrer* (junior assistant to the *hazzan*). Lyon also performed regularly as a tenor at Covent Garden under the name Michaele Leoni, and Braham made his first stage appearance at a benefit concert for Lyon in 1787.

Supported by the Goldsmid banking family, Braham's career went from strength to strength. His technique was mesmeric. 'The little Jew has bewitched me,' wrote Charles Lamb in 1808. 'I follow him like as the boys follow Tom the Piper. He cures me of melancholy as David cured Saul.'[10] Admiration, however, sometimes tipped into mockery. Braham's appearance was considered archetypally Jewish (short, with a large nose, dark hair and swarthy complexion), and he was widely caricatured. Critic Leigh Hunt, for example, believed Braham's singing was affected by his race: 'He had wonderful execution as well as force, and his voice could also be very sweet, though it was too apt to betray something of the nasal tone which has been observed in Jews, and which is, perhaps ... a habit in which they have been brought up.'[11]

In 1816, Braham married the niece of his Manchester concert promoter. In 1830 they leased the Grange, a fashionable eighteenth-century villa in Brompton. Their children grew up among fine things: 'splendid modern furniture', 'handsomely bound books' and 'foreign china'.[12] Even more impressive was the 'collection of antique paintings [and] drawings bronzes' assembled by 'the celebrated J Braham Esq'.[13] These included a Gainsborough portrait of the male soprano Giusto Tenducci, as well as works by Joshua Reynolds, David Wilkie, Richard Wilson and William Beechey. Among the Old Masters were paintings attributed to Breughel, Poussin, Wyck, Bronzino, Carlo Maratta, Canaletto, Teniers, Boucher, Greuze and Zuccarelli.[14]

Frances was nine when her parents moved to the Grange, and fourteen when they embarked on the biggest project of their lives: a London theatre. The savings nurtured by two banking houses – Goldsmid and Mitchell in London, and Rothschild Frères in Paris – were spent on the purchase of an expensive freehold plot on King

Street, St James's.[15] Braham approached London's leading theatre architect, Samuel Beazley, for the design. Frederick Crace and Son created the red-and-gold Louis XV-style interior, with a border of gilded flowers running round the dress circle, and scenes in the style of Watteau painted on the front of each box.

By founding an opera house, Braham hoped to take control of his own destiny, devising programmes where he could perform the lead, bringing new work to the London stage. Sadly, he was a better performer than impresario. The St James's Theatre Management Company folded with spectacular debts in 1839. Braham clung on to the freehold of the theatre, but he was forced to leave the Grange: its contents were dispersed by auction in June 1842.

The Strawberry Hill and Brompton Grange sales happened within the space of a few months, when Frances was only twenty-one. Although records survive for Strawberry Hill, it is difficult to know what she may have rescued from her family home. Among the heirlooms her adopted daughter inherited were the letters patent recording the coat of arms granted to John Braham in 1817. Braham's heraldry, illuminated on parchment by the Royal College of Arms, duly appeared in plaster, stone and stained glass at Strawberry Hill, given equal status to the Walpole and Waldegrave arms in all his daughter's residences.

Inheriting Strawberry Hill

Frances preferred to remember her father's triumphs. She was equally forgiving of her two Waldegrave husbands, who earned a reputation for drinking and wild living. Widowed twice by the age of twenty-five, Frances became, in 1846, sole heiress of Strawberry Hill and all the other Waldegrave property. The house was empty and dilapidated; retrenchment was needed before any repairs. Casting around for a new life partner to help manage a complex inheritance, Frances made a pragmatic choice: the eminently respectable Liberal MP George Granville Harcourt (1785–1861), known for his financial probity and mastery of estate management. According to Frances's biographer, Harcourt's father, the elderly Archbishop of York, was initially reluctant to see his family connected with 'the little Jewess'.[16]

Retaining her courtesy title of Countess Waldegrave, Frances travelled with Harcourt across Europe, seeking small objects to embellish her decaying houses. In Germany she bought glass and alabaster; in Italy, pictures and sculpture; in France, furniture, clocks, porcelain and enamels. The surviving bills date from 1848 onwards: all are made out to Lady Waldegrave. They record visits to specialist dealers, with repeat orders to luxury-goods suppliers like Monbro Fils Aîné in Paris, who sold both antiques and reproductions. Frances favoured richly ornamented goods in deep colours, with a preference for floral decoration and gilding.

These European purchases became more affordable when the Waldegrave estates returned to profitability. By the 1850s, Frances could expect a gross annual income of nearly £20,000, with a growing amount from the Radstock coalfields in Somerset. Her colliery bailiffs sent monthly reports. When the first railway engine arrived at Radstock, the bailiff wrote excitedly about the latest railway developments in the area. Frances invested in new railway schemes, the acquisition of trucks and the installation of underground lighting. She became a property developer and a housing provider, building terraces to house the workers, funding schools and chapels, and subscribing to hospitals. She also decided to fund a dignified retirement for her elderly father.

In March 1852, 'the world renowned & veteran singer Mr Braham' sang in public for the last time.[17] A crowd of 2,000 flocked to see Braham perform at Exeter Hall on the Strand. A few months later, Frances sat among even larger crowds in St Paul's for the state funeral of the Duke of Wellington. The streets were lined with

200,000 mourners, and she was one of the lucky few in the cathedral. Here she sat amid the grandees, listening to the Tory Chancellor of the Exchequer deliver a eulogy for the hero of Waterloo. The speaker was Benjamin Disraeli (Chaper 2), Britain's first Jewish-born cabinet minister, and Frances was thinking of her father. She turned to her neighbour and told him that she was proud of being a Jew.[18]

Restoring Strawberry Hill

By 1855, Lady Waldegrave was rich enough to repair Strawberry Hill. Harcourt's clerk of works, Mr Ritchie, provided drawings and supervised the works. Walpole's interiors were ornately decorated, but small in scale. If Frances was to entertain groups of any size, she needed to make the best of every space. Extra bedrooms for Braham relatives were squeezed into unlikely corners, and Walpole's chambers adapted for her own use. Walpole's Great Cloister was filled in to provide additional rooms, and the Little Cloister and Courtyard glazed over to create a sheltered foyer for arriving guests. Shiny Minton tiles appeared in the Entrance Hall, with gas lighting in key rooms, along with better heating. Work began in 1855, aiming for completion by Christmas 1856.

The main contractor was Edward Cobb, who sent Frances detailed updates. For the fitting out, she chose Nosotti and Hindley, two of the best-known Oxford Street suppliers. Walpole's first-floor Gallery, with its fan-vaulted ceiling, was the only space large enough for performances or parties: Frances made it gleam (see p. 108, top). Charles Nosotti was Milanese in origin, but had been established in London since the 1830s. Primarily a carver and gilder, he had built a reputation for working with mirrors and glass. His craftsmen provided the necessary adjustments to Walpole's gilded mouldings in the Gallery. Nosotti's firm is also thought to have supplied the little golden stars fitted to the vaults over the Staircase, against a background of cerulean blue.

Charles Hindley and Sons served a reassuringly aristocratic clientele, ranging from the Dukes of Newcastle, Argyll and Cleveland to the banking families of Hoare, Drummond and Rothschild.[19] Their specialty was cabinetmaking and flooring, but they also provided upholstery and general furnishings. Edward Cobb went to view the materials intended for the Gallery floor at Hindley's Oxford Street premises, assuring Frances they would look very fine.[20] Contrasting European and tropical hardwoods were laid by Hindley's in a diamond pattern. In each corner they fitted a large brass-and-pewter heraldic device, alternating between two designs: one with the date 1747 and a Saracen's head crest, representing Walpole; and the other with 1856 and an FW monogram and countess's coronet, representing Lady Waldegrave. Frances was bidding to be seen as co-creator of the revived Strawberry Hill House.

Frances's initials and countess's coronet appeared everywhere: engraved in gold on a set of crystal finger bowls purchased from Lahoche in Paris; carved in wood to form the backs of her gilded Gallery chairs; embossed in gold on her gilt-edged Strawberry Hill writing paper; picked out in lace and turquoise silk on the cushions for her Blue Dressing Room; stamped on the side of her leather dressing cases and travelling boxes for movement between houses. But the monogram was mostly known for its appearance on railway platforms. As the *Bristol Mercury* noted, the name Frances, Countess Waldegrave was familiar to railway travellers 'who often see it upon coal trucks, for this lady almost set the fashion by which the peerage now owns without shame when it is connected with trade'. As the owner of coalmines, 'she trades in her own name, and is no less known in trade than she is conspicuous in the aristocratic circles of the metropolis'.[21]

Louis William Desanges, *Lady Waldegrave and Her Friends in the New Drawing Room at Strawberry Hill*, 1865. Lady Waldegrave sits in the left foreground in a black dress, the prime minister Lord John Russell seated directly behind her. Her husband, Chichester Fortescue, stands rear centre, and the duc d'Aumale is on the left.

This time the contractor was Mr P. Chapman, who kept his patron regularly informed. On 6 September 1861, he told Lady Waldegrave that masons were fixing stone battlements to the Drawing Room, and the carvers finishing the pinnacles for the top of the buttresses.[32] By 3 October, the sashes were ready to fit to the windows, the ironwork was ready for the new gates, and Mr Plows, the carver, had finished the figures.[33] Inside, Frances decided to fill the walls of the Drawing Room with massive history paintings commissioned from Henry Wyndham Phillips (see p. 111). Chapman liaised between client and artist, ensuring that key paintings like *The Music Party* would actually fit in the spaces intended.[34] Judging from the surviving correspondence, the Tudor-Gothic details for the internal decoration were devised under Chapman's direction for approval by Frances.

Ceilings, cornices, window surrounds, door surrounds, panelling and fireplaces were all enlivened by floral decoration, interspersed with occasional heraldic emblems. Some of the vegetation is stylised, but much is almost organically naturalistic, with strawberries and vines predominating. There is a strong thematic link to the seventeenth-century Venetian needle lace collected by Frances and passed on to her adopted daughter Constance. Frances wears key pieces of this lace in several of her surviving portraits, one of which now hangs at Strawberry Hill, where the lace patterns are mirrored in the specially commissioned frame, and around the adjoining window frame (see p. 104).

Back in 1856, Frances had chosen rich floral papers from the firm Cowtan for the refurbished bedrooms, demonstrating a taste for overblown pink roses and brightly tinted birds. In the 1860s extension, colourful strawberry plants climb over the brass door plates and door handles, contrasting with the FW monogram picked out in deep blue, and the countess's coronet in red with white finials (see p. 98).

Charles Hindley and Sons supplied 358 yards of crimson satin brocade for the Drawing Room, and they are thought to have laid the parquet floor, which

Countess Waldegrave at the Sitting Room Window at Strawberry Hill, c.1871, photographer unknown. Lady Waldegrave's niece Constance included this image in her edition of the letters from Edward Lear to Chichester Fortescue and Lady Waldegrave (published in 1911).

was imported by Frances from Vienna. Whether they provided the set of gilded seat furniture upholstered in matching brocade is uncertain, but a few years later they were sending Frances bills for gilded cane-back chairs and side ottomans at Strawberry Hill.

By the time Bond Street photographer Philip Henry Delamotte was asked to take record-photographs in 1863, most of the Henry Wyndham Phillips paintings were in place, and other signature pieces were starting to appear. A large gilt cassone (wedding chest) supplied by Blundell Spence was installed against the far wall, of which the central panel is now in the Getty Museum. Pietro Magni's sculpture *The Reading Girl* (1861), lent to the London International Exhibition in 1862, appears to one side of the cassone. Not visible in the photographs, but illustrated in the same exhibition catalogue, was 'a superb cabinet, carved and gilt, the production of Nosotti of Oxford Street, a carver and gilder of high and established repute. This very elegant work was executed by him for the Countess of Waldegrave and graces her Drawing Room at Strawberry Hill.'[35]

Harcourt did not survive to see the completed Drawing Room. He died in December 1861, leaving the field open for the enthusiastic Mr Fortescue. Frances prepared the ground carefully. New trusts were set up to protect the Waldegrave property, with her two younger brothers as trustees. Neither had a permanent home, so they made their base with Frances. Charles Braham's wife had died in 1860, so Frances also provided a home for his little girl, Constance. Fortescue proved undaunted by the growing number of Brahams in residence, or his inability to exploit the Waldegrave fortune for personal gain. When the couple married on 20 January 1863, the *Illustrated London News* noted Frances's determination to retain her title: 'society, we believe, will see no harm in the beautiful and fashionable F. Cntess Waldegrave continuing a Countess to the end of the chapter'.[36]

Frances stepped up the Liberal Party entertaining she had begun with Harcourt, hosting Wednesday dinners in London, and regular Saturdays to Mondays at Strawberry Hill. Guests could expect to see the prime minister, members of the Liberal cabinet, diplomats, journalists, and representatives of the exiled French royal family, many of whom lived nearby. All these groups were represented in the portrait Frances commissioned in October 1865 to celebrate Fortescue's promotion as Chief Secretary of Ireland (opposite). Frances sits triumphantly in the foreground, with the duc d'Aumale to her right, and Prime Minister Lord John Russell to her left. Fortescue stands at the rear. The ladies' extravagantly flounced evening dresses gleam in the candlelight, but the star of the show is the Strawberry Hill Drawing Room, with its deep red walls, gilded furniture and picture frames, and highly polished Viennese floor.

Poor Louis Desanges took ten years to finish this conversation piece, sending increasingly desperate explanations regarding the difficulty of painting an ever-changing cast of characters. When it was finally delivered to Strawberry Hill in 1875, Frances had exchanged the Henry Wyndham Phillips paintings for Waldegrave and Walpole treasures. Desanges kept pace with the changing picture-hang as well as the people, and Reynold's *Ladies Waldegrave* is visible in the background. Frances looks thoroughly at home, in command of all she surveys. But to some she would always be a Jewish outsider who had appropriated another family's property. Adam Badeau, the US Consul, knew Strawberry Hill in the last years of Frances's life. Reminiscing for *The Cosmopolitan* magazine, he imagined Horace Walpole's reaction to her success: 'How little did the exclusive patrician imagine that the Hebrew daughter of a public singer would queen it in his galleries and absolutely inherit Strawberry Hill from an Earl of his own family.'[37]

5 Playing with the past at Waddesdon Manor

Juliet Carey

Waddesdon Manor is visible from far away on a hill in Buckinghamshire, turrets among trees. From a distance it seems knitted into the landscape but upon approach its silhouette and elaborate roofline assert themselves against the sky. A symmetrical central block is flanked by two wings, different from each other in plan and style; towers articulate corners and turnings, surmounted by an invigorating variety of domed and sloping roofs, spires and pinnacles. The entrance front pays homage to the French Renaissance and incorporates architectural quotations from Loire châteaux, including Chambord, Blois and Maintenon.[1] Close up, fantastical stone detail captures the eye. There are raised panels with carved frames, like empty pictures, and blocks faceted like jewels. There are baskets and swags of fruit and, everywhere, vases, embodying wealth and abundance. The covered entrance porch is deeply vermiculated, and the blind arcade on the far right is carved with giant scales that resemble the scales of a reptile or pangolin but also imitate medieval and Renaissance scale-plate armour. Part-animal, part-human heads animate the façade, many with open mouths, as though calling out or speaking. Those incorporated into the ground-floor window arches include a jester and a satyr with plants for hair. There is wit in unexpected places: water runs off the kitchen roof through the giant spouts of upturned ewers; the tallest chimney stacks are carved with upwards-scrolling smoke.

While the exterior is learned, but pretend, Waddesdon's interior assimilates architectural elements salvaged from real Parisian houses. Invention and innovation coexist with recycled old materials.[2] The house is steel framed, with the most advanced heating and lighting, period elements adapted to the demands of a Victorian 'palace of art'.[3] It is stuffed full of French seventeenth- and eighteenth-century decorative art, eighteenth-century British paintings, and the kind of treasure-cabinet wonders associated with German princely collecting. Further strands of what

Waddesdon Manor, photographed for the commemorative photographic album known as 'The Red Book', 1897, collotype prints.

Top left: North Front.
Top right: Smoking Room.
Bottom left: Dining Room.
Bottom right: Red Drawing Room.

was known as the '*goût* Rothschild' include a roomful of Dutch seventeenth-century paintings and two enormous Venetian views by Francesco Guardi. No category was particularly pioneering: the novelty lay in the combination, which integrated different lines of familial inheritance.[4]

As Waddesdon's creator wrote in his *Reminiscences*: '[the] British collector likes paintings; the average Frenchman chooses decorative art and the German waxes sentimental over a curio of minute workmanship.' Waddesdon brings together all three. It was the fulcrum of Ferdinand de Rothschild's self-fashioning as an aesthete and connoisseur, society host, country squire and public benefactor, all of which required different forms of cultural competence and different ways of playing with the past.

Ferdinand de Rothschild

Ferdinand (1839–98) was a member of the Austrian branch of the Rothschild banking dynasty, which originated in the Frankfurt ghetto, 'closed at night with heavy chains'.[5] Ferdinand described himself as 'cosmopolitan' and his European lineage was as central to his own idea of himself as it was to others' perception.[6] His memoirs self-consciously intertwine his family's story with that of the nineteenth century: born in Paris, in the house of his grandfather Salomon von Rothschild ('in the same room as that in which Napoleon III had first seen the light').[7] His name honoured both the ruler of Austria and the Kaiser Ferdinands-Nordbahn (Kaiser Ferdinand Northern Railway) founded by his grandfather.[8] Raised in Frankfurt and Vienna, Ferdinand was always drawn to England, particularly after the death of his English mother, and settled there in 1860. Within five years he had married his second cousin Evelina, lost his wife and son in childbirth, and taken citizenship. He would never remarry.

In 1874, Ferdinand acquired the land on which he built Waddesdon from the Duke of Marlborough: his father had just died and he inherited a vast fortune. Born into the third generation of the family firm, Ferdinand was free to fashion himself as a collector, whose life's work, as contemporaries acknowledged, was Waddesdon.

In 1885, Ferdinand was elected as Liberal member of parliament for the nearby town of Aylesbury. In London, where he lived at 143 Piccadilly, he chose not to run for a parliamentary seat in the East End, near to the Evelina Hospital for Sick Children he founded in Southwark. It was here that he most visibly embraced his leading role in the Jewish community. Unlike his strictly observant father, Ferdinand was relaxed about religious practice, joking in a letter written on Yom Kippur that although 'my coreligionists … [were] making to the dinner table after a fast of 24 hours, I have fasted today from 10–2 and again from 3'.[9] Yet he laid the foundation stone of the North London Synagogue and served as treasurer of the Jewish Board of Guardians from 1868 to 1875, and as warden of the Central Synagogue, endowing the Ferdinand de Rothschild Technical Scholarship at Stepney Jewish Schools and enjoining its pupils 'never [to] forget that you are Jews and Jewesses, but at the

Ferdinand de Rothschild in his private sitting room, from 'The Red Book', 1897.

same time be proud that you are Englishmen and Englishwomen. Determined to be worthy of the liberties which your fathers obtained for you.'[10]

Country life features vividly in Ferdinand's narrative: first Grüneburg, near Frankfurt, a neo-Baroque schloss, decorated inside in the Louis XV manner, where he and his siblings sat out the 1848 revolution; then Schillersdorf (see pp.273–5), 'an oasis in the wilderness'.[11] However, it was his grandparents' Regency villa at Gunnersbury, just outside London, that gave Ferdinand his first experience of 'old England'. In *Reminiscences*, memories of his joy in his cousins, the Gunnersbury glasshouses and a llama in the park are followed immediately by the royal, material and technological spectacle of the opening of the Great Exhibition of 1851.[12] The episode forms a crux in Ferdinand's narrative of Britishness: 'being denationalised, so to speak, on the one hand, and not renationalised on the other, being left more or less my own master at my dear Mother's death ... I severed the slender ties that bound me to the countries I had hitherto lived in' and eventually made 'England, the land of my dreams ... my permanent abode.'[13]

A competitive house

Ferdinand's bit of Piccadilly was sometimes called 'Rothschild Row',[14] and in Buckinghamshire he joined another Rothschild enclave.[15] Mentmore was the first of their houses, designed between 1852 and 1854 for Ferdinand's uncle Mayer by Joseph Paxton, of Crystal Palace fame. It is with Mentmore, built from scratch, in 'Jacobethan' style, that Waddesdon most clearly converses and competes, just as the château belonging to Ferdinand's great-uncle James at Ferrières did in France (see Chapter 3). At much the same time, Mayer's brother Anthony acquired an estate at Aston Clinton – alterations to that relatively modest neoclassical house by George Henry Stokes (Paxton's assistant at Mentmore) and then George Devey were ongoing as Waddesdon began. Tring, nearby, was bought in 1872 by Ferdinand's father-in-law, Lionel. Originally designed by Christopher Wren, it was transformed for the Rothschilds with stone dressings and a mansard roof. In 1873, Lionel acquired a farm at Ascott for his son Leopold, who expanded it into a rambling country house in an old English, half-timbered style to designs by Devey, who had also worked on Tring and designed so many Rothschild estate buildings. Here, as so often, several family members employed the same architect to create houses that are individual statements but with conspicuous, underlying affinities.[16] Indeed, Leopold's brother Alfred began building Halton House in a loosely French Renaissance style just as Ferdinand was building Waddesdon.

Building demonstrates wealth and stability. This kind of collective, self-reflexive country-house construction also asserts unity, essential to the success of a family enterprise, while providing a playful structure for competition and rivalry. It mattered to Ferdinand, who would enquire how high above sea level each Rothschild house was to ensure Waddesdon was the highest.[17] Collecting can work in a similar way, and Waddesdon is full of this duality. By the time it was created, the idea of a shared Rothschild taste was well established. They sometimes collected as a group, getting a good price buying *en bloc*. For example, Ferdinand and his uncle acquired a set of fourteen pierglasses by Pineau, among the earliest examples of what would become known as the Rococo style, and split them between Waddesdon and Mentmore.[18] Buying as a consortium gave a group of cousins the leverage to acquire the celebrated Van Loon collection of Amsterdam in 1877 and 1878, a painting by Gabriel Metsu being among those that came to Waddesdon.[19] However, the pleasures of ownership or one-upmanship were often solitary. Ferdinand hid his first important purchase, a turquoise Sèvres porcelain vase in the shape of a ship, paid for in instalments, afraid that his uncles would disapprove of his extravagance.[20]

The handling, acquiring and understanding of works of art is central to the story Ferdinand tells. Art surrounded him from childhood, and his father's collection formed the nucleus of his own. He helped to pack and unpack his father's 'curiosities' when the family left town, learning 'to distinguish a Teniers from an Ostade', and 'would kneel on the floor, fold my hands as if in prayer and screw up my eyes in mimicry of a head of a girl by Greuze'.[21] He remembered his joy when the German-Jewish painter Moritz Daniel Oppenheim, acting as his father's art agent, brought 'some quaint Nuremberg or Augsburg tankard, or the figure of a man, a lion or a stag.... Oh! For those good old days when the artistic merit of a cup was of no account to its possessor, and he merely valued it according to the number of ounces it contained!' Inherited possessions, particularly metalwork, are everywhere at Waddesdon, but the sarcasm here suggests a certain distance from earlier approaches to collecting and his father's 'limited' taste.[22] Ferdinand also recounts his own mistakes, and how, through experience and luck, he honed his judgement and grew confident in his taste, to create, in Waddesdon, a complex and complete work of art.

Waddesdon stages its creator in a lineage of great builder-collectors, made present through portraits of those, like Louis XIV and George IV, whom Ferdinand admired, and through works of art owned, for example, by Madame de Pompadour and Marie Antoinette, Rudolf II, William Beckford and the Duke of Hamilton. Ferdinand set himself apart from a type of younger collector, who 'need only sit in his chair, open his purse-strings and the mountain will come to him'.[23] He bought little contemporary art, but engaged, ludically, with centuries of princely and aristocratic collecting. He valued things both for their rarity and 'the memories they evoke, the trains of thought to which they lead, and the many ways they stimulate the imagination and realise our ideals'.[24]

Never intended as a museum, Waddesdon was created for modern living and the display of particular objects: art, architecture and sociability intertwined. When Ferdinand bought the Guardis, the East Gallery was redesigned around them; in the West Gallery, the careful placement of pieces of Gobelins tapestry against the wood panelling creates a dialogue between designs woven and carved, grotesques and arabesques.[25] In the Morning Room, a painting of a courtesan in the guise of Thaïs presides over the fireplace, just one example of the playfully ironic deployment of the collection.[26] The room is all about writing and papers, where letters were written and read, and books and albums shared: Thaïs was one of history's most infamous arsonists who, according to legend, goaded her lover Alexander the Great to burn down the palace of Persepolis with its famous library.

Playing with the past

Waddesdon does not pretend to have grown slowly, organically, out of the English landscape. Its creation was fast and spectacular. Ferdinand flattened the top of a bare hill and, a marvel of nineteenth-century logistics, turned it into a park with avenues and mature trees. A temporary railway hauled the materials. There is something performative, something of Versailles, about the earthworks and hydraulics, the fountains and sculptures brought from all over Europe, instant forests, vast glasshouses, the neo-Rococo aviary and the menageries installed on artificial crags. One visitor called it 'a real creation – not an old mansion taken over with its gardens, parks and stabling – but a vast château built by its owner, surrounded by endless gardens planned by him, and towering over a park reclaimed from agricultural meadows'.[27]

Excavations for the drive at Waddesdon Manor, photographed c.1876–7.

The Manor was designed by the French architect Gabriel-Hippolyte Destailleur (1822–93), who had renovated Schillersdorf for Ferdinand's grandfather and was then employed building his brother Albert's townhouse in Vienna. Destailleur had an international reputation for the mastery of historic styles in the construction of new buildings and the restoration of old ones. He had transformed the hilltop Mouchy-le-Châtel into 'a fairy tale castle' for a scion of the old aristocratic Noailles family, whose wife was a cousin of Napoléon III.[28] While building Waddesdon, Destailleur was also working on Louis Le Vau's Vaux-le-Vicomte, for the sugar baron Alfred Sommier, and the Louis XIII château of Courances for the Franco-Austrian Jewish banker Samuel de Haber. Also overlapping with Waddesdon were two commissions in England for the exiled Empress Eugénie, widow of Napoléon III: a funerary chapel for the Prince Imperial in Chiselhurst (then in Kent), and the Imperial Mausoleum in Farnborough, Hampshire.[29] Set against the ambiguity of the Rothschilds' status within European society, Eugénie's was a friendship that cemented Ferdinand's sense of his family as a kind of analogue to the interconnected royal houses of Europe.[30]

Although Waddesdon's eclecticism incorporates some French Gothic forms, the primary prototypes are from a later period. Destailleur's choice of French Valois and Bourbon styles, as opposed to the medieval, Italian Renaissance or antique models more common at the time, was tied to his promotion of a French national style in architecture, spanning and synthesising centuries. French Renaissance style was becoming the last word in quality and refinement, as appealing to private patrons as to hoteliers seeking to advertise themselves to cosmopolitan guests.[31] In the 1890s, Ferdinand acquired numerous works from Destailleur's library, especially topographical and architectural works, crucial for understanding his salvage work and the grasp of French decoration and ornament that underlies Waddesdon's witty erudition.[32]

Waddesdon's francophone interiors are predominantly eighteenth century in style. Ferdinand considered it a specifically Rothschild achievement to have 'first revived the decoration of the [French] eighteenth century in its purity, reconstructing their rooms out of old material, reproducing them as they had been during the reigns of the Louis, while at the same time adapting them to modern requirements'.[33] Many rooms are lined with panelling from French houses, the elements reconfigured to articulate modern spaces with different dimensions. The Breakfast Room repurposes panels of different origins from the 1730s Hôtel Dodun, but only the closest scrutiny disrupts the illusion of a symmetrical whole.[34] The wall lights are scaled-up versions of eighteenth-century models; the console tables modern riffs on their Rococo style. The Dining Room both displays and transgresses its historical references. The marble-clad walls recall seventeenth-century Versailles, and the principal elevation largely follows a design in an eighteenth-century architectural treatise. However, on either side of the fireplace hang Beauvais tapestries after pastoral designs by François Boucher, whose contemporaries frowned upon the hanging of precious textiles in eating rooms: at Waddesdon, these works are the trophy pieces around which an imaginative reiteration of an eighteenth-century space is arranged.[35]

Ferdinand was not nostalgic for the world in which these works of art originated. He saw the French Revolution as inevitable, the failed aristocracy '[making] way for a new order of things'.[36] Looking back at the *ancien régime* from his own time, with its own sense of historical transition, Ferdinand saw its art and literature as a high point of European cultural achievement, but believed (like many others) that it possessed a delicious decadence: from moral decay 'rose the perfume that surrounded it with so much glamour and glory'.[37] The books and albums he assembled, like the designs for the *Ballet Royal de la Nuit* masque in which Louis XIV first appeared as the Sun King, give insight into the theatre of state, but they also reveal his fascination with everyday life, from butchery to hairdressing, and include the Saint-Aubins' dangerous book of caricatures and albums of revolutionary ephemera (below).[38]

Below left
Charles Germain de Saint-Aubin and others, *Livre de caricatures tant bonnes que mauvaises*, c.1740–c.1775, a volume of 387 satirical drawings, which is a unique survival from an age of powerful censorship. These pages target (left) legislation outlawing the use of big shop signs in Paris and (right) the influence of his official mistress Madame de Pompadour on Louis XV.

Below right
Attributed to Henri Gissey, design for a stage set from *Ballet Royal de la Nuit*, 1653, a volume of designs for a court masque starring Louis XIV, performed at the Château de Versailles.

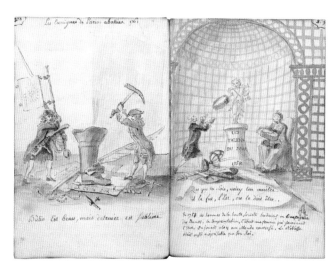

Ferdinand's revivalism at Waddesdon was shaped by his private reading and, as a collector-artist in a European mould, he also wrote. He tried out different literary genres – the country-house romance (*Lady Glendale*), oriental tale (*The Legend of Samandal*) and German *Novelle* (*Vroni*), but, above all, essays about French and British history, his collection enabling an imaginative immersion in the past. Viewing the French Revolution as a cautionary tale to the British establishment, he set the rupture in French history against the slow development of English liberty.[39] As well as privately published essays, he gave lectures to a variety of audiences. 'The Advent of the French Revolution', a warning against revolutionary anarchy, was delivered on 15 December 1888 at Toynbee Hall in the East End of London at a time of considerable social unrest, but he spoke about Queen Elizabeth I and about John Wilkes at the Reading Room he had built for the village of Waddesdon (alongside a Methodist Chapel, Hygenic Steam Bakery and Village Hall).[40] Here too, he spoke about Magna Carta, about the forward march of English liberties, placing emphasis on the issue of religious liberty with reference to Jews. His experience of other regimes, his foreign accent and the exuberant un-Englishness of Waddesdon gave these accounts of the institutions and relative security of his adoptive country a passionate urgency.

Ferdinand's cultural confidence in himself as a Briton fulfilling the duties of a local squire did not protect him from antisemitism. As a foreign Jew, he became a particular target in the wake of his 1885 electoral win, when Frederick Charsley, the defeated Tory candidate, accused him of electoral corruption. Ferdinand was cleared in the county court, but Charsley tried to drum up support against the village whose 'squire' was 'not an Englishman'.[41] The episode prompted a parson from Prestwich in Lancashire to make pointed claims about the 'vindictive savages' and 'special festivities and revellings' in the Waddesdon village hall every Sunday: 'The people have obviously put up their old English nature with their old English customs.'[42]

Faces for a house party

Up at the house, Ferdinand was playing with the past and with Britishness through his collection. Just as Waddesdon does not pretend to be something grown over centuries from an English landscape, the English portraits by Gainsborough, Reynolds and Romney do not mimic traditional country-house portrait galleries, manifesting long lineages and genealogical attachment to a place. Ferdinand was more interested in figures, especially women, with an ambiguous or mobile social status: actors, singers, courtesans (opposite). He was fortunate that during the 1870s and 1880s many aristocratic families encountered financial hardship due to the agricultural depression and began selling their possessions. No longer portraits of intimates or ancestors, these portraits were now valued as works of artistic merit, expressions of national character, and historical and social documents exhibited in exhibitions and museums.[43]

Throughout Waddesdon are images of women whose portraits were central to their own self-promotion within eighteenth-century cultures of celebrity. In his private sitting room, Ferdinand gazed upon three performers: the actress Mrs Jordan, the singer Elizabeth Linley and Emma Hamilton in one of her antique 'attitudes'.[44] Their portraits offered a flattering counterpart to the women who assembled at Waddesdon in real life, invoking, in English translation, something of the nineteenth-century (idealised) idea of the French eighteenth-century *salon*: a few exceptional women bringing together, through the civilising power of conversation, groups of people that transgress conventional social boundaries.[45] This model of elite society appealed to Ferdinand, not least for its embrace of

Joshua Reynolds, *Mrs Abington as the Comic Muse*, 1764–8 & 1772–3, oil on canvas. The portrait was central to the actress's self-promotion.

Joshua Reynolds, *Lady Anne Luttrell, Duchess of Cumberland*, 1772–3, oil on canvas. Reynolds imbued the sitter with regal magnificence just after she had angered George III by eloping with his brother. Both this and *Mrs Abington* hang in the Grey Drawing Room, a focus of Waddesdon's celebration of Reynolds; Gainsborough predominates in the Red Drawing Room next door.

The Prince of Wales and friends, photographed on the North Front at Waddesdon in the 1890s. The future Edward VII first visited Waddesdon in 1881 and was a regular guest until Ferdinand's death.

writers and performers; in the theatre 'a brilliant actor or actress became the darling of the world, of the mob and society alike'.[46] Nevertheless, the first paintings visitors encountered on arrival, in the Red Drawing Room, were men: the Prince of Wales, future George IV, with whose love of French art Ferdinand particularly identified, and his close friend and drinking companion Captain St Leger.[47] This pair of works, by Gainsborough and Reynolds respectively, invited conversational comparison of the two artists, a key theme in their nineteenth-century reception, and embedded the theme of princely friendship at the start of the visitor's progress through the house. When Ferdinand died, his close, informal friendship with Albert Edward, Prince of Wales (future Edward VII), was the starting point of many an obituary, stamping him with Britishness and status (above). 'Bertie', however, was fascinated by the Rothschilds' 'quizzical detachment' from the European class structure, relishing their flair and international outlook.[48]

Earlier generations of Rothschilds had been Court Jews serving the Elector of Hesse-Kassel, while Ferdinand's brother was the only Jew deemed presentable (*hoffähig*) at the court of Franz Josef. Yet for Bertie, whose family network, like Ferdinand's, spanned Europe, Waddesdon functioned as a kind of unofficial court.[49] Visiting in a private capacity, never with his wife and often with a mistress, he invariably determined the guest list, which included political and diplomatic figures to whom his mother refused him access. Ferdinand's sister Alice acted as her brother's hostess (she built a house at neighbouring Eythrope).[50] Together, they entertained figures from the worlds of culture: painters like Louise Jopling and John Everett Millais, and writers like Guy de Maupassant and Henry James. The shah of Persia visited in 1889, a year before Queen Victoria. He was besotted with Waddesdon's elephant automaton; she was impressed by the electricity. The

British public were fascinated by the queen's visit: an elaborate public spectacle that contrasted with the visits by her eldest son. Ferdinand, meanwhile, compared himself to an Elizabethan courtier, having knelt on one knee in the Green Boudoir to present Victoria with a little ivory fan studded with diamonds.[51] This comparison was not accidental. The year before he died, Ferdinand attended the Devonshire House Ball dressed as a sixteenth-century German Calvinist prince, shown favour by Henri III of France, who once sought to marry Elizabeth I (above). How carefully he chose his costume: a European prince, at home in the French and English courts.

The glasshouses, dairy, aviary and menagerie, music, carriage rides and visits to Alice's teahouse were all part of the entertainment, but the house and the collection were its heart. Like the Renaissance prince of his imagination, the host would show special favour to a guest by inviting them into his artistic inner sanctum. At the far end of the West Gallery, closed by mirrored doors, the Baron's Sitting Room led through into the Tower Drawing Room, a small, centralised space that housed his most precious works: private and apart, like an Italian *studiolo*; designed for close and conscious looking, like a French *cabinet*; a treasury of artful wonders like a German *Kunstkammer*.

Most of Ferdinand's acquisitions furnished spaces in which 'every object fulfils a fitting decorative function'; nothing acquired unless an appropriate place could be found for it in the general scheme of form and colour.[52] However, this roomful of treasures worked differently. This was his 'Renaissance Museum', and it comprised works of great mystery: Seychelles nuts, ostrich eggs and nautilus shells made into vessels with gold and silver mounts; misshapen pearls transformed into animals and people; wood, amber and ivory, glass and enamels, pottery and porcelain. Objects are layered with evidence of their provenance: the Lyte Jewel bears the monogram

of James VI of Scotland, and the case of a boxwood tabernacle, the arms of Emperor Charles V.[53] For the first time, we see religious works here. The Pressburg Cup, with its inscription from a Jewish burial society in Pressburg (Bratislava), is a discrete piece of Judaica, while the Holy Thorn Reliquary is the most spectacular of the goldsmiths' works Ferdinand inherited from his father (below).[54] There are also many examples of the intrinsically valuable, portable goods associated with Jewish merchants for centuries, and thus with the origins of the Rothschild fortune and the overlaps between the collections of banking and princely dynasties.[55]

How exactly the 'Renassiance Museum' was first displayed is uncertain, but in 1896 Ferdinand reinstalled it in the Smoking Room, in the Bachelors' Wing.[56] Here, Waddesdon's predominantly eighteenth-century idiom gives way to one associated in the late nineteenth century with masculine spaces, incorporating medieval and Renaissance, Moorish and Asian elements. The prominence of textiles, often adapted from ecclesiastical robes and furnishings, along with clever use of stained glass and lighting, heightened the textural and chromatic subtlety for which the house was known.[57] The arrangement of the vitrines emphasised shared types and materials, while drawing attention to star pieces like the Cellini Bell (opposite), once owned by Horace Walpole, who described it as 'the uniquest thing in the world' and which Ferdinand was the first to identify as German.[58]

Fascinated by the history of collecting in England, Ferdinand determined that the future home of these treasures should be in public hands. He saw himself as a new type of collector, who might have a 'beneficent influence on the tone and conditions of society at large' and to this end in 1898 he made a spectacular bequest to the British Museum. As a gift to a national museum, this forms part of a broader pattern of giving among the European Rothschilds. Ferdinand was also following the examples of Lady Wallace – who had given the Wallace Collection to the nation – and, in France, the duc d'Aumale and Chantilly.[59] The moral and patriotic purpose of his donation was clear to contemporaries: 'Many of [the works] were a hereditary

Right
The Holy Thorn Reliquary, c.1400, enamelled gold, sapphires, rubies and pearls. Made in Paris for Jean, duc de Berry, and later in the treasury of Emperor Charles V, it was acquired in the 19th century by Ferdinand de Rothschild's father, Anselm. The reliquary was made to contain a thorn, supposedly from the Crown of Thorns that was placed on Jesus Christ's head before the Crucifixion.

Far right
Hans Petzolt, the Pressburg Cup, c.1600, silver-gilt. Another object that Ferdinand inherited from his father, the Hebrew inscription around the lip of this standing cup attests to its ownership by a Jewish charitable fraternity in Pressburg (modern-day Bratislava) in 1739–40.

Glass Case Containing Works of Art of the Sixteenth Century, in the Smoking Room, photographed for 'The Red Book', 1897. The Cellini Bell is at the centre of the lower part of the case, which also contains boxwood sculptures, enamels and other medieval and Renaissance works of art that now form part of the Waddesdon Bequest at the British Museum.

possession of the late Baron, so that in bequeathing them to the nation he has done the highest service in his power to promote the education and add to the cultivated enjoyment of the community at large.'[60] But there is something more to this princely gift.

Ferdinand was a public man, who lived a public life, and Waddesdon was his only posterity. For this was a man without children, a man who never remarried, a man whose political career and literary output was, for all his sophistication and grand friends, not particularly distinguished. In Waddesdon, however, he created a total work of art, in which architecture and art were completely interwoven, the spaces inside and out animated, if only temporarily, by the guests with whom it was his pleasure to share them. It was through Waddesdon that he chose to be remembered. When he named the prize pieces from his collection that he bequeathed to the British Museum 'the Waddesdon Bequest', Ferdinand linked it forever to the house he built, underlining the fact that he understood it as a whole, the *Gesamtkunstwerk* that was his legacy – a fragile thing, but something worth remembering.

Before the house and the 'Renaissance Museum' were physically separated by this bequest, Ferdinand encapsulated the idea of Waddesdon, retrospective and complete, in a photographic album entitled *Waddesdon Manor*, and known today as 'The Red Book'. The text is full of the drama and activity of Waddesdon's making, individual items set within an overall visual narrative about its totality and haunted by fears for the future and probable annihilation in a time of rising death duties and an exodus of artwork across the Atlantic.[61]

In separating the Waddesdon Bequest from the Manor, Ferdinand destroyed something of what he had created. He knew that his heirs would change it, whatever it might become. Certainly, he never imagined that Waddesdon itself would be absorbed into the National Trust, and thereby made public too.

6 Two houses, two countries, one cosmopolitan family: Torre Alfina and Champs-sur-Marne

Alice S. Legé

Auguste Renoir, *Pink and Blue (Alice and Elisabeth Cahen d'Anvers)*, 1881, oil on canvas. This painting of two of the daughters of Louis Cahen d'Anvers and his wife Louise de Morpurgo is one of three that the family commissioned from the Impressionist Renoir, whom they met through the collector and art critic Charles Ephrussi. Alice, on the left, married a British army officer; Elisabeth died on the way to Auschwitz in 1944.

Who were they anyway, the Cahen d'Anvers? Just another family of German Jews who had gambled on the uncertainties of liberal revolution.[1] First in Belgium, where Meyer Joseph Cahen (1804–81) made a fortune out of the 1830 revolution, built a commercial empire and married Clara Bischoffsheim (1810–76), whose brother became the dominant figure in Belgian finance. Then in revolutionary Paris, where the family settled in 1849, just as the future Napoléon III tightened his grip. Only a year earlier, with all of Europe in turmoil, Meyer Joseph had dared finance the war of 'national liberation' led by Carlo Alberto of Piedmont against Habsburg rule in Italy. It proved a far-sighted decision. Within ten years, the constitutional rulers of Piedmont would join forces with Napoléon III and with the forces of nationalist revolution embodied by the military leader Giuseppe Garibaldi. Defeating the Austrians in the north and overthrowing the Bourbons in the south, they founded a new liberal state in 1861. The pope still ruled in Rome, and the Habsburgs in Venice, but Carlo Alberto's son became king of the rest of this new Italy; in 1866 he acquired Lombardy-Venetia as well. In that triumphant year, Vittorio Emanuele II of Italy finally repaid the money his father had borrowed and, as a token of his gratitude, made Meyer Joseph, known now as Cahen d'Anvers, a count.[2]

By now, Meyer Joseph and his wife were well-established figures on the Parisian financial and social scene. Here their five children grew to adulthood, and from Paris they and their descendants married into other leading families – not just Jewish dynasties like the Morpurgos, the Montefiores and the Camondos, but Catholic and Protestant families as well. Albert Cahen d'Anvers (1846–1903) became a composer; his brothers Édouard (1832–94), Louis (1837–1922) and Raphaël (1841–1900) followed their father into business and continued to thrive.[3] As part of this comprehensive social reinvention, Meyer Joseph and his descendants acquired a new, aspirational surname. 'Cahen d'Anvers' set them apart from other Parisian Jews of the same

Top row
Édouard Cahen d'Anvers and his wife Christina Spartali, photographed *c*.1875.

Bottom row
Louis Cahen d'Anvers and his wife Louise de Morpurgo, photographed *c*.1875.

Edouard Cahen

Christina Cahen

Louis Cahen

Louise Cahen

name, gestured towards the origins of the family fortune in Belgium, and lent them a certain aristocratic allure.

The family lived at the Hôtel du Plessis-Bellière on the place de la Concorde, an eighteenth-century masterpiece in a powerfully symbolic space. The guillotine had stood in this former royal square during the revolution, and it was now in the throes of transformation by Jacques Ignace Hittorff into a very different, and modern, idea of a city square. Over time, the Cahen d'Anvers would acquire thirteen houses in France, Italy and Belgium.[4] Collectively, their impressive property portfolio enabled the family to figure as a new phalanx of the old nobility, in a world where titles and land still carried enormous prestige.

This was no longer a family of sugar brokers from Antwerp, but a transnational Jewish business dynasty: one that embodied change, both economic and political. They embraced modernity unashamedly, even as they relished the glamour that attached to feudal Europe and the remnants of the *ancien régime*. The houses the family bought, built and developed reflected that tension. Here, we shall consider only two: Torre Alfina near Orvieto, acquired in 1884 by Meyer Joseph's eldest son, Édouard Cahen d'Anvers; and the Château de Champs-sur-Marne, just outside Paris, bought by his brother Louis in 1895. Torre Alfina was substantially rebuilt by the architect Giuseppe Partini (1842–95) in a neo-medieval style, while Walter-André Destailleur (1867–1940) privileged the eighteenth century with his restoration of Champs. Yet the French landscape designers Henri (1841–1902) and Achille Duchêne (1866–1947) contributed to the redesign of both. In this way, the brothers' restoration of these very different historic properties combined erudite respect for their pasts with an imaginative response to modern life. These were nineteenth-century country houses created out of historic ones; in this they mimicked the status of their owners.

Torre Alfina: an Italian fiefdom

The new Kingdom of Italy offered plenty of opportunities for a well-connected, liberally inclined Jewish banker. Old Meyer Joseph was canny enough to seize them: not in person, but by sending his eldest son. In 1866, Édouard Cahen d'Anvers became an Italian citizen. He then moved definitively to Italy, living first in Naples and later Florence, when both cities were competing for the role of capital. He reached Rome in 1871, immediately after the fall of the rump Papal State (below). Here, Édouard would become the driving force in the urbanisation and development of the Prati district near the Vatican.[5]

Despite the presence of the pope and his government, the Eternal City had long been a backwater in economic terms, dominated by clergy and living off the past glories that rendered it a focus for international writers and artists, and the goal of many an aristocratic Grand Tour. Suddenly, Rome was the capital of a

Rome: The Taking of Porta Pia, 20 September 1870, photographer unknown. This famous image of the Risorgimento was in fact constructed after the actual event, with a group of soldiers from the Italian army staged in front of Porta Pia. The breaching of Rome's city walls near this spot led to the integration of Rome into Italy.

148

great European nation, and a property speculator's paradise. These were decades of convulsive, overwhelming change, during which this crumbling provincial town reinvented itself as a modern metropolis, replete with grand avenues, new buildings and all the social problems that come with industrialisation and explosive population growth.[6] Jews were not incidental to this transformation, either politically or economically, or when it came to urban space. Piedmont had emancipated its Jews as early as 1848. Consequently, when the Italian army captured Rome in 1870, the Jews of that city were liberated from the ghetto in which they had been confined for centuries, receiving, at long last, civil and political rights. Even in the seat of St Peter, it was suddenly possible for Jews to acquire property, and exercise governmental functions as proud Italians. Neither Pope Pius IX nor his successor Leo XIII could accept the loss of papal power, or the emergence of a secular polity. They refused to acknowledge the Kingdom of Italy, and in his addresses to the pilgrims who flocked to Rome in the early 1870s, Pius attacked Jews as 'dogs' and 'beasts who know not God', a 'reprobate' nation, filled with 'the love of money', 'fomenters of lies and injustices against Catholicism … in so many European countries'.[7]

In this context, a man like Édouard Cahen d'Anvers seemed the visible expression of a new secularised society that opposed the Church, its works and the established order. Édouard's English wife, Christina Spartali (1846–84; see p. 146 and opposite), was a beauty celebrated for inspiring the Pre-Raphaelites. She had been born into the Greek Orthodox Church, but her husband never converted and theirs was most likely a civil union.[8] Achieving the rank of marquis in 1885, Édouard prided himself on his Jewish origins, adopting as his coat of arms a lion rampant holding the lyre of King David next to the heraldic symbol of Torre Alfina. Édouard's social position was correspondingly ambivalent. Yet in business, as on the social scene, the Cahen d'Anvers and their sons Rodolfo (1869–1955) and Hugo (1874–1956) interacted with established members of the Franco-Italian aristocratic and financial elite. Some (like the Torlonias) had close ties to the Vatican; others (like the Primolis and Bonapartes) had more complex political and social pedigrees.

The privileges and values of landownership were central to aristocratic life, and houses served as important markers of the Cahen d'Anvers' new social status. After renting the first floor of the seventeenth-century Palazzo Núñez-Torlonia in Rome, a princely palace with recent Bonaparte associations, Édouard set about acquiring a country residence appropriate to his new status.[9] The ancient castle of Torre Alfina, formerly owned by the Monaldeschi della Cervara and the Bourbon del Monte families, was just the thing (see pp. 150–1).[10] It cost 165,000 Italian lira in 1884, and Édouard paid an additional 30,000 lira for the furniture.[11] But he had no intention of simply reproducing the style of its former owners.

Situated near Orvieto, the Castello di Torre Alfina's romantic renown went back to the thirteenth century, when it had been a strategic stronghold in the struggles between the popes and the Holy Roman Empire.[12] Centuries later, the castle had played a key role in the battle for Italian unity, sheltering the troops of Giovanni Acerbi during Garibaldi's 1867 uprising.[13] This association with Italian nationalism was still etched into local memory when Édouard bought the castle seventeen years later. With its layers of history, the building offered certain prestige to the freshly minted marquis, superimposing his own ambitions on the new ideal of *italianità*. Now, Édouard commissioned Giuseppe Partini to transform the property into a neo-medieval fortress, imbuing the Cahen d'Anvers with all the associations of ancient feudal power.

Through the nineteenth century, the revival of medieval architecture across Italy provided an element of cultural unity in a deeply fragmented country, harkening back to an era of powerful landed families and proud city-states. In parallel with

The gallery at Castello di
Torre Alfina in 2022.

Left
Castello di Torre Alfina,
photographed before 1884.

Below
Castello di Torre Alfina,
photographed by the Fratelli
Alinari studio, c.1890.

the Renaissance Revival, the vision of a revised and reinterpreted Middle Ages appealed to a new class of patrons and collectors.[14] As a former member of the Commission for the Enlargement and Embellishment of Rome, Partini was a safe choice.[15] He was well known in intellectual and political circles, having partially reconstructed the cities of San Gimignano and Siena, where he restored such national monuments as the fifteenth-century Fonte Gaia by Jacopo della Quercia.[16]

At Torre Alfina, Partini's intervention was radical. Nothing remained of the eighth-century military tower originally built here, but the ruins of a later medieval tower now abutted a Renaissance villa with a horseshoe plan. This villa had two floors and a central façade articulated by three arches. The house had been remodelled by Ippolito Scalza between 1556 and 1580 for Sforza Monaldeschi della Cervara and his wife Dianira Baglioni.[17] Several spaces, including the monumental staircase, were decorated with frescoes, probably by Cesare Nebbia and his school, all inevitably in poor condition. Surprisingly little of this now survives.[18] One contemporary who visited during Partini's rebuilding described how, by 'rebuilding on the old, gradually demolished and disappearing', the Cahen d'Anvers were creating 'a new and colossal medieval castle … in the pure style of the thirteenth century'.[19]

The result was impressive. Five towers, including the turreted courtyard entrance, gave the castle a fairy-tale allure. The castellated central tower, 45 metres high, directly recalls Florence's town hall, the Palazzo Vecchio, which was a powerful symbol of secular authority.[20] Édouard's coat of arms, in white marble, stands out against the grey-basalt ashlar on the front of the central tower and on the top of the turreted courtyard entrance. Combining historical motifs and genealogical references, Partini and his patron showed their mastery of the power of imagery; the marquis used architecture to legitimise his recently acquired nobility, while giving visual expression to the civil rights long denied to Italian Jews.

Édouard was even bolder when, in 1890, he donated a stained-glass window incorporating the figures of Moses and King David to the cathedral of Orvieto. Importantly, he convinced the cathedral authorities to change the inscription from *Edoardi Cahenis* to *Edoardi Caheniorum Comitis*, explaining that 'Cahen' was not 'the name of a single family, but that of a distinct population'.[21] By inscribing his name alongside bishops and powerful Christian patrons in one of the greatest Italian cathedrals, Édouard perpetuated his memory to posterity, and identified this action with the Jews of Italy, so long excluded from many aspects of social, cultural and economic life. In this way, he affirmed his Jewish identity and his claim to be recognised both as a free individual and as part of a community with a place in the public life of the new nation.

Édouard chose to be buried not on consecrated ground but in a mausoleum near the castle he had transformed – a monument originally conceived as a family tomb.[22] Hidden in the forest of Sasseto, it asserted his desire to determine his own path into the next world, while reinforcing the family's connection to the founding fathers of Italian unity through its emulation of Vittorio Emanuele II's catafalque in Siena Cathedral.[23] Édouard's son Rodolfo later commissioned Henri and Achille Duchêne to link the mausoleum to a new garden below the castle; their design combined Italian and French elements.[24] Édouard's grave bound the Cahen d'Anvers dynasty to its Italian fiefdom for eternity, but Rodolfo's choice of designer underlined the family's cosmopolitan orientation and international roots.

A French château for a French banker:
Louis Cahen d'Anvers and Champs-sur-Marne

Back in France, Édouard's younger brother Louis had already embarked upon
a similar process of property construction and status acquisition, consciously
entwining the fate of his own family with that of his chosen nation. Raised in London
and Paris, Louis studied at the École des Mines before joining his father at the
helm of the family firm in 1868.[25] This was a time of upheaval: over the next few
years France became first a liberal empire, then a revolutionary regime at war
with Prussia, and finally a reluctant republic. High society did not lose its allure
under these new circumstances, and Louis became a well-known man about
town, joining prestigious associations such as the Jockey Club, the Cercle de
l'Union Artistique and the Automobile Club.[26] In 1880, he employed a fashionable
Parisian architect, Gabriel-Hippolyte Destailleur (father of Walter-André), to build
an *hôtel particulier* on a triangular plot at 2 rue Bassano, near the Champs-
Élysées.[27] Completed three years later, the result was a cleverly historicising
building in which a brick-and-stone neo-Renaissance courtyard contrasted with
an eighteenth-century-style street front. Inside, Destailleur integrated historic
elements such as the Regency panelling from Germain Boffrand's remodelling
of the Hôtel de Mayenne. Then, in 1895, shortly after his elder brother's death,
Louis too acquired a country house rich with historical associations (above).[28]

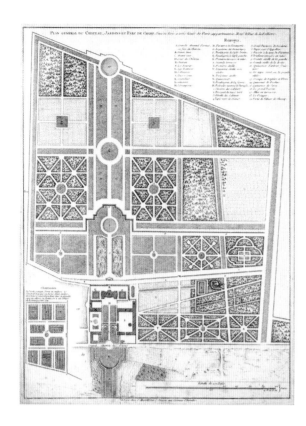

Left
Jean Mariette, general plan of the château, gardens and park of Champs, engraving, published in *L'architecture françoise ou Recueil des plans, elevations, coupes et profils des églises, palais, hôtels & maisons particulieres de Paris [...] et de plusieurs autres endroits de France*, Paris, 1727.

Below
Henri and Achille Duchêne, bird's-eye view of the Château de Champs-sur-Marne, 1895, graphite and charcoal on paper. The high viewpoint recalls depictions of 17th- and 18th-century châteaux that emphasise the geometry of a landscape design that enforces a sense of power; the vigorous draughtsmanship and treatment of light and dark made it a persuasive proposal of how historic designs might be brought to life for the new owners of Champs.

The Château de Champs-sur-Marne was built between 1703 and 1708 by the architects Pierre Bullet and Jean-Baptiste Bullet de Chamblain, for the financier Paul Poisson de Bourvallais.[29] However, the house is principally known for the years spanning 1757 and 1759, when it was rented by Louis XV's official mistress, Jeanne Antoinette Poisson, Madame de Pompadour. Its 85-hectare park recalled the gardens of Versailles, and in their restoration of the property, Louis and his wife, Louise de Morpurgo, chose a particular kind of French style with long-standing international currency.[30] Louise, indeed, stemmed from a dynasty of Italian Jews headquartered in Trieste, and shared her husband's passion for the French eighteenth century.[31] Gabriel-Hippolyte Destailleur had already built important buildings imbued with this spirit, not least Ferdinand de Rothschild's Waddesdon Manor (see Chapter 5). By choosing Destailleur's son Walter-André, and landscape designer Henri Duchêne (opposite, bottom), to renovate their domain, the Cahen d'Anvers embraced a vision of pre-revolutionary France made fashionable earlier in the century through popular novels like Alexandre Dumas's Le collier de la reine.

Unexpectedly, perhaps, the old monarchy retained much of its symbolic power in the early decades of the Third Republic.[32] Both reflecting and influencing aristocratic fashion, intellectuals like the Goncourt brothers dictated much of what passed for good taste. They famously considered the years between the end of Louis XIV's reign and the French Revolution as the period in which French art was most uniquely French, and Paris the European capital of style.[33] It was a world in which witty, enlightened women, the 'queens of the Rococo', ruled over society and culture, with Madame de Pompadour chief among them. Acquiring a château known for her brief stewardship embedded this foreign-born Jewish family in a place imbued with the magic of her mythmaking, and emblematic of the very idea of Frenchness. Barely a year after Captain Alfred Dreyfus had been convicted on false charges of treason by antisemitic elements within the French establishment, it was an audacious act, to say the least. Through their distorted reporting of the collapse of the Union Générale bank in 1882, the crash of the Comptoir d'Escompte de Paris in 1889, and the Panama Scandal of 1892 (see p. 156), polemicists like Édouard Drumont and Auguste Chirac were drumming up widespread hatred of Jewish bankers.[34] When they railed against 'Jewish France' and decried the Jewish financial elite as veritable 'Kings of the Republic', this was precisely the kind of thing they had in mind.[35] Yet the house Louis bought was no resplendent trophy; it was in a sorry state of disrepair. Walter-André Destailleur initially estimated that the restoration would cost 500,000 or 600,000 francs. In the end, it cost nearly five times as much, excluding the park and plantations.[36]

Work began in 1896, and a plan drawn up in 1899 shows the château to the south of the River Marne, with 318 hectares of woods and agricultural land to the west.[37] There were two farms, a Louis XIV dovecot (the privilege of the seigneurial lord) and an eighteenth-century dairy. Destailleur emptied the château, stabilised it, and restored the structure. He removed the terraced roof (installed in 1832) and replaced it with the kind of French mansard roof it had had originally, adding an extra floor that would allow him to demonstrate his deep knowledge of eighteenth-century spatial distribution, construction and style (see p. 153).

Henri Duchêne approached the gardens with a similar interest in restoring their quintessentially eighteenth-century form, as designed by Claude Desgots.[38] Duchêne used a 1727 engraving to recreate the original geometrical design, with two round fountain basins and Italianate parterres.[39] To decorate these spaces, the Cahen d'Anvers commissioned neoclassical marbles from the Carrara workshops of contemporary Italian sculptor Carlo Nicoli – mostly versions of works in the gardens at Versailles, which promoted a sense of continuity, and a visual conversation

for protocol. Women changed three times daily, while riding, hunting and fencing took up most of everyone's days.[55]

In these houses, the Cahen d'Anvers brothers adopted and transformed an aristocratic mode of rural living derived from the villa retreats of sixteenth-century Italy.[56] Industrialisation and the democratisation of wealth forced the aristocracy to share its privileges and havens with a new financial elite. As settings for family life and delight, country houses became the ideal locus for the architectural and social expressions of distinction. Radically different political systems prevailed in Italy and France, but etiquette and a court aesthetic epitomised social achievement and good taste for both branches of the family. Essentially, they adopted a top-down model of integration, whereby their spectacular houses and collections served as the material manifestation of the civil rights they now enjoyed. Antisemites like Drumont and the Goncourt brothers might declare 'true good taste' a 'matter of race', lambasting the Cahen d'Anvers and other rich Jews for their aesthetic inadequacy and cultural inauthenticity,[57] but these attacks obscured a more complex truth.

Through their houses and gardens, Édouard and Louis Cahen d'Anvers revealed deep awareness of the political and social dynamics of their time. They demonstrated familiarity with contemporary Italian and French taste, marshalled the possibilities of different versions of European historicist style, and linked their own lives to the patriotic narratives of their adopted homelands. Integrating the aesthetics of the past with new political goals and shared ambitions, Meyer Joseph's sons showed they knew what it took to belong. Money was not enough; prestige and social acceptance necessitated the most sophisticated cultural literacy. Far from being a synonym for bad taste, opulence served a particular function for a new generation of businessmen seeking their place in society during turbulent times.

7 Agriculture et ars: Villa 'La Montesca' in Città di Castello

Luisa Levi D'Ancona Modena

Educators, philanthropists and politicians were among the many guests Leopoldo Franchetti (1847–1917) and his wife Alice (1874–1911) entertained at their country house in northern Umbria.[1] The Villa 'La Montesca' had been built in the 1880s by Leopoldo and his brother Giulio (1840–1909), a well-known art collector and donor in Florence. Leopoldo himself was a liberal politician who applied his ideas about agriculture at the villa. He married the American Alice Hallgarten in 1900, and in the following years she transformed La Montesca into a centre for pedagogical and philanthropic innovation, particularly for women.[2] The combination of agriculture et ars, and the Franchettis' approach to rural philanthropy, made a strong impression on their visitors, and changed the lives of many of the peasants who lived in the hills near Città di Castello.[3]

La Montesca: architecture and decoration

The Franchetti brothers first started buying land in the fertile hills of the Upper Tiber in 1881; by 1900 they owned 1,000 hectares, divided into fifty farms. They had inherited the money from their father, Baron Isaac Franchetti, who came from a Sephardic business dynasty that had grown rich trading between Livorno, Tunis, Smyrna and France.[4] For the Franchetti brothers, land was a new dimension of their social capital: at once a social, symbolic, economic and political asset. Not only did they belong to an urban elite that still invested heavily in land, but the grain crisis of the 1880s had meant it was also a profitable investment, enabling the brothers to buy up mortgaged landholdings from Florentine and local aristocratic families. Within two years of purchasing his first farm in the region, Leopoldo had entered politics: he would represent this constituency in parliament for the next twenty years.

A page from the Montesca visitors' book, 1901–6. This page, from 1901, includes inscriptions by the German art historian Aby Warburg and the Anglo-Italian politician Ernesto Nathan. Nathan described the view from the house, 'to where heaven and earth meet', as the mirror of the Franchettis' lives.

Back in the early 1870s, Isaac Franchetti had engaged Giuseppe Poggi – Florence's most prominent architect – to restructure his sumptuous Palazzo delle Cento Finestre.[5] His sons opted instead for a younger architect for their country house: Giuseppe Boccini (1840–1900), who had launched his career by designing Isaac's tomb as a family mausoleum in the city's old Jewish cemetery.[6] This commission enabled him to establish himself as an architect for funerary, religious and private buildings in Florence, including Palazzo Levi, which occupies part of the site of what had been the Jewish ghetto. Meanwhile, Giulio Franchetti was developing a local reputation as a cultural philanthropist, collector and, eventually, donor of ancient and oriental textiles.[7] He invited Boccini to teach at the Istituto d'Arte, a school for applied arts he had founded in Florence, which was to play a crucial role in forming talent for the city's new artistic–industrial sector (including several decorators engaged to work on La Montesca).[8]

Built between 1883 and 1889, La Montesca stands on a hill overlooking Città di Castello. In the 1890s it was used as the Franchetti brothers' country house, also hosting their mother Elena Tedeschi, who received her extended family there. In September 1897, for example, her granddaughter Isabella Goldschmidt Errera visited from Brussels with her husband, who recorded that La Montesca was 'admirably situated … est tres reussi'.[9] Approached through its nineteenth-century park via a path leading to the side entrance, La Montesca 'has a surprising and sudden impact'.[10] The two-storeyed main building is constructed in a neo-Renaissance style and enclosed by two towers, which are crowned with loggias that provide views over the estate and towards the city. Here, the combination of yellow plaster and grey-ashlar decoration is a clear architectural reference to the *pietra serena* of Florentine Renaissance buildings.

While the exterior is uniformly neo-Renaissance, the interior is an exercise in different styles, with a Renaissance-inspired coffered wood ceiling, neoclassical statues, and a *salottino* (small sitting room) decorated in the grotesque style. This eclectic approach, which included genres considered the basis of the Italian tradition, was typical for late nineteenth-century Italian villas. The brothers commissioned the Umbrian painter Cleomone Marini, who had trained in Florence and taught at Giulio's school there, to produce both the *salottino* and a second sitting room: the Perspective Room. The latter is a synthesis of illusionistic architecture, classical ruins and *trompe l'oeil*, with La Montesca itself featured in a landscape that culminates in a balustrade opening onto a sky full of clouds, putti and flowers. By contrast, the grotesque *salottino* depicts 'an imaginary world, full of colour ... and irony, with mythological figures, animals, flowers', realistic fruit and vegetables, female figures representing wisdom and the arts, sensuous women, and African scenes (the latter probably a reference to Leopoldo's activities as head of the Colonisation Office of Eritrea between 1889 and 1890).[11] The arabesque decorations of the Perspective Room were painted by Giovanni Panti, an artist born in Perugia but active in Florence, best known for his polychrome geometric frescoes of the city's Moorish revival synagogue (1882).[12] Like Marini and Boccini, Panti was closely connected to the school Giulio had founded in Florence, as was the sculptor Augusto Passaglia, whose bas-reliefs and doors adorned the new façade of the Florentine Duomo. At Montesca, Passaglia was responsible for the statue of a naiad (water nymph) positioned at the base of the staircase, and for other sculptures in the house and park. Local artisans made the furniture, and the glass and ironwork in the grounds and stables.[13] Naturally, the villa also contained valuable articles of furniture, as well as majolica, paintings, silver, and a beautiful wooden library on the ground floor.[14]

Unquestionably, La Montesca was an extravagant project: 'the most sumptuous villa of the zone', according to one local guidebook.[15] Disputes over the cost reputedly precipitated the 1899 quarrel between the brothers that left Leopoldo (see p. 168, left) sole owner of the property. Architecture, decorations and landscape – all made a profound impression on visitors. As the American feminist writer and activist Vida Scudder wrote on her second visit in 1910:

> We've been in Umbria, living with my precious little friend Baroness Franchetti in a big, cool high-studded villa on the slopes of the Apennines, adorned with the most amazing frescoes on which the eye of man – or modest woman – ever rested – (in the full modern Italian taste for a princely residence) – and overlooking the whole wide sweep of the valley of the Upper Tiber and the encircling hills. Oh, La Montesca is a wonderful place!.... An upper loggia commanding such a sweep of sacred earth and sky that at any moment a Perugino cherub, or more likely, a solemn grotesque seraph, might have appeared silently, floating in the blue.[16]

Leopoldo: agriculture and politics

Born in the Tuscan port of Livorno, Leopoldo Franchetti received a broad education influenced by time spent in schools in Paris, and on long sojourns in England and Germany. Like many newly emancipated Italian Jews, he graduated from university and threw himself into public life, becoming a prominent politician. A firm patriot and strong believer in a constitutional regime based on private property, he was, nonetheless, an unusual liberal: Leopoldo believed the state had a duty to address the growing social and economic gulf between city dwellers and the rural masses, particularly in the south.[17] During the 1870s – the first decade of an independent, unified Italy – Leopoldo had engaged in public policy as a writer. Inspired by forms of self-government in England, his first book (1872) proposed that the rural municipality serve as a true representative body for citizens, landowners, and those 'with the same interests as the peasant *mezzadri* of our Tuscany'.[18] Here, he was referring to the sharecropping contract typical of central Italy's agrarian landscape. *Mezzadria* has since been interpreted as an obstacle to rural modernisation and a paternalistic method of preventing social unrest. Nevertheless, Leopoldo and his close friend, the future liberal prime minister Sidney Sonnino, saw the *mezzadria* both as an economic contract and as a model of 'collaboration between elite and masses, which could develop a rural democracy in which they fervently believed'.[19]

In 1876, Leopoldo, Sonnino and Enea Cavalieri – all men of Jewish origin – conducted a famous enquiry into the condition of Sicily: a crucial matter for the new Italian state. Their book about the 'Southern question' is still debated today, and is usually criticised for the paternalistic, orientalist approach adopted by northern political elites towards the 'uncivilised' south.[20] With time, Leopoldo would realise that the *mezzadria* model he knew from his own lands could not be applied to southern Italy. However, the peasant problem remained central to his political and philanthropic agenda, and the focus of his parliamentary activity. He argued that, in Umbria, in the south and in Eritrea (which he proposed colonising to provide land for Italian emigrants), the state must help peasants to become self-sufficient landowners.

Leopoldo began his political career as a liberal deputy from Umbria in 1882, consolidating his position as the largest landowner in the Città di Castello region. Other Jewish deputies in Italy also used rural constituencies to build and consolidate the political networks necessary for their political careers, but Leopoldo, who publicly denounced electoral clientelism, was no absentee liberal deputy interested only in his constituency.[21] Although he participated in debates about issues such as the navy and public finances, the rural masses remained at the heart of his politics: he proposed government enquiries into rural labour, favoured rural credit, promoted universal (male) administrative suffrage, and championed the role of the state in combating land speculation. Inevitably, he became a target for local socialists. Articles in *La Rivendicazione* described him as 'nothing more than a boulder that, for more than twenty years, has oppressed the stomachs of workers to their total detriment'.[22] The journal published a letter from several peasants in the same issue, complaining that when the *fattore* told them to vote for him, 'we did not know that he did not belong to the Christian religion and was not even baptized'.[23] In 1904, the same journal ran a column entitled 'Baroneide', attacking Leopoldo as an 'exploiter', who represented the 'parasite land-owning class'.[24] His philanthropy was also derided as too modest and, later, ineffective.[25]

Leopoldo's parliamentary campaigns reflected his own experiences as a landowner. Familiar with rural poverty, he revised *mezzadria* contracts and introduced better conditions for his workers, alongside innovations in the hydraulic system, crop rotation and vine-growing.[26] Life on his rural estate inspired Leopoldo's view of 'a democracy of small owners': a vision that was crucially influenced by his wife Alice.[27]

Alice: progressive pedagogy and philanthropic activism

Alice Hallgarten (opposite) was born in New York to a well-known Jewish banking family. Her grandfather Lazarus had left Germany after the 1848 revolution and later founded the international banking firm Hallgarten & Co.[28] Her parents, Adolph Hallgarten and Julia Nordheimer, and their extended family network were renowned for their philanthropic engagement in Jewish and non-Jewish causes in Germany, the United States and Canada.[29] The wealth and ethos of her relatives shaped Alice's cosmopolitan upbringing, world-view and subsequent activism in Italy, where she settled in the mid-1890s after a decade in Hamburg. She became one of several notable foreign-born Jewish women to influence Italian civil society through their activities in academia, philanthropy and politics.[30] Like many of her German compatriots, and some Jewish friends, Alice was fascinated by Italian art.[31] However, the move to Italy with her mother and younger brother had also been for health reasons; tuberculosis stalked the family and would take them all, including Alice, who died at thirty-seven. Their diagnosis affected the Hallgarten sisters' marital prospects and may have been a factor in Alice's decision to 'dedicat[e] all her energy to charitable works'.[32]

In Rome, Alice cultivated cosmopolitan networks, initially around the venerable German feminist and intellectual Malwida von Meysenbug.[33] She soon became involved with several projects in underprivileged neighbourhoods – activities through which, according to most biographical accounts, she met Leopoldo, whom she described as 'everything I could wish for in terms of goodness and idealism'.[34] The couple's acquaintance through philanthropic activism may, in retrospect, have been overly emphasised by their biographers, but their marriage, celebrated with a civil ceremony in Rome in July 1900, was to become a union 'of soul and deeds'.

Projects such as the Colonia Agricola – an agricultural colony for forty boys – belonged to a constellation of philanthropic activities in Rome in which Italians, foreigners, Jews, atheists and Catholic modernists collaborated. These resembled and overlapped with similar circles in *fin de siècle* Paris.[35] Scholars have studied the latter in the context of the Dreyfus affair (see p. 191, bottom), but in Italy such activities have largely been considered within studies of Christian modernism.[36] Alice, however, cultivated a spirituality that was foreign to binary Italian and Jewish categories of religious/secular. Her activism makes more sense if we contextualise her spirituality within contemporary debates about religion, morality, social reform and theosophy – highlighting the cluster of initiatives associated with German–American progressives of Jewish origin like Felix Adler, whose schools she visited.[37] In Rome, Alice was also active in secular women's institutions like the Consiglio Nazionale Donne Italiane (CNDI), where she displayed her talents as a social entrepreneur committed to advancing women's work.[38]

Alice's major impact was as the 'Lady of La Montesca', where she founded institutions to 'raise, guide, illuminate, effectively help'.[39] We can see her influence clearly in the Montesca charitable registry: before his marriage, Leopoldo distributed aid to individuals; after it, only through the centralised congregation of charity.[40] The most innovative and effective of Alice's philanthropic projects relied upon education as a source of empowerment. She founded co-educational schools and kindergartens, deploying new pedagogical methods, as well as opportunities for female adult education, and a textile workshop for women with childcare facilities known as the Tela Umbra Laboratory (see p. 176, bottom). Revitalising the local embroidery industry through women's work, Tela Umbra was the concrete expression of Alice's commitment to 'substituting almsgiving with a paid job', as Aurelia Josz, her friend and first biographer, explained. It empowered women through labour, and showed the 'value of Umbrian work' by conserving traditional craft cultures.[41] In addition to providing a workshop space in Palazzo Tomassini, in the centre of town, Alice purchased modern looms, paid teachers, publicised Tela Umbra products in Rome, and brought her guests to the workshop.[42] Nevertheless, after it opened in 1908 it received criticism from socialists who believed that philanthropy could not replace 'the big secret of human emancipation, the elevation from down up'.[43] Alice had a different approach to social change, and the role of La Montesca in the institutions she created is particularly striking.

In October 1901, Alice inaugurated her first school at La Montesca itself (see opposite and p. 176, top). As she wrote to her friend Mary Warburg:

> I set up an elementary school for the children of our tenants in the large *loggia* room of the Montesca.... It does not teach dead knowledge but educates people to live. You can imagine what a strong connection I get to the people, what new interest in them all has been kindled in me & what dreams for the future I cherish!![44]

In the *scuola grande*, as it was called by the pupils (as opposed to the *scuola piccola* that Alice founded in 1902, 10 kilometres away in Rovigliano), children 'climbed the staircase behind the house' and had lessons in the loggia and adjacent rooms. When in residence, Alice began her morning with the pupils, descending later to her rooms to attend to her guests.[45] Her commitment to the school, bolstered by its location inside the villa, was apparent in her hands-on approach to everything from operations and curricula to introducing new pedagogical practices and subjects such as botany and meteorology. The school was also innovative in employing the villa to teach history and geography:[46]

Alice Franchetti and pupils of her school at the Villa 'La Montesca', photographed c.1905–10.

The loggia is particularly apt for the teaching of geography as the landscape lends itself to the practical analysis of mountains, planes, water courses, train tracks, roads.... History teaching is also based as much as possible on the landscape under the students' eyes ... following part of the road traveled by Raffaello on his way from Urbino to Perugia, St. Francis' lowlands, the valley trotted by Garibaldi in 1849.[47]

Sacred history, based on the Old and New Testament and taught on Saturday mornings, also mattered to Alice, although she demonstrated her complex attitude to religion when she voted against abolishing religious education in schools at the CNDI's first National Congress of Italian Women in 1908 – a tense debate in liberal Italy's culture wars.[48]

Alice continuously sought out new pedagogical methods to use in her schools. In England, where she studied botany through a correspondence course, she was a member of the School Nature Study Union and communicated with Lucy Latter, a proponent of kindergartens and the role of nature in education.[49] Alice's meticulous notebooks reveal that the garden at La Montesca became a site for her own botanical experiments.[50] Even from afar, she ensured that pupils had *orticelli* (vegetable gardens) and cultivated them (see p. 177).[51] After Latter visited La Montesca in April 1907, Alice made the *orticelli* an integral part of the curriculum. The Montesca park, with its trees and gardens, was now a crucial element in the life of the school.

Alice was also in touch with the German pedagogical reformer Hermann Lietz, who brought seventeen students from his rural boarding school in Germany to visit La Montesca in 1906. In Milan, Alice visited the first Italian agricultural school

Opposite top
A class of the school founded by Alice at La Montesca, date unknown. After the Franchettis visited Maria Montessori's 'Casa dei Bambini' in Rome, they invited her to La Montesca to write her book on her ground-breaking teaching method. Alice applied Montessori's method to her school; here, the loggia is transformed into an outdoor classroom in which children learn through play.

Opposite bottom
The Tela Umbra weaving workshop in Città di Castello, photographed in 1908. Alice established the workshop along cooperative lines to train and employ local women. They used traditional methods, preserving an artisanal craft that was threatened by industrialisation. To enable young mothers to work, Alice also provided for a nursery – a novelty for the area – and was involved in all stages of production and sale through her networks in Rome and internationally.

Below
Pupils in the vegetable garden at La Montesca, photographed 1900–10.

for women, founded by her friend Aurelia Josz, whom she supported financially and in other ways.[52] Above all, Alice embraced the innovative methods of Maria Montessori, who wrote and published the first book on her method in 1909 while staying at La Montesca, and held the first Montessori teacher-training seminar there. Montessori's concept of the child's freedom as the basis of learning, with an emphasis on cultivating a strong relationship with nature, resonated deeply with Alice, who adopted the method in her schools and became central to the early transnational circulation of these ideas.[53] Indeed, contemplating Montessori, alongside Lietz, Latter and the American Goldman sisters (who visited in the spring of 1906, when they invited her to Bryn Mawr women's college), allows us to see the role of both Alice and La Montesca in the dissemination of new educational concepts. As the British author Edith Bradley, a champion of agricultural education for girls, wrote in the visitors' book in May 1906:

> At Montesca I have learned many things, how it is possible – when there is the will – to have a school for the peasants' children at the top of the *Padroni's Villa*, without causing the local inconvenience or annoyance; how it is possible to take an interest in both scholars + teachers, that the former regard the *Signora* with the deepest affection, + the latter as a true + sympathetic friend. I have seen how these peasants' children can be shown how to use a lending library + a lending picture gallery + to be taught as well the first principles of thought, in the opening of saving bank accounts into which are put the rewards of their attention + industry. Further that the love of nature, & the delights of gardening are brought home to them in their *orticelli*.[54]

Bradley was just one of many who passed through La Montesca. Family visited constantly, including Alice's mother Julia, her great-uncle Jacob Nordheimer, her cousins Emma and Henriette Hallgarten, and their brother Robert and his wife Constanze, who became an important feminist and pacifist in Germany and the United States. The villa also became a place where friends like the renowned art historian Aby Warburg (see p. 162) came 'to take a break from strenuous work'.[55] Others, like the German architect Ernst Ziller, marvelled at the harmony between the house and its owners: 'I "as an architect" felt a constant joy about the good solid architectural taste that animates the whole property and "as a person" about the warm kindness of my hosts, whose way of thinking stands in rare harmony with that of the architecture.'[56]

Politicians came too: Leopoldo's colleague Giustino Fortunato, and the Jewish freemason and Mazzinian democrat Ernesto Nathan, with whom Leopoldo collaborated in Rome on projects like the Colonia Agricola, as well as schools in the Agro Romano, before Nathan became mayor in 1907.[57] James Loeb, the American philanthropist and art patron, who was of German-Jewish descent, was even prompted to paraphrase Dante after a week-long visit in October 1904: *Trovate ogni speranza o voi che entrate* ('Find all hope, oh you who enter'). His protégé, the German–American conductor Frank Damrosch, founding director of the New York Institute of Musical Art, dedicated a few notes to 'the beautiful dreamland' after staying with his family in July 1908.[58]

Another group of guests reflected Alice's spiritual interests. The Christian feminist authors Hope Malleson and Mildred Tuker came from England in November 1901, while the German philosopher and pacifist Friedrich Forster visited in October 1905. Alice was so enthusiastic about his *Lebenskunde* that she funded an Italian translation (*Il Vangelo della vita*) and distributed the book to her guests.[59] Some visitors were fascinated by the figure of Saint Francis, whose legacy in his native

Umbria was particularly strong: the Canadian painter James Kerr-Lawson; French modernist Paul Sabatier, 'the first modern biographer of St Francis'; and Professor Vida Scudder from Wellesley College, a settlement-house pioneer who worked with Italian immigrants.[60] Scudder was invited by 'my first Jewish friend'[61] to stay at her 'beautiful summer home' in June 1906, and admired Alice's 'activities, which St. Francis would have liked'.[62] Some have argued that their continuing friendship, and Alice's fascination with Saint Francis, reflected a desire to convert, although Scudder recognised that Alice's 'passionate loyalty to her race withheld her'.[63] We might do better to interpret Alice's Franciscan rhetoric in the light of Saint Francis standing as a 'transversal icon' of contemporary modernist literature and, above all, a figure local teachers and pupils could relate to.[64]

The books Alice left in the library at La Montesca – especially Felix Adler's *Life and Destiny* (1903) and *Essentials of Spirituality* (1905) – suggest that, as with so many American Jews of her generation, her distance from Jewish ritual life was transformed into an ethical culture based 'on progressive education and good works'. Indeed, she seems to have functioned as a vector for the Ethical Culture movement Adler founded. Forster was general secretary of the International Ethics Association in Zürich. Adler's nieces, the Goldman sisters, who had visited Alice at Montesca in 1906, came to see her again on her deathbed in Leysin; they made a donation to her schools, which she intended to use to 'build gymnastic machines for children, as suggested by Montessori, and books for the school library and Tela Umbra'.[65] Until her final days, Alice was a pivotal player in the transfer of money, people and ideas about education and philanthropy across national borders.

Legacy

Shortly after their marriage, Alice and Leopoldo began to think innovatively about the future of La Montesca. After 1903, they donated all the income from their Montesca and Rovigliano farms to the local schools. In 1907, the annual obligations of the *mezzadri* were abolished. Written three months before Alice's death in 1911, Leopoldo's will ensured a future for her schools and their peasantry. He committed suicide six years later, broken by the loss of his wife and deeply troubled by the Italian defeat at the Battle of Caporetto in 1917. He left his farms, some 65 per cent of all his real-estate holdings, 'to the heads of the families who will keep them in *mezzadria*'. He donated the remainder to the Opera Pia Regina Margherita in Rome, a secular institution focused on schools for women and directed by some of Alice's collaborators in the CNDI. As with Leopoldo's secular burial in Rome's Non-Catholic Cemetery, this bequest followed a common pattern among liberal Jews in Italy; the focus on his country house was distinctive. Here, Leopoldo left money to maintain the Tela Umbra, schools in and around La Montesca, and a rest home for teachers established in the villa. The twin preoccupations with peasants and schools reflected his own desire to create a class of 'medium-wealthy peasants', and Alice's vision of empowerment through education. The school at La Montesca closed in 1980, but the Tela Umbra thrives, housing a museum that preserves the couple's memory. And from its base in the villa, the Hallgarten–Franchetti Foundation continues to promote education and social inclusion. The time has now come to grasp the Jewish dimensions of this legacy.

8 Kérylos: 'the Greek Villa'

Henri Lavagne (translated by Abigail Green)

In this book, Villa Kérylos appears to be an anomaly. Ever since it was first built, between 1906 and 1912, this remarkable house has been known as 'the Greek Villa' because its architecture, décor and furnishings all draw explicit inspiration from ancient Greece. Situated on the edge of a rocky promontory between the bays of Villefranche and Monaco (see p. 190, bottom), Kérylos stands bright white against the raw irregularity of rocks, mountains and vegetation behind it, rising from and surrounded by the sea. The squares and rectangles of the exterior, with simple, shuttered openings, and terraces and belvederes at differing heights, call to mind ancient buildings yet anticipate modern ones. Inside, the colours are earthy. Polished and matt stucco, reliefs, mosaics and wall paintings, inlaid wood, bronze and textiles all capture and modulate the light, drawing the visitor through courtyard and colonnade – and through sequences of spaces and rooms that express a continuity with classical antiquity while offering a seductive and luxurious environment for modern living. Here, on the French Riviera, Théodore Reinach and his architect Emmanuel Pontremoli created a masterpiece in which the 'Greek spirit' found powerful expression.[1]

Théodore (1860–1928) was one of three brothers known in Parisian high society as 'les frères Je Sais Tout', a pun on their respective initials (Joseph, Salomon and Théodore), and a nod towards their eclectic academic interests and intellectual brilliance. Like the Rothschilds, the wealthy Reinachs acted as a lightning rod for political antisemitism in France. Théodore's uncle, Baron Jacques de Reinach, had committed suicide at his château in Nivillers after being implicated in the infamous Panama Canal scandal of 1892 (see p. 156, bottom), which helped to launch the career of Édouard Drumont, the author of the notorious antisemitic text *La France juive*. Théodore's elder brother Joseph was a prominent republican politician and protégé of Léon Gambetta, who became one of the most effective

Below
Frances Benjamin Johnson,
*Villa Torre Clementina, the
Riviera House of Louis Antoine
Stern in Roquebrune-Cap-Martin*,
1925, glass lantern slide, looking
towards the Mediterranean
past the mock-Gothic ruins.

Below right
Emmanuel Pontremoli on the site
of the Temple of Apollo, Didyma,
Turkey, photographed in 1895–6.

Bottom
Beaulieu-sur-Mer, early 20th
century, photographic postcard,
with the recently built Villa
Kérylos on the right, at the
end of the promontory called
the Pointe des Fourmis.

Théodore Reinach, photographed in 1913.

and influential defenders of Alfred Dreyfus, after the imprisonment of this Jewish officer in 1894 on false charges of espionage shook the Third Republic to its core (below). Another brother, Salomon, was a philologist, archaeologist and historian of religion, keenly engaged with a number of international Jewish causes. Théodore, meanwhile, was a lawyer, politician and classically minded polymath. But Théodore's attitude to Judaism differed from his brothers since he was, in fact, a very sincere Jew, whose engagement in communal affairs became particularly intense after he was elected to the National Assembly in 1907.

Théodore was the founder of the Union Libérale Israélite de France. This was the country's first reform synagogue, which aimed to rediscover the richness of Judaism's spiritual and religious traditions. Not always in agreement with Jewish religious authorities, Théodore was greatly respected for the depth and seriousness of his beliefs. He was, moreover, the general secretary of the Société des Études Juives: a body described by the pre-eminent scholar of French Jewry, Pierre Birnbaum, as the veritable ideological progenitor of Franco-Judaism.[2] How then could Villa Kérylos, the visible expression of so many of Théodore's most deeply felt convictions, be so completely lacking in references to Judaism, a faith to which he remained passionately committed? After all, Théodore could have furnished his principal residence with a private synagogue, just as James de Rothschild did

Henri-Gabriel Ibels, 'Pitié!' ('Have Mercy!'), published in an album of prints entitled *Les légendes du siècle album de dessins par H.-G. Ibels, Le Siècle*, Paris, 1901. The Dreyfus affair (1894–1906) divided France and revealed the depth of European antisemitism, with the press and public opinion playing a central role. The Jewish army officer Alfred Dreyfus was wrongly accused of treason, and evidence that exonerated him was suppressed. The miscarriage of justice led to his imprisonment. This political cartoon is dedicated to the politician and journalist Joseph Reinach, who was one of Dreyfus's most prominent supporters.

at Ferrières (see Chapter 3); with the fashionable fresco painter Gustave Jaulmes (1873–1959) at his disposal, we might expect to find Old Testament motifs decorating the villa walls here, as they do at Doornburgh in Holland. But Théodore eschewed anything so explicit.

That, in itself, is hardly surprising. Nearby on the Côte d'Azur, only a couple of years before Théodore began work on Kérylos, the Triestine-born Jewish *salonnière* Ernesta Stern (1854–1926) had commissioned and built the Villa Torre Clementina at Roquebrune-Cap-Martin (see p. 190, top left). Designed by the architect Lucien Hesse, who was known for his work on synagogues and Jewish private houses, this luxurious villa, with its Italian name, is, above all, Venetian, much as Kérylos is Greek. But then Ernesta saw herself principally as an author of Venetian tales – the villa is the image of her inspiration. Marcel Proust, meanwhile, noted nothing specifically Jewish about the château at Illiers-Combray in which he would later install the fictional Charles Swann as a neighbour of the young Marcel's Aunt Léonie. Yet a closer examination of this bourgeois home, which had belonged to the Drache-Lelièvre family when Proust visited as a child, reveals no hint of 'Jewish' taste in what is essentially a rather pompous Second Empire château. Nor is there anything about Théodore Reinach's other country house, near Chambéry in the Savoie (which he represented in parliament between 1906 and 1914), to suggest that its owner was a proud Jew, passionately invested in religious renewal and the reform of Jewish services. For this was essentially an eighteenth-century property, which Théodore bought in 1901 and reworked in a Louis XIII revival style, well suited to a man who planned to run for public office (below).

Château Reinach, La Motte-Servolex, early 20th century, photographic postcard.

If Villa Kérylos is not, then, a site of Jewish memory, we may wonder why its Greek aspect appears so compelling, and what sets it apart from other luxurious villas built in the early twentieth century by members of the Jewish elite. This is a house that attracts up to 50,000 visitors a year, but there is little here to tempt the connoisseur of classical Greek masterpieces.

A villa *à l'antique*

Of all his brothers, Théodore was the best Hellenist and the most steeped in Greek culture.[3] A brilliant archaeologist and numismatist, who had joined digs led by the École Française d'Athènes in his youth, his deep knowledge of Greek literature and applied arts led him to dream, at an early stage, of building a 'Greek house'. The idea came to him in 1900, but he only began work in 1902, after his encounter with Emmanuel Pontremoli (1865–1956; see p. 190, top right), a talented architect who shared his Greek passions. Together, they conceived a villa that would bring to life the latest archaeological discoveries, while serving as a comfortable family home and a scholarly retreat where Théodore could study the Greek texts he so loved. The emergent friendship between architect and patron, and the freedom he allowed Pontremoli when designing the layout and interiors, help to explain the unity and harmony of the whole.

Like Théodore, Pontremoli was Jewish. The son and grandson of rabbis, he had worked at the Pergamon Museum in Berlin, and with Bernard Haussoullier at the temple of Apollo at Didyma; he remained, like Théodore himself, closely connected to leading French archaeologists at the École d'Athènes – men such as Joseph Chamonard, then excavating the theatre quarter at Delos and the most important private houses there. This deep knowledge of Greek and Roman buildings permeates Kérylos, a house that anticipates Pontremoli's adaptation of other architectural traditions for modern use: the Byzantine synagogue at Boulogne-Billancourt (1911), commissioned by Edmond de Rothschild, and the neo-Renaissance Institute for Human Paleontology in Paris (1914).

To begin with, Pontremoli made the most of the isolated position at the end of the Pointe des Fourmis, to build 'a terraced villa, over the sea, protected on one side by high cliffs, recalling the site of the sanctuary at Delphi'.[4] Following the great Charles Garnier, architect of the Paris Opéra, whom he knew at the end of his life, Pontremoli did not hesitate to give the house a high corner tower, like that of Garnier's 1872 villa in Bordighera on the Italian coast, which demonstrates a similar freedom from the constraints of time. The interior layout at Kérylos cleverly incorporates rooms from an ancient Greek plan, but on a larger scale than in classical times. Their names have been similarly transposed, into a transliterated Greek (*triklinos*, *balaneion*, *andrôn*...) that creates a delicious impression of the idea of a Greek house as it existed in the European imagination before the first archaeological excavations. The interiors were overseen by Jaulmes, a former architect then becoming known for his neoclassical brand of Art Deco decoration, and Adrien Karbowsky (1855–1945), an innovator in the Art Nouveau style, celebrated for murals and textiles. The stucco reliefs are by the academic sculptor Paul Jean-Baptiste Gascq (1860–1944). Reinach commissioned some bronze copies of objects in the National Archaeological Museum in Naples, and asked Pontremoli to design the furniture, taking inspiration from the ancient *klismos* chairs, tabourets, tripods and chests from Pompei that were displayed there. These were then made up in exotic woods by the Parisian cabinetmaker Louis-François Bettenfeld. Not once, however, did Reinach and Pontremoli sacrifice modern comfort for the careful accuracy of historical reconstruction. Thus, the arrangement of corridors and staircases reserved for servants reflects the bourgeois practices of the Parisian society to which the

Reinachs were accustomed. Only the owner, a philhellene par excellence, could appropriate the lifestyle that Emperor Hadrian (who was himself enamoured of the Greek way of life) had made fashionable at his villa at Tivoli.

Looking back on their efforts in 1934, Pontremoli elaborated: 'I knew – and previous experiments enabled me to understand this fully – that every restoration, reproduction or reconstruction of a building from the past is empty of meaning if one sticks exclusively to what one believes to be the truth, or to what appears to be archaeologically truthful.'[5] This clear-sighted understanding guided his work. Through it, we can see that Kérylos is not a pastiche of a classical Greek house, but rather an attempt to revive the 'Greek spirit': a spirit reconceived and transformed through the addition of identifiably Latin elements.

Take, for example, the sculpture displayed at the villa. The art historian Alain Pasquier, who has studied it in depth, stresses that few of these sculptures are authentic – indeed, they are consistently mediocre; whether made from marble, stone or bronze, almost all are copies of celebrated works.[6] The villa is consequently far from being a 'Greek museum' put together by a collector with enough money to acquire the original pieces then still in circulation.[7] An essay by Pierre Gros points to similar conclusions.[8] Here, Gros shows that archaeologists were engaged in 'inventing' the Greek house during precisely this period, starting from a reading of the Roman author and architect Vitruvius, to which were added lessons drawn from the first discoveries of the houses on Delos. In short, for all its 'self-proclaimed Hellenism', Villa Kérylos is arguably as Roman as it is Greek; it 'emerges simultaneously from Vitruvius, Delos and Pliny the Younger'. One might even talk of a reappropriation of the Greek spirit, revisited through Roman culture. These insights do not diminish the exceptional achievement that is Kérylos, wonderfully integrated into a natural setting, in a part of France deeply connected to Greece and which, as Reinach and Pontremoli grasped, resonates mysteriously with the Greek landscape.

How, then, can we understand the Jewish dimensions of Kérylos, if we reject the idea of a 'Jewish villa' and minimise the traditional interpretation of this house as 'Greek' in favour of the idea that is a villa à l'antique? Risky though it may seem, we might attempt a symbolic interpretation of Théodore Reinach's project from the moment he first began work on the villa.

Here, the first obstacle we encounter is the absence of personal archives and, in particular, of all correspondence between Théodore, his architect and his decorators. These documents were no longer at the villa when it was occupied by an SS commando in September 1943, having been sent to the home of Théodore's second son, Léon Reinach (1893–1944), in Neuilly-sur-Seine.[9] There, they were seized by the German police and dispatched to the Einsatzstab Reichsleiter Rosenberg in Frankfurt, which served as a central depot for all the archives and libraries looted from Jewish owners.[10] A further collection of papers preserved by Léon seem to have been taken to the Château de Chambord, where they too fell into German hands.[11] Some literary and musical manuscripts belonging to Théodore were recently identified at the National Library of Belarus, in Minsk. None relate to Villa Kérylos, and we can only hope that the remaining Reinach archives, stolen by the Germans and later sent on to the Soviet Union, will eventually be found in a German or Russian library. For now, we are reduced to speculating on what may have been Théodore's state of mind when he set about putting his plan into action.

Despite his immense learning and mastery of Greek, Théodore (who then held the Chair in Greek Numismatics at the Collège de France) was not – and certainly not in his youth – an austere scholar, preoccupied with his studies and uninterested in mixing with the fashionable celebrities of the day. In 1900, when Théodore acquired the rocky promontory known as the Pointe des Fourmis at Beaulieu-sur-Mer, the area boasted large hotels frequented by European royalty, with the most sumptuous residences already sprouting up around them. Like other well-known figures, Théodore ate at La Réserve, a restaurant first established in 1880, where King Léopold II of Belgium kept a table. We know that while Kérylos was under construction, Théodore lived at the Métropole, one of the grandest palace-hotels in Beaulieu, which he later used as a lodging house for his guests. Once the villa was completed, he clearly enjoyed hosting prominent political and cultural figures: King George of Greece; Léopold II, who owned a large estate at Cap Ferrat; his relative-by-marriage Béatrice Ephrussi de Rothschild, who built her own villa just opposite; and his neighbour, the world-famous engineer Gustave Eiffel. There is also a well-known photograph of Théodore with Armand Fallières, then president of the French Republic.[12] Both the actress Sarah Bernhardt (at the height of her fame) and the acclaimed American dancer Isadora Duncan were likewise entertained there.[13] For the Riviera was, far more than Paris, a space where individuals from quite different classes and cultural milieux could overlap and intermingle.

All this helps us to understand Kérylos as a site of integration: social and political. It testifies to Théodore's desire for acceptance by members of the official and cultural elite. For both his republican political ideas and his personal ambitions inclined him to seek to move beyond the confines of the privileged Jewish world into which he had been born, which formed a kind of exclusive Parisian 'ghetto'. Bear in mind that the opposition between 'Hebraism' and 'Hellenism' as cultural archetypes, developed for example in Matthew Arnold's *Culture and Anarchy* (1869), was already a staple of European intellectual culture. Ancient Greece was a motif that the French nationalist philosopher and political activist Charles Maurras had sought to make peculiarly his own: Greece could stand for many things, but for Maurras it represented an ideal of social cohesion, the Greek *polis* providing the perfect environment, a model for modern polities, in which humans could thrive. The hateful right-wing critique, voiced by the monarchist and anti-Dreyfusard Léon Daudet, may have failed to articulate this clearly, but Théodore's appropriation of Greece was experienced as a provocation by the ultra-nationalist milieu associated with Action Française. Thierry Maulnier, another disciple of Maurras, even felt prompted to write of 'that Greece, where we were born', underlining their sense of spiritual ownership.[14] Yet Théodore's philhellenism was no less passionate, as he demonstrated in a 1908 article entitled 'Greece, Rediscovered by the Greeks'.[15]

Reinach's blissful retreat

Perhaps, however, we should ponder the enigmatic name of the villa itself. For the *kérylos*, a mythical bird, comes as something of a surprise in a home that we might have expected Reinach to place under the auspices of Athena and her owl, as symbols of wisdom, intelligence and the arts of civilisation. Athena is certainly present at Kérylos, but relegated to the gloomy ground-floor *amphithyros* (and she is, in any case, just a plaster copy of the Lemnian Athena, skilfully patinated).[16] Symbolically, the owl and the goddess carry little weight; it is the *kérylos* that matters. This melodious word, which appears only very rarely in Greek and Roman literature, denotes an imaginary bird known sometimes as the 'Halcyon of the seas'. And perhaps Théodore settled upon that word because Greek and Roman naturalists ascribe to this bird a particular characteristic: it flies over the water when the sea is stormy, only to nest on the water when it is perfectly still. In short, he chose the bird as a symbol of the Jewish people, tossed on the seas of human history and condemned to wander in search of a moment's rest: those joyous few days of peace known in Latin as the *alcyonia*, the 'halcyon days'.

Here, like the *kérylos* of the Greeks, Théodore pursued the quiet and scholarly family life he longed for. Facing the sea, in the library where he liked to pass his time, he commissioned the following inscription in Greek: 'It is here in the company of Greek orators, scholars and poets that I have created a peaceful retreat among immortal beauty.' For Reinach, then, Kérylos was a place of retirement: a place to read, reread and write about the riches of Greek literature, and even Greek music (in which he began to specialise when the French archaeologist Théophile Homolle uncovered the two Delphic Hymns in 1893). What greater joy could he know than listening to the brilliant composer Gabriel Fauré play one of his scholarly transpositions on the piano he had commissioned from Pleyel for his wife, Fanny? When closed, this state-of-the-art French instrument is disguised as a version of an antique storage chest, but it bears the playful Greek inscription *Pleyelos epoiesen* ('Pleyel made [me]').[17]

With the same teasing humour, Reinach selected a small mosaic for the paved floor of the entrance hall, depicting a hen, a cock and their chicks (see p. 201) – a feature that tells the visitor precisely what he aimed to achieve here, while serving as a counterpoint to the imaginary bird that is the *kérylos*. Interestingly, this is not, in fact, an antique mosaic from the Alexandrian period, as has often been suggested. It is, instead, a relatively modern mosaic, purchased in 1901 when the decorative scheme of the villa was still evolving. This kind of barnyard subject, and particularly the motif of hens and chicks, had been fashionable in the studios of Roman artists like the Bohemian painter Wenceslaus Peter (1742–1829), who sold the cartoons of these paintings to the mosaicists of the Vatican.[18] Reinach was too much the connoisseur of Greek art to purchase this piece in error, mistaking it for an authentic fragment of a Roman mosaic. More likely, he brought it for its subject, as a subtle and ironic allusion to the imaginary bird whose name he had chosen for his home. Rather than finding an image of the legendary *kérylos*, Théodore Reinach preferred to present his visitors with the most prosaic image of family life imaginable: one that came straight from the farmyard.[19] He wanted to let his visitors know that even though the villa walls were decorated with elevating tales from Greek mythology, this was still a family home: a nest in which they could live happily together.

Home of the founder of French liberal Judaism

There are, indeed, three elements at Kérylos that can best be understood as allusions to the Judaism of the man who created it. The first is the altar to an unknown God that takes pride of place against one wall of the 'gentleman's salon', the *andrôn*, which is the principal room on the ground floor (see p. 197). This altar is made, very simply, from white plaster, inscribed with a dedication to *agnostos theos* ('the unknown God'); it occupies the place of honour, even if it has failed to attract the attention of visitors or experts in Reinach's iconography. To begin with, it is worth noting that this room opens onto the peristyle (interior courtyard) via a monumental bronze grille decorated with medallions depicting the twelve principal Greek deities: a feature to which this little altar to an unknown God serves as a response. The text from which Théodore derived this inscription was well known, and would become even more so with the 1913 publication of Eduard Norden's celebrated and controversial book *Agnostos Theos: Untersuchungen zur Formengeschichte Religiöser Rede* ('*Agnostos Theos*: Investigations into the History of Forms of Religious Speech').[20] Norden tells us that when the Apostle Paul visited Athens in the mid-first century CE, he addressed the Athenians from the Areopagus rock and congratulated them on their religiosity, because he had encountered in their city not just expressions of veneration for the twelve Gods of Olympia, but also an altar to 'an unknown God'. This, Paul explains, is the God he will reveal to them – a god they venerate already, without knowing him. It is a much-discussed text, frequently deployed by Jewish theologians in their polemics against idol worship and to shore up the monotheistic tradition of Israel: the sole true and living God is the 'God of Abraham, Isaac and Jacob'.[21] Let there be no doubt about it: when a man as familiar with Jewish history and theology as Théodore commissioned an altar bearing this inscription for the *andrôn* of his villa and placed it opposite a group of medallions representing the twelve deities of ancient Greece, then he accorded that altar a fundamental importance, reflecting his personal religious beliefs.

We may find Jewish meaning, too, in the small room by the entrance to the villa, which is loosely described as the *thermae*, but is probably a deliberate allusion to the laws of ritual purity. It is, in fact, a bathroom with an octagonal pool that calls to mind the Jewish *mikveh* (see pp. 202–3). This pool is accessed via a short flight of steps, something out of place in a *nymphaeum* (indeed, Greek *nymphaea* are not deep enough to stand in – something that is even truer of the Roman variety). It seems far more likely that what Théodore had in mind was a reference to the *mikveh,* and the Jewish rite of ritual immersion.[22]

Finally, the geometric motif that characterises the mosaic on the library floor (see p. 200), insistently repeated across the whole surface of the room, must be intended as a reference to that star we call the Star of David, known both as the emblem of King David and a symbol of the Messiah and Davidic line. This is something of which the art historian Ernst Kitzinger was utterly convinced: the schematic geometrical composition may already be known from Pompei and other straightforwardly Roman contexts, but here it has an undeniably Jewish quality.[23] For while there is nothing remarkable about the hexagonal pattern that covers the floor, the stars composed of two equilateral triangles, superimposed on one another and placed at the centre of each hexagon, are certainly intended to conjure up that pre-eminent Jewish symbol. Not many among the thousands who pass through this library, where Reinach loved to work, give any thought to it, and some consider this hidden symbolism too far-fetched. But Théodore Reinach certainly knew the old Jewish story about the spider who spun a web with this motif across the mouth of the cave in which David was hiding from Saul.

Perhaps then, we need to challenge the assumption that Kérylos is a Greek villa first and foremost, acknowledging instead the decisive importance of these allusions to the Judaism of the two men who made it: Théodore Reinach and his architect Émmanuel Pontremoli, both deeply committed Jews. Scholars have failed to identify this dimension because it is expressed discreetly. Yet in the words of that great philosopher of the visual, Gaston Bachelard, 'we must always look behind the obvious images, for the images that are in hiding'.[24] These hidden Jewish images reflect an aspiration to neutrality that characterised both the ideology of French secularism and Reinach's own historical writing. It was an aspiration affirmed in the first issue of the *Revue des études juives,* to which Théodore and his brother Salomon gave much time and effort. Here, the new periodical declared to its readers: 'we do not wish to engage in religious propaganda, and our aim is not to edify'.[25] The *Wissenschaft des Judentums* (as this new Jewish scholarship was called) assumed a scientific detachment; in the privacy of his home, Théodore attempted to maintain the same rigour.

'Where is your Delos, where your Olympia?' asked the German Romantic poet Friedrich Hölderlin of the muse Urania, when he urged her to pass the torch of Greek civilisation to a Europe still in search of a future. Théodore Reinach's response to this question was to build the Villa Kérylos.

9 Schloss Freienwalde: the Jewish restoration of a Prussian legacy

Martin Sabrow

In Mark Brandenburg, on the easternmost edge of present-day Germany, lies an almost forgotten country house: its history speaks powerfully to the shattered promise of Germany's Jewish past. Built between 1798 and 1799 by David Gilly for Friederike Luise – the discarded wife of Frederick William II, the most insignificant of Prussian monarchs – this little palace, 80 kilometres from Berlin, has always been a place of resigned seclusion. So it seemed to the great German writer Theodor Fontane, who came upon it, empty, during his *Wanderungen durch die Mark Brandenburg* ('Rambles through Mark Brandenburg') in the mid-nineteenth century, and discovered a dusty barrel organ amid the forgotten detritus of the interior: '[w]e turned the crank, hidden under a bale…. But the harmony is gone. Spritely tones no longer leap cheerfully from the barrel; lame, broken and out of tune, they creak slowly through the air, echoing grim and eerie against the basement wall.'[1] He could hardly guess that only a few decades later, the outline of an alternative path into twentieth-century modernity would be briefly illuminated from this remote little Hohenzollern palace, rendering it a site of European importance. This particular history began in 1909, when the Prussian Crown sold the dilapidated property, complete with contents, park and outbuildings, to an entrepreneur from Berlin.

The new owner was Walther Rathenau (1867–1922; see p. 211), a seminal figure in German and European history. Rathenau's father, Emil Rathenau – founder of Allgemeine Elektrizitäts-Gesellschaft (AEG) – was a pioneer of the German electrical industry in the new Prussian-dominated German Empire that came into being in 1871. His son is remembered as an industrialist and businessman, an intellectual polymath and widely read social philosopher, and a gifted amateur painter and architect – a combination of entrepreneurial activity and cultural reflection that, together with his political aspirations, often antagonised his contemporaries. A critic of turn-of-the-century German society in what is known as the Wilhelmine period, Rathenau's

Jewishness prevented him from serving as a Prussian reserve officer. Yet he would oversee the supply of raw materials to the German military during World War One, and develop ambitious proposals for social renewal and European unification. Rathenau's widely rejected call to fight on in October 1918 meant he could take no credit for rebuilding the country. After operating behind the scenes as a financial expert, he took office when the Kapp Putsch of 1920 threatened the survival of the newly formed Weimar Republic – as Minister of Reconstruction and, from 31 January 1922, Foreign Minister. In this role, Rathenau's name became synonymous with *Erfüllungspolitik* – the attempt to rebuild relations with the victorious Allied powers – and with the Treaty of Rapallo with revolutionary Russia that ended Germany's diplomatic isolation. However, his efforts to reintegrate a defeated and reconstituted Germany into the family of nations lasted less than six months: he was murdered in Berlin on 24 June 1922 by right-wing ultra-nationalists hoping to destroy the new democratic order.

Rathenau was assassinated principally because he was one of the most important members of the new government. Yet he had been the target of antisemitic attacks all his life and always experienced his Jewish origins as a social embarrassment. As he wrote, '[t]here is a painful moment in the youth of every German Jew that he remembers all his life: when he first truly understands that he has been born a second-class citizen, that neither hard work nor merit can free him from this condition.'[2] At first, Rathenau responded to his ambiguous status – a leading industrialist and a stigmatised outsider – by calling for assimilation, criticising Jewish immigrants from the East for their distinctive culture. However, in 1911, he took a different tack in a polemic that decried both sides:

> [i]t's true that the Prussian nobility created the old Prussian system that is now sadly dying out ... it is hard that it must share its ancient privileges.... However talented and specially trained, a thousand ruling families are neither numerous nor active enough to meet the massively increased need for administrative staff ... I stand by my conviction...: the state cannot dispense with any of its intellectual or moral forces; it must and shall accord a role in our collective efforts for the public good to the bourgeoisie, very broadly understood, including the Jews – and this sooner than those involved anticipate.[3]

This prophecy was realised with the Weimar Republic. When he was appointed Foreign Minister, Rathenau refused an official request that he state his religious affiliation, pointing out that the question did not 'conform to the constitution'.[4] Yet the social and economic repercussions of military defeat stimulated an atmosphere of increasingly aggressive German nationalism. Rathenau was attacked as a Jew and denigrated as a traitor in the service of foreign powers; he even received death threats. When he asked a fellow politician, the pacifist journalist Hellmut von Gerlach, 'Why do these men hate me so?', Gerlach's answer illuminated the tragedy of his position: '[s]imply because you are a Jew who is making a success of German foreign policy. You are the living contradiction of the antisemitic belief that the Jews harm Germany.'[5] The fatal outcome of his career still lay ahead in the summer of 1919, when Rathenau recorded:

> [i]n 1909 the Prussian royal treasury sought to dispose of several properties; one was Schloss Freienwalde...; a one-storey country house, five windows wide and four windows deep, in a modest park on the edge of the town of Freienwalde. A friend took me there because he knew I loved the architecture of Prussian classicism, which was hardly heard of then, and little valued.[6]

Edvard Munch, *Walther Rathenau*, 1907, oil on canvas. Rathenau's choice of the Norwegian artist to paint his portrait bears witness to his progressive artistic taste. Munch found both controversy and fame in Germany, where he was championed by the Berlin Secession, a group of artists whose first president was Rathenau's cousin Max Liebermann (see Chapter 11).

Opposite top
The Allgemeine Elektricitäts-
Gesellschaft (General Electric
Company) turbine factory,
Berlin, photographed in 1909.
The pioneering nature of AEG's
industrial production methods is
reflected in the innovative design
of its buildings. The turbine hall,
by the architect Peter Behrens
and engineer Karl Bernhard,
built 1908–9, was a turning
point in architectural history.

Opposite bottom
Walther Rathenau's villa in the
Berlin suburb of Grunewald, date
and photographer unknown.
The house, designed in 1910 by
Johannes Kraaz, incorporates
details copied from Schloss
Freienwalde. In the Nazi era,
Rathenau's sister was forced to
sell the house before emigrating.

Schloss Freienwalde as a socio-political programme

Here, with deliberate understatement, Rathenau indicated there was more to this acquisition than a summer retreat for a rich Wilhelmine entrepreneur and industrialist. For Schloss Freienwalde recalls a silent culture war before World War One: the stakes were Jewish integration and exclusion in the German national community – that is to say, Germany's route into twentieth-century modernity. To understand how, we must explore Rathenau's promotion of early Prussian classicism. Two years before buying Freienwalde, he had stepped down from the helm of the Berliner Handels-Gesellschaft; as crown-prince of AEG, he hoped his informal advice to the government might lead instead to a real political appointment. Instead, 1909 to 1911 saw the gradual destruction of his political ambitions, reawakening in him the old conflict between literary and entrepreneurial vocations. Schloss Freienwalde, like Rathenau's Berlin home, became the site of memory in which this frustrated spirit realised his vision for the country – for the moment, an aesthetic programme rather than political action. In the elegantly simple, delicately detailed, classicising villa he built in the Berlin suburb of Grunewald in 1910, Rathenau installed a strikingly narrow door, whose modesty was in stark contrast to the opulence of the imperial capital (opposite bottom). Through his restoration of a forgotten and neglected architectural jewel, designed for the Prussian royal house with quintessential eighteenth-century modesty, Rathenau silently articulated his protest against the immoderate bombast that characterised the neo-Romanesque Kaiser Wilhelm Gedächtniskirche (1891–5) and the neo-Baroque Berlin Cathedral (1894–1905).

Rathenau found congenial collaborators for his architectural undertakings. The 'friend' he had mentioned was a young Hermann Schmitz, then working on a study of late eighteenth-century Berlin master builders and devoted to the rediscovery of early Prussian classicism. Here was a kindred spirit who shared Rathenau's critique of Wilhelmine stylistic decadence and urged him to preserve the 'simple creations of old Prussian culture' for art-historical reasons. 'It is,' Schmitz wrote later, 'no coincidence that – precisely in the early 20th century, when the neo-Baroque was in full flow in Berlin, intermingled with every possible stylistic imitation – a few subtle artistic spirits became aware of the … [forgotten] relics of the simple old-Prussian style of building and living produced in Mark Brandenburg around 1800.'[7] Rathenau was, according to Schmitz, one of the first to 'motor through the Mark, seeking out the sequestered monuments of *altmärkisch* palace and country-house architecture'. This was probably how he came across the neglected little palace, then scheduled to be repurposed as a courthouse, its overgrown park sold off – and likely broken up – by the royal estate 'due to the high costs of maintenance'.[8]

Rathenau would appropriate and restore this ensemble with the same care he showed in choosing it, at the cost of considerable time and effort. Supported by the art historian Schmitz and the architect Johannes Kraaz, who had designed his recently completed villa in Berlin-Grunewald, Rathenau took charge of repairing the dilapidated property. A Berlin sculpture studio was tasked with preparing a plaster model of the building so that they could experiment with different approaches. Together, Rathenau and Schmitz motored through the Brandenburg area, where '[s]o many classic examples of this school between Freienwalde and Berlin' were visited and discussed, including 'the 1803 *Chausseehäuser*' in Berlin, the Eberswalde hammer mills and 'the tower Gilly built for the Humboldt family tomb in the village of Falkenberg near Weissensee'.[9] Written after Rathenau's death, Schmitz's memoirs make clear how consciously Rathenau situated himself in the tradition of Gilly and his student Karl Friedrich Schinkel, who had made architectural history *circa* 1800 in their search for a 'harmony of historical form and pure function', thereby anticipating the modern. This search for a lost political

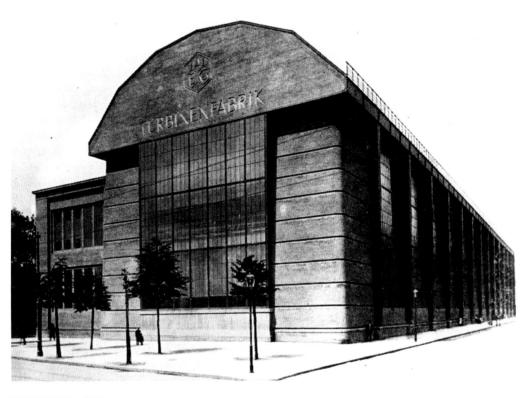

These photographs, commissioned by Rathenau in 1912, show interiors at Schloss Freienwalde that were destroyed in 1945.

Top left: Summer Sitting Room. Rathenau restored this room, which had been Queen Friederike Luise's sitting room. The wallpaper was painted with trees and shrubs, including viburnum ('snowball bush').

Top right: Dining Room, with floral walls, ceilings, curtains and furniture. On the south side, this was the largest room in the house.

Bottom left: Music Room. On the upper floor, decorated with scenes from the story of Cupid and Psyche, this was furnished with historic pianos and a harpsichord, all of which Rathenau played.

Bottom right: Blue Salon. Rathenau restored the other rooms on the main floor to their 18th-century appearance, but the Blue Salon was his own invention. He joined two separate rooms to create one large reception room; gilded columns mark the original division. The light blue wallpaper had borders printed with roses.

and aesthetic harmony led Rathenau and Schmitz to explore Brandenburg's architectural landscape together:

> [w]e affirmed each other's conviction that preserving and studying these simple creations of the old Prussian culture of the late 18th century was necessary for the revival of a healthy architectural tradition ... in our contemporary Mark Brandenburg – naturally not in the sense of copying its forms, but with a view to following true architectural principles, taking purpose as a starting point and paying attention to the native area.[10]

And so the schloss acquired a new face, creating a classical impression that chimed with Rathenau's Berlin-Grunewald villa (which also referenced Gilly and Schinkel) without simply restoring its original condition. The pilasters, a later addition that helped provide clearer form to the building's exterior, now received greater emphasis, at the expense of the cornice originally running between the main and upper floor. The projecting cornices on the *piano nobile* were set higher and provided with brackets. The proportions of the house, originally plastered in yellow, and later white, were emphasised by repainting the façade pink, and the pilasters grey. Above all, the new owner had a semicircular balcony supported by Doric columns set out from the east front, out of keeping with Gilly's formally strict classicism, but enhancing the living quarters with an outlook across the park towards the River Oder: this synthesis between old Prussian architecture and modern life could be read more generally as a broader programme of Prussian cultural renewal.

A similar intention guided Rathenau in the interior, which lacked grand staircases and large spaces, but instead opened behind a deliberately inconspicuous rear entrance into a square staircase, with narrow corridors leading to the individual rooms. The palace's loss of relevance meant that these spaces had mostly retained their original decorative schemes. 'Here,' Schmitz recounted, 'was one of the very rare examples of a Brandenburg summer residence, whose reception and living spaces – wallpaper, stoves, furniture, light-fittings and other effects – had been kept almost exactly as their inhabitants left them in about 1800.'[11] Like the white ceilings and simple doors, windows and fireplaces, the upright, unshowy furniture embodied a programmatic rejection of the Baroque, and the embrace of the deliberately plain, quasi-bourgeois style that had come into fashion during Queen Friederike Luise's time. Rathenau largely kept the original layout, conserved the wallpaper wherever possible, and replaced what was missing in a neoclassical style. Here, too, he was careful to preserve the overall impression without worrying excessively about historical accuracy. The same applied to the contents: several dozen chairs, wardrobes, mirrors, chests of drawers and tables from the same period. Rathenau originally contracted to purchase the entire inventory of fifty-three objects, only to discover that court officials had dispatched them 'in error', to be put into storage at Schloss Charlottenburg.[12] Rathenau insisted the furniture be returned piece by piece, to be renovated and displayed in its original setting, complemented by some specially purchased pieces. A few rooms on the top floor were set aside for his personal needs and furnished as an apartment with sanitary facilities.

Little wonder that after Rathenau had finished his restoration, Schloss Freienwalde gave, as Schmitz put it, a 'complete impression of the lifestyle associated with the final achievements of the 18th century'. This was no museum; it appeared 'still animated by the breath of its inhabitants'.[13] Rathenau was clearly pleased. He commissioned a photographer from Berlin to record palace and park, and kept the images together in a portfolio (opposite). When Rathenau sent a set to the writer Gerhart Hauptmann for Christmas 1911, he wrote with restrained pride: '[t]hese pictures, which I had taken this autumn, show house and garden still surrounded with bloom; the photographer, a good sort, seems to me to have produced something very serviceable.'[14]

In Freienwalde, Rathenau had restored an old Prussian *lieu de mémoire* to public consciousness. Its aura was artificial, and its authenticity re-created, but Rathenau understood Freienwalde as an aesthetic counter-programme to a Wilhelmine ambition that was oblivious to history because it rejected the policy of self-restraint and reform Prussia had embraced after its 1806 defeat at Jena by Napoléon. This symbolism was apparent when Rathenau recorded a March 1911 encounter with Wilhelm II in his diary, noting that the Kaiser had spoken about Freienwalde and 'architecture (opposing Schinkel)'.[15] At Freienwalde, Rathenau turned once more to political writing. Here, in 1911, he produced the essay collection *Zur Kritik der Zeit* ('On the Critique of the Times'), which became his first real public success, a literary counterpart to the alarm he had sounded in bricks and mortar. In it, Rathenau articulated the paradox 'that Prusso-Germany, the country leading European mechanisation, the much-feared and much-admired land of technology, the strongest industrial power in the Old World ... neither manages its public affairs itself, nor produces sufficient talent to take decisive responsibility, nor possesses clear and significant political goals'.[16]

Rathenau's masterpiece, *Von kommenden Dingen* ('In Days to Come'), took shape in the rural seclusion of Freienwalde during 1915 and 1916. Even in wartime, he ventured to look to an uncertain future: 'I now work fairly regularly for most of the day. The weather is cold and damp, a slight hint of autumn in the vegetation. Guests come rarely, every week I am in Berlin for a day, which impresses me each time with its narrow-minded lack of judgement.'[17] Writing in quasi-monastic seclusion, his

call for the moral reform of German society and a kind of state socialism made the book a bestseller. Some were enthusiastic, others sceptical, but all recognised the far-sighted vision that proclaimed Rathenau one of the country's seminal intellectual voices. 'Curious, how little Jewish – i.e. sceptical – his thought is,' noted General Hans von Seeckt after Rathenau gave him the book in February 1917; 'instead, it's constructive – admittedly, castles in the air'.[18]

Through his purchase, rescue and use of Schloss Freienwalde, Rathenau proved he could understand the roots of 'Prussianness' better than the hordes who beat the drum of 'Germanness', invoking the national spirit while actually betraying it. Through the stiff reserve of these spaces, through his insistence on a complete inventory and the title of 'Royal Palace', the Jew who could never be a Prussian reserve lieutenant showed himself and the world that Freienwalde was more than a picturesque relic. This Prussian–Jewish symbiosis expressed a critique of overblown Wilhelmine style that was fundamentally political:

> I am fighting against all that is wrong in Germany, for I see shadows encroaching wherever I look. I see them when I pass through the blaring streets of Berlin at night; when I contemplate the insolence of our insane wealth; when I absorb the emptiness of power-hungry words or hear talk of pseudo-Germanic exclusivity.... An era is not trouble free just because the lieutenant beams and the attaché is hopeful. For decades, Germany has not experienced a more serious juncture...; the best you can do in such times is: to undo harm.[19]

Contemporary reception

To Rathenau, the restoration of this little royal palace amounted to a political programme for emancipation; its rapid realisation evoked the modernisation of Prussia during the famous Reform Era. By and large, Rathenau's contemporaries interpreted his interest in Freienwalde rather differently. Even confidantes, like his friend Lili Deutsch, saw Rathenau's desire for a Hohenzollern property as a quest for ennoblement: compensation for the social recognition he lacked. She wrote to her brother:

> [n]ow at last Walther has bought something, and really found exactly what suits him. It is the little royal palace 'Freienwalde' with a large park, old, respectable, 1¼ hours from here by car. And the Rathenau old folks are building too, the old man bought the house in Victoria str. where Walther lives, and a second one next door, and they are building themselves a great palace; we have all become very spendthrift in these good times.[20]

Others attributed the house's cool, museum-like quality to Rathenau's own character. Among the first guests was Carl Fürstenberg of the Berliner Handels-Gesellschaft, who, as the banker behind AEG, had been party to the Rathenaus' rise:

> [w]ork on the garden was still underway, when I, with my wife and children, paid a first visit to Walther at Freienwalde. The little *Märkisch* spa ... lay in friendly sunshine. The trees just beginning to turn green. Under these circumstances the fresh design of the new part of the Freienwalder *Schlosspark* still emerged rather abruptly. Rathenau's height made the low, newly planted hedges look even tinier ... he stepped over them easily as he came towards us.[21]

The East Front at Schloss Freienwalde, photographed by Franz Kullrich in 1916. Kullrich's low viewpoint emphasised the house's height, the impression of which Rathenau increased by removing the cornice between the two floors.

Fürstenberg meant no harm and wanted to acknowledge Rathenau's achievement. But he could not hide his unease:

> [w]e spent a few pleasant hours at Freienwalde, though I must admit that to my taste the house was too museum-like to be habitable. The even distribution of the furniture along the walls may have been completely in keeping with the style of the period when the house was built, but it did not invite the visitor to linger.[22]

As Fürstenberg went on to explain, 'Walther, though he had great human qualities, was never really given to *Gemütlichkeit* [cosiness].'[23] Fürstenberg was not the only one of Rathenau's friends to read the remodelled schloss in psychological terms. Writer and royal tutor Gustav Hiller-Steinbömer had already noted the contradiction in Rathenau's Grunewald villa between the completely impersonal atmosphere and what was, for Rathenau, a deeply personal undertaking:

> [w]henever I was a guest at Freienwalde ... I felt he had furnished his dream with the Prussian past, without actually inhabiting it. Walking through the masterfully assembled ground-floor rooms with their hand-painted wallpaper and landscapes, cheerful curtains hanging over the deep windows between commodes, mirrors, vases and pictures, I would be overcome by the feeling that without felt slippers I was not properly equipped ... I was afraid to sit on the flowery covers of the gently curving furniture, or to take my place on an ornate little chair in the heavenly Chinese salon with its braided treasures. And we sat in the bright dining room, its leafy decoration flowering across wall, ceiling, chair and sofa, more in admiration than to eat.[24]

The Austrian writer Stefan Zweig also used a memory of Freienwalde to capture its owner's chilly, restrained personality: '[o]ne could never really get warm in his feudal Queen Louise palace in Brandenburg: its order was too obvious, its arrangement too studied, its cleanliness too clean.'[25] Intended as a manifesto for civic equality and unity, Schloss Freienwalde became instead a symbol of Rathenau's isolation. His inability to lure his long-time friend and mentor Maximilian Harden there underlined the point. In 1910, when the works had just been completed, Rathenau wrote to Harden, telling him to 'come on a voyage of discovery in the Oderbruch. Sunday presents a good opportunity. The Fürstenbergs are coming to breakfast; perhaps my parents too.… You will always get a good seat and lively company in the Fürstenberg Omnibus.'[26] But Harden never came, and in Schloss Freienwalde, Rathenau remained what he was in his equally overwhelming Berlin villa: an intellectual, alone.

Symbol of a failed symbiosis

In this way, a house intended as an aesthetic beacon came to be seen, contrary to its creator's intention, as the key to Rathenau's peculiar and contradictory personality. Over time, the affinity this bourgeois son of an industrialist felt with the lifestyle of the Prussian royal house would impact his public image. It was noted, for example, that the new owner set great store by the fact that the property remained a 'royal palace'.[27] The Expressionist writer Fritz von Unruh described his first encounter with Rathenau's summer home thus:

> 'Here…', Rathenau began … 'you can get the best view of my "Schloss"! Look how the crown glitters in the sun on top of the flagpole! Oh yes, they wanted me to unscrew it!' He smiled. 'The Kaiser insisted after he had closed the deal with me. But I told the Hofmarschall, Graf Eulenburg, I had bought the Schloss and everything in and on it, and did not plan to remove the crown from the flagpole.' His smile brightened. '*Nee!* I bought this Prussian royal crown, and it's shining there now!' – 'For how long?' I asked… 'Well, it's already been 500 years.'[28]

Such stories gave rise to the myth of the marginalised Jewish nabob whose wealth could not buy respect, and whose country house was less a publicly useful cultural gesture than a self-serving status symbol. Most contemporaries preferred to understand this aesthetically articulated critique of Wilhelmine society as a rich outsider's barely disguised longing for belonging. Harden, for example, was to disparage Rathenau's relationship with Freienwalde as a transparent bid for social recognition, lumping him in with the other *Kaiserjuden*: men like the banker Fritz von Friedlaender-Fuld, one of the first Jews in the Prussian House of Lords, and James Simon, the 'cotton king', a notable collector and philanthropist. 'Who presents [the Kaiser for his birthday] with Fredericiana? Herr Simon. Who gathers the rural nobility of Mark Brandenburg around him? Herr Friedlaender. Who buys a Hohenzollern palace, complete with Queen Luise's sewing table? Herr Rathenau.'[29]

The idea that Rathenau hoped thereby to purchase the fabled entry ticket into Wilhelmine society affirmed the cliché of the Jewish *arriviste* and seemed in keeping with Rathenau's own calls on Germany's Jewish minority to assimilate. Even after his death, antisemitic attacks on Rathenau gained credence from the *topos* that 'Emil Rathenau's son, who got rich by founding businesses' had turned himself into the noble 'lord of a royal castle' by coming into 'possession of Queen Luise's desk' and fastening 'Hohenzollern eagles to his walls'.[30] *Völkisch* agitators even claimed that Rathenau had set a series of sculptures above the gate of his

Berlin mansion, featuring the heads of European dynasties in a sacrificial bowl. Such libels went unpunished, as did the lie that Rathenau had declared that 'the revolution and overthrow of the German monarchy had been envisaged and agreed by the Jews before the war'.[31]

In this way, the elevated message Rathenau sought to convey was turned against its author and served to undermine him. Even a neutral observer like the Swedish painter and writer Ernst Norlind noted that it was difficult to refute the critique of Rathenau that emerged amid the terrible poverty of the last years of the war. The way that Rathenau envisaged the state was, Norlind wrote, 'reminiscent … of communism', explaining that as someone who had 'always stressed equality and community, he was soon the target of a hateful agitation'. Was Rathenau, 'a millionaire living in a "royal palace", in "princely surroundings", entitled to say such things?', Norlind asked.[32]

Unable to grasp that such symbolism rendered his situation untenable, Rathenau sought to defuse this critique after the war with an apologetic tract:

> 'Freienwalde. Philosopher and *Schlossbesitzer*. He owns a palace! A royal palace! And' – or so well-meaning and upright humanitarians say – 'he insisted on retaining this royal epithet in the deed of sale'…. I bought the house to rescue it, and over the years I have carefully restored it; much that was of value could be re-acquired, which is caricatured as: 'I filled the palace with antiquities and fake ancestral portraits.'[33]

The funeral of Walther Rathenau, 27 June 1922, photographer unknown. After the state funeral service, thousands of people gathered outside the Reichstag to pay their respects to the murdered man.

During the revolution, Freienwalde had been briefly threatened with expropriation; afterwards, Rathenau's reputation was such that his nomination as President by a foreign-born German prompted the Reichstag to erupt with laughter. Yet he had been right about something. Before the war, Rathenau prophesied that 'within less than a decade we will see the final phase of Jewish emancipation'.[34] Many things, including his appointment as Foreign Minister of the Weimar Republic, seemed to confirm that assessment, yet Rathenau's murder would prove the contrary. Long before the Nazis set in motion the persecution and elimination of European Jewry and, with it, the death of a civilisation, Rathenau's manifesto for German–Jewish symbiosis was revealed as nothing more than a noble dream in a hostile world.

In 1926, Rathenau's heirs gave Schloss Freienwalde to the district of Oberbarnim, which committed to establishing a Walther Rathenau Foundation and 'making park and palace accessible to the public ... as a memorial to the old Prussian culture of 1800 and to Foreign Minister Dr. Walther Rathenau'.[35] As Gerhart Hauptmann noted at the 1927 inauguration ceremony, this reflected Rathenau's original intentions: '[f]rom a broken relic of monarchy he created a royal gift to the [country's] citizens. Now the hospitable gates of Freienwalde's park and palace are open to all, as they were to me in a happier hour, a blessing for many generations and a beautiful and permanent monument to its donor.'[36]

All that came to an end in 1933. The Nazis preserved the Prussian legacy, but eliminated all traces of the Jew Rathenau. His remaining associates rapidly left the Walther Rathenau Foundation, which was dissolved on 30 June. Thereafter, palace and park were used primarily by the National Socialist Cultural Association. Nothing recalled Walther Rathenau, from the moment that the Nazis took power until the fall

of the communist dictatorship in the German Democratic Republic half a century later. The estate barely survived looting during the Russian invasion of spring 1945. Then, on 9 September 1953, the authorities announced a new use for the building: '[d]uring the years of reconstruction, the nationally conscious inhabitants of Freienwalde had established a "Pushkin-Haus" of German–Soviet friendship within the palace (see p. 225). It was hoped that "this would be a source of education, elevation, relaxation and joy for all those who desired a peaceful and prosperous Germany"'.[37] And so, until 1990, the palace served as a district cultural centre, library and offices for the German Democratic Republic Cultural Association. In all this, Rathenau's memory played only a marginal role.

Only after 1989 was it possible to re-establish the memorial to Walther Rathenau in Schloss Freienwalde. A permanent exhibition was created in 1992 and has since been further enhanced. Today this little palace resonates powerfully as a site of European memory, embodying a missed historical opportunity. Near the River Oder, which now marks the border with Poland, Rathenau's country house speaks to us of a lost utopia and a historical road not taken – one that might have led more happily into the twentieth century and towards a more civilised, less power-hungry modernity: a modernity shaped more by integration than exclusion, and more by a serene liberalism than imperial excess.

10 Nymans: an English house and garden

John Hilary

When the German-Jewish stockbroker Ludwig Messel bought the West Sussex country estate of Nymans in 1890, the house looked essentially the same as it had done for the previous fifty years. A fine lithograph from the first years of Queen Victoria's reign shows the ivy-clad Regency villa as seen from the south-west, framed by a morinda spruce and monkey puzzle tree growing out of the lawn (see p. 232). A Messel family photograph taken from precisely the same angle in 1891 demonstrates how little had changed in the intervening period. Yet the house would be altered again and again over the next three decades in a succession of redevelopments as the Messels refashioned the building to express their changing identities. While its first expansions still reflected the hybrid nature of the immigrant family, the later redesign became the vehicle for the Messels' appropriation of an English identity. Even when the second generation had assimilated entirely, however, the fabric of the country house would still bear intriguing traces of their German-Jewish roots.

Ludwig Messel was born in 1847 into one of the leading Jewish families in Darmstadt, capital of the Grand Duchy of Hesse. As the eldest of five children, he would normally have taken over the running of the family bank, but it passed instead to an uncle when Ludwig's father died prematurely in 1859. Ludwig moved to London six years later, established himself as a stockbroker and founded his own company, L. Messel & Co., in 1873. The firm carved out a niche for itself in foreign securities and prospered from the trading boom in international equities during the final three decades of the Victorian era. By the end of the nineteenth century, Ludwig Messel was reputedly the richest man on the London Stock Exchange.[1]

*Nymans House, c.*1838, lithograph published by Kell Brothers of Holborn, showing the original Regency villa at Nymans.

Expansion

As soon as he bought Nymans, Ludwig Messel embarked on a project to enlarge the property and make it the focal point of his rapidly expanding family. The house would become a hive of activity at Christmas and New Year, when the visitors' books are full of close friends and relations, and in the summer months, when younger parties could use Nymans as a base from which to attend the race meetings of Glorious Goodwood. Ludwig helped each of his married children to buy their own properties in the Sussex or Surrey countryside, near enough for them to make it over to Nymans in time for Sunday lunch. In a parallel statement of intent, he also began the process of enlarging the Nymans estate towards the 600 acres it encompasses today.

For the expansion of the house itself, Ludwig first commissioned the architect Leonard Stokes, still in his early thirties but already president of the Architectural Association and widely seen as a rising talent. Stokes produced a design that recast the Regency villa of Nymans in neo-Jacobean style, with a modest tower and three gabled bays on the south front, as well as a new east wing with a sizeable billiard room. The design was exhibited at the Royal Academy and published in the *Architectural Review* for 1891, but Stokes never realised the project. The architect was known for his violent temper and for falling out with clients. Equally, the German-Jewish immigrant Ludwig may not have wished to remodel his country seat as an Old English manor house.

Ludwig turned instead to his younger brother Alfred (1853–1909), the only one of the Messel siblings to have remained in Germany when the rest of the family emigrated to Britain. Already making a name for himself as an architect in Berlin, Alfred would later become one of the pioneers of early German modernism as well as an arbiter of taste for the Kaiser himself.[2] According to the *Architektonische Rundschau*, which published Alfred's designs together with a ground plan showing the distribution of the new rooms, Ludwig himself wanted the Nymans extension to be constructed in the continental European style (opposite left).[3] Echoing the fashion

Above left
'Extension to Nymans Country House near Crawley (England) by Professor A. Messel in Berlin', published in the *Architektonische Rundschau* in March 1896. The architect was Ludwig's younger brother Alfred, the only one of his siblings to have stayed in Germany when the rest of the family emigrated to Britain.

Above right
Nymans, photographed c.1910, showing Alfred Messel's extension in its final manifestation.

adopted by family villas outside Berlin, Alfred set a four-storey tower on the south side of the house to provide a visual link between the original building and the new wing. Several more bedrooms were added, plus a protruding two-storey extension with symmetrical roof. The upper floor of the extension was to be devoted to the all-important billiard room, while the downstairs plan added yet another bedroom, together with a French window leading out onto the south-facing porch.

Construction followed the spirit of Alfred's design, but with noticeable simplifications. The extension was built without the arcades on the ground floor or the open veranda to the upper storey, with the result that it lost much of its grandeur. The initial tower was a more faithful reproduction of the original design, its viewing platform surmounted by a steeply pitched roof with hexagonal lantern in the Germanic style.[4] The most striking visual difference came with the exaggerated sweep of the new roof over the east wing, now markedly asymmetrical and more dramatic than in Alfred's original. This variation speaks to the developing English idiom of the 1890s, as seen in the designs that Edwin Lutyens would draw up for Fulbrook House and Berrydowne Court (in Surrey and Hampshire, respectively), or Charles Voysey for Moor Crag at Windermere.[5] Alfred incorporated similar roof plans into his own houses for German-Jewish industrialists outside Berlin, notably the Landhaus Wilhelm Wertheim and Landhaus Ferdinand Springer, both of which were understood by the Germans to reflect the English style of the Arts and Crafts movement.[6] It is doubly ironic that the Nymans extension, an anglicisation of a Germanic design, ended up looking so much like an Alpine chalet.

The new house would undergo a series of further changes over the years (above right). The open belvedere was filled in to create an enclosed space with Italianate designs on the exterior walls, an alteration supervised by the architect Sir Ernest George, whom Ludwig knew as a fellow member of the Arts Club and who would become a Messel family friend. The timber detailing that had been introduced to integrate the tower with the main body of the house was reversed, so that the wood was now picked out in white on a dark plaster background (and removed from the tower altogether). An ornamental bay was added to the west end of the south front and, as a final flourish, a neoclassical portico replaced the undistinguished awning over the door to the right of the bay, creating a grander transition when walking out of the house into the garden. These improvements certainly added to the elegance of the property, even if they could not disguise the bewildering jumble of architectural styles that now characterised the whole. Looking back nostalgically after it had been pulled down and rebuilt in the next generation, Ludwig's grandson Rudolph Messel remembered the house with affection:

> I myself shall never cease to regret the disappearance of the tower, the fantastic conservatory, the Greek porticoes and the heavenly Swiss chalet roof that covered the vast billiard room. We used to have tea on the Greek portico, we played (on wet days) hide & seek among Grandad's priceless plants in the conservatory and were allowed, but only on rare occasions, to climb the tower. The old Nymans was I suppose an architectural freak but what a freak![7]

Reconstruction

Ludwig Messel's elder son Leonard (1872–1953) inherited Nymans on his father's death in 1915, but Leonard's wife Maud was unhappy about living in the property as it now looked, so pressed for a wholesale reconstruction. Based largely on her vision, the Messels set out to create an Old English manor house modelled on fifteenth-century originals such as Great Chalfield Manor in Wiltshire, or Brede Place in Sussex. This radical building project would consume most of the following decade and the Messels appointed Norman Evill (1873–1958), the celebrated pupil of Sir Edwin Lutyens, to turn their dream into reality (below and opposite top). Working to designs he drew up in 1922, Evill oversaw the construction of the west front of the building as it exists today, including the Forecourt Garden and dovecote, but he fell out with Maud and withdrew from the project within a couple of years.

On Evill's departure, the Messels turned to the ecclesiastical architect Walter Tapper (1861–1935) to carry the transformation of Nymans through to its completion. Influenced in his youth by the teachings of John Ruskin and employed for many years by the Gothic Revivalist firm of Bodley and Garner, Tapper was by now at the

John Buckland Wright, *Alterations to Nymans, Handcross, Sussex*, 1922, watercolour on paper. In this rendition of Norman Evill's design, the Great Hall is imagined as an Elizabethan long gallery, complete with 16th-century figures; there are stained-glass windows, arms and armour on the walls, and furniture with a rather Arts and Crafts look about it.

Norman Evill, *Nymans, Handcross, Sussex*, 1922, ink and watercolour on paper. This drawing imagines the west front of Nymans as an old English manor house, inhabited by figures in 17th-century dress.

very top of his profession; while overseeing the final stages of the Nymans rebuild, he would also serve as president of the Royal Institute of British Architects and as Surveyor of the Fabric of Westminster Abbey, where his restoration of the royal chapels earned him a knighthood.[8] He was responsible for designing the main living spaces of the new house at Nymans, including the drawing room, library and book room, as well as the reconfiguration of the exterior to relocate the main entrance to the east side of the house. Even in the ruined form we see today, the majestic south front bears witness to the scale of his ambition.

The most imposing room in the new Nymans was the Great Hall. Norman Evill's interpretation had evoked the spirit of the Elizabethan long gallery, with an enclosed ceiling and regular window seats harking back to its function as a space for cultural recreation as well as exercise.[9] In Tapper's conception, however, the Great Hall

Right
G. L. Walls, *Interior of the Great Hall, Nymans, Handcross, Sussex*, 1927, watercolour on paper. The architect Walter Tapper made the Great Hall the formal centre of the manor house, and this presentation drawing emphasises its height and the architect's knowledge of medieval and ecclesiastical spaces. In the end, the organ above the minstrels' gallery was not installed.

Far right
The Great Hall, Nymans, photographed for *Country Life*, published 10 September 1932.

at Nymans was restored to its traditional status as the formal centre of the manor house, and the design for it was correspondingly impressive (see p. 235, left). The roof space was open and far loftier than in Evill's gallery proposal, while a monumental fireplace was inserted into the east wall along with a large tapestry and wood panelling at the south end. Tapper had previously worked on the restoration of Penshurst Place in Kent, and there are close similarities between the Great Hall at Nymans and the fourteenth-century Baron's Hall at Penshurst, most notably in the treatment of window tracery and roof beams. Echoing his practice as an ecclesiastical architect, the presentation drawing of Tapper's design for Nymans included an organ above the minstrels' gallery, but none was ever installed. The Great Hall was finally completed in time for Christmas 1927; the sole concession to modernity was a subterranean billiard room, out of sight under the hall floor.

Not everything in the new Nymans was designed to look medieval. The Old English style that Maud Messel favoured did not seek to recreate a single moment in architectural time; rather, it suggested the organic development of a manor house over centuries of accretion, allowing for later styles and furnishings to take their place within the overall framework. Making use of this licence, Maud's own bedroom boasted a fine ceiling of Jacobean derivation, as did the Bristol Room above the library (opposite, top right and bottom left). The inclusion of stylistic features from later periods contributed to the natural feel of the whole, and architectural historians were overwhelmingly enthusiastic in their response. Christopher Hussey hailed the new Nymans as 'an exquisite example of pastiche', while Nikolaus Pevsner approved the result as 'amazingly deceptive'.[10]

For Maud, who played such an active part in the creation of the new Nymans, the opportunity to live in an Old English manor house was the realisation of a long-held dream.[11] For Leonard, the reconstruction set the seal on a new identity for the Messel family that was distinct from their German-Jewish heritage. He had already obtained the official grant of a Messel coat of arms from the College of Arms in 1911, and the design is shown together with the family motto, *Dirigat Deus*, alongside his entry in the centenary edition of *Burke's Landed Gentry*.[12] Leonard used the coat of arms on his bookplate, and its central motif – a fir tree – was incorporated into the masonry at prominent points around the exterior walls of Nymans. Guests arriving at the new Postern Gate on the east side of the building would pass under a carving of the Messel escutcheon as they entered the house (see p. 238).

Other relief carvings embedded in the walls around the new entrance hint at the multiple layers of identity that made up the Messel family history. Below an image of the Sussex county martlets (heraldic birds) is an English rose, national emblem of the country in which the family had put down roots and prospered. Near it on the same wall is a Star of David, the most tangible indication that Leonard Messel, a practising member of the Church of England, had not forgotten his Jewish roots (see p. 243). Yet even this symbolism is ambiguous. Leonard had become an avid Freemason at the same time as the new Nymans was being constructed, and the six-pointed star bears an important significance in the Masonic tradition, appearing prominently on the façades of famous lodges such as Mary's Chapel on Hill Street in Edinburgh, and the Masonic Hall at Barnard Castle in County Durham.[13] As well as recalling the Messel family's Jewish background, the Star of David embedded in the wall at Nymans points forward to the new identity that Leonard had forged for himself within the British establishment.[14]

The creation of a faux medieval manor house from scratch was a bold venture to undertake in the 1920s. One of the few local comparisons would be Bailiffscourt on the West Sussex coast, a similar undertaking begun by the Guinness family's Lord and Lady Moyne a few years after the Messels started work on Nymans, while

Photographs of Nymans taken for a series on the property featured in *Country Life*, September 1932.

Top left: The South Front and Great Hall.
Top right: The Bristol Room.
Bottom left: Maud Messel's Bedroom.
Bottom right: The Drawing Room. *The Rest on the Flight into Egypt* attributed to Bonifacio de' Pitati (called Bonifazio Veronese), hanging above the door on the left, is one of the paintings that Leonard inherited from his father Ludwig, who had acquired it from the Marquess of Exeter's sale in 1888. Its current whereabouts are unknown.

the extensive restoration of Leeds Castle in Kent by the Anglo-American heiress Lady Baillie also qualifies as a contemporary parallel. Paradoxically, the sourcing of original materials was made easier by a boom in the architectural salvage trade, as many old English country houses put on the market in the wake of World War One failed to find buyers and were instead cannibalised for their masonry, fixtures and fittings.[15] Leonard and Maud benefited from this commercial recycling and were able to set their fine collections of antique furniture, tapestries and armour alongside period doors, fireplaces and staircases. The photographs of the new interior published in *Country Life*'s three-part series on the finished property reveal what a sumptuous effect they managed to achieve (above).[16]

The new Nymans also provided a backdrop for the display of Leonard and Maud's most important paintings. The large Bonifazio Veronese *The Rest on the Flight into Egypt (Repose of the Holy Family)*, which hung in the drawing room, was one of the artworks that Leonard had inherited from his father Ludwig, as was the Velázquez *Portrait of an Advocate*, which held pride of place in the library. This last room also contained Leonard's exceptional collection of English herbals and other botanical books, including several rare fifteenth-century incunabula.[17] When presenting him with the Victoria Medal of Honour at the Royal Horticultural Society's annual meeting in 1946, Lord Aberconway remarked that, after the society's own library, Leonard had put together 'the finest collection of horticultural books in the world'. Tragically, the entire library was lost in the fire that took hold of Nymans in the early hours of 19 February 1947, destroying all the main rooms and turning Leonard and Maud Messel out of the home they had worked so hard to build.

Below

Bracelet made of pinchbeck (a metal alloy) and the plaited hair, entwined, of the three daughters of Lina Messel (Ludwig Messel's sister) and Isaac Seligman; made as a keepsake for the girls' grandmother back in Germany. When the last German Messels fled the Nazis and came to Britain in 1939, they were able to take it with them because the hair was mounted on base metal rather than silver or gold and was thus of no monetary value.

The garden

While successive redesigns of the house reflected the changing identity of the Messel family, the garden at Nymans provided an important sense of continuity. For the first-generation immigrant Ludwig Messel, whose German accent branded him an outsider the moment he opened his mouth, horticultural experimentation offered a passport into the society of other landowners in this part of the High Weald. The botanist Sir Edmund Loder had turned Leonardslee into a famous array of gardens with a wildlife park, while his younger brother Wilfred planted his own woodland garden at High Beeches, the neighbouring property to Nymans. Frederick DuCane Godman and his wife created a celebrated garden at South Lodge, as did the naturalist Colonel Stephenson Clarke at Borde Hill and the Hendersons at Sedgwick Park. In the midst of so much local activity, Ludwig Messel embraced gardening with a passion and together with his head gardener James Comber succeeded in establishing Nymans as a centre of horticultural excellence. Their joint achievements are catalogued in the compendium of plants grown at Nymans that was published by Ludwig's youngest daughter Muriel Messel shortly after the end of World War One.[18]

The importance of the garden to the Messels' social integration is revealed in the visitors' books for Nymans, which cover a full 100 years from 1894 to 1994. As well as professional botanists William Robinson, Henry Elwes and Richard Lynch, early visitors included horticulturalists from among the Sussex gentry, such as the Loders, Stephenson Clarke, John G. Millais (son of the artist), and the Nix brothers of Tilgate Park. Ludwig Messel was elected a Fellow of the Royal Horticultural Society in 1898, but it is telling that he chose not to exhibit the new plant varieties being cultivated at Nymans at the society's fortnightly London shows. Whatever his worldly success or social standing, the diffident Ludwig remained conscious of his status as a first-generation immigrant throughout his life.

Ludwig's son Leonard, with the privilege of an education at Eton and Oxford behind him, had no such inhibitions. He retained James Comber as head gardener at Nymans and the two men were soon exhibiting regularly at flower shows in London and elsewhere, winning numerous awards for the new varieties of plants they had cultivated. On the back of this success, Leonard established himself as a leading figure in the world of horticulture between the wars. As well as becoming a fellow of the Linnean Society and serving on the Royal Horticultural Society's council for many years, Leonard was elected a member of the Garden Society, the exclusive (and male-only) dining club of serious horticulturalists from the higher echelons of the landed gentry. Jewish country-house owners held prominent roles in the society: Lionel de Rothschild was a founder member, as was Sir Frederick Stern of Highdown in West Sussex, who served as honorary secretary for almost forty years. Nor were Leonard Messel's achievements confined to horticulture. In addition to his other civic roles, Leonard was appointed Lieutenant for the City of London and High Sheriff of Sussex in 1936.

Like many country houses bought by Jewish owners in the nineteenth century, Nymans was destined to have a public afterlife, and it was the garden that guaranteed its survival. Prior to World War Two, the National Trust had never assumed responsibility for gardens unless they were an adjunct to an historic house. As part of a joint initiative with the Royal Horticultural Society, provision was now made to receive gardens of national interest on their own account, with the Trust's acceptance of Bodnant in Wales, and Hidcote in the Cotswolds, paving the way for similar transfers in the future. Nymans was an important example of the new style of 'English' garden where the focus was on exotic trees and shrubs brought back by plant hunters from across the world as well as new varieties raised by professional plant breeders at home.[19] Leonard Messel introduced a codicil to his will bequeathing the garden and ruined house of Nymans to the National Trust, with the proviso that his children Anne and Oliver should retain a life interest in the habitable parts of the property. Nymans was duly handed over in a formal ceremony on 26 March 1954 – a 'happy day', as Anne described it in her speech on the occasion, seeing that the future of the family's creation was now assured.[20] Twenty-five years later, Anne did indeed take up residence in the rehabilitated west wing. Today, with house and garden both open to the public, Nymans is one of the National Trust's most popular properties, enjoyed by well over 300,000 visitors a year.

Belonging

The successive reconstructions of Nymans act as material indicators of the changing identity of the Messel family and their progressive assimilation into English society. The Messels had established their London homes in Tyburnia, the fashionable district north of Hyde Park that was much favoured by continental Europeans and had a strong Jewish presence by the second half of the nineteenth century.[21] In contrast to this cosmopolitan milieu, Ludwig Messel's decision to acquire a country estate in rural West Sussex represented a bold move into a more homogeneous and non-Jewish environment, where his foreign background and German accent made him instantly recognisable as an alien presence.[22] This 'otherness' was brought out most emphatically during World War One, when waves of anti-German feeling swept the country and Ludwig's loyalties became the object of intense local suspicion. The redevelopment of Nymans was itself reinterpreted in a sinister light, as the viewing platform in the new tower designed by Ludwig's brother Alfred was suddenly seen as the perfect vantage point from which the German family could spy on its neighbours.[23]

Within a single generation, however, Nymans came to symbolise the quintessential Englishness of the Messel family. The transformation of the property into an Old English manor house confirmed Leonard Messel as a member of the landed gentry, a designation that his elder son Linley duly inherited.[24] Moreover, the remodelling of Nymans was accepted on its own terms without any of the charges of ethnic mimicry or counterfeit 'passing' so often levelled at Jews in earlier times.[25] The Messels were recognised as an immigrant family who had chosen to integrate into English society like so many other families before them, while the garden they created was celebrated as one of the horticultural wonders of the Weald. When Leonard Messel died in 1953, aged eighty, his obituary in the *Mid-Sussex Times* affirmed without qualification that he would always be remembered as 'a fine old English gentleman'.[26]

The Messels' successful metamorphosis from German-Jewish immigrants to English gentry carried special significance in light of their origins. It is commonly understood today that individuals from ethnic minorities can construct their own identities from the options available to them, and revise those identities at different points throughout their lives.[27] For Jews in *fin de siècle* Europe, however, this freedom was far from assured. In much of the antisemitic discourse of the time, Jews were held to be essentially different from non-Jews, and their efforts to fashion any identity beyond Jewishness doomed to failure.[28] The prejudice assumed an added urgency precisely because there was no somatic difference distinguishing Jews from non-Jews.[29] The claim that Jews were irredeemably 'other' was thus forced to fall back on pseudo-scientific myths of indelible, if invisible, racial determinism.[30]

Such essentialist thinking held little sway in the German-Jewish community, where 'only very few Jews accepted the argument of the racial antisemites that they could never be assimilated'.[31] The Messels certainly assumed that they could fashion their own identities to suit their social and professional ambitions: while his two brothers living in Britain felt no need to convert to Christianity, Alfred Messel was baptised in 1899 and his children were brought up as Protestants. Yet the last generation of Messels to remain in Germany were forced to flee in the face of the Nazi regime's 1935 Nuremberg Laws, which codified the racial myth into a taxonomy for genocide. With help from her English cousins, Alfred's daughter Irene managed to escape Berlin with her husband and two children shortly before the outbreak of World War Two (see p. 241). Her husband's family, all of whom had also converted to Christianity, remained in Germany and perished.

German Jews migrating to Britain were alive to the politics of integration and proceeded to establish themselves within British society while remaining, to varying degrees and for varying lengths of time, both German and Jewish.[32] As a first-generation immigrant, Ludwig Messel retained several aspects of his native identities, but his primary concern was that his family should assimilate into English society within the shortest time possible. Purchasing the country estate of Nymans was the vehicle for making this ethnic choice visible, just as the remodelling of the house in the next generation set the seal on the family's new English identity. The fact that the Messels retained their surname at a time when many Germans (Jewish and non-Jewish) were anglicising theirs ensured that their ethnic background remained discernible, so that even the third generation faced occasional stigmatisation: the stage designer Oliver Messel was bullied during World War One as soon as fellow schoolboys discovered his surname to be of German origin, while his cousin Rudolph Messel was heckled when campaigning as a parliamentary candidate years later, and was forced to make a 'vigorous denial' that he was anything but English.[33] As with the Star of David still visible in the wall at Nymans today, however, these were the last traces of a multidimensional ethnic history that became ever more distant with each passing generation. In the final analysis, such vestiges of difference serve as a reminder of the Messels' successful integration into the adopted country they now called home.

11 Max Liebermann's villa at Lake Wannsee: a public retreat

Lucy Wasensteiner

The Berlin-born painter Max Liebermann (1847–1935) stands among the most successful and best-known artists of his generation. He found fame in the 1870s and 1880s as an early German proponent of painterly realism, applying the lessons of the Barbizon school to his depictions of workers in the Dutch countryside. In 1899 he was announced as a founding member and the first president of the Berlin Secession. This pioneering organisation sought to provide opportunities for artists outside the conservative imperial establishment, encouraging freedom of expression and the inclusion of foreign artists, and thus paving the way for later waves of artistic experimentation in the city. Liebermann's increasingly Impressionist canvases brought international modernist ideas to Berlin and were collected widely, both by private individuals and the country's leading museums. A constant stream of portrait commissions from around 1900 onwards provided him with a highly lucrative sideline.

In the summer of 1909, Liebermann acquired one of the last free plots at the Alsen villa colony on the banks of Lake Wannsee, around 25 kilometres south-west of his main residence in the centre of Berlin. Here he constructed a lakeside home where he and his family would spend the summer months over the following quarter century. Though born to a wealthy Jewish family, Liebermann was proud to be able to finance the villa himself, as expressed in a letter he wrote shortly after its completion to his friend, the then-director of the Hamburger Kunsthalle, Alfred Lichtwark: 'You see, these ten fingers have painted all of this in just two years: land, house, garden and furniture.'[1] Liebermann commissioned the Berlin architect Paul Otto Baumgarten (1873–1946) with the design of the villa, and the landscape designer Alfred Brodersen (1857–1930) with the construction of the garden. Liebermann was, however, centrally involved in the conception of both elements, much of which he discussed in a dense exchange of letters with Lichtwark.

Max Liebermann, *Self-portrait*,
1922, oil on canvas.

Max Liebermann,
*Martha Liebermann with
Her Granddaughter Maria*,
1922, oil on canvas.

In many respects, the villa at Wannsee was a private space for Liebermann and his family. He clearly valued it both as a retreat from the crowds and obligations of the capital, and as a place to work in peace.[2] Nonetheless, there are numerous indications – including his detailed control over the design of the house and garden – that the public impact of the villa was of central importance. This chapter attempts to trace the significance of Liebermann's Wannsee property as a means of self-positioning. What was the artist saying about himself with the design of this villa and its garden? And what was the lasting impact of these efforts after his death in 1935?

The Liebermanns in Berlin

Max Liebermann was descended from a family of fabric merchants from the town of Märkisch Friedland (present-day Mirosławiec, in Poland).[3] His grandfather had moved to Berlin at the start of the nineteenth century, following the signing of the so-called *Judenedikt* ('Jews' Edict', or Prussian Edict of Emancipation), which among other benefits bestowed relative freedom of movement on Prussia's Jewish citizens. In Berlin, the family's textile businesses flourished from their base in the city's old town – today, the area around Alexanderplatz. By the time of Max's birth, his father Louis was a multimillionaire. In 1857, just short of Max's tenth birthday, Louis Liebermann acquired the so-called Stüler Palace at Pariser Platz 7, right by the Brandenburg Gate – one of the most prominent addresses in the city. It was a further sign of the family's prosperity that the young Max, unlike his two brothers, was not required to join the family business. After training at the Academy of Arts in Weimar, he spent four years in Paris followed by four years in Munich, painting, exhibiting and building his network. He returned to Berlin in 1884, in the same year marrying Martha Marckwald, also descended from a prosperous Jewish Märkisch Friedland family. Their only child, a daughter Käthe, was born in 1885. Over the following decades, Liebermann established himself as one of the most popular, influential and widely collected artists in Berlin. He also became a prominent public figure in the city, not least as a result of his role in the Berlin Secession. Following the death of his parents in the mid-1890s, Liebermann moved with his wife and daughter to the palace on Pariser Platz.

The west side of Pariser Platz, Berlin, *c.*1890, photographic postcard. The Liebermann house is directly to the right of the Brandenburg Gate.

The idea of the villa

The notion of a country residence, removed from the crowds of the city, had been introduced to Liebermann during his childhood. In the mid-1800s his grandfather, Joseph Liebermann, had built himself a country house in Charlottenburg – then far beyond the boundaries of Berlin – which Max and his siblings would visit regularly. As the artist later recalled: 'the house had a large garden. It extended down to the River Spree and was cared for carefully by my grandfather. He knew every tree, every shrub and every flower.'[4]

Joseph Liebermann was by no means the only wealthy European to build himself a country house during those years. The mid-nineteenth century saw a number of villa colonies springing up around the continent's major cities. Among the most fashionable near Berlin was the Colonie Alsen, on the banks of Lake Wannsee.[5] The colony had been founded in 1863 by the banker Wilhelm Conrad, and many of its earliest residents belonged, like Conrad, to the Club von Berlin – a private club known for the wealth and liberalism of its members, many of whom were Jewish. Some of the first buyers at Wannsee were members, including the publisher Julius Springer and the Berlin branch of the Oppenheim family. In the closing years of the nineteenth century they were joined by other prominent Jewish figures in Berlin, including the coal baron Eduard Arnhold and the banker Barthold Arons.

It was around this time that Max Liebermann first articulated his own interest in the idea of a country residence – albeit not in his letters, but in his artistic work. In the summer of 1901 he painted *Country House in Hilversum*, capturing an imposing residence on the outskirts of Amsterdam.[6] Liebermann had spent almost every summer in Holland since the mid-1870s, dedicating his work to the daily life of rural workers, their villages and their families. Although the *Country House in Hilversum* had a rural motif, its imposing architecture and carefully tended garden meant that it was certainly not the home of a farmer or fisherman. With this painting, Liebermann depicted, for the first time, a country house for people who did not need to work on the land.

In the following year, Lieberman returned again to the idea of the country house. In the summer of 1902 he was invited to Hamburg by Alfred Lichtwark, to paint scenes of the city for the Kunsthalle's collection. Exploring Hamburg, Liebermann discovered the classicist villas of the Nienstedten district, built during the eighteenth and nineteenth centuries for the city's wealthy merchants. Liebermann dedicated a series of sketches to these villas, among them the Godeffroy house, with its surrounding deer park, and the Wesselhoeft house. This interest in the villa as a retreat from city life was further strengthened in the autumn of 1902, during a trip to Florence with his wife and daughter. Liebermann was deeply impressed by the city's unique combination of landscape and architecture, as his sketchbooks testify, with numerous pastel drawings depicting the walled Renaissance old town surrounded by hilltop villas.

In the spring of 1903, immediately after his trip to Florence, Liebermann wrote for the first time of acquiring a country house for himself. As he articulated in a letter to Lichtwark on 10 May 1903: 'Do you perhaps know of a modest house with a large garden near Hamburg? ... it needn't be as large as [Hamburg's] Jenisch Park, but with old trees, where my models can pose in the shade.'[7]

The Liebermann Villa, 1925, photographer unknown, showing the entrance on the street side of the property.

The villa at Wannsee

It was ultimately not in Hamburg but on the outskirts of Berlin that Liebermann would realise his country-house dream. In the summer of 1909, he acquired two of the last remaining plots in the Colonie Alsen, combining them to form a 6,700-square-metre plot stretching from the street down to the banks of Lake Wannsee.

The design of the house was entrusted to Paul Otto Baumgarten, a student of the renowned Berlin architect Alfred Messel (see pp. 232–3).[8] Liebermann did not give Baumgarten free rein, however. Although the house was to be a country retreat, it also needed to reflect a sense of the city, as Liebermann explained to Lichtwark after rejecting Baumgartner's early plans: 'we're clear about the floor plans ... but not about the façade, which looks too much like a farmer's house: I want a country house that has been built by a city dweller. As always, the simplest thing is the most difficult.'[9]

Liebermann was also clear that the house and garden should comprise a single, united, complete work of art. According to one anecdote, he summarised his goals to Baumgarten as follows:

> When I stand here on the banks of the lake, I want to be able to see through the house, to that part of the garden that lies on the other side. In front of the house, a simple lawn should be planted, so that I can see the lake from every room without difficulty. And left and right of the lawn I want straight paths. That is most important. And one more thing – the room in the central axis should be the dining room, so ... now start building.[10]

The final design of the villa did, in fact, incorporate many of Liebermann's wishes. The house was relatively modest compared with its neighbours. On the ground floor, alongside an entrance hall and a salon, the central axis was occupied by the dining room, with French doors on both sides allowing continuity between house and garden. On the first floor, the northern corner housed a large studio, while facing the lake were bedrooms for Max, Martha and Käthe. The two façades of the villa also illustrate Liebermann's influence, both echoing houses he had seen on his tours around Hamburg. Facing the street, a small garden house was constructed, providing a home for Liebermann's gardener and his family.

The garden itself also satisfied Liebermann's requirements, with a simple lawn leading down to the lake, flanked by straight pathways. Various other elements were introduced, however, following an extensive exchange of letters between Liebermann and Lichtwark. Lichtwark was a leading proponent of the reform movement in garden design, which proposed a move away from the staged naturalism of the English country garden, towards divided, geometric 'garden rooms', the use of block colours, and the allocation of space to growing produce as part of a modern, healthy lifestyle.[11] According to these principles, the street-facing garden at Wannsee was divided into a geometric grid of beds for shrubs, fruit and vegetables, framed by box hedging, and a geometric lawn by the house. In the lakeside garden, floral terraces were planted according to a rigid regime: purple and yellow pansies in spring, and red geraniums in summer. The northern stretch of the lakeside garden was transformed into three hedged gardens, with each of these individual spaces dedicated to shade-giving linden trees, an oval lawn with a flowerbed and a rose garden respectively. Liebermann did allow some deviance from these strict reform ideas, however. A copse of birch trees on the southern side of the garden was allowed to remain, providing a natural interruption of the lawn and its bordering pathway.

The entrance hall, looking through into the dining room and out onto the Wannsee garden beyond, photographed in 1914. The paintings, from the Liebermanns' private collection, are: Édouard Manet, *Portrait of M. Arnaud on Horseback*, 1875; Liebermann's copy of a head from *Banquet of the Officers of the St George Militia Company* by Frans Hals (1627), 1876 (left of door, top); not identified (left of door, bottom); Max Liebermann, *The Artist's Daughter, Seated in Full Figure*, 1989 (right of door).

The modern ideas behind Liebermann's garden were echoed in the interior of the house. Compared with the family's residence on Pariser Platz, the rooms were bright and simply decorated, as Liebermann's biographer Erich Hancke noted following the house's completion: 'airy, light … with colourful wallpapers' making a 'beautiful, bright impression'.[12] Indeed, the artist's studio on the first floor was, according to Hancke, somewhat too airy, as he wrote in 1927, and 'uncomfortable to a point. With its bare whitewashed walls, and almost no furniture, it still looks … like a new build, waiting for its décor'.[13] The pared-back furnishings also provided the ideal backdrop for Liebermann's impressive collection of modern art.[14] His first purchases had been made in Paris during the 1870s; by 1910 he possessed key works not only by Germans such as Adolph Menzel and Carl Blechen, but also by the greats of French painting, including Courbet, Monet, Renoir, Cézanne, Degas and at least seventeen paintings by Manet.

A public retreat

The house at Wannsee was completed in the summer of 1910, and Liebermann was thrilled with what he had achieved for his family. As he wrote to Lichtwark, 'it is among the most delightful things that a man can experience, to build a house and garden for himself and his own'.[15] The importance of creating his own space was expressed again in a further letter to Lichtwark, shortly after moving in: 'I have the feeling, for the first time in my life, that I'm on my own clod of earth.'[16]

The audience for the Wannsee villa was not, however, restricted to Liebermann's family. The artist's letters from 1910 to 1913 illustrate his systematic promotion of the house among his friends and contacts. These include correspondence with Max Sauerlandt, director of the City Museum in Halle;[17] Fritz Wichert, director of the Kunsthalle Mannheim ('I find it more beautiful, than I had hoped … come and be astounded');[18] his Berlin patron Harry Graf Kessler; and the critic and journalist Franz Servaes ('if you come in summer, I will show you my castle on the lake; it really is worth seeing').[19] As Liebermann proudly reported in a letter to Lichtwark, Hugo von Tschudi, former director of the Berlin National Gallery and prominent defender of modernism, visited the Wannsee villa in July 1910 and 'found it very beautiful'.[20] Eduard and Johanna Arnhold were also early visitors, as Liebermann again reported to Lichtwark: 'Frau Arnhold was here, and couldn't say enough about the beauty of the garden.'[21]

Liebermann was also keen to invite journalists and photographers to his villa. Early images capture the exterior of the house, the interior of the downstairs rooms, and Liebermann in his garden. Photographs of the garden were reproduced in trade journals and literature.[22] Throughout the 1920s and 1930s, Wannsee became a favourite location for portrait photographs of Liebermann and his family, or shots of the artist at work, particularly following his appointment as president of the Prussian Academy of Arts in 1920. The dozens of images now held in the archive established by the Ullstein publishing empire stand as testament to the frequency of these press visits.[23]

It was, however, in Liebermann's paintings that the property at Wannsee was most comprehensively publicised. Between 1910 and 1934, Liebermann created more than 200 oil paintings and countless drawings depicting the house and garden, returning again and again to views of the street-facing and lakeside gardens (opposite). Characterised by their glowing colours and careful capturing of the light, these works remained faithful to the Impressionism Liebermann had brought to Berlin decades earlier. They thus became his calling card, passing immediately into some of the most prominent collections of the time: Henry Newman in Hamburg,

Eduard Arnhold and Hans Ullstein in Berlin, the Berlin National Gallery and the Hamburger Kunsthalle, among many more.[24]

Liebermann's villa may not have been the most architecturally avant-garde property in Berlin, but almost every aspect of the house and garden reflected the modernist ideas that characterised his work throughout his career. Compared with the residence at Pariser Platz, the house was simple, functional, light and airy, with a garden that supported healthy living. The studio was not the highly decorated salon of old, but clean and minimal – a space for work. The house was also filled with international modernist art. And in this respect, perhaps somewhat ahead of his time, Liebermann carefully used the house, and the art he created there, to construct and preserve his personal brand: a modern artist, made in Berlin.

The Liebermann family after 1933

Though in many respects assimilated, the Liebermann family had never sought to deny or renounce their Judaism, as Max himself neatly summarised: 'All my life, I have always asked myself: What kind of person are you? But never: Are you a Jew, a Christian or a pagan? I was born a Jew and I will die a Jew.'[25] There were certainly moments in his long life when he felt his Judaism more acutely – for example, during the scandal surrounding his depiction of *The Twelve Year Old Jesus in the Temple* in 1879[26] – but he never considered conversion. He is said once to have responded to this suggestion with, 'Do you think it would make me a better painter?'[27]

After 1933, the downfall of the family was accordingly swift and devastating. In April 1933, Liebermann's son-in-law Kurt Riezler lost his professorship in Frankfurt. The following month, Liebermann was forced to renounce his public office at the Academy of Arts. As he wrote in a statement published two days after his resignation: 'During my long life I have tried, with all my strength, to serve German art. Because of my conviction that art has nothing to do with either one's politics or one's ancestry ... I can no longer belong to the Prussian Academy of Arts ... because they no longer consider my standpoint valid.'[28]

Liebermann died in February 1935 at the age of eighty-seven, confused and disappointed by political developments, as he had recounted to a visitor to his Pariser Platz home in November the previous year: 'You know, I live now only from hate. Every day, when I go down the steps of this house that belonged to my father, the hate rises up in me ... my entire life, I have been German ... my entire life I believed I was German and now – what do I have left!'[29]

In 1936, the Liebermann family were banned from their property on Pariser Platz. Two years later, Käthe was able to emigrate with her family to the United States. The widow Martha Liebermann was thus left alone in Berlin. In 1940, she was forced to sell the Wannsee villa to the Reich. The following year, at another Baumgarten-designed villa less than 500 metres from Liebermann's former home, the 'Final Solution to the Jewish Question' was resolved by a group of high-ranking National Socialist officials at the Wannsee Conference. On 4 March 1943, Martha received notification that she would be deported to the Theresienstadt concentration camp the following day. She chose instead to take an overdose of sleeping pills, dying in the Berlin Jewish Hospital five days later, at the age of eighty-five.

From Reichspost to diving club

With the death of Martha, the Liebermann family were eradicated from Berlin. Their palace on Pariser Platz was also destroyed, hit by enemy bombs in 1943. Directly adjacent to the Berlin Wall from 1961, the plot remained empty until German reunification.

The Liebermann Villa viewed from the lakeside garden, photographed in 1971.

The villa at Wannsee, meanwhile, survived the war unscathed. Used from 1940 as a training centre for postal workers, in the final years of the war it was converted into a hospital, a use that continued in the newly formed West Berlin. In 1951, the house was restituted to Käthe Liebermann. She leased the house back to the hospital, and in 1958 it was sold by the family to the State of Berlin. The hospital moved out in 1969. From 1971 the villa was leased to a diving club, part of an organised policy of the West Berlin government to encourage water sports at Wannsee, the lake being one of few bodies of water still accessible to residents of the walled-in city.

Throughout these years, Liebermann's reputation as the father of twentieth-century German art was slowly restored. Significant museum collections of his works had remained intact during the war years, so they could be put back on public display, and solo exhibitions were staged – at the Kunsthalle Bremen in 1954, for example, and at the Hamburger Kunsthalle in 1968.[30] In 1979, the National Gallery of West Berlin staged what remains to this day the largest solo exhibition of Liebermann's works.[31]

At Wannsee, however, there was little left of Liebermann's carefully planned ensemble. The family's furniture and papers had all been lost during the war years. With the exception of fourteen pieces that had been shipped to Zürich in 1933, the family's art collection had also been lost: sold or gifted by Martha Liebermann after 1935, confiscated by the Gestapo after her death in 1943, or stolen from the premises.[32] Inside the villa, the rooms had been divided and repeatedly repurposed. Outside, the gardens were completely destroyed, flattened and combined with those of the neighbouring villa.

The significance of the villa was not entirely forgotten, however. At some point before 1969, *Hier wohnte und wirkte Max Liebermann* ('Here lived and worked Max Liebermann') was engraved into the stonework at the top of the front façade. The exact origins of this engraving are unknown, though it is rumoured to have been instigated by a Jewish doctor assigned to work at the hospital. In 1971, a newspaper article by the renowned architectural historian Julius Posener, himself born to a Jewish family from Berlin and who had spent the war in Britain, mourned the lease of the villa to the diving club, and the city's failure to establish a museum on the site.[33] Partly in response to Poesner's campaigning, the garden of the villa, though still largely unrecognisable, was listed as a historical monument in 1987.

Slowly but surely, the process of reclaiming the villa continued during the 1990s. In 1992, Liebermann paintings were hung in the villa for the first time since 1940, in a commercial exhibition organised by the Leipzig-based Kunstsalon Franke. And, in the debates surrounding the construction of Pariser Platz following the fall of the Berlin Wall, attention was drawn explicitly to Liebermann and the possibility of a dedicated museum. In 1995, the Max Liebermann Society was founded in Berlin. The stated aim of the original fifteen members was to establish a Liebermann Museum in the artist's villa at Wannsee.[34] In the same year, the villa too was listed as a historical monument. In 1997, the Berlin Senate agreed that the society could establish a museum on the premises, as long as it could finance the project itself, and find and finance alternative premises for the diving club.

The Liebermann Villa as museum

Despite these challenging conditions, the society was able to raise the necessary funds over the next five years. From 2002, both house and garden were restored, under the guidance of architects Nedelykov Moreira and the landscape architect Reinhold Eckert, and in 2006 the museum opened. While the ground floor houses a documentary presentation covering Liebermann's life and career, the exhibition rooms on the first floor – including the artist's former studio – house a display of his paintings, alongside twice-yearly special exhibitions dedicated to Liebermann and his contemporaries.

The Liebermann Villa today sets out to continue the project started by Liebermann in 1909: to provide a space for retreat and relaxation outside the city, but also to bolster the artist's reputation as a central figure in the story of Berlin modernism. At the same time, the villa now serves additional, and perhaps even more vital, purposes. Embodying the changes that occurred here between 1940 and 2002, the house confronts visitors with the racist persecution suffered by the Liebermanns at the hands of the Nazi regime; it illustrates clearly how a family of status and success was able to lose everything in a little over a decade. The museum also stands as proof of the fragility of this history. It is purely by chance that Liebermann's villa survived the war, the years of a divided Berlin, and the changing needs of the Wannsee community. It is also purely by chance that the villa, though set in a beautiful lakeside location, nonetheless remains easily accessible for visitors from the city, thus facilitating a flow of funds sufficient to support it. And it is solely thanks to the engagement of the Max Liebermann Society and its many supporters that the house could be reclaimed and repurposed as a museum. The villa thus stands as a representative of the many thousands of now destroyed and forgotten Jewish houses across Europe, whose owners suffered a similar fate to Max and Martha Liebermann in the years after 1933.

12 From the palatial to the modern: industry and luxury in Habsburg Europe

Petr Svoboda

The year 1825 saw the inauguration of the world's first steam railway; it linked the English towns of Stockton and Darlington but affected the whole of Europe. So it was at precisely this juncture that a Viennese professor conceived the idea for another railway – more than 400 kilometres long – connecting the Habsburg capital with the Polish town of Halicz.[1] Four years later, Professor Franz Riepl announced his plan for a line running northwards from Vienna, through Moravia and Silesia to Galicia, with branch lines to Brünn (Brno), Olmütz (Olomouc), Troppau (Opava), and Bielitz-Biala (Bielsko-Biala). This proposal caught the attention of the man whose credit ensured the smooth running of the entire Habsburg monarchy: Salomon Mayer von Rothschild (1774–1855).

Rothschild immediately grasped how railways could transform the trading of goods and commodities in Central Europe. He commissioned a geological survey, acquired the ironworks in Ostrau (Ostrava) – which would become the celebrated Witkowitz Mining and Ironworks Company – and established the joint-stock railway and mining company that would enter history as the Imperial and Royal Kaiser Ferdinand Privileged Northern Railway (or Kaiser Ferdinands-Nordbahn; see p. 272).

This railway was the catalyst for a great industrial leap forward – a process in which, for the first time, Jewish entrepreneurs played a major role. Some Jews had managed to break into the upper echelons of society during the first part of the century, but it was not until the Austrian constitution of 1867 that they acquired full civil and political rights. Serfdom was only abolished in Austria during the revolutions of 1848, and throughout the nineteenth century an aristocratic title remained the ultimate goal of the rich. Members of the nobility were expected to own a city palace and a network of country houses, valued as much for their cutting-edge technology as for their antiquity. Great houses, art collecting and philanthropic activity all served to enhance an individual's social prestige.

Leopold Müller, *Arrival of the First Train to Brno on 7 July 1839*, coloured lithograph.

What exactly this meant changed over time. The first generation of these newly ennobled families typically bought historic country estates, taking care not to erase the splendour of former times when they restored the houses. In this way they distinguished themselves from the urban bourgeoisie, who also sought to emulate the aristocracy in terms of lifestyle, art collecting and charitable works. For those born into the nobility, things were quite different. They sometimes built completely new houses, although the style tended to reflect the political and social order around them. When that order disintegrated in the conflagration of World War One, noble titles lost significance, along with the link to any associated land and property. Everywhere, 1918 heralded a new era. The elite of the country that was now Czechoslovakia no longer hankered after the trappings of aristocracy, creating instead estates that proudly mirrored the modernity of the emergent republic.

Schillersdorf (Šilheřovice)

To understand the Rothschilds' role in Central Europe, we must return to 1811. During the final phase of the Napoleonic Wars, Austria declared bankruptcy. Few European banking houses were able or willing to bail out the Habsburg polity. Not even the Rothschilds would provide a loan without preconditions: they wanted titles. This was unpalatable, but when the search for alternative funding failed, Emperor Francis I elevated Amschel and Salomon Rothschild to the nobility on 25 September 1816. It was not the first such ennoblement. Israel Hönig von Hönigsberg had become the first Jewish nobleman in 1789, but many court officials had found that intolerable. Nevertheless, in September 1822, each of the five Rothschild brothers received a baronetcy, along with the title Freiherr von Rothschild.[2]

Noble status traditionally presupposed ownership of a grand city residence and at least one rural property. Yet, for the time being, Jews only had the right to reside in certain parts of the empire. In towns like Pressburg (Bratislava), they were confined to the ghetto, and throughout Habsburg Austria they were barred from owning real estate. After 1819, when he relocated his operations to Vienna, Salomon opted to live as a guest in the Hotel zum Römischen Kaiser. Arguably, he had little choice. But in 1843, the city made him an honorary citizen, enabling him to buy the hotel and several other properties. Outside Vienna, things remained difficult. Salomon needed a country estate, but his efforts to buy land in Hungary or Moravia

Above right
Artist unknown, *Schloss Schillersdorf from the Southwest*, before 1850, hand-coloured engraving. This is probably the only surviving image of the courtyard after the reconstruction by Gabriel-Hippolyte Destailleur and before the reconstruction by Friedrich Flohr.

Right
Artist unknown, *View of the Greenhouses at Schloss Schillersdorf from the House*, before 1850, hand-coloured engraving.

273

failed. The City of Brno even refused a donation of 40,000 gold coins in exchange for the privilege.[3] Nevertheless, between 1843 and 1844, Salomon managed to acquire three large estates with showpiece castles: Oderberg (Bohumín), Hultschin (Hlučín) and Schillersdorf (Šilheřovice). The largest of the three, Schillersdorf was within sight of the city of Ostrau, but actually located outside the Habsburg lands in Prussian Silesia. A railway was built along the border of both territories.

Salomon's first step was to instruct the head forester, Karel Exner, to buy more property to expand the park. Relatively few changes were made to the property itself, although it is believed that at some point between 1842 and 1855 Salomon added a narrow new extension with a gallery to the central wing, extending into the side wings to about half their length. He also added an entrance wing with a horseshoe staircase. Two floor plans found among Gabriel-Hippolyte Destailleur's workshop papers indicate he was directly involved; the French architect later became a firm favourite of the Austrian Rothschilds.[4]

The revolutions of 1848 nearly bankrupted Salomon. His son Anselm (1803–74) took over first the business, then work on the château, together with his younger brother Albert (1844–1911). Gradually, the family consolidated its position at the imperial court, and Anselm eventually became a life member of the Austrian upper house: the first Jew to receive this honour.[5] During this time, the park at Schillersdorf was transformed beyond recognition. Exner, whom the Rothschilds likened to Sir Joseph Paxton, tripled it in size to nearly a kilometre square. It now included three lakes, a new garden, and a manor house built on the site of a former brewery and distillery. There was a new orangery, a hothouse, a dairy, a house for servants, apartments for the gardener and coachmen, a stable for horses, a coach house and a gatehouse. A steam engine (added in 1855) powered the fountains and irrigation system. In 1870, the Rothschilds also built a pool with a fountain in the park below the château, which featured a sculpture representing Neptune and Salacia, in a rather familial arrangment with putti and a dolphin, surrounded by shells and sea creatures.[6] (The creator of this impressive work is unknown, but it may have been Henri Chapu, the French sculptor then working for Anselm's brother Nathaniel in Vienna.[7]) The whole of this technologically remarkable complex was executed in a variety of historicising architectural styles, even drawing inspiration from contemporary English fashions in rustic dwellings and their landscapes.[8]

Anselm's son Ferdinand visited Schillersdorf during his honeymoon. Writing home, his wife Evelina described how Anselm had 'surrounded his mansion with large stones, waterfalls and bridges…. Like all the Rothschilds, father-in-law Anselm was fond of the water fountain that was set up on one of the lakes when pipes were laid to irrigate the lawns. A picturesque red-brick castle near the Oder River hid the machinery for the waterworks.'[9] Evelina died young, but it is said that she liked to sit on the banks of the small lake in the park that still bears her name.

The full extent of subsequent work on the château is unclear, though the scant archival sources reveal that in 1878, for example, three leading Viennese masons were dispatched to Schillersdorf to carry out modifications to the windows and roof in the Baroque style of the façade.[10] Other elements, such as the form of the roof and the rusticated ground floor, infuse the building with the spirit of French classicism. Destailleur was probably only responsible for the first stage of remodelling the house, but his sophisticated staircase and galleries imbued the interior with a distinctly eighteenth-century French atmosphere. The current form of the house was finalised by the Viennese architect Friedrich Flohr in the 1860s.[11] The first floor comprised four reception rooms connected by an enfilade, the central hall opening onto the terrace. Some of the paintings set into carved and gilded wood panelling and stucco ceilings survive to this day, in addition to marble fireplaces and parquet floors inlaid with the Rothschild coat of arms, despite the upheavals of World War Two and decades of misuse during which the building served different functions.

Long deserted and left to decay, Salomon von Rothschild's country house is now an events venue, yet it still testifies to his family's aspirations. Free to choose from the many historicising styles then in vogue, the Rothschilds opted for an exterior that enforced the visual connections between Schillersdorf and quintessential landmarks in the imperial capital, such as the Schwarzenberg Palace.[12] This architecturally conservative, if technologically ambitious, solution was also the choice of another recently ennobled Jewish family – the Gutmanns.

Nathaniel von Rothschild, 'Entrance Gate Evelinen-Thor [the "Evelina Gate"] to the Grounds at Schloss Schillersdorf', heliogravure, from the album *Schillersdorfer Ansichten* ('Views of Schillersdorf'), 1900.

Tobitschau (Tovačov)

Let us return for a moment to the Kaiser Ferdinand Northern Railway. In 1842, the section that ended in Leipnik (Lipník nad Bečvou) opened for business, before financial difficulties forced a halt of almost five years. There was an opening here for local business: the Gutmann brothers took it. The elder, Wilhelm (1826–95), had already been trading quite successfully in various commodities, but he only really started to prosper when he began to sell coal to large companies like the Kaiser Ferdinand Northern Railway, the First Danube Steam Navigation Company and the Austrian State Railway.[13] Without the new railway, such deals would have been unthinkable. As the business grew, Wilhelm invited his younger brother David (1834–1912) to join him. Even when the Northern Railway purchased its own Ostrau coal mines, the brothers managed to turn this potential setback to their advantage: not all coal was suitable for powering locomotives, so they established a near monopoly on the supply of household fuel to Vienna, Pest and Brno.[14] Recognising their abilities, the Rothschilds involved the brothers in their own enterprises, including, of course, the Witkowitz works.

It was not long before the Gutmann brothers relocated to Vienna. Here they initiated several high-profile philanthropic projects, hoping (perhaps) to be rewarded with the hereditary knighthood that they would in fact receive in 1878. Wilhelm's daughter Marianne married Sir Francis Montefiore of Worth Park (see pp. 36 and 330), a British Jew whose family was closely allied with the Rothschilds. Other Gutmann girls married into Christian branches of the European aristocracy: Wilhelm's daughter Rosalie married Count Robert Charles Henri de Fitz-James; her sister Elisabeth married the Hungarian nobleman Géza Erös de Bethlenfalva and, much

Artist unknown, *Blast Furnace Complex with the Anselm Smelter in Ostrau*, illustrated on a postcard, 1950.

Artist unknown, *Panoramic View of the Morava River between Charváty and Kroměříž* (detail showing the town of Tobitschau), first half of the 18th century, ink on paper.

later, Prinz Franz of Liechtenstein; meanwhile David's youngest daughter Helene became the Countess di Carrobio. Yet their fathers remained central players in Vienna's Jewish community, continuing their philanthropy and social activism, both within and outside it.

A palace on the Ringstrasse was a *sine qua non* in these circles, and the Gutmann brothers shared the spectacular mansion at Beethovenplatz 3 designed by Carl Tietz. Wilhelm invested in property close to Vienna and, as his summer residence, bought a villa designed in the German Renaissance style by Alexander Wielemans von Monteforte in the nearby spa town of Baden. He later bought the châteaux of Dross and Jaidhof. David, however, directed capital into a country estate in his native Moravia, just 30 kilometres from his birthplace. This was the castle of Tobitschau (Tovačov; above), which he bought from Franz Count Küenburg for 2.7 million florins in 1887.[15] Originally a moated medieval fortress, it had been remodelled in the late fifteenth century, with a distinctive tower and the earliest Renaissance entrance portal north of the Alps,[16] but this historic landmark had been severely neglected and lacked the modern comforts the Gutmanns required.

David considered two Jewish architects who knew the local area. Both candidates were Moravians who had studied in Vienna, and had experience designing public and residential buildings. Jakob Gartner (1861–1921), now celebrated for his magnificent Moorish synagogues, did much to shape the city of Olomouc. Max Fleischer (1841–1905), also known for synagogue architecture, preferred the neo-Gothic style. He had served his apprenticeship under Vienna's leading architect, Friedrich von Schmidt, best known for his restoration of St Stephen's Cathedral, and had assisted him on the splendid new town hall. This was the architect Gutmann chose.

Fleischer began by probing the foundations of the building to find out why the masonry was cracking. Investigations in the tower revealed fire damage and long-term water ingress. Fleischer reinforced the foundations, restored the tower, and added a completely new roof inspired by a recently discovered historic painting (since lost). He also enhanced the well-preserved entrance portal by adding a large stone tablet carved with the Gutmann coat of arms and an inscription commemorating the *Ritter* David von Gutmann. However, the most important work took place within, with Fleischer renovating the interiors and restoring the elaborate three-storey arcade that, in the manner of an Italian Renaissance palazzo, opened onto an internal courtyard.

Having only one staircase in such a grand house was a significant constraint. This was the main inspiration for a completely new wing, on the site of an old building previously used as a granary, which became the new entrance for visitors.[17] Passing through the vestibule, they found themselves at the bottom of a magnificent double staircase made of limestone. Cut-and-polished limestone was also used for the columns and balusters. Giant stone lions bearing the owner's coat of arms presided over the start of the final flight of steps.

Inside, walls, vaults and ceilings decorated in a sober colour scheme of soft greys, blues and yellows were lit first by kerosene, and later electricity. Central heating ensured maximum comfort, with outlets for warm air built into the staircase between each step. The water-supply system was another state-of-the-art feature. Operating fountains and fire hydrants, it was served by a reservoir holding 53,000 cubic metres of water and a steam engine capable of pumping three times that amount every day. The new wing also housed the principal reception room, the centrepiece of the range of rooms leading through to the old palace, and, like the staircase, featured a stucco-decorated vaulted ceiling. The walls were articulated with pilasters and covered with imitation damask wallpaper, and the room centred on a modern fireplace combining marble, cast iron and wood, with hot-air distribution controlled to increase its efficiency. From the staircase or reception hall, one proceeded into the vast, vaulted Knights' Hall, and thence to a second vaulted hall decorated with modern frescoes and stained glass depicting the early history of the site, by the Viennese painters Franz Renner and Hans Schok respectively.[18] In this way, as with the prominent use of heraldry, Gutmann connected his family to the castle's deep past.

Fleischer's alterations for Gutmann recall the Vienna opera house designed some twenty years earlier by August Sicard von Sicardsburg and Eduard van der Nüll, both of whom had taught the architect. One can only guess at how deliberately Gutmann meant to invoke a building that was emblematic of high culture in Central Europe, but these visual references, like the decision to invoke Tobitschau's medieval past, contrast strikingly with those aspects of the estate that demonstrate his enthusiasm for industrial modernity. In 1890, he built a sugar factory there, connecting Tobitschau to the Kaiser Ferdinand Northern Railway from Kojetín via the so-called 'beet railway'. Later, between 1903 and 1905, he tamed the Morava River, providing electricity to the castle and the entire town of Tobitschau at the same time.[19] In short, Gutmann approached his newly acquired estate with the same mindset that he used to run the industrial enterprises and trade that formed the basis of his wealth.

The courtyard at Tobitschau, early 20th century, photographer unknown. The Italian Renaissance-style arcades are already bricked up.

De Sandalo photography studio, Villa Gutmann, Brno, c.1923. One of the first modernist houses in the city, the only decorative elements are the ceramic window and door frames.

For Gutmann's heirs, Tobitschau was primarily an economic asset. After World War One it lost its role as a showpiece; thereafter, alterations were purely utilitarian. The impressive cycle of paintings narrating the castle's history was whitewashed, and some of the corridors that opened onto the courtyard, together with their columns and vaults, were walled up and covered with unsightly plaster (opposite). The younger generation preferred cities, where their homes reflected different values. David's great-nephew Wilhelm was, after all, the builder of one of Brno's first modernist houses (above).

Villa Stiassni

On 7 July 1839, there was cause for celebration when the first train arrived from Vienna's Floridsdorf station, connecting Brno to the Northern Railway (see p. 272). Ten years later, a second railway linked the city with Prague, Dresden and Berlin.[20] The local textile industry dated back to 1764, but the railways heralded the large-scale relocation of manufactories and factories to Brno from other towns in the vicinity. The city became a veritable 'Austrian Manchester', and Jewish entrepreneurs contributed much to its success.[21]

Hermine Stiassni (1889–1962) was a daughter of the coal wholesaler Jakob Eduard Weinmann, one of the richest, most important men in northern Bohemia. Jakob was a prominent local philanthropist whose involvement in professional associations had a political dimension. The Weinmann home in Aussig (Ústí nad Labem), a magnificent, historicist villa with neo-Baroque elements, was consequently the venue for important cultural, charitable and political functions. In this respect, much changed for Hermine when she married Alfred Stiassni (1883–1961), one of Brno's leading textile manufacturers.

Stiassni Brothers (Gebrüder Stiassni/Frères Stiassni) had operated in Brno since 1868. Young Alfred joined the management in 1907, but the war transformed the scale of the firm's operations. When peace came, Alfred began working with Walter Neumark, a textile entrepreneur and honorary British consul, whose family connections stretched all the way to Manchester. Together, they expanded into new European markets and the Middle East. By the 1930s, Stiassni Brothers was one of the most modern factories on the continent, but social recognition did not come as quickly as commercial orders.

The present story unfolds after the collapse of Austria–Hungary, in the newly formed Czechoslovakia, when Brno became the country's second-largest city. Many new public buildings were created there, by architects like Ernst Wiesner (trained in Vienna), Bohuslav Fuchs (trained in Prague), and graduates of the brand-new Brno Technical College, then positioning itself as a leader of the emerging architectural avant-garde. In 1924 and 1925, the editors of *Bytová kultura* ('Housing Culture') magazine organised a lecture series in Brno entitled 'For a New Architecture', which attracted such leaders of architectural modernism as Le Corbusier, Amédée Ozenfant, Jacobus Johannes Pieter Oud, Theo van Doesburg, Walter Gropius and Adolf Loos.[22] Brno's rise during the interwar years contrasted sharply with the fate of Vienna, which was changing from the proud capital of an imperial monarchy into a satellite of Nazi Germany, its population sinking into unprecedented poverty.

In a city steeped in modern architecture, Hermine Stiassni, a young, ambitious woman, threw herself into the real-estate business. Between 1921 and 1938, she built (or rebuilt) seven tenement buildings, mostly in the white functionalist style then in vogue. Another venture was the construction of a high-rise hotel that, for planning reasons, was eventually built as a large, five-storey multipurpose building, later called the Morava Palace. Hermine even launched an international competition to design it, approaching both Peter Behrens and Jacobus Oud. She settled, however, on the Brno-based Ernst Wiesner (1890–1971), who later designed the Stiassni family home.

Wiesner had returned to Brno in 1919 after an apprenticeship with Friedrich Ohmann in Vienna, and military service. His designs were a revelation. They combined a fresh, individualist Viennese modernism with the spare, unornamented architecture of Adolf Loos, an emphasis on high-quality natural materials, and the latest technical advances in heating and ventilation. Wiesner's first major work had been a house for Wilhelm Gutmann, whose grandfather we encountered earlier. Gutmann's villa, which housed individual apartments intended for the exclusive use of family members, was an overnight sensation. It introduced to this city, full of Art

Interior of the factory for woollen and knitted goods, Stiassni Brothers, Brno, *c*.1930, photographer unknown.

De Sandalo photography
studio, Villa Stiassni, 1930.

Nouveau and historicist façades, a smooth, bright surface whose only decoration
was the coloured ceramic window and door frames (see p. 279). Wiesner's
modernism gradually became even more progressive, as evidenced by the hotel he
designed for Hermine. The brief for her family villa was different. It was also a project
that took an unusually long time to develop, undergoing several revisions.

The villa was to stand on a hillside above a fine residential avenue, V Hlinkách,
at the interface between residential and recreational areas in what were then the
outskirts of Brno. Here, the Stiassnis consolidated a plot of over 300 square metres,
one of the largest in the city. Unusually, the house was not situated at the edge of
the plot but nearly in its centre, approached by a lime-tree-lined drive that led to an
enclosed courtyard; access to the garden was via the house (above). This layout,
as well as the internal arrangement of the formal reception rooms, recalled English
domestic traditions, known in Moravia through the works of the German architect
and theoretician Hermann Muthesius and the Slovak architect Dušan Jurkovič.[23]

Wiesner's first design shows a stone-clad building of three wings.[24] A large hall
opens via a trio of French windows onto a balustraded terrace with floral parterres
below. At this stage, there was already a large loggia to the east, with a sightline
terminating in a semicircular rest area of considerable size with a group of mature
trees. This plan, like the final design, suggests that the Stiassnis always envisaged a
home that would work for large social occasions. Its proportions were of a different
order to those of other luxurious villas nearby, which belonged to doctors, judges
and bank directors.

The house, as finally built, consisted of two wings, with a separate space for
servants and a detached dwelling for the head gardener, which included an
apartment and two garages. The buildings created a kind of courtyard, with roof
gardens on both the villa and the gardener's house. The façades were plain, in a
greenish plaster, with sculptural plasticity and a play of light and shade introduced
by the stone tracery of the windows and doors, the stone-clad columns of the
entrance wing, or loggia, the prominent cornice, and the slatted wooden louvres
and pulley awnings. All this lent the building a Mediterranean air. Screening
was a necessity, given the south-facing aspect of the bedrooms and reception

rooms. The grounds were further enhanced by a driver's house, stables, a pair of greenhouses, a tennis court and a swimming pool.

The ground floor was reserved for the most public spaces. A sumptuous guest cloakroom lined with Paonazzo marble signals the house's function as a setting for social gatherings. In the staircase hall, the expensive coffered ceiling (elm-root veneer) made a deliberately luxurious statement. That hall then connected to a music room, a dining room, a smoking room and a ladies' boudoir. The dining room connected to the kitchen in the service wing, and both were linked by a narrow corridor to the loggia and the main garden parterre, which allowed the Stiassnis to host events for nearly a hundred people. Upstairs, the first floor was an intimate family area, with three suites for its individual members. Each consisted of a dressing room, a bedroom and a bathroom; their daughter also had a playroom and access to a terrace (above). This style of living was without precedent in Brno; the family spaces in the nearby Villa Tugendhat are much more modest.

For the furnishings and the wood panelling, the Stiassnis called in the Viennese architect Franz Wilfert, former director of the famous Portois & Fix furniture company, and an art broker with a largely Jewish clientele. The relatively traditional interior of the main house contrasts with the functionalist interior of the servants' wing. In this respect, the grandeur of the staircase, with its voluminous skylight, seems an anomaly. Its location, in a servants' area, suggests a stylistic rather than economically motivated choice. Presumably the Stiassnis liked Wiesner's design and, since money was no object, agreed to implement it.

The house was completed by November 1929, with final approval following in June 1930, but the Stiassni family spent less than nine years there. They fled Czechoslovakia in 1938, shortly before Hitler invaded, and headed first to Britain and then to the United States. The Stiassnis were luckier than most Jewish refugees: they transported most of their artworks and other furnishings to London in two railway carriages procured through Alfred's brother-in-law, who owned one of the largest shipping companies of the time.

Villa Tugendhat

Grete Löw-Beer (1903–70), the daughter of another prominent Jewish textile family, moved in the Stiassnis' social circle. Fifteen years younger than Hermine, she too considered employing Ernst Wiesner to design her family home. Yet her requirements differed in almost every respect from the purpose of Villa Stiassni. Grete had returned to Brno from Berlin after her second marriage to Fritz Tugendhat in 1928. In her memoirs, part of which she delivered as a lecture in 1969 at the Brno House of Arts, she recalled: 'I very much wished to have a spacious, modern house with clean and simple shapes. My husband was quite terrified of the rooms full of figures and all kinds of blankets he remembered from his childhood.' To understand why, we need to know something of her family and upbringing.

Grete's father, Alfred Löw-Beer, came from a line of very successful textile manufacturers. A leading representative of the Moravian Association of Wool Industrialists in Brno, and a founder of the League of Moravian Industrialists, he served as vice president of the Brno Chamber of Commerce and Trades throughout the interwar period. Like many Jews, the Tugendhats identified culturally as German. Between 1919 and 1937, Alfred was also active in the Deutsches Haus, a social and cultural hub for Germans living in the city.[25]

Grete grew up in splendid houses designed for large-scale entertaining. Fritz Tugendhat came from a less prominent family, but his experience was broadly similar. This was the environment they sought to escape. In Berlin, Grete had often visited the art historian Eduard Fuchs, whose house had been designed by Ludwig Mies van der Rohe (1886–1969) in a style based on classical forms. We know that it was a source of inspiration for Grete, who may even have encountered the architect there, along with his friend and colleague Lilly Reich. The Weissenhof development in Stuttgart was a further source of inspiration. Completed in 1927, this was the very first modern housing estate, part of an urban development planned by Mies.[26] Even bolder designs were still sitting in his drawer, but his German Pavilion for the 1929 International Exhibition in Barcelona, which is often compared with Villa Tugendhat, was already nearing completion. Both buildings were designed almost

Main living area at the Villa Tugendhat, view from the entrance to the winter garden, c.1931, photographer unknown. The dominant feature is the onyx wall.

A

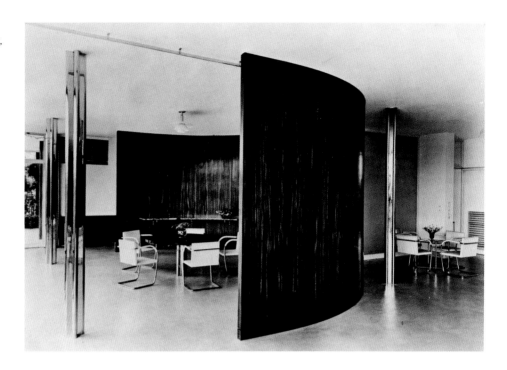

Main living area at the Villa Tugendhat: view of the dining part, showing the semi-circular wall veneered with macassar ebony, c.1931, photographer unknown.

simultaneously. They use the same steel structural system, continuous space and luxurious materials, but there are also significant differences. While the Barcelona Pavilion was more of a sculptural work – an ephemeral building with limited practical use – Villa Tugendhat was a proper home. The former immediately became a modernist icon, but the latter only established itself in the history of architecture after World War Two.

Grete's father Alfred gave his daughter a plot of land and an unlimited budget. In September 1928, Mies came to Brno for an initial inspection. The plot was situated at the top of a garden in the city's oldest villa district, with her parents' villa at the other end. It offered a beautiful view of Špilberk (Spielberg) Castle and the rest of the city skyline. Mies was enchanted – and impressed by the local architecture and standards of construction. He had no reservations about entrusting the project to the Eisler brothers: the very same company that had built Villa Stiassni. Mies, in fact, had long dreamt of clients like the Tugendhats: wealthy, knowledgeable, sophisticated, and willing to let him get on with it. In one respect, however, the result did not meet their requirements. As Grete testifies in her memoirs: 'we naturally imagined a much smaller and more modest house than Mies then designed'.[27]

Villa Tugendhat and Villa Stiassni were not country houses. Nor were they typical townhouses because they were constructed on the very edge of a built-up area. While Villa Stiassni looked out towards the forests, Villa Tugendhat offered its inhabitants and guests a magnificent view of the city. Therein, indeed, lay its novelty.

The house is too well known to merit more than a few observations.[28] The spatial arrangement contrasts the conventional layout of the bedroom floor with the open plan of the living area on the main floor (see pp. 283–5). The family's own rooms are actually quite modest, and probably reflect the Tugendhats' initial desire for simpler living. A large terrace takes up the rest of the floor plan: it opens out onto a view of the city but is, thanks to the terrain, set high above the surrounding houses, offering an intimate, safe, outdoor space, just steps away from the bedrooms and children's rooms. Much has been written about the flexibility of the main floor, its connection to the garden, and the architect's ingenious minimalism.

The main living area of the
Villa Tugendhat being used
for therapeutic gymnastics,
photographed by Miloš Budík
in 1959, when the house was
part of the Brno University
Children's Hospital.

We should also note the use of precious materials in a way that was deliberately functional – for example, veneers of macassar ebony on the dividing walls and, most famously, a partially translucent wall of solid onyx. Manufactured by the Brno Standard Housing Company after designs by Mies and Lilly Reich, the furniture was conceived in much the same spirit.[29] A technologically innovative central-heating system allowed the air to be cooled as well as heated, and an electric motor lowered the windows, connecting the inside to the outside.

Villa Tugendhat was completed in December 1930, just six months after the Villa Stiassni. It is now recognised as an icon of modern architecture, but it was Wiesner's villa that was more likely to make the pages of prestigious architectural magazines at the time of its completion. The reception of the house Mies built was shaped by the crisis then engulfing the economy. The leader of the Czech avant-garde, writer and critic Karel Teige, wrote: 'A machine for living? No, a machine for showing off, for splendour, for the workless, lazy life of gentlemen playing golf and bored ladies in boudoirs.'[30] This was the critique of a left-wing activist; others had more practical concerns: a debate even broke out in *Die Form* magazine as to whether it would be possible to live in the Villa Tugendhat at all.[31]

Despite its generous spaces, ostentatious materials and state-of-the-art technology, Villa Tugendhat appears to represent a rupture with the tradition of the Jewish country house. The continuous space on the main floor is a living room: a large but ultimately private area. However, a family like the Tugendhats could not avoid social contact. They even held bridge tournaments and film screenings in the house to raise money for the Human Rights League, a fashionable cause on which Grete collaborated with Hermine Stiassni. The couple could not – and did not want to – break completely with their parents' lifestyle. The house, although not directly built for such purposes, made that possible.

In the event, the Tugendhats' enjoyment of this modernist masterpiece proved brief. They too were forced to emigrate when the Nazis closed in on Czechoslovakia, travelling in the opposite direction along the very same railway that would carry most of Brno's large Jewish community to their deaths. A total of twelve transports were dispatched from Brno, carrying 10,080 people. Only 841 lived to see the end of the war.

Legacies

Jewish entrepreneurs had ample warning, but many did not flee in time. Even those who survived the Holocaust could not return to their homes as another totalitarian regime seized control in Czechoslovakia. Under the Communists, Villa Stiassni met a relatively dignified fate as a hotel for state visitors. The other houses served different purposes: Schillersdorf became a young people's home and mining school; Tobitschau, the site of a small museum, health centre, canteen and academy of folk art; Villa Tugendhat, which was significantly damaged by the Red Army, was first a dance school, then a rehabilitation centre for children. With the exception of Schillersdorf, all have since become museums. Visitors can admire the beauty of times gone by and learn something of their history, but these houses no longer represent the future. What does continue to serve its purpose, however, still connecting cities and states despite national borders, is the railway.

13 Trent Park: a house under German occupation

Helen Fry

John Singer Sargent, *Sir Philip Sassoon*, 1923, oil on canvas.

In 1912, Sir Philip Sassoon came into possession of Trent Park, a Victorian mansion near Enfield, just north of London; between 1925 and 1931, he commissioned substantial alterations. Its unobtrusive rooms and restrained style, combined with a level of luxury many visitors perceived as distinctly un-English, functioned as a kind of stage-set: first for Sassoon's sociability, then for His Majesty's Government when it repurposed the property to house top-ranking German officers after their capture by the Allies during World War Two. This is a Jewish country house with a multilayered history, one at the centre of high society and politics during the inter-war period, and then at the heart of intelligence gathering during the war.

The English and the oriental

Originally consisting of over 400 acres of parkland, the Trent Park estate was a gift in 1777 from George III to Sir Richard Jebb, physician to the royal household, in recognition of Jebb's help bringing the king's younger brother back to health at Trento in Italy. Jebb built the first house on the site and commissioned Sir Humphrey Repton to landscape the grounds. After Jebb's death, the estate was sold several times and the house extended to roughly its current footprint before being purchased in 1833 by the Bevan family, who rebuilt much of the house, including the south front. In 1908, the lease was acquired by Sir Edward Sassoon, the Indian-born MP for Hythe whose Baghdadi-Jewish family had made a fortune from opium and other commodities, benefiting as local intermediaries from the opportunities created by British imperialism.[1] Sir Edward married Aline de Rothschild, thus cementing an alliance between two great Jewish families, one supremely well established, the other newcomers from the east. On his death in 1912, the lease passed to Sir Edward's only son Philip (1888–1939), who also inherited 25 Park Lane in Mayfair (see p. 301) and other family properties in Brighton and Mumbai.[2]

David Sassoon and his sons, photographed in Baghdad, c.1850. David Sassoon is seated, with his sons standing behind him; left to right, Elias David, Albert Abdallah and Sassoon David.

William Orpen, *Park Lane Interior*, 1913, oil on canvas. Philip Sassoon and his sister Sybil are depicted in his London house, whose emphasis on French furnishings and works of art associates it with his Paris-born Rothschild mother, Aline.

Sir Philip was a politician, art collector and socialite, a pillar of the establishment with a touch of the exotic. He purchased Trent Park from the Duchy of Lancaster in 1923, and the alterations he began three years later included major changes to the façade. The exterior of the house was clad in rose-coloured bricks and off-white stone purchased from Devonshire House, one of the great London palaces of the eighteenth century (designed by William Kent). This 'dream of another world' incorporated elements salvaged from other historic houses too, including Stowe, Chesterfield and Wrest Park.[3] *Country Life* magazine described the changes as having been handled 'with such understanding that the exterior can be regarded as typical of the traditional English house unaffected by foreign example or architectural vogue'.[4] The interior remained structurally unchanged, but Sassoon added Georgian furniture and conversation pieces, a genre he had brought back into fashion through the ten loan exhibitions he staged at his London home. He commissioned Chinese wallpaper for the middle reception room on the ground floor, as well as a number of murals by the voguish Rex Whistler, in the Library and Long Salon. He also installed a modern telephone system, a luxury and uncommon feature in 1920s houses. Indeed, Sassoon had installed the first hotline in Britain at his other country house, Port Lympne (see p. 302).

There he had adopted a very different aesthetic. Designed before World War One by Herbert Baker in Dutch Cape style, and completed afterwards by Philip Tilden, Port Lympne's orientalising extravagances included a dining room whose decoration was inspired by the Ballets Russes, and a bachelor's wing with a Moorish courtyard. So confidently did Sassoon play with these stereotypes that the Conservative politician Robert Boothby later recalled finding his host in the gardens there, 'sitting reading alone in a fez'.[5] (To his contemporaries, Sassoon looked un-English, but it is said that he much preferred to be seen as Parsee than Jewish).[6]

Below left
Port Lympne, photograph published
in *Country Life*, May 1923; an early
20th-century country house in
Cape Dutch style, designed by
Herbert Baker and Philip Tilden.

Bottom left
The dining room at Port Lympne,
published in *Country Life*,
4 February 1933. The walls
were cobalt blue, the ceiling
opalescent pink and the frieze
was painted by Glyn Philpot.

Below right
The Tent Room at Port Lympne,
published in *Country Life*,
4 February 1933. The *trompe l'oeil*
tent was designed by Rex Whistler.

Tilden described this, his first Sassoon house, as 'a challenge to the world, telling people that a new culture had risen up from the sick-bed of the old, with new aspirations, eyes upon a new aspect, mind turned to a new burst of imagination'.[7] Port Lympne revelled in the sense of otherness that contemporaries emphasised about Sassoon. Murals by the Catalan artist José María Sert, whose creation (in the drawing room) Sassoon directed even while serving in France, incorporated elephants and other Asian elements into an allegory about the war with Germany. They were painted over shortly before Port Lympne hosted an important diplomatic delegation, but another set of murals, this time by Glyn Philpot, were the focus of much fascination in the cobalt-blue dining room (whose ceiling was opalescent pink). Philpot's frieze depicted naked black Egyptians and white bullocks (bottom left). Its startling style combined Greek, African and Mesopotamian influences, as well as the Ballets Russes and *fin de siècle* book illustration.[8]

Trent Park was conspicuously more restrained (opposite). At Port Lympne, Whistler had transformed the billiard room into a *trompe l'oeil* Tent Room, with riverside landscapes populated with real and imaginary figures and places – many, like Paris, linked to Sassoon himself. At Trent Park he was confined to overmantel panels with classical trophies. In the garden, some of the statuary was given gilded highlights and there were flamingos on the lake, in addition to a scarlet ibis and flocks of penguins that Sassoon fed himself, but despite these flourishes, Trent Park was an exercise in a particular kind of Englishness. Writing in *Country Life* in 1931, the architectural historian Christopher Hussey described it as 'unpretentious, practical yet civilized', 'an ideal example of English domestic architecture unalloyed by fashion or fantasy'.[9]

The paintings, particularly, created the congenial atmosphere of the light-filled rooms, made comfortable with spacious arrangements of understated furniture, rugs and ceramics. Sassoon was a pioneer in the collecting of conversation pieces by

Johann Zoffany and Arthur Devis, among others. He mounted the first exhibition of this type of portraiture in his London house in 1930, describing it as a 'representation of two or more persons in a state of dramatic or psychological relation to each other.... A half-way between the portrait group and the genre picture, drawing upon the qualities of both and adding one of its own, intimacy'. For Sassoon, these works were peculiarly English and characteristic of English eighteenth-century life, an age he characterised as 'one of commercial expansion and political development, which gave increasing scope for the expression of individual character'.[10]

The grounds were extensively re-landscaped to include an avenue of lime trees and the Wisteria Walk: a secluded pergola of Italian marble wound round with wisteria and clematis, leading to a sunken garden. On the east side of the house, an outdoor heated swimming pool was built, the first in Europe, with an orangery at the rear. Boothby wrote that 'the blue bathing pool surrounded by such a profusion of lilies that the scent at night became almost overpowering, the flamingos and ducks, the banks of exquisite flowers in the drawing-room, the red carnation and the cocktail on one's dressing table before dinner, were each and all perfect of their kind'.[11] This description draws the imagination and senses into Sassoon's world, as redolent of the French Riviera as it is of India.

A socialite world

During the 1920s and 1930s, Trent Park was the setting for lavish and theatrical parties that brought together figures from the worlds of high society, politics, literature and showbusiness. Sassoon was an extravagant, enthusiastic host whose weekend retreats here became legendary. Guests included the Duke and Duchess of Kent, the Duke and Duchess of York, Lord Louis Mountbatten, Charlie Chaplin, George Bernard Shaw, T. E. Lawrence (Lawrence of Arabia), Winston Churchill, Neville Chamberlain, Stanley Baldwin, David Lloyd George and the future Edward VIII, who abdicated in 1936 to marry Mrs Wallis Simpson. Prior to their wedding, they used the house as a secret love nest.

Early on the morning of the weekend guests' arrival, a cavalcade of horse-drawn carts could be seen leaving Covent Garden for Trent Park, each cart laden with lilies, roses and azaleas. The flowers filled every room of the house. Boothby described the scene: 'white-coated footmen serving endless courses of rich but delicious food', with 'Winston Churchill arguing over the tea-cups with Bernard Shaw, Lord Balfour dozing in an armchair, Rex Whistler absorbed in his painting'. Trent Park also had its own airfield, and guests were entertained with 'flights over the grounds in [Sassoon's] private aeroplane after tea, with a fire-work display over the lake after dinner ... and with songs from Richard Tauber, which we listened to on the terrace by moonlight before going to bed'.[12]

Once Hitler seized power in Germany, the parties took on a sense of urgency. During the 1930s, Sassoon hosted weekend political meetings, almost a parliament outside parliament. The secluded location enabled frank and confidential discussions about the situation in Europe and the growing threat of war. He also played an important role preparing the RAF for the coming conflict. At this time, Sassoon befriended a number of young airmen and had a relationship with the rich and handsome Sir Paul Latham. Homosexuality was still illegal, and Sassoon's houses were a refuge for his homosexual friends. Like many of his bachelor circle, who became fierce anti-Nazis, he was shocked by the murder of many homosexuals by the Nazis in the Night of the Long Knives (1934).[13]

Max Beerbohm, *Philip Sassoon in Strange Company*, 1913, pen, ink and wash on paper. Beerbohm's depiction of the newly elected Sassoon plays on his otherness, seated on a bench of the House of Commons, cross-legged and rarefied, between two rotund and bellowing fellow Conservative MPs.

Many English country houses harboured aristocrats who wanted to appease Germany, sometimes out of sympathy with Hitler's politics, and sometimes because they sought to preserve peace at all costs.[14] Meanwhile, Sassoon's Rothschild relatives were actively engaged in supporting Jewish refugees and speaking out against their persecution. His father had publicly embraced Jewish causes, but Sir Philip never did so. The style in which he visited Germany as Under-Secretary of State for Air, when he was entertained by Goering, was neither forgotten nor forgiven by some British Jews.[15] Yet Sassoon's Jewishness was known, and his high profile made him a target for antisemitism: in 1937, Trent Park itself was vandalised with graffiti spelling out the words *Perish Judah*.[16]

That year, Sassoon became First Commissioner of Works and Public Buildings, with responsibility for requisitioning sites for special government purposes. His unexpected and premature death on 3 June 1939 closed a chapter in the life of Trent Park. However, a new era was about to begin – one of supreme national importance in wartime – in which the house provided a stage-set for a new cast of guests.

During World War Two, Trent Park came under a strange kind of German occupation while at the same time harbouring a group of Jewish refugees whose task it was to monitor and record the residents' unguarded conversations. Known to the War Office as 'secret listeners', their activity rendered Philip Sassoon's elegant country retreat a site of monumental significance for the war effort. As the focus for one of Britain's longest, most important intelligence-gathering operations against Nazi Germany, its significance has been formally recognised by Historic England as of 'considerable national and international historical interest which bears comparison to the codebreaking work at Bletchley Park'.[17]

A house for the secret purposes

None of the paintings or original furnishings were in situ when British Intelligence, under the auspices of the War Office, requisitioned Trent Park in October 1939 for 'special purposes'. Now, MI6 spymaster Major (later Colonel) Thomas Joseph Kendrick arranged for a team of specialist engineers to 'wire for sound' the empty mansion house and stable block.[18] Tiny microphones were hidden in the light fittings, fireplaces, billiard table, and even trees in the grounds. Five interrogation rooms and six bedrooms were wired to conceal microphones supplied by the Radio Corporation of America (RCA). The wiring was deeply embedded in small cavities behind the plasterboard in each of the rooms, behind fireplaces and skirting boards. The cabling on each floor was wired ultimately to one central point in the house: a cavity that ran from floor to ceiling behind the plasterboard at the back of a front bedroom on the first floor.

On the ground floor, the two long reception rooms at the rear of the house were fitted with false ceilings. The space between these ceilings and the floorboards of the rooms above was at least double the depth of the cavity usually found between floors, and with an extra layer of wooden supporting beams. Some cabling ran through this space, although why it should have been so deep remains a mystery. The alterations dovetailed perfectly with the original architecture and did not arouse suspicion. Later, in May 1940, some ground-floor rooms were divided up and further soundproofing was added. False panels were erected to stop the German 'guests' from straying accidentally into the basement or other sealed-off parts of the building. The site was never referred to as a prisoner-of-war camp but 'Cockfosters Camp', or 'Camp 11'.[19]

By the end of December 1939, Kendrick moved his listening operation from the Tower of London, where it started with a team of six officers, to Trent Park, which afforded relative safety from the bombs falling on London. The location meant this intelligence operation could function in secret away from the prying eyes of the public. Kendrick now commanded over 500 intelligence officers, a third of whom were women, and a team of 30 secret listeners who recorded the conversations of the German POWs. Results were swift.

Prisoners from the German submarine U-35 began to talk among themselves about German codes, decoding methods and ciphers (all picked up by the hidden microphones). Erich May, a telegraphist, was soon giving up information about the German Naval Enigma, a vital development when Bletchley Park had not yet broken the German Enigma codes. May was befriended by a British naval interrogator, Lieutenant Colonel Bernard Trench. On 28 December 1939, Trench travelled to Bletchley Park to meet with Alastair Denniston, the first head of the Government Code and Cypher School (GC&CS). Two days later, naval interrogator Lieutenant Pennell visited Denniston to ascertain how to secure Enigma intelligence from the prisoner at Trent Park. Pennell took May for trips into central London where he was given 'a very good meal and drank only champagne and port'.[20] This preferential treatment was designed to soften him further. In this way, Pennell sweet-talked May into giving away more information about the German naval Enigma machine.[21] On 8 January 1940, he even drew a diagram explaining to Pennell how Enigma worked.[22]

The official history of Bletchley Park now recognises that Alan Turing and his colleagues were only able to crack the German naval Enigma thanks to the intelligence from Trent Park.[23] At the time, Admiral John Godfrey (head of Naval Intelligence Division) wrote: 'I have reviewed the results obtained from naval prisoners of war [at Trent Park] since the outbreak of war ... they are of such operational importance as to make it vital to develop this source of information to the full.'[24]

At this stage of the war, the 'secret listeners' were not Jewish refugees, but British personnel. Not until 1943 did the difficult colloquial language overheard render the use of native German speakers a necessity. Now, Kendrick enlisted Jewish refugees serving in the British Army's Pioneer Corps, who were native German speakers. Many, like Fritz Lustig, who wrote an extensive memoir, and Eric Mark (see p. 310, left), whose parents had sent him to Britain as a child refugee at the age of twelve, had spent time in internment camps on the Isle of Man in 1940, where nearly 30,000 Germans were crammed together behind barbed wire.[25] Some Jewish refugees were also deployed in other roles. Ernst Lederer from Teplice in the Sudetenland worked as an interrogator and 'stool pigeon', who pretended to be a fellow officer and mixed with the German generals to lead their conversations in a particular way and gain relevant information (see p. 310, right).

Thousands of transcripts of the overheard conversations survive in the National Archives at Kew. This secret unit, which went by the obscure cover name of Combined Services Detailed Interrogation Centre (CSDIC), rapidly became a factory of information on the enemy. The secret listeners sat at desks with specialist listening and recording equipment in the 'M Room' (M for 'miked'), overhearing conversations about German technology being developed or used in warfare, references to *X-Gerät* and *Knickebein* (new kinds of navigational beam systems on German aircraft for bombing targets), as well as huge quantities of information on the U-boat campaign, new weapons for the German navy, and aircraft and tanks.

Copies of Kendrick's intelligence reports were passed to the relevant intelligence organisations (MI6, MI5 Naval Intelligence, Political Warfare Executive and the Air Ministry) as well as Bomber Command, various departments within the Admiralty, Fighter Command, government scientists working at other secret locations, and other branches of military intelligence. The transcripts of bugged conversations shed much light on German radar, including night-fighter radar appliances and tactics. It was estimated that by the end of the war the intelligence gained from Trent

Park and its two sister sites of Latimer House and Wilton Park in Buckinghamshire gave the Allies knowledge of '95% of the whole developed and developing field of German radar and anti-radar devices with accuracy little short of 100%'.[26] In short, Trent Park provided vast amounts of information from lower-rank Axis prisoners during the early years of the war.

Charming Hitler's generals

From May 1942, Trent Park was reserved for a new class of German occupant: generals and senior officers recently captured from the battlefields, first of North Africa (1942–3), then Italy (1943), and Normandy after D-Day (June 1944), who were greeted like honoured guests (below). It was a haven for weary, disillusioned men who had suffered bitter defeats. Housing them here played right into their inflated egos and sense of self-importance, which was exactly how Kendrick had planned it. In this country house, these top commanders were duped into believing they were being held as befitted their status as military gentlemen. Everything was choreographed to extract intelligence that would not be given up in interrogation.

Little did these senior Nazi officers suspect that tiny microphones had been placed in light fittings, fireplaces, the billiard table, the plant pots, behind picture frames and under windowsills. Their conversations were recorded from three M Rooms in the basement. The generals had been warned before they left for the battlefields that if they were captured, the British would be listening in to their conversations. Thanks to Kendrick's charm offensive, that caution went unheeded.

At Trent Park, Sassoon's vision of an English country house lulled the generals into a sense of security. Run like a gentleman's club, with wine at suppertime, the elegant Green Room became their dining room. Every Friday evening after supper, they organised an hour's lecture on aspects of the German military. The generals were permitted to walk along the terrace at the back of the house, with views over the lake, and enjoy a quiet stroll anywhere within the barbed-wire fence of their compound. During the day they could wander between the ground-floor rooms and their bedrooms on the first floor, but the basement was sealed off. They devoted their time to the arts and painting, playing cards and billiards. A room was set aside for creative activities. They also received newspapers and could listen to BBC radio broadcasts.

Below left
German prisoners go for a walk, photographer unknown, 1943 or 1944. The man in the left foreground is believed to be General Ludwig Crüwell, probably with General Hans-Jürgen von Arnim walking behind him to the left, and General Wilhelm Ritter von Thoma to the right.

Below right
General von Arnim arrives at Trent Park, photographer unknown, May 1943.

With Kendrick's careful planning, conditions were created to enable Hitler's senior commanders to relax yet further. They were taken by a 'Lord Aberfeldy' for occasional trips into central London, and lunch at Simpson's in the Strand. Aberfeldy, they were told, was their welfare officer and a man of distinguished Scottish ancestry, an aristocrat, and second cousin of the king, with a castle in Scotland. In fact, he was a fake — one of Kendrick's intelligence officers whose real name was Ian Thomson Munro.[27] The German generals took him into their confidence, and never discovered his true identity. The ambience of the country house rendered him entirely credible.

Conversations between Hitler's generals and senior officers were not confined to the weather. At Trent Park they first learned through newspapers and radio broadcasts about the fall of Stalingrad on 2 February 1943, the failed assassination attempt on Hitler on 20 July 1944, and Hitler's suicide on 30 April 1945. Events like these provoked much discussion, all of it recorded. Bitterness and rivalry were never far from the surface as the generals quickly aligned themselves into pro-Nazi and anti-Nazi camps. This led to intense arguments. Sometimes they even shouted at each other, oblivious to the presence of others in the house.

During 1944, the question of how to celebrate Hitler's birthday on 20 April provoked fierce argument. In the end, Generaloberst von Arnim made a short speech during the officers' lunch and glasses were raised to the Führer.[28] The set-up enabled British Intelligence to learn much about the internal politics of the highest military leaders of the Nazi command. While Hitler's commanders wrangled over politics and loyalty to the Third Reich, they began inadvertently to reveal some of their country's most closely protected military secrets to the hidden microphones.

War-winning intelligence

Distilling the vast quantities of information provided by POWs at Kendrick's sites and understanding the consequence of that intelligence for particular outcomes in the war is still a major work for historians. We do know that one huge revelation obtained from the generals in captivity at Trent Park drastically affected the course of the war. It pertained to Hitler's secret V-weapon programme. British Intelligence needed to corroborate information coming from behind enemy lines about a German programme to develop long-range rockets.[29] The intelligence was clinched at Trent Park in March 1943. Events had taken a dramatic turn on the Russian Front, where Generalfeldmarschall Paulus, in charge of the German 6th Army trying to take Stalingrad, had surrendered to the Soviets. Relaxing in Sassoon's former drawing rooms as they listened to radio broadcasts detailing their military losses, the generals and senior officers at Trent Park now believed the war was lost for Germany. It was then that General von Thoma gave some vague information about rockets reaching 15 kilometres into the stratosphere, with no limit to the range.[30] His statement 'represented a crucial point in the intelligence picture at that date'.[31] In the coming weeks, the generals talked about rocket technology, the V-1 (doodlebug), V-2 and Germany's experimental site at Peenemünde on the Baltic coast. Within months they would also be discussing the V-3, a new super gun in development. These unguarded conversations led the RAF to send reconnaissance aircraft over the Baltic coast. An analysis of their photographs was delivered to British Intelligence within a matter of days.[32]

The photographs confirmed Hitler's V-weapon programme at Peenemünde. On the night of 17/18 August 1943, the site was heavily bombed in a secret mission and rendered non-operational.[33] Consequently, the first V-1 did not fall on London until 13 June 1944, approximately a week after D-Day. This bought nine months of grace, during which Allied troops were able to continue their offensive through Italy and launch the invasion of Normandy on 6 June 1944. Intelligence about the V-weapons was described by Lieutenant Colonel Pryor of the Air Ministry as 'near to being a war-winner as any single report I have met'.[34]

Towards the end of the war, British Intelligence was holding fifty-nine German generals and forty senior German officers at Trent Park. In the words of Lieutenant Colonel St Clare Grondona (Kendrick's deputy at Wilton Park): 'Had it not been for the information obtained at the centre, it could have been London and not Hiroshima which was devastated by the first atomic bomb.'

Painful revelations

The generals discussed more than military information. Their unguarded conversations revealed important evidence about the systematic extermination of Europe's Jews and the mass killings of Russians and Poles. Hitler's generals boasted about the number of people killed, speaking in chilling and graphic detail. Increasingly, they worried about discovery. 'What will they say when they find our graves in Poland?,' Generalleutnant Neuffer was overheard saying to his Luftwaffe colleague, Generalmajor Bassenge. 'The OGPU can't have done anything worse than that. I myself have seen a convoy at Ludowice, near Minsk. I must say it was a frightful, a horrible sight. It is ghastly, this picture. The women, the little children who were, of course, absolutely unsuspecting – frightful! Of course, I didn't watch while they were being murdered.'[35] As they worried, the generals divulged their own guilt to each other, hardly expressing remorse even as the war turned, and they realised they could face charges of war crimes and the death penalty. General von Choltitz confessed to General Wilhelm Ritter von Thoma (see p. 307) on 29 August 1944: 'The worst job I ever carried out – which, however, I carried out with great consistency – was the liquidation of the Jews. I carried out this order down to the very last detail.'[36]

All the major concentration camps are mentioned in the transcripts, including Mauthausen, Dachau, Buchenwald and Auschwitz. One can only begin to imagine the pain of those in the basement as they recorded the details. Listening to the POWs talk about gas lorries or the mass shootings of Jews into shallow-dug pits in Russia, Poland or Latvia, it could have been a description of the murder of their own families. Eric Mark learned that his parents had been murdered in Treblinka; most of Ernst Lederer's family died of maltreatment in Terezin. How did they cope? 'Listening to them talk was one of the most difficult times I ever had, but I could not show any emotion,' recalled Eric Mark, who would sit in the cellar recording conversations on a disc, which was taken away for translation. 'Most of them liked to boast about how many Jews they had killed, saying things like "I knocked off about 1,500," which was tough for me to take, being a Jew.'[37]

Below left
Eric Mark, one of the secret listeners at Trent Park, who said of the prisoners: 'Most of them liked to boast about how many Jews they had killed ... which was tough for me to take, being a Jew.'

Below right
Ernst Lederer, whose intelligence work at Trent Park included chatting to German generals while pretending to be a fellow officer.

Bergen-Belsen

On 15 April 1945, British troops liberated Bergen-Belsen. Nothing prepared them or the world for what they saw. Lustig recalled:

> when I saw film footage of Belsen for the first time, I was deeply shocked at the emaciated survivors and heaps of naked dead bodies lying around. Although coming from Nazi Germany I had known about concentration camps, I was not prepared for this. Seeing the extent of the Nazi disregard for human life raised questions about how such unspeakable acts could have been committed in the civilized country of my birth.[38]

Kendrick determined that every German general officer and senior officer would be shown Pathé news footage of the liberation of Belsen, forcing them to confront Germany's war crimes. He made it compulsory viewing. The footage is believed to have been screened in the Sassoon sports hall where the generals had exercised regularly. In the M Rooms below, the secret listeners recorded the generals' responses. When photographs of Belsen, Buchenwald and Dachau were circulated by their British minders, some prisoners suggested they had been faked.[39] Generalleutnant Dittmar and Generalleutnant Holste felt the scenes were revolting, but could not be compared with what had happened to Germans in Russian camps. They could not understand why the SS had not destroyed the damning evidence. 'It's a very effective film,' Generalleutnant Siewert acknowledged, '... a fine sort of recommendation from us! It really was like that, I saw it.'[40] Barely ten years later, he would resume his military career in the Bundeswehr.[41] Kendrick had always imagined that the transcripts would be used as evidence against the generals and POWs in war crimes trials, but for complex reasons, ranging from standards of proof to security considerations, this proved impossible.[42] As for the secret listeners below, they could not tell anyone about what they had heard. Having signed the Official Secrets Act, many went to their graves never speaking about their work.

The hidden drama that has now emerged from the shadows of official secrecy reveals a very different side to the history of Trent Park, a property long regarded as the quintessential inter-war country house. The house became the ideal stage for senior spymaster Colonel Kendrick when he turned it into a pivotal element of his intelligence operation and a vital source of war-winning information. It was in this context that a different kind of Jew, and a different layer of Jewish history, would enter the house. All over Europe, country houses that had been Jewish homes were seized and appropriated by members of the Nazi elite, who revelled in the comfort and luxury they afforded while the rightful owners fled or were sent to be murdered in the east. Here, thanks to Trent Park's secret listeners, that all too familiar story acquired an unexpected British twist.

14 An American postscript

Juliet Carey and Abigail Green

Otto Kahn playing golf,
photographer and date unknown.

War and the Holocaust brought an end to the era of the Jewish country house, although a few families lingered on. In Europe, such houses were part of the fabric of rural society, where they had traditionally fulfilled a very particular set of social, political and cultural functions rooted in the *ancien régime*. That world, and the place of country houses within it, had been disrupted by revolutions, by Jewish emancipation, by the economic and social transformations wrought by industrialisation and, in the east, by communism; now it was comprehensively destroyed. Yet, when the fashion entrepreneurs Rosalinde and Arthur Gilbert (né Abraham Bernstein) moved from London to California in 1949, they built a mock Tudor villa in Beverly Hills for their collection of English furniture and then, when their collecting turned to European princely treasures, an Italian-style palace. This final chapter will explore how country houses, although not necessarily a defining attribute of social success, could nonetheless play a central role in the self-fashioning of wealthy Jews: immigrants, émigrés and those long made good.[1]

Belonging meant differently in the United States – a society shaped by settler colonialism, slavery and the drama of the North American landscape in ways that created a unique relationship between people and the land. Houses meant differently here too, for this was a context in which race not class was the primary determinant of social status. In some ways, the plantation houses of the South bear comparison with the European archetype of a country house at the heart of a landed estate, the keystone in the economic and political organisation of a locality. Not coincidentally, the planter class was sometimes known as the Southern aristocracy, although that term described a radically different set of social, political and economic relationships to those that prevailed on the other side of the Atlantic. In Europe, of course, the aristocracy was by definition Christian; in both colonial

Right
C. W. Uhl, *Rebecca Isaiah Moses (née Phillips, 1792–1872)*, 1843, oil on canvas.

Far right
Theodore Sidney Moïse, *Isaiah Moses (1772–1857)*, c.1835, oil on canvas.

America and the antebellum United States, this Southern aristocracy was by definition white. Jews in this quite different social setting, of whom there were, in 1800, perhaps 2,000, could acquire and own Southern plantation houses without occasioning much remark.

Take Isaiah Moses (1772–1857; above), an immigrant from Bremerhaven in Hannover, who settled in South Carolina after some years in England. The Oaks, which he purchased in 1813, was a well-established plantation 18 miles from Charleston, consisting of 794 acres of cleared land, woods, and about 60 acres of rice fields, worked by some fifty enslaved people at its peak (opposite). It was an economic investment that also carried social cachet, but the couple retained a business and house in town, using the land as security, before selling it in 1841 to settle a debt. Isaiah's West Indian-born wife Rebecca (1792–1872; above) came from a Jewish family long-established in the Americas: her parents owned a plantation in the South Caroline upcountry, near the vast estate belonging to the Salvador family known, tellingly, as 'the Jew's Land'.[2]

This specific Southern context created entirely different possibilities. The emancipation campaigner Moses Levy (1782–1854) was one of east Florida's largest landowners, and it was on this basis that he established, in 1822, a pioneering Jewish agricultural settlement, conceived as a refuge for European Jews.[3] 'Pilgrimage Plantation' defined itself against the oppressive social order of the old continent: the house Levy built here was self-consciously modest, and the estate supported five other Jewish families. But despite Levy's abolitionist commitments, most of the work was done by enslaved people. This was an exceptional episode. Most Jewish immigrants settled in the North, where they encountered a different set of challenges and opportunities.

Through the nineteenth century, the Jewish population of the United States expanded exponentially, as did the general population. Only in the 1880s did Eastern European Jews start to arrive in significant numbers, doubling the number of Jews in the United States to roughly one million, between 1890 and 1900. Before that, Jews came overwhelmingly from the German lands of Central Europe: a distinct subgroup of the much larger wave of transatlantic migration that rendered New York, by the 1850s, the third capital of the German-speaking world after Vienna and Berlin.[4] To begin with, most were poor or came from lower-middle-class families, but as Europe changed so did the emigration of Jews from these areas. A few were political refugees active in the 1848 revolutions, and a few were intimately connected to the European world of the Jewish country house.[5] The Warburgs,

Seligmans and Hallgartens, for example, were transatlantic business dynasties, whose relatives feature in different chapters of this book; August Belmont, who represented the Rothschilds in New York, was a connection of Baron de Hirsch. Unlike their European cousins, none of these American Jewish financiers had titles, nor did they seek to acquire them.

Such Jews also owned country houses, but country houses in Gilded Age America were never the essential accoutrement of a political career or social status they remained in Europe.[6] They were instead private family spaces that came with relatively small acreages. As country 'homes' they resonated with a distinctively American set of moral and spiritual values, often expressing a certain ambivalence about display. Not for nothing were the lavish summer retreats of the New York elite in Newport, Rhode Island, known as 'summer cottages'. It was here, in 1860, that Belmont and his Episcopalian wife Caroline (née Perry) built By-the-Sea, one of the earliest of the grand Newport mansions: an Italianate house with a mansard roof and a three-bay entrance-front pavilion, located on 14 acres of land off Bellevue Avenue. Their son Oliver had Richard Morris Hunt design and build Belcourt, an eclectic house in a mixture of European styles, on part of the property (see p. 316, top). This was the third largest of all the Newport cottages, and his entertainments were legendary. Newport was a place New Yorkers went to see and be seen; class may have operated differently here, but houses like By-the-Sea and Belcourt were certainly intended to facilitate integration in the social life of the Four Hundred. To some extent, Jewishness too carried different connotations. After all, Newport was also the site of the oldest synagogue in the United States. In 1870, Emma Lazarus's father, the sugar merchant Moses Lazarus, had built a Second Empire-style property he called The Beeches (see p. 316, bottom) not far from the Belmont residences, and the synagogue is celebrated in one of Emma's most famous poems.[7]

With time, new barriers began to be erected. This reflected the influence of European antisemitic ideas and discourse, and the changing legal and social boundaries between whites and African Americans that characterised the Reconstruction and Progressive eras.[8] As in Europe, the late 1870s represented something of a watershed, for it was in 1877 that the prominent banker Joseph Seligman was barred from staying at the Grand Union Hotel in the fashionable New York spa resort of Saratoga because he was a Jew. Social exclusion of this kind would become an ingrained feature of American life in the cities of the East Coast and the surrounding countryside, as high social mobility brought the so-called Uptown Jews into spaces controlled by established Protestant families like the

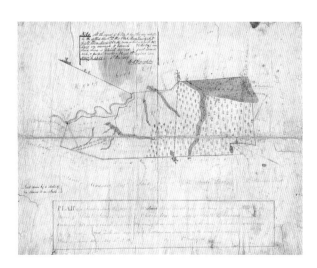

'Plan of a tract of land, the property of Mr. Isaiah Moses, situate lying and being in Goose Creek in the Parish of Saint James: District of Charleston: and State of South-Carolina', based on a survey by William Brailsford, 1817, ink and watercolour on paper.

Right
Belcourt, Newport, Rhode Island, loggia and courtyard, photographed by Frank H. Child in 1895. The house was designed by Richard Morris Hunt for Oliver Hazard Perry Belmont.

Far right
Belcourt, front elevation, photographed by Frank H. Child in 1895.

Astors, the Vanderbilts and the Roosevelts. Famously, in 1893, Joseph's nephew Theodore Seligman was blackballed by the Union League Club 'solely because of his race', prompting his father Jesse to resign from an institution of which he had been one of the earliest members.[9] This kind of thing began earlier in New York and Boston than it did in newer cities like Chicago. Antisemitism, of course, functioned differently from the racial barriers that African Americans encountered. Yet in 1904, J. P. Morgan did not hesitate to classify his and the British bank Barings' representative in the United States as the only 'white firms in New York'.[10] Exclusion, however, did not imply social isolation. Jews with money often engaged philanthropically with a wide range of social and cultural causes; this enabled figures like Henry Morgenthau Sr to navigate the informal constraints rather well.

Europe, of course, had its spas and seaside resorts, but the Rhode Island cottages spoke to a distinctive American context in which, as the architectural historian Clive Aslet has noted, country houses might conjure up the illusion of European country living, but never its substance.[11] Thus Jacob Schiff, Morgan's competitor at Kuhn, Loeb & Co. and arguably the most prominent of New York's Jewish grandees, owned a 'farm' at Red Bank in New Jersey that recalled an English village, with shingle thatch and stucco walls imitating clunch: 'like a true *ferme ornée*, it included a tea house as a "retreat for afternoon gatherings"'.[12] Self-consciously European resonances of this kind spoke to the culture and heritage of the Uptown Jews, and to the transatlantic lives they led; they were also one way in which such properties, and their owners, could be coded 'white'. Here we focus on two particularly celebrated East Coast Jewish houses, both in their way American archetypes, in which readers will nonetheless find many resonances with their European counterparts.

The Beeches, Newport, Rhode Island, photographed c.1875. The Jewish-American poet Emma Lazarus spent the summers here with her family.

OHEKA Castle

Otto Kahn (1867–1934; see p. 312), an immigrant from the Grand Duchy of Baden sometimes known as the 'King of New York', built his country house, from scratch, looking out over the great expanse of Long Island Sound two miles away. Just as Ferdinand de Rothschild had measured the height of Waddesdon Manor against that of the other Rothschild houses in the Vale of Aylesbury (Chapter 5), so Kahn insisted his house be the highest of the many hundred mansions on Long Island. To this end he created an artificial hill.[13]

Kahn had been born in Mannheim after his father, a political refugee who fled to the United States after the revolutions of 1848, returned there. It was here that the young Otto began a brilliant career in merchant banking that brought him, via a ten-year stint in *fin de siècle* London, to the United States. Working alongside Schiff, he became a partner in Kuhn, Loeb & Co., known for his role in railroad consolidation and his championship of the civic virtues of art. In Manhattan, Kahn and his wife Addie's Florentine Renaissance-style house was directly opposite the Carnegie mansion on the Upper East Side. Their first country home, originally owned by Addie's banker father Abraham Wolff, was Cedar Court, Morristown, New Jersey. It burned down in 1914 and the move to Cold Spring Harbor on Long Island's Gold Coast was motivated partly by the Kahns' desire to distance themselves from the antisemitism that had barred them from local social clubs, including the golf club adjacent to the property.

OHEKA Castle, Long Island, photographed from the air, probably in the 1920s.

OHEKA Castle's garden front and library, photographed probably in the 1920s.

The prominence of the new site and its combination of stately-home spectacle and self-sufficiency, with Norman-style turrets, gatehouses, an eighteen-hole golf course, clubhouse, stables, bridleways, working farm and dairy, had more than a hint of swagger in the face of hostility, as did the capitalisation of its name. Initially known as Cold Spring Harbor, it became OHEKA Castle: an abbreviation of O(tto) He(rmann) Ka(hn). It was technologically innovative, with its own generators and an unprecedented system of wind tunnels and air ducts for cooling, but OHEKA's aesthetic played with historical models. The double staircase that wowed visitors as they entered was designed after the exterior staircase at Fontainebleau, which the Kahns had admired during their European honeymoon, while the fireproof walls gave the impression of wood panelling, though it was achieved with plaster, paint, graining combs and rollers. The property also boasted a French formal garden (designed by the Olmsted Brothers) with fountains and reflecting pools.

During World War One, Kahn's German origins generated resentment and suspicion. Work had begun on the earthworks at Cold Spring Harbor in 1914, but he only began the construction of the house as he finished the process of naturalisation in 1917.[14] He presciently became an American citizen shortly before the United States entered the war. A tree motif, integrated into the metalwork of the balconies, which must have been among the last elements to be completed, expresses his complex personal identity, for it is a linden tree, invoking the land of his birth (below).

Designed by Delano and Aldrich, OHEKA was the largest residential building in the United States after the Vanderbilts' Biltmore, and it too adopted historicising European styles filtered through a stylistic prism familiar from some of the Jewish country houses discussed in this book, which proved highly appealing to the American industrial and financial elite at the turn of the twentieth century.[15] The stark abstraction of the exterior and lack of ornament are nevertheless striking and unusual.

Kahn was a Broadway angel and big investor in the cinema industry, but it is the grand old European tradition of opera with which his efforts to modernise and democratise high culture are particularly associated. These were rooted in the German concept of *Bildung,* which became a pillar of German-Jewish identity: that is to say, the self-cultivation through education and the arts of an individual within broader society.[16] That Jews were forbidden to own boxes at the Metropolitan Opera for most of the time that it depended on Kahn's money epitomises the concurrent social integration and exclusion he had to navigate, in order to achieve the kind of transcultural collaboration that brought the Ballets Russes to New York in 1916.[17] As the biographer Theresa Collins has argued, this allowed Kahn to play the priest of culture, consecrating the soil of artistic modernism in the United States, and fashioning a comeback for cosmopolitanism and the avant-garde.

The metalwork on the balconies at OHEKA Castle incorporates a linden tree.

The extravagant sociability of OHEKA was another theatre in which to express continuities between the Old and New Worlds, and the attendees encompassed Wall Street power brokers and industrialists, international high society, writers and Hollywood celebrities: Enrico Caruso sang there, Arturo Toscanini conducted there, and the guest list included the Prince of Wales (the future Edward VIII), Sergei Eisenstein, Hart Crane, George Gershwin, Paul Robeson, Douglas Fairbanks and Charlie Chaplin, combining distinctively American figures with stalwarts of the European country-house scene.

Sold off after Kahn's death, OHEKA had a string of institutional residents, including New York City sanitation workers, World War Two radio trainees and military school cadets, before falling into ruin – a fate not unlike that of many European country houses. It was eventually restored and is now a hotel and events venue that makes much of its Gilded Age past. In its heyday, the house had provided a model for the estate of Jay Gatsby in Scott Fitzgerald's *The Great Gatsby* (1925) and for Orson Welles' vision of Charles Foster Kane's Xanadu, that fantastical amalgam of millionaires' houses in *Citizen Kane* (1941), in which it is seen from the air in the opening montage. This association with two great American fables about owning and belonging perpetuates a kind of mythological life.

Fallingwater

Fallingwater, in Pennsylvania's Laurel Highlands, could hardly be more different (see opposite and p. 323). Like the Villa Tugendhat in Brno (see pp. 283–97), it is widely regarded as a modernist masterpiece. Famous even before it was completed in 1937, Fallingwater has become a site of pilgrimage for students of Frank Lloyd Wright (1867–1959), the second phase of whose career it helped to launch. It was built as a mountain retreat for the Pittsburgh department-store millionaire Edgar Jonas Kaufmann (1885–1955) and his wife (and cousin) Liliane (1889–1952), whose social position, as Jews, was not straightforward. The site they chose for Fallingwater is at some distance from where the non-Jewish Pittsburgh elite, including Fricks, Mellons and Carnegies, focused their country life. The Kaufmanns were not welcome in country clubs such as the Rolling Rock Club in Ligonier Valley.

The Kaufmanns were confident in the use of architecture to create settings for both their retail and family lives. Benno Janssen had built them a family home inspired by old Norman manor houses in 1924: La Torelle, in the wealthy enclave of Fox Chapel, in the suburbs of Pittsburgh (see p. 322). Three years previously, Janssen had designed the stables at the Rolling Rock Club and, the following year, the Kaufmanns commissioned his Art Deco modernisation of the main selling floor of their flagship store. In 1946, after Fallingwater, with its superfluity of water, they asked Richard Neutra to build them, in Arizona, one of the first American desert houses. Hailed in Pittsburgh as a merchant prince and innovative master of the science of retail, Edgar, like his wife Liliane, was philanthropically engaged, moving in intellectually and socially progressive artistic circles. Edgar had been born in the United States, but his studies had taken him to Hamburg and Paris, and his interest in the modern architecture being developed there encompassed its possibilities for civic renewal as well as private commissions.

Cantilevered over Bear Run's rushing waterfalls, and intimately, geologically enmeshed in the landscape, Fallingwater exemplifies Wright's organic, transformational architecture, in which building, furnishings and environment are treated as one, embodying a relationship between man and nature that grows out of a specifically American experience of the landscape. As the distinguished scholar of English country houses Mark Girouard recognised long ago – echoing Edgar Kaufmann jr's own interpretation of how it played with country-house conventions –

for all its game-changing modernity, Fallingwater is rooted in the English eighteenth-century idea of the picturesque, and Romantic ideas about the relationship of buildings and nature, the *cottage ornée* and faux-ruined hermitages.[18] It comes to the Allegheny Mountains by way of nineteenth-century mountain houses, and the subsequent creation of holiday houses and camp houses, with their rough-hewn stonework and exposed logs, in wild country all over America.[19]

From 1890, Bear Run had been the site of vacation clubs run by various Masonic groups. In 1916, Kaufmann's Department Stores started to use it as an employees' camp, and in 1921, Edgar and Liliane built a little prefabricated cabin there for their own use, buying the property outright in 1933. So the place was already stamped with associations of rest, recreation and restoration in nature, whether in a collective and philanthropic holiday mode or as a more individual retreat into wilderness and simplicity.

The Kaufmanns rejected Wright's suggestion that they put gold leaf on the concrete; it is instead painted the pale earthy colour of the underside of the rhododendron leaves that grow in the woods all around it. Fallingwater is full of quiet luxury in the beautifully worked materials and meticulous engineering, for its service as both an intensely private family retreat and for sophisticated entertaining. Edgar Kaufmann jr recalled: 'What we wanted at Fallingwater was neither lordly stateliness nor a mimicry of frontier hardihood, but a good place for city people to renew themselves in nature.'[20]

The house was full of works of art from many periods and cultures. The Kaufmanns were friends with Frida Kahlo and Diego Rivera and acquired their work, alongside Mexican pottery and pre-Columbian art. Accessible from New York City, Fallingwater was also oriented eastwards and, with Edgar jr's curatorial position at the Museum of Modern Art as a catalyst, the guest list included figures such as the Alfred Barrs, Marcel Breuer, the Moholy-Nagys, Walter Gropius and Alvar Aalto. The rise of Nazism brought Europe to Fallingwater too. As chairman of the General

Council for Jewish Rights after September 1938, Kaufmann (Sr) worked to unite different sectors of American Jewry in dealing with the federal government. It was in this context that Albert Einstein came to Fallingwater for a conference that aimed to help Jews still trapped in Germany.

Edgar Kaufmann jr stressed that Fallingwater was not static and that the family never intended or expected it to be there for centuries. It was, in this sense, the very opposite of a dynastic edifice. However, in 1957, after his parents' death, he built a mausoleum for them, with great bronze doors by the Swiss sculptor Alberto Giacometti. In this way, when Kaufmann gifted Fallingwater to the Western Pennsylvania Conservancy in 1963, he ensured its survival as a shrine not just to modern architecture but also to his parents.

Crossing a little bridge to this private place one sees, on the left, a standing male figure; on the right a seated woman; distanced but contained, in a mysterious space with tree-like forms rising like swirling air above them. The iconography is suggestive of Adam and Eve and of Everyman, and the doors themselves call to mind Ghiberti's *Gates of Paradise* and Rodin's *Gates of Hell*. The material speaks of the greatest antiquity, from the bronze doors of Greek temples and treasuries, of arms and commemorative busts, to the bronze of the sacred vessels and ritual objects in the spaces outside the inner sanctum in the Temple of Jerusalem (only inside did God direct that gold should be used). But the site itself is modest. Both the footprint and the old stone wall, a remnant of one of the summer-camp buildings that predated Fallingwater, belie its sombre permanence.

In Europe, though not in North America, the country-house mausoleum is an established form. Through the double staircase and the French formal gardens at OHEKA, Otto Kahn had deliberately sought to inscribe his country home on Long Island within the European country-house tradition. Consciously or otherwise, Edgar Kaufmann jr did the same when he removed his parents from their original resting place in Pittsburgh and reinterred them in the mausoleum at Fallingwater. Here, as in Britain and Italy, this, like country houses themselves, was a tradition Jews too made their own.[21]

Edgar and Liliane Kaufmann
on the terrace at Fallingwater,
photographed in 1940.

Exploring the traces

The Low Countries

The Netherlands was unusual in not restricting either Jewish landownership or Jewish residence before the French Revolution. Little now recalls that early period, though material traces remain. Instead, two very different houses, one in the Netherlands and one in Belgium, evoke the more recent history of Jews in this part of Europe.

Kasteel de Haar in Utrecht was commissioned by Baron Étienne van Zuylen and his wife, Hélène de Rothschild, in the 1890s (see p. 26). Designed by the acclaimed Dutch architect Pierre Cuypers, it blends his signature medievalism with stylistic, heraldic and ornamental references to the baroness's family background, including the Star of David and the Rothschild coat of arms. All attempts by the Nazis to expropriate De Haar during the German occupation were frustrated by the family's steward, and the property remains in their ownership. Once denounced as an un-Dutch neo-Gothic fake, it is now admired as an eclectic *Gesamtkunstwerk,* attracting hundreds of thousands of visitors each year.

By contrast, the **Château de Seneffe**, a neoclassical architectural gem, has only recently begun to engage with its twentieth-century history as home, first, to the Philippson banking dynasty, and then to General von Falkenhausen, who presided over the Nazi occupation of Belgium (see pp. 23, 32–3). Restituted to the Philippsons after the war, it eventually passed to the region of Wallonia, which removed all traces of its Jewish owners and their English garden, restoring the house and its charming grounds to their eighteenth-century condition.

France

Paris was a focus for many of the great Jewish business dynasties of the modern era. Three French houses feature in this book: the **Château de Ferrières**, **Château de Champs-sur-Marne** and **Villa Kérylos** (Chapters 3, 6 and 8). Ferrières is now an events venue. All three were eventually donated by their Jewish owners to the French state. Champs, in particular, illuminates the passion of French Jews for the refinement of the *ancien régime*, whose forms were invoked and extended by specialist architects, artisans and gardeners. Several other houses, more or less accessible to the public, also speak to this history.

The **Château de Courances** in Essone was acquired in the 1870s by the German-Jewish banker Samuel de Haber, who had it renovated by Gabriel-Hippolye Destailleur, the architect of Waddesdon Manor. Opposite Kérylos at Saint-Jean-Cap-Ferrat, the Jewish architect Aaron Messiah was responsible for constructing the rose-coloured **Villa Ephrussi de Rothschild**, which blended French and Italian influences appropriate to its Riviera setting, and was filled with panelling, furniture and collections transported from the Rothschild mansions in Paris. Famed also for its exquisite gardens and musical fountains, Béatrice de Rothschild bequeathed Villa Ephrussi to the Institut de France. Yet the Jewish revival of Louis XVI style surely reached its apogee at the **Château Porgès de Rochefort-en-Yvelines**, constructed between 1899 and 1904 for the Austrian-born diamond magnate, Jules Porgès. Bringing together the cream of contemporary designers, including Charles Mewès, the Jewish architect behind the Ritz in Paris and London, this vast château was modelled on the Palais de la Légion d'Honneur in Paris, but with its neoclassical forms and dimensions doubled in size.

The importance of such houses as symbols of French culture is now recognised, but their Jewish histories are rarely celebrated. Partly this reflects the French tradition of state secularism, which treats Judaism as a religion and relegates all religion to the private sphere, and partly it reflects the legacy of the Nazi period. Memories of 1941 make it especially difficult to label individuals in public as Jews.

Right
Villa Kérylos

Italy

Jews have lived in Italy since Roman times. This deep, continuous history was shaped by the power of the Catholic Church, which chose to preserve a Jewish presence for theological reasons, while later dictating the segregation of Jews from Christians into urban ghettos. Jewish museums, synagogues and ghettos are now established features of the heritage landscape. Jewish country houses have been neglected, their Jewish associations forgotten and often left to decay, which is not, perhaps, an unexpected outcome in a country so rich in beautiful old buildings.

Neither of the two Italian houses that feature in this book are museums, although both **Castello Torre d'Alfina** and **Villa Montesca** are accessible and well preserved (Chapters 6 and 7). So too is **Villa Varda** in the Veneto, recently reopened as a museum, which was acquired by the Triestine Jewish businessman Baron Carlo Morpurgo de Nilma in 1867. He added an English park and a mausoleum to the original Renaissance house, and in 1941 his last male descendant bequeathed the property to the Catholic Church, which allowed his sister access to some parts for the next twenty years. You can learn more about this family and its cultural enthusiasms at the **Civico Museo Morpurgo** in nearby Trieste. **Villa Lattes** at Istrana, on the other hand, has managed against all the odds to preserve in situ the collections assembled by the lawyer Bruno Lattes during his extensive travels.

Most surviving houses are less attentive to their Jewish heritage. The monumental neoclassical **Villa Pignatelli** in Chiaia, Naples, built in 1826 and later acquired by Carl von Rothschild, who kept one room as a prayer room, now tells the story of a different family. Others, like **Villa Ottolenghi** at Marina di Ravenna, or the splendid Gothic Revival **Villa Adele** in the Colli Euganei, have become luxury hotels.

Germany

Jewishness weighs differently in the German context, for this has become a country eager to recall its Jewish past. At the time of writing, we believe two properties are open to the public: **Schloss Freienwalde** and the **Liebermann Villa**. Both are within easy reach of Berlin, both feature in this book (Chapters 9 and 11), and both were restored and reconfigured as museums in the aftermath of 1990, as part of the broader reconstruction that accompanied reunification.

These houses, whose owners were cousins, reflect several facets of German-Jewish life before the Holocaust: on the one hand, the socially aspirational Jewish business elite of the capital, many of whom acquired noble estates in the Brandenburg area or commissioned grand villas in the suburbs of Grunewald and Wannsee; on the other, Berlin's artistic and intellectual avant-garde, some of whom found inspiration in rural retreats. The Nazis, the war and several decades of communism have left few traces of these lost social worlds.

Those seeking to explore the remnants may seek out the **Einsteinhaus** in Caputh, a deceptively simple, modernist holiday home made of wood for the famous physicist; **Schweizerhaus Seelow**, an experimental farm established by the radical Jewish banker Hugo Simon; and the **Landhausgarten Dr Max Fraenkel** in Kladow, designed by Erwin Barth, one of Berlin's greatest garden designers. In addition, the **Museum Falkensee** honours the memory of the German-Jewish lyric poet Gertrud Kolmar, who lived in her father's nearby mansion and took inspiration from the pines, sandy paths and animals of this rural landscape. She was murdered in Auschwitz.

Other cities nurtured similar clusters. Close to Hamburg, at Blankenese on the River Elbe, the Warburg family provided shelter to young concentration camp survivors in their **White House,** now named for the Swedish Red Cross nurse, Elsa Brandström, a family friend.

Left
Villa Liebermann

327

The Habsburg lands and further east

After Jewish emancipation in 1867 and before its dissolution in 1918, the Habsburg empire proved surprisingly conducive to the acquisition, construction and development of country houses by Jews. The reasons for this varied. In Austria, it reflected the dominant position of the great Jewish business dynasties in Viennese high finance. In the Czech city of Brno, it reflected the dominance of Jewish families in industries like textiles and mining. In Hungary, it reflected the willingness of Jews to embrace the dominant Magyar nationality – and the eagerness of Magyars to assimilate them. In Galicia, it reflected the role that unemancipated Jews had played in estate management. Since then, Austria, the Czech and Slovak lands, Hungary and Poland have become separate polities, but only Hungary retains a significant Jewish presence.

All four of the Habsburg houses featured in this book (Chapter 12) are now located in Czechia. **Schillersdorf**, formerly in Prussian Silesia, has become a hotel, **Tobitschau castle** a local museum, and the **Brno villas** commissioned by the Stiassni and Tugendhat families are a major focus for local tourism. It is also possible to visit nearby **Eichhorn (Veveří) Castle**, acquired and restored by the banker and philanthropist Maurice de Hirsch, most likely for its excellent hunting.

Less is made of this heritage in **Austria**, which notoriously cultivated a self-image as the first victim of Nazism. Take **Schloss Rothschild**, in Waidhofen an der Ybbs: extensively remodelled after 1875, this thirteenth-century castle signalled the family's status as major landowners in Lower Austria, with a large forestry enterprise and some forty properties in the surrounding area. Restituted after the war and later transferred to public ownership, it is now a regional museum; little apart from the name recalls its former owners. In this context, eighteenth-century **Schloss Leopoldskron**, just outside Salzburg, is a rare exception. Its stunning interiors were lovingly restored during the 1920s by Max Reinhardt, one of the founders of the Salzburg Festival; he hosted many exclusive theatrical performances here before the palace was confiscated by the Nazis. A memorable shooting location for *The Sound of Music*, today it is a hotel and home to the Global Salzburg Seminar.

Jews occupy a more difficult space in present-day **Hungary**, where the Orbán regime promotes an ethnocentric, Christian nationalism. Significant Hungarian properties survive, but their Jewish dimension – and particularly the fate of their owners during the Holocaust – is rarely well addressed. Chief among them is **Schossberger-kastély** in Tura, a luxury hotel built in 1883 by Baron Sigmund Schossberger and inspired in part by Halton House, the Buckinghamshire home of Alfred de Rothschild. Sixty kilometres from Budapest, in Hatvan, the Hatvany-Deutsch family built and acquired numerous properties around the vast sugar factory and communal institutions they built in the town, including the historic **Grassalkovich-kastély**. Emptied of the family's collections, it now contains the Széchenyi Zsigmond Hunting Museum.

Further east, the parts of **Poland** and **Ukraine** that made up Galicia were once a unique centre for Jewish culture and Jewish landowning. However, processes of military occupation, genocide, forced emigration, spoliation and communist rule have left little for the tourist or the historian. Typical are the remains of a house in the village of **Svyatoi Dukh** in **Belarus**, which once belonged to Leiba Strugach/ Strugacz, owner of a wine and yeast factory (see p. 35). Inhabited in Soviet times, most recently by families of local schoolteachers, it deteriorated rapidly once it passed into private hands and cannot be visited, although it is now entering a new phase of renovation. An exception is **Villa Gartenberg**, just outside Lviv, seat of the Drohobych State Pedagogical University's history department, which has been in public use since 1911.

Finally, it is worth mentioning that Leopold Jan Kronenberg's Renaissance revival manor **Wieniec**, outside Toruń, in what was once Congress Poland, is also still standing. Although it lost its interior detailing after nationalisation in 1945, the building is now being restored for long-term use by the Kujawsko-Pomorski Teatr Muzyczny (Musical Theatre).

Scandinavia

The fascinating story of Jewish life in Scandinavia will be unknown to most readers of this book. In **Denmark**, the most famous country houses built by Jews are no longer standing. These include **Rolighed** (see pp. 20–1) in the district of Østerbro, where Hans Christian Andersen died, which belonged to the Melchiors, and **Skraenten** by the coastal town of Skodsborg in Sjaelland, which was the summer residence of the tobacco manufacturer and art collector Heinrich Hirschsprung, whose collection is preserved in Copenhagen's **Hirschsprunske Samling museum**.

In **Sweden**, however, there is more to see. In the seaside resort of Saltsjöbaden, where the industrialist Carl Robert Lamm and the noted collector Ernest Thiel both built summer villas, it is still possible to visit the **Grünewaldvillan**: named for the Russian-born Swedish-Jewish expressionist painter Isaac Grünewald, who lived and worked here from 1937. North of Stockholm, at Täby on the Baltic Sea, stands **Näsby Slott**, the seventeenth-century castle renovated by Lamm in 1903, and which now serves as a hotel.

Two other properties, both now museums, became important centres of local philanthropy. **Nääs estate**, outside Gothenburg, was home to the German-born Jewish merchant August Abrahamson, who died in 1898 and transferred the estate to the Swedish state through his will, establishing a foundation to protect the school for handicrafts he had created there (see p. 19). His niece Sophie Elkan also loved this place, sharing it with her close friend the novelist Selma Lagerlöf, who immortalised it in her fiction. Meanwhile, the **Zornsamlingarna** in Mora, on Lake Siljan, celebrates the work of painter Anders Zorn. Zorn's Jewish wife Emma (née Lamm) turned their rural home into a public museum in 1942 and spearheaded the couple's extensive philanthropic activity in Mora (see pp. 19–20). Swedish neutrality during World War Two protected such families and their heritage.

Britain

No fewer than six British houses feature in this book: **Salomons Estate**, **Hughenden Manor**, **Strawberry Hill**, **Waddesdon Manor**, **Nymans** and **Trent Park**. We could have included many more. Nowhere else does the country house occupy such a central place in the heritage landscape, thanks in large part to the National Trust, the largest mass-membership organisation in Europe. There are other factors too: the persistence of the monarchy and the House of Lords, which gives the trappings of aristocracy a continuing salience; the importance of the City of London as both the imperial capital and a global financial centre in which Jewish businessmen historically played an important part; and, of course, the fact that Jewish life in mainland Britain was not directly affected by the Holocaust.

Among National Trust properties, we would highlight especially **Upton House** (see p. 22), home to Lord Bearsted's extraordinary collection of Old Masters, both for its great art and for the family's important role in Jewish life. Many other National Trust properties have Jewish stories to tell: **Ightham Mote**, a medieval manor house whose owner Sir Thomas Colyer-Fergusson married into the Cousinhood, became the leading expert on Anglo-Jewish genealogy and set great store by his own Jewish heritage; **Mottisfont Abbey**, whose châtelaine Maud Russell (née Nelke) brought a taste for European modernism into rural Hampshire; **Monk's House**, the rural retreat of Leonard and Virginia Woolf; and even **Croft Castle**, saved for the nation by Diana Uhlman and other members of the Croft family. Her husband Fred, a German-Jewish artist who authored the classic novel *Reunion*, never learned to love his wife's ancestral home, but he spent a great deal of time there. Curators are committed to thinking harder about the role Jewishness plays in the history of these properties.

Other houses survive, many with an imperial dimension. **Houghton Hall**, one of the greatest English country houses, now cultivates the memory of Sybil Sassoon, who did so much to restore it. Two empire houses, **Port Lympne** (see pp. 301–2) and **Tylney Hall**, have become hotels, as has **Sea Marge** in Overstrand, home of the banker Edgar Speyer, notoriously accused of spying during World War One. Garden lovers, meanwhile, may visit the recently restored Pulham garden designed for Sir Francis Montefiore at **Worth Park**; **Exbury**, home to Lionel de Rothschild's extensive collection of rhododendrons, azalias and camellias; and **Highdown Gardens**, where Sir Frederick Stern created a celebrated garden in the chalk cliff face at Worthing and hosted annual summer camps for Jewish East Enders.

Two unique sites in Kent underscore the complexity of this heritage. The **Montefiore synagogue and mausoleum** in Ramsgate (see pp. 8–15 and opposite) tells a very Jewish story, while the twelve stained-glass windows designed by Marc Chagall and commissioned by the last of the d'Avigdor-Goldsmid family for the small medieval church in **Tudeley** (see p. 29) speak of integration, syncretism and assimilation.

Endnotes

A note on style

In this book we attempt to balance consistency, accessibility and scholarship. For example, we have not attempted to standardise different modes of Jewish identity. Individuals are described on a case-by-case basis, in ways that reflect their specific biographies and cultural frameworks: Max Liebermann was a German-Jewish painter, while the poet Emma Lazarus sought to popularise the idea of a hyphenated Jewish-American identity, and Felix Adler – who founded the Ethical Culture movement – was a German–American progressive of Jewish origin.

Where possible we have also sought to give this book a properly European flavour. Towns like Prague, Venice and Vienna retain their commonly anglicised forms, but in other ways we have tried to retain the original foreign-language forms for proper nouns: Napoléon not Napoleon, Walther not Walter and so on. Where place names are contested, for example in parts of Central and Eastern Europe, we have tried to use both forms. In the case of books, organisations and institutions, we have opted to use both the full foreign-language titles and their English translations in the first instance only.

A Jewish and a European story (pp. 8–37)

1. Our thanks to Michael Hall, Peter Mandler, Elizabeth Emery, Lila Corwin Berman, Esther da Costa Meyer and Petr Svoboda for their feedback on an earlier draft of this introduction.

2. Abigail Green, *Moses Montefiore: Jewish Liberator, Imperial Hero*, Cambridge, Massachusetts, Harvard University Press, 2010.

3. Ibid., p. 98.

4. Rev. D. A. Jessuran Cardozo & Paul Goodman, *Think and Thank: The Montefiore Synagogue and College, Ramsgate*, Oxford & London, Oxford University Press, 1933, pp. 192–3.

5. Joseph Mallord William Turner RA, *East Cliff Lodge, Ramsgate, the seat of Lord Keith* (c. 1796–7): www.bonhams.com/auction/28250/lot/80/joseph-mallord-william-turner-ra-london-1775-1851-east-cliff-lodge-ramsgate-the-seat-of-lord-keith [accessed 9 September 2023].

6. Susannah Avery-Quash & Kate Retford (eds), *The Georgian London Townhouse: Building, Collecting and Display*, London, Bloomsbury Publishing, 2019; Christopher Simon Sykes, *Private Palaces: Life in the Great London Houses*, London, Chatto & Windus, 1985.

7. Ruth Sebag-Montefiore, *A Family Patchwork: Five Generations of an Anglo-Jewish Family*, London, Weidenfeld & Nicolson, 1987, p. 36.

8. The Judith Lady Montefiore College, now transferred to London, continues to train rabbis to this day.

9. Helen Rosenau, 'Montefiore and the Visual Arts', in Sonia & Vivian D. Lipman (eds.), *The Century of Moses Montefiore*, Oxford, Oxford University Press, 1985, pp. 118–28; Sebag Montefiore, *A Family Patchwork*, plates between pp. 28–9.

10. 'Missverständnis 69. Reiche Juden haben weder Geschmack noch Manieren' and 'Missverständnis 70. Goût Juif ist schlechter Geschmack', *100 Missverständnisse über und unter Juden,* exhibition catalogue, Vienna, Jüdisches Museum Wien, 2022, pp. 152–5. This exhibition underlines the continued relevance of this trope.

11. It was in this spirit that an early assessment of this book dismissed Montefiore as a subject because 'he was not a collector, except of Jewish things'. Review commissioned by Yale University Press and the National Trust.

12. Trying to come up with a catalogue of properties that captured the architectural trends of the era, Clive Aslet acknowledged it was no easy thing to differentiate between 'country houses proper and smaller country houses or houses in the country'. Clive Aslet, *The Last Country Houses*, New Haven & London, Yale University Press, 1982, p. 309. See also Jill Franklin, *The Gentleman's Country House and its Plan, 1835–1914*, London, Routledge & Kegan Paul, 1981. Mark Girouard too engaged with many different scales and kinds of country house in his work: Mark Girouard, *Life in the English Country House: A Social and Architectural History*, New Haven, Yale University Press, 1978; *The Victorian Country House*, New Haven, Yale University Press, 1979; and *Life in the French Country House*, London, Cassell & Co., 2000.

13. Amid the excellent studies of the country-house tradition in France, Spain, Sweden and Czechia there exists no general survey of country houses in Europe; however, for an earlier British perspective on European houses, see Marcus Binney & Alex Starkey (eds), *Great Houses of Europe: From the Archives of Country Life*, London, Aurum, 2003. In Scandinavia and the Low Countries, the term 'estate architecture' is preferred, as part of a larger nexus of 'manorial worlds'; see Jonathan Finch, Mikael Frausing & Signe Boeskov (eds), *Estate Landscapes in Northern Europe*, Aarhus, Aarhus University Press, 2019.

14. Project researchers Silvia Davoli and Luisa Levi d'Ancona Modena have identified over 100 in Italy; Marcus Roberts has identified a similar number in Britain; Mia Kuritzén Löwengart has identified over 80 in Sweden within the project 'Judiska herrgårdar i Sverige – en pilotstudie'; in the Netherlands, Sietske van der Veen estimates the total to be at least several dozen. In Galicia, there were 561 Jewish landowners by World War One. Antony Polonsky, *The Jews in Poland and Russia: A Short History*, Liverpool, Liverpool University Press, 2013, p. 121.

15. Pauline Prevost-Marcilhacy, *Les Rothschild: bâtisseurs et mécènes*, Paris, Flammarion, 1995, and *Les Rothschild: une dynastie de mécènes en France (1873–2016)*, 3 vols., Paris, Somogy, 2016; Esther da Costa Meyer & Claudia Nahson, *The Sassoons*, New Haven, Yale University Press, 2023; Malcolm Brown, 'Anglo-Jewish Country Houses from the Resettlement to 1800', *Jewish Historical Society of England: Transactions and Miscellanies*, vol. 28 (1981–2), pp. 20–38.

16. Stephanie Barczewski, *How the Country House Became English*, London, Reaktion Books, 2023.

17. See, however, Abigail Green, Juliet Carey & David Rechter (eds), 'Beyond the Pale: The Country Houses of the Jewish Elite', special issue of the *Journal of Modern Jewish Studies*, vol. 18, 2019.

18. See the argument made in David Sorkin, *Jewish Emancipation: A History Across Five Centuries*, Princeton, Princeton University Press, 2019.

19. See Matthew M. Reeve, 'Gothic Architecture and the Liberty Trope' in Joan Coutu, Jon Stobart & Peter Lindfield (eds), *Politics and the English Country House, 1688–1800*, Montreal, McGill-Queen's University Press, 2023, esp. pp. 93–5.

20. Laura Leibman, 'From Pastoral to Georgic: The Dutch Jewish Country House as a Rhizome', *Journal of Modern Jewish Studies*, vol. 18, 2019, pp. 399–423.

21. Brown, 'Anglo-Jewish Country Houses', p. 21.

22. Robert Liberles, 'The Jews and Their Bill: Jewish Motivations in the Controversy of 1753', *Jewish History*, vol. 2, 1987, p. 34.

23. 'East Tytherley Manor': research.hgt.org.uk/item/east-tytherley-manor [accessed 12 December 2022].

24. Abigail Green & Marcus Roberts, 'A Jewish Landed Interest', in Christopher Ridgeway & Miles Taylor (eds), *The British Aristocracy and the Modern World*, London, British Academy (forthcoming).

25. The situation in the colonies was very different; see Leibman, 'From Pastoral to Georgic'.

26. Malcolm Cross, *A House by the River. West Indian Wealth in West Devon: Money, Sex and Power over Three Centuries*, Oxford, Oxford University Press, 2022, Chapters 8–10.

27. Members of 'the Cousinhood' barely figure in the database of the Centre for the Study of the Legacies of British Slavery, a

complex source that needs to be interpreted carefully. Thus John Montefiore, whose name appears, was actually a person of colour, while Nathaniel de Rothschild received compensation not because he owned slaves (he didn't) but because he held a mortgage from a deceased owner. See Catherine Hall, Nicholas Draper, Keith McClelland, Kate Donington & Rachel Lang (eds), *Legacies of British Slave-Ownership: Colonial Slavery and the Formation of Victorian Britain*, Cambridge, Cambridge University Press, 2014.

28. William D. Godsey, 'Nation, Government, and "Anti-Semitism" in Early Nineteenth-Century Austria', *The Historical Journal*, vol. 51, 2008, pp. 49–85; Lisa Silverman, 'On Jews and Property in Provincial Central Europe: Leopold Kompert's 1848 Publications', *Journal of Modern Jewish Studies*, vol. 18, 2019, pp. 1–19.

29. Gabriele Schneider (ed.), *Freundschaftsbriefe an einen Gefangenen: Unbekannte Briefe der Schriftstellerin Fanny Lewald an den liberalen jüdischen Politiker Johann Jacoby aus den Jahren 1865 und 1866*, Frankfurt, Peter Lang GmbH, 1996, pp. 7–8.

30. Roman Sandgruber, *Rothschild: Glanz und Untergang des Wiener Welthauses*, Vienna, Molden Verlag in Verlagsgruppe Styria GmbH & Co., 2018, pp. 82–6.

31. Sandgruber, *Rothschild*, pp. 245, 268–72. On Jewish ennoblement, see William O. McCagg, *A History of Hapsburg Jews, 1670–1918*, Bloomington, Indiana University Press, 1992, pp. 145–58.

32. Sorkin, *Jewish Emancipation*.

33. Polonsky, *The Jews in Poland and Russia*, p. 121. See also Yehosua Ecker, 'From Plunder to Refuge in the Galician Countryside', unpublished conference paper presented at *Jewish Country Houses and the Holocaust in History and Memory*, Brno, 11 May 2023; Yehoshua Ecker, 'The Beautiful Manor House: Glimpses of Jewish Childhood in the Galician Countryside', *Polin: Studies in Polish Jewry: Childhood, Children and Childrearing*, vol. 36, 2024, pp.65–88.

34. Stanley Weintraub, *Charlotte and Lionel: A Rothschild Marriage*, London, Pocket Books, 2004, p. 78.

35. Jarosław Kurski, *Dziady i dybuki,* Warsaw, Agora, 2022, p. 238; page numbers and quotes refer to the English translation of the manuscript kindly shared by Jarosław Kurski.

36. Christine Oliwkowki, *Die Familie Mosse und das Rittergut Schenkendorf 1896–1996: Ein Beitrag zur Regionalgeschichte*, Berlin, Bebra Verlag, 2017; Elisabeth Kraus, *Die Familie Mosse: Deutsch-jüdisches Bürgertum im 19. und 20. Jahrhundert*, Munich, C. H. Beck, 1999.

37. George Mosse, *Confronting History: A Memoir*, Madison, University of Wisconsin–Madison, 2000, pp. 7–16.

38. On Salomon's educational work, see Anders Hammarlund, *A Prayer for Modernity: Politics and Culture in the World of Abraham Baer (1834–1894)*, Stockholm, Svenskt Visarkiv, 2013, pp. 224, 228. Thanks to Mia Kúritzen Löwengart and to Matilda Eriksson, who is working on a comparative study of the musealisation of the Zorn House and the Liebermann Villa.

39. Fredric Bedoire, *The Jewish Contribution to Modern Architecture, 1830–1930*, New York, KTAV Publishing House, 2004, p. 475.

40. Louis Hyman, *The Jews of Ireland: From Earliest Times to the Year 1910*, Jewish Historical Society of England, London, and Israel Universities Press, Jerusalem, 1972, p. 150.

41. András Koerner, *How They Lived: The Everyday Lives of Hungarian Jews, 1867–1940*, Budapest, CEU Press, 2015, pp. 157–8; J. M. Cohen, *The Life of Ludwig Mond*, London, Methuen, 1956, pp. 141–2, 145–6.

42. On the less well-known 'Rothschild-Viertel' in Lower Austria see Sandgrüber, *Rothschild,* pp. 245–56.

43. Here see Leora Auslander, 'The Modern Country House as a Jewish Form: a Proposition', *Journal of Modern Jewish Studies*, vol. 18, 2019, pp. 466–88.

44. Arne Vestbø, *Moritz Rabinowitz: en Biografí*, Oslo, Spartacus Forlag, 2011.

45. Jackie Wullschläger, *Hans Christian Andersen: The Life of a Storyteller*, London, Allen Lane, 2000, pp. 389–92. The dedication is from a plaque at Rolighed, where he died.

46. Robert Henriques & Marcus Samuel, *First Viscount Bearsted: Founder of 'Shell' Transport and Trading Company*, London, Viking Press, 1960, pp. 20–21.

47. Michael Stevenson, *Art & Aspirations: The Randlords of South Africa and their Collections*, Cape Town, Fernwood Press, 2002, pp. 63–8, 75.

48. da Costa Meyer & Nahson, *The Sassoons*, pp. 139–41. See also Stanley Jackson, *The Sassoons*, London, Arrow, 1968, p. 32.

49. See Tom Stammers, 'Patriarch's Society', *Apollo*, vol. 197, 717, March 2023, pp. 146–57; da Costa Meyer & Nahson, *The Sassoons*.

50. Eva Isaacs Reading, *For the Record: The Memoirs of Eva, Marchioness of Reading*, London, Hutchinson, 1973, pp. 109–11; Tom Stammers, 'Jewishness, Antiquity and Civilization; Alfred Mond, Lord Melchett (1868–1930) and the Renewal of a Collecting Legacy', *Journal of the History of Collections*, vol. 34, 2022, pp. 427–40.

51. Cyril Grange, *Une élite parisienne: les familles de la grande bourgeoisie juive (1870–1939)*, Paris, CNRS Editions, 2016.

52. This story was explored in a 2018–19 exhibition at the Musée Nissim de Camondo, *L'art de vivre selon Moïse de Camondo*.

53. Margot Finn & Kate Smith (eds), *The East India Company at Home, 1757–1857*, London, UCL Press, 2018, pp. 4, 9. See also Jon Stobart & Mark Rothery, *Consumption and the Country House*, Oxford, Oxford University Press, 2016.

54. Peter Stansky, *Sassoon: The Worlds of Philip and Sybil*, New Haven, Yale University Press, 2012, pp. 263–6.

55. Alice S. Legé, *Les Cahen d'Anvers en France et en Italie: demeures et choix culturels d'une lignée d'entrepreneurs*, Paris, LGDJ / Institut Louis Joinet, 2022, pp. 229–62.

56. René Brion & Jean-Louis Moreau, *Franz Philippson: aux origines de la Banque Degroof*, Brussels, Devillez, 2016, pp. 145–8.

57. James McAuley, *The House of Fragile Things: Jewish Art Collectors and the Fall of France*, New Haven, Yale University Press, 2021, pp. 198–203.

58. Bedoire, *The Jewish Contribution*, p. 37.

59. Sietske van der Veen, 'A Rothschild Legacy in Utrecht: Hélène de Rothschild and the Rebuilding of De Haar Castle': jch.history.ox.ac.uk/article/rothschild-legacy-utrecht [accessed 9 September 2023].

60. Emily Russell (ed.), *A Constant Heart: The War Diaries of Maud Russell, 1938–1945*, Dorset, Dovecote Press, 2017, p. 20.

61. Milantia Errera-Bourla, *Une histoire juive, les Errera: parcours d'une assimilation*, Brussels, Editions Racine, 2000, p. 102.

62. Michael Hall, '"Le Goût Rothschild": The Origins and Influences of a Collecting Style', in Inge Reist (ed.), *British Models of Art Collecting and the American Response: Reflections across the Pond*, Farnham, Routledge, 2014, pp. 101–16.

63. Christoph Sattler, 'My Grandfather Carl Sattler, James Loeb's Friend and Architect', in *James Loeb: Collector and Patron in Munich, Murnau and Beyond*, Hermann Mayer (ed.), Munich, Hirmer, 2018, p. 128.

64. Tom Stammers, 'Old French and New Money: Jews and the Aesthetics of the Old Regime in Transnational Perspective c.1860–1910', *Journal of Modern Jewish Studies*, vol. 18, 2019, pp. 489–512.

65. Elana Shapira, *Style and Seduction: Jewish Patrons, Architecture and Design in Fin-de-Siècle Vienna*, Waltham, Brandeis University Press, 2016, pp. 18–19.

66. Jonathan Freedman, *The Jewish Decadence: Jews and the Aesthetics of Modernity*, Chicago, University of Chicago Press, 2021; William Whyte, 'The Englishness of English Architecture: Modernism and the Making of a National International Style, 1927–1957', *Journal of British Studies*, vol. 48, 2009, pp. 441–65.

67. See the essays in Elana Shapira (ed.), *Designing Transformation: Jews and Cultural Identity in Central European Modernism*, London, Bloomsbury Publishing, 2021.

68. Kurski, *Dziady i dybuki,* p. 259.

69. McAuley, *House of Fragile Things*, pp. 4–5.

70. Mary Neervort-Moore, *The History of All Saints' Tudeley*, London, Bloomsbury Publishing, 2014.

71. W. T. Stead, *The Splendid Paupers: A Tale of the Coming Plutocracy*, London, Review of Reviews, 1894, pp. 48, 57, 62.

72. H. G. Wells, *Tono-Bungay*, London, Penguin Classics, 2005, pp. 16, 65.

73. Tom Stammers, 'Catholics, Collectors, and the Commune: Heritage and Counterrevolution', *French Historical Studies*, vol. 37, 2014, p. 84. In a debate in the Chambre des Députés on 27 May 1895, Alfred Naquet tried to dispel the perception that the majority of plutocrats were Jews.

74. Luisa Levi-D'Ancona, 'Italian-Jewish Patrons of Modern Art in Nineteenth- and Twentieth-Century Italy', *Ars Judaica*, vol. 16, 2020, p. 6.

75. Sietske van der Veen, 'Novel Opportunities, Perpetual Barriers: Patterns of Social Mobility and Integration among the Jewish Dutch Elite, 1870–1940', doctoral thesis, Utrecht University, 2024; Peter Sutton, *Reclaimed: Paintings from the Collection of Jacques Goudstikker*, New Haven, Yale, 2008. A collaborative project, led by Elyze Storms-Smeets, is investigating the fate of all Dutch houses in the war: 'War in Arcadia: Country Houses in the Dutch-German Border Area, 1940–44'.

76. Flora Aghib Levi D'Ancona, *La Nostra Vita con Ezio e Ricordi di guerra*, ed. Luisa Levi D'Ancona Modena, Florence, Florence University Press, 2021, pp. 179–80.

77. For an initial exploration of these issues, see Abigail Green, 'Insider-Outsiders', *London Review of Books*, 18 February 2021.

78. Hannah Arendt, *The Origins of Totalitarianism*, New York, World Publishing Company, 1958, p. 40.

79. Kraus, *Die Familie Mosse*.

80. See David Cannadine, *The Decline and Fall of the British Aristocracy*, New Haven, Yale University Press, 1990; Joseph Mordaunt Crook, *The Rise of the Nouveaux Riches: Style and Status in Victorian and Edwardian Architecture*, London, John Murray, 1999.

81. Selma Stern, *The Court Jew: A Contribution to the History of the Period of Absolutism*, Philadelphia, Jewish Publication Society of America, 1950; Daniel Schroeter, *The Sultan's Jew: Morocco and the Sephardi World*, Stanford, Stanford University Press, 2002.

82. David Cannadine, 'Cousinhood', *London Review of Books*, vol. 11, 27 July 1989. In contrast, see Israel Bartal, 'Nationalist Before His Time or a Belated *Shtadlan*? – Guidelines for the Activities of Moses Montefiore', in Bartal (ed.), *The Age of Moses Montefiore*, Jerusalem, Misgav Yerushalayim, 1987, pp. 5–24.

83. ChaeRan Freeze (ed.), *A Jewish Woman of Distinction: The Life & Diaries of Zinaida Poliakova*, trans. Gregory Freeze, Waltham, Brandeis University Press, 2019, p. 7.

84. Deborah Cadbury, *The School that Escaped the Nazis*, London, Public Affairs, 2022.

85. Hildegard Feidel-Mertz & Andrea Hammel, 'Integration and Formation of Identity: Exile Schools in Great Britain', *Shofar*, vol. 23, 2004, pp. 71–84.

86. Amy Zahl Gottlieb, *Men of Vision: Anglo-Jewry's Aid to Victims of the Nazi Regime*, London, Orion University Press, 1998, pp. 33, 56–8, 61–72, 104–8.

87. Natalie Livingstone, *The Women of Rothschild: The Untold Story of the World's Most Famous Dynasty*, New York, St Martin's Press, 2021, p. 298.

88. Laura Hobson-Faure, 'Exploring Political Rupture through Jewish Children's Diaries: Kindertransport Children in France, 1938–1942', *Journal of Modern European History*, vol. 19, 2021, pp. 1–16.

89. 'Reopening of the Jewish Museum, 1947', Archives of Jewish Museum London, box 3, JML/1/C/3. Jewish house owners were involved in protecting other precious collections, see

Caroline Shenton, *National Treasures: Saving the Nation's Art in World War II*, London, John Murray, 2022.

90. Association for Researching the History of the Jews in Blankenese and Erhard Roy Wiehn (eds), *Cherries on the Elbe: The Jewish Children's Home in Blankenese 1946–1948*, trans. Judy Grossmann, Konstanz, Hartung-Gorre, 1996.

91. Luisa Levi D'Ancona Modena, 'Villa Mayer: A Space for Jewish Displaced Persons in Italy', unpublished conference paper presented at *Jewish Country Houses and the Holocaust in History and Memory*, Brno, 11 May 2023.

92. On the Lingfield children, see Rebecca Clifford, 'The Picture of (Mental) Health: Images of Jewish "Unaccompanied Children" in the Aftermath of the Second World War', *Journal of War & Culture Studies*, vol. 15, 2022, pp. 133–56.

93. See the testimony of Steven Mendelssohn for the Association of Jewish Refugees: www.ajrrefugeevoices.org.uk/RefugeeVoices/Steven-Mendelsson [accessed 9 September 2023].

94. Taking our cue from Michael Graetz, *The Jews in Nineteenth-Century France: From the French Revolution to the Alliance Israélite Universelle*, trans. Jane Marie Todd, Stanford, Stanford University Press, 1996, Chapter 8.

95. Peter Mandler, *The Fall and Rise of the Stately Home*, New Haven & Oxford, Yale University Press, 1997, part 4.

96. Michael Hall, *Waddesdon Manor: The Heritage of a Rothschild House*, New York, H. N. Abrams, 2002, p. 256.

97. 'The National Heritage', *Hansard*, vol. 380, cc.1039–150, 9 March 1977.

98. 'The first thing that strikes one about the Jewish country house is that it displays an extraordinary and individual taste.' Peer review commissioned by Yale University Press and the National Trust.

99. On Villa Antonini-Brunner, the splendidly embellished home of Rodolfo Brunner, a Jewish textile merchant from Trieste, see Daria Brasca, 'The Dispossession of Italian Jews: The Fate of Cultural Property in the Alpe Adria Region during the Second World War', *Studi di Memofonte*, vol. 22, 2019, pp. 81, 98; also Tullia Catalan, 'A Lost Jewish Heritage: Villa Antonini-Brunner during the Fascist and Nazi Persecution and Beyond', unpublished conference paper presented at *Jewish Country Houses and the Holocaust in History and Memory*, Brno, 12 May 2023.

100. Kurski, *Dziady i dybuki*, p.12.

101. However, there was also evidence of revival, with old houses restored and new ones built. See John Martin Robinson, *The Latest Country Houses*, London, Bodley Head, 1984.

102. Terence Dooley, Maeve O'Riordan & Christopher Ridgway (eds), *Women and the Country House in Ireland and Britain*, Dublin, Four Courts Press, 2017; Jeremy Musson, *Up and Down Stairs: The History of the Country House Servant*, London, John Murray, 2009; Lucy Lethbridge, *Servants: A Downstairs View of Twentieth-Century Britain*, London & New York, W. W. Norton, 2013; Stephanie Barczewski,

Country Houses and the Empire, 1700–1930, Manchester, Manchester University Press, 2016; Finn & Smith, *The East India Company*; Madge Dresser & Andrew Hahn (eds), *Slavery and the British Country House*, Swindon, English Heritage, 2013.

103. For details see jch.history.ox.ac.uk [accessed 5 July 2023].

104. Fiona Carnarvon, *Lady Almina and the Real Downton Abbey: The Lost Legacy of Highclere Castle*, New York, Crown, 2011.

105. Season 5 [list of errors]: there were secret Jews in Tudor England, but the great Sephardic families only arrived in the seventeenth century; rich Jews in Edwardian England never had 'Russian' origins – those who fled the pogroms were still poor immigrants; and no rich City Jew would have contemplated a country seat so far from the metropolis as Yorkshire.

106. Kurski, *Dziady i dybuki*, p. 531.

107. See *Light Lines: The Architectural Photographs of Hélène Binet*, exhibition catalogue, Royal Academy of Arts, London, 23 October 2021 – 23 January 2022.

Chapter 1
The stories we tell: Salomons Estate (pp. 42–57)

1. Abigail Green & Chris Jones, 'Vera Frances Salomons', *Shalvi/Hyman Encyclopedia of Jewish Women*, 31 January 2022: jwa.org/encyclopedia/article/salomons-frances-vera [accessed 10 September 2023].

2. 'Opening of David Salomons House', *The Courier*, 8 July 1938.

3. Deed of trust between Vera Salomons and Jewish Board of Guardians, 8 November 1937.

4. Chaim Bermant, *The Cousinhood: The Anglo-Jewish Gentry*, London, Eyre & Spottiswoode, 1971.

5. Michele Klein, 'The Young Photographer at Broomhill', *Jewish Country Houses*: jch.history.ox.ac.uk/article/young-photographer-broomhill [accessed 10 September 2023].

6. Salomons Estate: Dsh.m.00471.

7. M. D. Brown, *David Salomons House: Catalogue of Mementos*, privately printed, 1968, no. 522, p. 83.

8. D. L. Salomons, *A Souvenir of Broomhill, Kent*, Tunbridge Wells, Courier Printing, 1898, p.5; Salomons Estate: Dsh.m.00471.

9. See the auction catalogue *Sassoon: A Golden Legacy*, New York, Sothebys, 17 December 2020, pp. 46–7.

10. Brown, *David Salomons*, no. 79, p. 18; Salomons Estate: dsh.m.00079.1.

11. Moses Montefiore to D. L. Salomons, 3 March 1880, University of Southampton Special Collections (SSC), Ms 378/ A4162/1 no. 51.

12. D. L. Salomons, 'In the Days of My Youth', 19 January 1901, *The Courier* in Broomhill Scrapbook (I).

13. *Transactions of the Jewish Historical Society of England*, vol. 7, 1911–14, p. 325.

14. Abigail Green & Peter Bergamin, 'Vera Salomons and the Kotel: Reading International Jewish History through a Jewish Country House', *Journal of Modern Jewish Studies*, vol. 21, 2022, pp. 261–71; Salomons Estate: dsh.m.00823.

15. Albert Hyamson, *David Salomons*, London, Methuen, 1939, p. 105.

16. On Salomons' political career, see Geoffrey Alderman, 'Salomons, Sir David, baronet (1797–1873)' Oxford Dictionary of National Biography, 2004: www.oxforddnb.com [accessed 1 September 2023].

17. Seymour to D. Salomons, 29 September 1851, SSC, Ms 378/ A4162/1 no. 7.

18. Birmingham United Hebrew Congregation to D. Salomons, SCC, Ms 378/ A4162/1 no. 17.

19. Brown, *David Salomons*, no. 40, p. 10.

20. Alderman, 'Salomons, Sir David, baronet'.

21. See letter of thanks from the Guildhall to P. Salomons, SCC, MS 378/ A4162/1 no.6.

22. D. L. Salomons, *Bréguet (1747–1823)*, London, printed for the author, 1921, p. 6.

23. Salomons Estate: dsh.m.00016.2.

24. Salomons, *Souvenir of Broomhill*; Salomons Estate: Dsh.m.00471.

25. 'Electricity in the Home', *House Beautiful*, 15 February 1905.

26. 'Sir David Salomons motor stables, Broomhill', Historic England, listed 1 June 2012: historicengland.org.uk/listing/the-list/list-entry/1408552?section=official-list-entry [accessed 1 September 2023].

27. D. L. Salomons, *Breguet*, p. 5.

28. See letters about the donation in SSC MS378/A4162, 2/63–4, 66–70, 73.

29. Brown, *David Salomons*, pp. 58–9.

30. Hyamson, *David Salomons*, p. 105.

31. D. L. Salomons, *An Address to the Ladies of England*, Southborough, A. K. Baldwin, Steam Press, 1876.

32. Salomons Estate: dsh.m.00094. For more on Jewish women, family memory and material culture, see Laura Leibman, *The Art of the Jewish Family: A History of Women in Early New York in Five Objects*, New York, Bard Graduate Center, 2020.

33. Brown, *David Salomons*, nos. 57, pp. 1–2; Salomons Estate: dsh.m.0003, dsh.m.0006, dsh.m.0007.

34. Brown, *David Salomons*, no. 325, p. 63; Salomons Estate, dsh.m.00325 (1).

35. James Parkes, *The Story of Three David Salomons at Broomhill*, privately printed, 1950, p. 16.

36. Last Will and Testament of David Lionel Salomons, 7 June 1924, p. 7; Salomons Estate, dsh.m.00929.

37. *Catalogue of the Collection of Pictures, Engravings, Etchings and Sculpture at Broomhill, Kent*, Tunbridge Wells, A. K. Baldwin, 1881: no. 31 (Meditating on the book of Ecclesiastes), 32, 35, 80, 115, 122, 127; for Simeon Solomon see no. 39 (Abraham on the road to sacrifice his son Isaac); for Grant, no. 81. Abraham Solomon 'Doubtful Fortune' no. 103; Rebecca Solomon nos. 111, 119, 137.

38. Salomons Estate: dsh.m.00279.

39. A. Solomon to D. Salomons, undated, SCC, Ms 378/ A4162/1, no. 18.

40. For instance, Salomons owned Frederick Leighton's *The Knuckle-Bone Player*, *Broomhill Scrapbook* (I).

41. *Catalogue of the Library at Broomhill, Tunbridge Wells*, privately printed, 1916, p. vii.

42. Émile Bertaux, 'Préface' in Vera Salomons, *Charles Eisen*, London, John & Edward Bumpus, 1914, p. 9.

43. Vera Salomons, *Gravelot*, London, John & Edward Bumpus, 1911; *Choffard*, London, John & Edward Bumpus, 1912.

44. See the American Art Association/Anderson Galleries auction catalogue: *Rare & Valuable Colour Plate Books, from the Library of the Late Sir David Lionel Goldsmid-Stern Salomons*, London, American Art Association Anderson Galleries, 1930.

45. Trust deed, 23 November 1946, Warburg Institute Archives, Otto Kurz Bequest, Box 10.

46. Hansard vol. 366: debated on 10 December 1975.

Chapter 2
Hughenden Manor: a home for a prime minister (pp. 58–79)

1. William Flavelle Monypenny & George Earle Buckle, *The Life of Benjamin Disraeli, Earl of Beaconsfield, 1860–1881*, vol. II, London, John Murray, 1929, p. 1507; cited after Hannah Arendt, *The Origins of Totalitarianism*, London, Harvest, 1968, p. 70. Among the many biographies of Disraeli, see Robert Blake, *Disraeli*, London, Eyre & Spottiswoode, 1966; and Sarah Bradford, *Disraeli*, London, Weidenfeld & Nicolson, 1982.

2. Benjamin Disraeli, *Vivian Grey*, vols. 1 & 2, London, Henry Colburn, 1826, p. 50.

3. Arendt, *Totalitarianism*, p. 68.

4. Nathaniel Parker Willis, *Rural Letters and Other Records of Thoughts at Leisure: Written in the Intervals of More Hurried Literary Labor*, New York, Baker and Scribner, 1849, p. 57.

5. The popular handbook of the Cambridge Camden Society, first published in 1841. Initially offering guidance on the construction and conservation of ecclesiastical structures, but due to its growing influence, eventually offering criticism also.

6. Queen Victoria's Journals, RA VIC/MAIN/QVJ (W), 1 April 1852 [Princess Beatrice's copies].

7. Disraeli dubbed Queen Victoria his 'Faery Queen' in homage to Edmund Spenser's romantic reference to Elizabeth I.

8. Yvonne Lewis, Tim Pye & Nicola Thwaite, *100 Books from the Libraries of the National Trust*, Swindon, National Trust, 2023, pp. 78–9.

9. Martin Goodman, 'The Disraeli Family and the History of the Jews', *Journal of Jewish Studies*, vol. 71, 2020, pp. 141–60.

10. Thanks to Emma Hills for drawing my attention to this paper, and to Martin Goodman for interpreting its contents.

11. Benjamin Disraeli, 'Preface' in Isaac D'Israeli, *Curiosities of Literature*, London, Edward Moxon, 1849, p. xlii.

12. M. G. Wiebe et al. (eds) *Benjamin Disraeli Letters: 1852–1856*, Toronto, University of Toronto Press, 1997, vol. 6, no. 2572.

13. Marquis of Zetland (ed.), *The Letters of Disraeli to Lady Bradford and Lady Chesterfield: Volume I, 1873 to 1875*, London, Ernest Benn, 1929, p. 296.

14. Ibid.

15. M. G. Wiebe et al. (eds), *Benjamin Disraeli Letters: 1860–1864*, Toronto, University of Toronto Press, 2009, vol. 8, no. 3499.

16. Ibid.

17. Ibid., no. 3853.

18. Ibid., no. 3582.

19. Recent National Trust research indicates the historic inclusion of sainfoin in the fields to the west, close to and clearly visible from the manor.

20. Roy Jenkins, *Gladstone*, London, Papermac, 1996, p. 459.

21. Blake, *Disraeli*, p. 504.

Chapter 3
The Château de Ferrières: a European powerhouse (pp. 80–95)

1. Pauline Prevost-Marcilhacy, 'James de Rothschild à Ferrières: Les projets de Paxton et de Lami', *Revue de l'art*, no. 100, 1993, pp. 58–73; Pauline Prevost-Marcilhacy, *Les Rothschild: bâtisseurs et mécènes*, Paris, Flammarion, 1995.

2. Paul-André Lemoisne, *L'oeuvre d'Eugène Lami (1800–1890): lithograpies, dessins, aquarelles, peintures / essai d'un catalogue raisonné…*, Paris, H. Champion, 1914; *Eugène Lami: peintre et décorateur de la famille d'Orléans*, exhibition catalogue, Musée Condé, Château de Chantilly, 2019.

3. Anka Muhlstein, *James de Rothschild, Francfort, 1792 – Paris, 1868: une métamorphose, une légende*, Paris, Gallimard, 1981; Niall Ferguson, *The World's Banker: The History of the House of Rothschild*, London, Weidenfeld & Nicolson, 1998.

4. On all the Rothschild properties, see Prevost-Marcilhacy, *Les Rothschild: bâtisseurs et mécènes*.

5. Pauline Prevost-Marcilhacy, 'Un hôtel au goût du jour: L'hôtel de James de Rothschild', *Gazette des beaux-arts*, no. 1506–07, 1994, pp. 35–54.

6. Charles Raphaël Peyre, 'Les galeries célèbres et les grandes collections privées. II. Ferrières', *Le Correspondant*, 1892, pp. 440–53.

7. Mathieu Georges Dairnvaell, *Histoire édifiante et curieuse de Rothschild 1, roi des Juifs*, Paris, 1846; Alphonse Toussenel, *Les Juifs, rois de l'époque: histoire de la féodalité financière*, Paris, Librairie de l'École Sociétaire, 1845.

8. Quoted in Bertrand Gille, *Histoire de la Maison Rothschild 1848–1870*, vol. 2, Geneva, Librairie Droz, 1967, p. 98.

9. Jean Autin, *Les frères Pereire*, Paris, Librairie Académique Perrin, 1984; Frédéric Barbier, *Finance et politique: la dynastie des Fould XVIIIe – XXe siècle*, Paris, Armand Colin, 1991.

10. David Cohen, *La promotion des Juifs en France à l'époque du Second Empire (1852–1870)*, Aix en Provence, Université de Provence, 1980; Michael Graetz, *Les Juifs en France au XIXe siècle: de la Révolution française à l'Alliance israélite universelle*, Paris, Éditions du Seuil, 1989; Jean-Yves Mollier, 'De Rachel aux Rothschild: la place des Juifs dans la bourgeoisie parisienne entre 1850 et 1914', *Quarante-huit/Quatorze*, no. 4, 1990–1, pp. 37–43.

11. *L'Illustration*, 1852, p. 245.

12. Dominique Jarassé, *L'âge d'or des synagogues,* Paris, Herscher, 1993; *Les Rothschild en France au XIXe siècle,* exhibition catalogue, Bibliotèque Nationale de France, Paris, 2012.

13. Pauline Prevost-Marcilhacy, 'Les lotissements autour de la gare du Nord: le rôle de James de Rothschild', in Frédéric Jiméno, Karen Bowie & Florence Bourillon (eds), *Du clos Saint-Lazare à la gare du Nord: histoire d'un quartier de Paris*, Rennes, Presses Universitaires de Rennes et Comité d'Histoire de la Ville de Paris, 2018, pp. 201–18.

14. Prevost-Marcilhacy, *Les Rothschild: bâtisseurs et mécènes.*

15. In 1853, the Pereire brothers purchased important grounds in the Opéra area, thanks to a loan of 11 million from the Crédit Mobilier. They also built the Grand Hotel (designed by Alfred Armand, 1861–2), which would go on to become a model for many other hotels. François Loyer (ed.), *Autour de l'Opéra: naissance de la ville moderne,* Paris, Délégation à l'Action Artistique de la Ville de Paris, 1995.

16. Letter from Charlotte de Rothschild to Lionel de Rothschild, ARL RAL C/21/63.

17. Melun, Archives Départementales de Seine-et-Marne, 1585, 'Journal' 111 (1855) and 112 (1856), Travaux de construction du château. Id 'Journaux de Caisse', 158J 388-391 (1855–8).

18. Prevost-Marcilhacy, *Les Rothschild: bâtisseurs et mécènes.*

19. Edmond de Goncourt, *Journal des Goncourt: mémoires de la vie littéraire*, Paris, G. Charpentier et E. Fasquelle, 1912.

20. Françoise Bercé, 'Le château au XIXe siècle', in Jean-Pierre Babelon (ed.), *Le château en France,* Paris, Berger-Levrault, 1986, pp. 370–86.

21. On the collections, see Pauline Prevost-Marcilhacy, 'Le Château de Ferrières', in Pauline Prevost-Marcilhacy (ed.), *Les Rothschild: une dynastie de mécènes en France*, vol. 3, Paris, Musée du Louvre Éditions/BNF Éditions / Somogy Éditions d'Art, 2016, pp. 326–39.

22. See Laurent Haumesser (ed.), *Un musée éphémère: le musée Napoléon III au Palais de l'Industrie, mai–octobre 1862*, Paris, Musée du Louvre Éditions / Mare & Martin, 2021.

23. Édouard Drumont, *La France juive: essai d'histoire contemporaine*, vol. 2, Paris, Marpon et Flammarion, 1886, p. 116.

24. Prevost-Marcilhacy, 'Le Château de Ferrières', pp 326–9.

25. See Adrienne Childes, *Ornamental Blackness: The Black Figure in European Decorative Arts*, (forthcoming with Yale University Press), in which there is a substantial section about Cordier's Ferrières caryatids.

26. Isabelle Leroy-Jay Lemaistre (ed.), *Henry de Triqueti, 1803–1874: le sculpteur des princes*, exhibition catalogue, Orléans, Musée des Beaux-Arts, and Montargis, Musée Girodet, 2007–8. This exhibition demonstrated that the drawings for the Ferrières vase were the same as those created for the choir of St Paul's Cathedral.

27. Jean-Pierre Fournet, 'Les cuirs dorés des collections Rothschild dans les institutions publiques françaises', in Pauline Prevost-Marcilhacy, Laura de Fuccia & Juliette Trey (eds), *De la sphère privée à la sphère publique*, Paris, Publications de l'Institut National d'Histoire de l'Art, 2019.

28. *Archives israélites*, 7 October 1863.

29. 'Prince Napoleon has asked the Baron through Nigra to let him see Ferrières, which charms the great Baron,' wrote Leonora to Lionel de Rothschild in 1862. Archives Rothschild de Londres, RAL, RFAM/C/17/45.

30. Th. L, 'Visite de S.M l'empereur au château de Ferrières', *Almanach du département de Seine et Marne et diocèse de Meaux*, 1864, p. 141ff.

31. *Le monde illustré*, 27 December 1862; *The Times,* 10 December 1862.

32. ARL RAL 000 23 Evelina letters, Ferriéres, Tuesday morning, 16 December 1862.

33. *Almanach de Seine et Marne*, Diocèse de Meaux, Meaux, 1864.

34. Ibid., 1862.

35. Melun, Archives Départementales de Seine-et-Marne, 158J, Journal, 1867.

36. Fritz Stern, *L'or et le fer: Bismarck et son banquier Bleichröder,* Paris, Fayard, 1990.

37. Ferguson, *The World's Banker*, pp. 715–21.

38. Stern, *L'or et le fer.*

39. ARL, RAL, Londres RFamC /1/167 Hannah de Rothschild to Mayer, 12 September 1842.

40. Prevost-Marcilhacy, *Les Rothschild: bâtisseurs et mécène*; all the household linen from Paris, Boulogne and Ferrières was washed in this huge laundry, outside the castle near the Taffarette pond.

41. A. Gervais, *Petite monographie de Ferrières en Brie,* 1929, held at Archives Départementales de Seine-et-Marne, p. 9.

42. Melun, Archives Départementales de Seine-et-Marne: 'The Journaux de Caisse'. 1853–66: 158J 384–158J398, and 'Grand Livre 1856–1862': 158J 112–158J118.

43. James de Rothschild gave different works of art to Ferrières church in 1864, first testimony of the important Rothschild sponsorship in France: a sculpture, *Saint Jean Baptiste*, and a large painting, *Clovis Baptem*, both anonymous.

44. Melun, Archives Départementales de Seine-et-Marne, Ecole, Mairie, Asile, 1853–1903, 1MI92EDT.

45. For example, Worth Park in Sussex had a ballroom and theatre for the servants.

46. Reported by Leonora de Rothschild in a letter to her mother Charlotte Lionel de Rothschild, 12 September 1861: ARL, RAL, Londres RFAM C/6/ 16.

47. ARL RAL, Londres RFAM C21/ 67 Charlotte to Lionel, 29 March 1867.

48. Melun, Archives Départementales de Seine-et-Marne, 1703 W3: Ferrieres is sequestered by 'L'administration des Domaines for the Secours National', 1 April 1941.

49. Guy de Rothschild, *The Whims of Fortune*, London, Random House, 1985, p. 7.

50. Ibid., pp. 12, 35.

51. Ibid., p. 286.

Chapter 4
In Walpole's footsteps: Lady Waldegrave at Strawberry Hill (pp. 96–117)

1. Horace Walpole to his cousin Henry Seymour Conway, 8 June 1747, quoted in Anna Chalcraft & Judith Visconti, *Strawberry Hill: Horace Walpole's Gothic Castle,* London, Frances Lincoln, 2007, p. 16.

2. Matthew Reeve, *Gothic Architecture and Sexuality in the Circle of Horace Walpole*, University Park, Pennsylvania State University Press, 2020.

3. Thomas Babington Macaulay, *The Edinburgh Review*, October 1833.

4. Admiral William Waldegrave, quoted in Christopher Simon Sykes, *Black Sheep,* London, Chatto & Windus, 1982, p. 191.

5. Abraham Hayward, 'Strawberry Hill', *The Quarterly Review*, October 1876, p. 296.

6. David Conway, 'John Braham – from *Meshorrer* to Tenor', *Jewish Historical Studies,* vol. 41, 2007, p. 44.

7. *The Times*, 19 February 1856.

8. *The Bath Chronicle*, 15 December 1796.

9. Charles Lamb to Thomas Manning, 2 January 1810, from Thomas Noon Talfourd, in *The Life and Letters of Mr Lamb*, Philadelphia, Willis P. Hazard, 1856, p. 195.

10. Charles Lamb to Thomas Manning, 28 February 1808, in Edwin Marrs (ed.), *The Letters of Charles and Mary Anne Lamb,* vol. 2, Ithaca, Cornell University Press, 1976–8, p. 273.

11. J. E. Morpurgo (ed.), *The Autobiography of Leigh Hunt*, London, Cresset Press, 1949, pp. 125–6.

12. Somerset Heritage Centre, Strachie Papers, DD/SH/48/37, sale catalogue for the Grange, George Lewis, May 1842.

13. Ibid.

14. Ibid.

15. Ibid., DD/SH/48/38.

16. Osbert Wyndham Hewett, *Strawberry Fair*, London, John Murray, 1956, p. 60.

17. Playbill for Exeter Hall, 13 March 1852.

18. Osbert Wyndham Hewett, *And Mr Fortescue*, London, John Murray, 1958, p. 36.

19. Furniture History Society, British and Irish Furniture Makers Online database: bifmo. furniturehistorysociety.org

20. British Library Add MS 89287/1/2/1.

21. *Bristol Mercury*, 4 July 1863.

22. British Library Add Ms 89287/1/2/1.

23. British Library Add Ms 89287/1/2/5.

24. *The Illustrated London News,* 18 February 1860.

25. *The Athenaeum*, 25 February 1860.

26. Lady Strachey (ed.), *Letters of Edward Lear*, London, T. Fisher Unwin, 1907, pp. 132–3.

27. British Library Add MS 89287 1/1/1 Letter from John Hamilton Braham to Lady Waldegrave, 18 December 1858.

28. *Catalogue of the Third and Concluding Exhibition of National Portraits … on Loan to the South Kensington Museum*, 13 April 1868, London, Strangeways and Walden, p. 9.

29. Somerset Heritage Centre, Strachie Papers, DD/SH/64/358 Chichester Fortescue's Diary, 1 November 1860.

30. Ibid.

31. British Library Add Ms 89287/1/2/2.

32. British Library Add Ms 89287/1/2/1.

33. Ibid.

34. Ibid.

35. *The Art Journal Illustrated Catalogue of the International Exhibition*, London and New York, James Virtue, 1862, p. 310.

36. *The Illustrated London News*, 28 January 1863.

37. Adam Badeau, 'Strawberry Hill and the Countess Waldegrave', *The Cosmopolitan*, March 1892, pp. 535–41.

Chapter 5
Playing with the past at Waddesdon Manor (pp. 118–43)

1. Anthony Blunt, 'Destailleur at Waddesdon', in Denys Sutton (ed.), *Waddesdon Manor: Aspects of the Collection*, originally published in *Apollo*, vol. 105, no. 184, June 1977, pp. 9–15; the fullest account is Michael Hall, *Waddesdon Manor The Heritage of a Rothschild House*, London, Scala, 2002 (revised 2009). For the collections, Anthony Blunt & Geoffrey de Bellaigue (gen. eds.), *The James A. de Rothschild Bequest at Waddesdon Manor*, 16 vols., 1967–2013, including Bruno Pons, *Waddesdon Manor: Architecture and Panelling*, London, Philip Wilson, 1996; and Giles Barber, *Printed Books and Bookbindings*, 2 vols., Aylesbury, the Rothschild Foundation, 2013, cited here.

2. Pons, *Waddesdon Manor*.

3. Even the journalist Thomas Hay Sweet Escott, who deplored what he saw as 'the ascendency of the Jews', used this phrase and praised Ferdinand de Rothschild as a collector: Thomas Hay Sweet Escott, *Society in London*, New York, Harper & Brothers, 1885, p. 47.

4. The term '*goût* Rothschild' appears later in Britain, although the idea was long established; see Michael Hall, '"Le Goût Rothschild": The Origins and Influences of a Collecting Style', in Inge Reist (ed.), *British Models of Art Collecting and the American Response: Reflections Across the Pond*, Farnham, Surrey & Burlington, Vermont, Ashgate, 2014, pp. 101–15.

5. Ferdinand de Rothschild, *Reminiscences*, 1897 (bound typescript, Waddesdon Archive at Windmill Hill [WAWH hereafter], acc. no. 177.1997), p. 10; Chapter 3 of *Reminiscences*, which focuses on collecting and is entitled 'Bric-à-Brac', is published, Michael Hall, 'Bric-a-Brac – A Rothschild's Memoir of Collecting', *Apollo*, vol. 166, 2007, pp. 50–77.

6. Rothschild, *Reminiscences,* p. 19.

7. Ibid., p. 1 (at 17 rue Lafitte).

8 Victor Gray & Melanie Aspey (eds), *The Life and Times of N M Rothschild 1777–1836*, London, N. M. Rothschild and Sons, 1998, p. 112.

9. 29 September 1884, quoted in Hall, *Waddesdon Manor*, p. 151.

10. The chief rabbi called it 'the key-note of his entire career' in his address at Ferdinand's funeral, which was much reported, including in the *Evening Post*, 4 March 1899 (supplement).

11. Rothschild, *Reminiscences*, pp. 37, 54; the most comprehensive account of Rothschild houses is Pauline Prevost-Marcilhacy, *Les Rothschild: bâtisseurs et mécènes*.

12. Rothschild, *Reminiscences*, pp. 22–33.

13. Ibid., p. 55; for Gunnersbury see Diana Davis, 'A Rite of Social Passage: Gunnersbury Park, 1835–1925, a Rothschild Family Villa', in Abigail Green, Juliet Carey & David Rechter (eds), 'Beyond the Pale: The Country Houses of the Jewish Elite', special issue of the *Journal of Modern Jewish Studies,* vol. 18, 2019, pp. 443–65.

14. For Lionel de Rothschild's 148 Piccadilly, see Diana Davis, *The Tastemakers: British Dealers and the Anglo-Gallic Interior 1785–1865*, Los Angeles, Getty Publications, 2020, pp. 231–7.

15. David Kessler, 'The Rothschilds and Disraeli in Buckinghamshire,' *Jewish Historical Studies*, vol. 29 (1982–6), pp. 231–52.

16. For Devey's estate villages, see Cathy Soughton, 'George Devey and the Rothschild Estate Buildings in the Vale of Aylesbury 1850–1910', *Records of Buckinghamshire*, 55 (2015), pp. 261–85.

17. H. Wyatt to Ferdinand, 12 September 1891, WAWH, acc. no. 55.2004.

18. Pons, *Waddesdon Manor*, pp. 324–48.

19. Gabriel Metsu, *A Lady Playing a Lute, and a Cavalier*, 1662–5, acc. no. 2571.

20. Rothschild, *Reminiscences*, p. 83 (Hall, 'Bric-a-brac', p. 60); Sèvres porcelain manufactory, pot-pourri vase, 1762, acc. no. 2315.

21. Ibid., p. 71 (ibid., p. 56).

22. Ibid., p. 74 (ibid., p. 57).

23. Ibid., p. 69 (ibid., p. 55).

24. Ibid., p. 65 (ibid., p. 54).

25. Francesco Guardi, *The Bacino di San Marco with the Molo and the Doge's Palace, Venice* and *The Bacino di San Marco with the Churches of San Giorgio Maggiori and Santa Maria della Salute, Venice, c.*1755–70, acc. no. 2212, 1 & 2.

26. Joshua Reynolds, *Emily Warren as Thaïs*, 1781, acc. no. 2556.

27. John Vincent (ed.), *The Crawford Papers: The Journal of David Lindsay, Twenty-Seventh Earl of Crawford and Tenth Earl of Balcarres, 1871–1940, During the Years 1892–1940*, Manchester, Manchester University Press, 1984, p. 49 (18–20 June 1898).

28. Anthony Geraghty, *The Empress Eugénie in England: Art, Architecture, Collecting*, London, Burlington Press, 2022, p. 46; Diana Davis recently found evidence in Ferdinand's account books that craftsmen from Mouchy also worked on Waddesdon.

29. Geraghty, *The Empress Eugénie in England Art*, pp. 171–225.

30. One obituarist wrote: 'the family is the sphere of its own aristocracy. It is an aristocracy of its own. It is a universality.' *Manchester Evening News,* 17 December 1898.

31. Edward Morris, *French Art in Nineteenth-Century Britain*, New Haven and London, Yale University Press, 2005, pp. 202–3.

32. See Barber, *Printed Books and Bookbindings.*

33. Rothschild, *Reminiscences*, p. 67 (Hall, 'Bric-a-brac', p. 55).

34. See Pons, *Architecture and Panelling*, pp. 209–88.

35. Beauvais tapestry manufactory after designs by François Boucher, *The Flute Player* and *The Fountain of Love* from the 'Noble Pastorale' series, 1755–78, acc. nos. 2438.2-2438.3; for 'this misuse' see Bruno Pons, *Grands décors français, 1650–1800*, Quétigny, Éditions Faton, 1994, p. 144.

36. Ferdinand de Rothschild*, Personal Characteristics from French History*, London, Macmillan, 1896, p. 74.

37. See Guillaume Faroult, Monica Preti & Christoph Vogtherr (eds), *Delicious Decadence: The Rediscovery of French Eighteenth-Century Painting in the Nineteenth Century,* Farnham, Ashgate, 2014; Ferdinand de Rothschild, *Personal Characteristics from French History*, p. 75; see also Colin Jones, Juliet Carey & Emily Richardson, *The Saint-Aubin Livre de Caricatures: Drawing Satire in Eighteenth-Century Paris*, Oxford, SVEC, 2012, pp. 17–21.

38. For the *Ballet de la nuit*, 1663, acc. no. 3666, see Michael Burden and Jennifer Thorp (eds), *Ballet de la Nuit,* New York, Pendragon Press, 2010; *Livre de cariatures*, 1740–*c.*1775, acc. no. 675.

39. 'Lady Glendale' exists in manuscript, 1882, WAWH, acc. no. 176.1997, while *Vroni*

and *The Legend of Samandal* were privately printed, 1885 and 1879 respectively. For a list of Ferdinand's printed lectures, articles and books, including contributions to the Liberal monthly *The Nineteenth Century,* see Barber, *Printed Books and Bookbindings*, vol. 1, pp. 73–4.

40. Ferdinand de Rothschild, *Village Lectures*, privately printed, London, 1885, WAWH, acc. no. 227.

41. The trial took place 2–4 March 1886: hansard.parliament.uk/Commons/1886-03-08/debates/b0cc2895-355f-490d-baca-ce29ba965e43/Commons Chamber [accessed 25 September 2023]; *Bucks Herald*, 5 December 1885.

42. *Bucks Herald*, 12 December 1885.

43. Michael Hall, 'Baron Lionel de Rothschild (1808–1879): The Biography of a Collector of Pictures', PhD dissertation, Courtauld Institute of Art, London, 2005, pp. 296, 307.

44. George Romney, *Dorothea Bland, 'Mrs Jordan', as 'Peggy' in 'The Country Girl'*, 1786–7, acc. no. 2467; Joshua Reynolds, *Elizabeth Linley, Mrs Richard Brinsley Sheriden as Saint Cecilia*, 1774, acc. no. 2468; George Romney, *Emma Hart, Lady Hamilton, as Calypso*, 1791–2, acc. no. 2469.

45. In this context, see Emily D. Bilski & Emily Braun, *Jewish Women and their Salons: The Power of Conversation*, New York & New Haven, Yale University Press, 2005.

46. Rothschild, *Personal Characteristics*, p. 135; for the theatre's place in French society, see p. 132ff.

47. Thomas Gainsborough, *George, Prince of Wales, Later George IV*, 1781, acc. no. 2258; Joshua Reynolds, *Captain John Hayes St Leger*, 1778, acc. no. 2259.

48. Philip Magnus, *King Edward the Seventh*, London, John Murray, 1964, p. 106.

49. For example, Escott, *Society in London*, pp. 47–50.

50. Alice was a significant landowner, architectural patron and collector in her own right; see Rachel Jacobs, *Eythrope*, Waddesdon & Eythrope, Rothschild Foundation, 2020; *Alice's Wonderlands*, exhibition, Waddesdon Manor, 2022–3.

51. Ferdinand's account of the visit is published in Mrs James de Rothschild, *The Rothschilds at Waddesdon Manor,* London, Collins, 1979, pp. 46–60.

52. *Westminster Gazette*, 19 December 1898.

53. For 'The Renaissance Museum' see Dora Thornton, *A Rothschild Renaissance: Treasures from the Waddesdon Bequest*, London, British Museum Press, 1998; the Lyte Jewel, London, 1610–11, British Museum WB.167; boxwood tabernacle, northern Netherlands, *c*.1510–25, WB.233.

54. The Pressburg Cup, WB.104; Dora Thornton, 'Baron Ferdinand Rothschild's Sense of Family Origins and the Waddesdon Bequest in the British Museum', *Journal of the History of Collections*, vol. 31, 2019, pp. 181–98; the Holy Thorn Reliquary, Paris, *c*.1400, WB.67.

55. Thornton, 'Baron Ferdinand', p. 193.

56. The Tower Drawing Room and the Bachelors' Wing were remodelled, with Destailleur nominally in charge, but largely designed by his son, Walter-André Destailleur (who worked on Champs-sur-Marne for the Cahen d'Anvers), with the collaboration of the French interior designer Alfred André.

57. Rachel Boak, *Sacred Stitches: Ecclesiastical Textiles in the Rothschild Collection at Waddesdon Manor*, exhibition catalogue, Waddesdon, the Rothschild Foundation, 2013; for contemporary responses to the use of colour in Ferdinand's Waddesdon, see Hall, *Waddesdon Manor*, p. 122.

58. For the 'Cellini Bell,' Nuremberg, mid-sixteenth century, WB.95, see Thornton, *A Rothschild Renaissance*, pp. 310–17.

59. Ferdinand de Rothschild, 'The Expansion of Art', *The Fortnightly Review*, vol. 37, 1885, pp. 56–69 (57). For more on the historical self-awareness of collectors in this period, see Tom Stammers, *The Purchase of the Past: Collecting Culture in Post-Revolutionary Paris, c.1790–1890*, Cambridge, Cambridge University Press, 2020; Rothschild, *Reminiscences*, pp. 113–20 (Hall, 'Bric-a-brac', pp. 76–7).

60. *Daily Telegraph*, 21 December 1898.

61. 'The Red Book', Waddesdon Manor, acc. no. 54.

Chapter 6
Two houses, two countries, one cosmopolitan family: Torre Alfina and Champs-sur-Marne (pp. 144–59)

1. For an introduction to the European Jewish elite, see Catherine Nicault, 'Comment "en être"? Les Juifs et la haute société dans la seconde moitié du XIXe siècle', *Archives juives*, vol. 42, 2009, pp. 8–32.

2. On coat of arms, see Alice S. Legé, 'A Nineteenth-Century Entrepreneur, Owner and Collector: Meyer Joseph Cahen d'Anvers and the Permeable Boundaries of Nationality', *Journal of the History of Collections*, vol. 34, 2022, pp. 469–80. For context on Jewish ennoblement in Italy, see Paolo Pellegrini, 'Uscire dal Ghetto, ritornare nel Ghetto. Le resistenze alle nobilitazioni di ebrei in Italia dopo l'emancipazione', *Rivista di storia del cristianesimo*, vol. 14, 2017, pp. 83–102.

3. On the Cahen d'Anvers' investments, see Alice S. Legé, *Les Cahen d'Anvers en France et en Italie: demeures et choix culturels d'une lignée d'entrepenuers*, Paris, LGDJ & Institut Louis Joinet, 2022, pp. 48–54, 315–72.

4. Archives de la Ville de Paris, Registres de Déclarations Fiscales, *Déclaration de succession de Meyer Joseph Cahen d'Anvers*, DQ 7 11830, nos. 1399, 1436.

5. For context, see Glauco Schettini, 'Building the Third Rome: Italy, the Vatican, and the New District in Prati di Castello, 1870–1895', *Modern Italy*, vol. 24, 2019, pp. 63–79.

6. See Giuseppe Cuccia, *Urbanistica edilizia infrastrutture di Roma capitale 1870–1990*, Rome, Laterza, 1991; Piero Della Seta & Roberto della Seta, *I suoli di Roma: uso e abuso del territorio nei cento anni della capitale*, Rome, Editori Riuniti, 1988.

7. Giovanni Miccoli, 'Santa Sede, Questione ebraica e antisemitismo fra Otto e Novocento', in Corrado Vivanti (ed.), *Dall'emancipazione a Oggi, Gli Ebrei in Italia*, vol. 2 – *Storia d'Italia*, Annali 11, Turin, Einaudi, 1997, p. 1,399.

8. The couple married in London on 4 December 1868. Florence, Archivio Storico del Comune di Firenze, registration and transcription of marriage certificate, 28 December 1870, vol. 1870/8, no. 1517.

9. See Roberto Valeriani, *Palazzo Torlonia,* Rome, De Luca Editori d'Arte, 2018.

10. For a fuller description of Torre Alfina, see Legé, *Les Cahen d'Anvers*, pp. 397–500.

11. Rome, Ufficio Centrale degli Archivi Notarili, Notaio Ercole Buratti, *Istromento di ratifica di vendita di beni in Torre Alfina [...] fatta dal Sig. March. Guido Ubaldo B. del Monte a favore del Sig. Conte Edoardo Cahen a dì 25 settembre 1884*, reg. 56590, rep. 468–297.

12. Mario Montalto, *Vicende storiche di Torre Alfina: dalle origini al XIX secolo,* Grotte di Castro, Tipografia Ceccarelli, 2000.

13. Mario Montalto, '*Lasciato alla difesa di Torre Alfina terrò fermo finché avrò un sol uomo': fatti, personaggi e documenti dell'impresa garibaldina del 1867*, Grotte di Castro, Tipografia Ceccarelli, 1999.

14. Thomas Renard, *Dantomania: Restauration architecturale et construction de l'unité italienne (1861–1921)*, Rennes, Presses Universitaires de Rennes, 2019. More generally, Silvana Patriarca, *Italian Vices: Nation and Character from the Risorgimento to the Republic*, Cambridge, Cambridge University Press, 2013.

15. Italo Insolera, *Roma moderna: un secolo di storia urbanistica, 1870–1970*, Turin, Einaudi, 1983, p. 12.

16. On Partini's career, see Cristina Buscioni, *Giuseppe Partini: architetto del purismo senese*, Florence, Electa, 1981.

17. Busts of the couple were removed from the façade by the Cahen d'Anvers, but retained in their collections (Florence, private collection). See Francesco Piagnani & Lorenzo Principi, 'La scultura del Cinquecento in Orvieto', in Carla Benocci et al. (eds), *Storia di Orvieto: Quattrocento e Cinquecento*, vol. 2, Orvieto, Pacini, 2010, pp. 585–636.

18. Two painted friezes survive in the east wing of the castle, in two rooms never completed by Partini: the Sala della Caminata and the Sala dello Sforza. See Rhoda Eitel-Porter, *Disegni per Orvieto: dell''illustre concittadino Cesare Nebbia'*, Orvieto, Istituto Storico Artistico Orvietano, 2004, pp. 31, 140 and pl. XI, XIII.

19. Tommaso Pompei, *Torre Alfina e il suo castello*, ed. Benito Camilletti, n.c., n.p., [1892] 1999, p. 29.

20. See Axel Körner, *Politics of Culture in Liberal Italy: From Unification to Fascism*, London, Routledge, 2008, p. 103ff.

338

21. Édouard Cahen d'Anvers, *Lettres à Carlo Franci, 1888–1890*, Archivio dell'Opera del Duomo di Orvieto, Fenestroni nuovi delle pareti laterali del Tempio, Restauri, b. 12, VI.

22. For context, see Luisa Levi D'Ancona Modena, 'Giving and Dying in Liberal Italy: Jewish Men and Women in Italian Culture Wars', in Abigail Green & Simon Levis Sullam (eds), *Jews, Liberalism, Antisemitism: A Global History*, Cham, Palgrave Macmillan, 2021, pp. 153–82.

23. See Buscioni, *Giuseppe Partini*, pp. 43, 141.

24. On the Duchênes, see Michel Baridon, Michel Duchêne, Patrice Notteghem et al., *Les jardins des Duchêne en Europe*, exhibition catalogue, Le Creusot, Ecomusée Château de la Verrerie, 16 September 2000–27 February 2001, Paris: Le Creusot Neuilly, Association Duchêne Ecomusée du Creusot-Montceau Ed. Spiralinthe, 2000. On Torre Alfina's gardens, see Alice S. Legé, 'L'opera di Henri e Achille Duchêne: architetti paesaggisti al servizio dei Cahen d'Anvers tra Umbria e Lazio', *Saggi e memorie di storia dell'arte*, vol. 41, 2019, pp. 152–65.

25. Archives Nationales, Minutier Central des Notaires de Paris, Étude LXIV, 850, 1868, 28 December, *Procuration par M. Cahen (d'Anvers) à MM. Ses fils*; Bibliothèque de l'École des Mines, MINES ParisTech, *Journal d'un voyage en Belgique et en Piémont par Louis Cahen et E. Étranger (1858),* J 1858 (200) M 1858 194/199–201.

26. For comprehensive details of Louis's club membership, see *Bottin Mondain: annuaire du commerce Didot-Bottin*, Paris, Société du Bottin Mondain, 1920, p. 338.

27. On Destailleur, see Anne Dugast & Isabelle Parizet (eds), *Dictionnaire par noms d'architectes des constructions élevées à Paris aux XIXe et XXe siècles*, vols. 1–4, Paris, Service des Travaux Historiques de la Ville de Paris, pp. 1990–6; for the Hôtel Bassano, see Legé, *Les Cahen d'Anvers*, pp. 204–27.

28. Archives Nationales, Paris, Minutier Central, LXIV, 989, 1895, 5 August, *Vente par M. Santerre à M. Cahen d'Anvers [Louis]*; Archives Nationales, Paris, Minutier Central, LXIV, 989, 1895, 5 August, *États des meubles et objets mobiliers vendus par M. Santerre à M. Cahen d'Anvers [Louis]*.

29. Renaud Serrette, *Le Château de Champs*, Paris, Éditions du Patrimoine, 2017.

30. See, for example, Laurent Salomé, Claire Bonnotte & Catherine Pégard, *Versailles Revival 1867–1937*, exhibition catalogue, Château de Versailles, March 2019–March 2020, Paris, In Fine Éditions d'Art, 2019.

31. See Tullia Catalan, 'I Morpurgo di Trieste: una famiglia ebraica fra emancipazione ed integrazione (1848–1915)', in Filippo Mazzonis (ed.), *Percorsi e modelli familiari in Italia tra '700 e '900*, Rome, Bulzoni, 1997, pp. 165–86.

32. On the political connotations of the *ancien régime* aesthetic, see Daniel Brewer, '(Re) constructing an Eighteenth-Century Interior: The Value of Interiority on Display', in Denise Amy Baxter & Meredith Martin (eds), *Architectural Space in Eighteenth-Century Europe*, Farnham,

Ashgate, 2010, pp. 215–32; Stammers, 'Old French and New Money: Jews and the Aesthetics of the Old Regime in Transnational Perspective, c.1860–1910', *Journal of Modern Jewish Studies*, vol. 18, 2019, pp. 489–512.

33. See, for example, Domenica De Falco, *La femme et les personnages féminins chez les Goncourt*, Paris, Honoré Champion, 2012.

34. See Jean-Yves Mollier, 'Financiers juifs dans la tourmente des scandales fin de siècle à Paris (1880–1900)', *Archives juives*, vol. 29, 1996, pp. 65–82.

35. Édouard Drumont, *La France juive: essai d'histoire contemporaine,* Paris, Marpon et Flammarion, 1886; Auguste Chirac, *Les Rois de la République, histoire des juiveries*, Paris, Dentu, 1888.

36. Collection Cédric Rabeyrolles-Destailleur, Paris, *Mémoires de Walter-André Destailleur*, 1935.

37. A. Soyez, *Plan général du Domaine de Champs appartenant à M. le Comte Cahen d'Anvers*, 1899, ink on paper, Paris, Médiathèque de l'Architecture et du Patrimoine, PA00086861.

38. On Desgots, see Michel Racine (ed.), *Créateurs de jardins et de paysages en France de la Renaissance au début du XIXe siècle*, Arles, Actes Sud, 2001, pp. 73–5. This garden was later replaced by an Anglo-Chinese one.

39. Jean Mariette, *L'architecture françoise ou recueil des plans, elevations, coupes et profils des églises, palais, hôtels & maisons particulieres de Paris … & de plusieurs autres endroits de France…*, vol. 3, Paris, Mariette, 1727, pl. 363.

40. On the taste for antiquities in modern Europe, see Francis Haskell & Nicholas Penny, *Taste and the Antique: The Lure of Classical Sculpture 1500–1900*, New Haven & London, Yale University Press, 1988.

41. Achille Duchêne explained this proceeding to Ernest de Ganay in a letter dated 9 June 1926. This choice provoked a quarrel between the landscaper and Destailleur, analysed in Jean-Michel Sainsard, 'Histoire d'une vue brisée…', *L'année du jardinier,* Paris, 28 October 2016: www.anneedujardinier.blogspot.com [accessed 10 July 2023].

42. See Jean-Michel Leniaud, *Viollet-le-Duc ou les délires du système,* Paris, Mengès, 1994.

43. Serrette, *Le Château de Champs*, pp. 186–8.

44. Charles Cahen d'Anvers, *Le Château de Champs, notice historique,* Paris, 1928, p. 31.

45. On Cahen d'Anvers portraits, see Legé, *Les Cahen d'Anvers,* pp. 133–42; Guy Saigne, *Léon Bonnat: le portraitiste de la IIIe République. Catalogue raisonné des portraits*, Paris, Mare & Martin, 2017, cat. 100, 101, 101E, 102, 103, 104, 105.

46. Guy-Patrice & Michel Dauberville, *Renoir: catalogue raisonné des tableaux, pastels, dessins et aquarelles*, vol. 1, Paris, Bernheim-Jeune, 2007–12, cat. 253, 506, 558. See also Alice S. Legé, 'Irène Cahen d'Anvers et la Petite fille au ruban bleu. Biographie d'un tableau de Renoir', *Saggi e memorie di storia dell'arte*, vol. 46, 2024, pp. 103–14.

47. See Nicole Garnier-Pelle, Anne Forray-Carlier & Marie-Christine Anselm, *Singeries & exotisme chez Christophe Huet*, Saint-Rémy-en-l'Eau, Monelle Hayot, 2010, pp. 97–111.

48. See Alice S. Legé, 'Louise Cahen d'Anvers, née Morpurgo', in Ariane James-Sarrazin & Pauline d'Abrigeon (eds), *Collectionneurs, collecteurs et marchands d'art asiatique en France 1700–1939*, Paris, INHA, 2022.

49. On the Zalaffi and Corsini ateliers, see Alessandra Marzuoli, 'Le officine Zalaffi e l'arte del ferro battuto artistico a Siena tra Ottocento e Novecento', master's thesis, Università degli Studi di Siena, 1997; Mario Bandini and Renata Grappio, *Tito Corsini: ebanista intagliatore al Castello di Torre Alfina,* Turin, 2015.

50. Ridolfi achieved the decorations of Torre Alfina in 1912: Francesco Ridolfi, *I Ridolfi, artisti romani dal 1800 a oggi*, Rome, Bellini, 2009.

51. See Silvia Paoli (ed.), *Luca Beltrami 1854–1933: storia, arte e architettura a Milano*, Milan, Silvana Editoriale, 2014.

52. See Legé, *Les Cahen d'Anvers,* pp. 109–51.

53. For context, see Monique Eleb & Anne Debarre, *L'invention de l'habitation moderne: Paris 1880–1914*, Paris, Hazan, 1995.

54. Cubain, a French firm, also equipped the Hôtel de Camondo in Paris: Marie-Noël de Gary & Gilles Plum, *Les cuisines de l'hôtel Camondo*, Paris, Union Centrale des Arts Décoratifs, 1999.

55. Sonia Cahen d'Anvers (born Warschawsky), *Baboushka Remembers: Followed by a Diary of My Trip to Paraguay*, Bristol, 1972, p. 37.

56. James S. Ackerman, *The Villa: Form and Ideology of Country Houses*, Princeton, Princeton University Press, 1990.

57. More generally, see Stammers, 'Collectors, Catholics, and the Commune', *French Historical Studies*, vol. 37, 2014, pp. 53–87, 78ff. Drumont openly attacked the Cahen d'Anvers, see Drumont, *La France juive,* pp. XXXI, 231, 517–20; and *La dernière bataille: nouvelle étude psychologique et sociale*, Paris, Dentu, 1890, pp. 4, 12–15.

Chapter 7
Agriculture et ars: Villa 'La Montesca' in Città di Castello (pp. 160–83)

1. Rome, Associazione Nazionale per gli Interessi del Mezzogiorno d'Italia (ANIMI), carte Franchetti, 31 *Registro dei visitatori della Montesca* (from now *Registro*).

2. For a recent bibliography, see Rossella Pace (ed.), *L'eredità di Leopoldo Franchetti*, Soveria Mannelli, Rubbettino, 2020; Maria Luciana Buseghin, *Leopoldo Franchetti: passioni e progetti nel suo carteggio e nel rapporto con Alice Hallgarten*, Perugia, Deputazione di Storia Patria per l'Umbria, 2022.

3. Gian Battista Cerletti, 21–4 April 1901, *Registro*.

4. Mirella Scardozzi, 'Una storia di famiglia: i Franchetti dalle coste del Mediterraneo all'Italia liberale' *Quaderni storici*, vol. 114, 2003, pp. 697–740.

5. Sandra Carlini, Lara Mercanti & Giovanni Straffi, *I Palazzi: arte e storia degli edifici civili di Firenze*, vol. 2, Florence, Alinea, 2004, pp. 22–7.

6. Francesco Cotana, 'Giuseppe Boccini architetto', PhD thesis, Università di Perugia, 2021, p. 68; I refer to this thesis for all information on the architect Boccini. On the Franchetti tomb, see also Giulia Mariucci, 'L'antico cimitero ebraico fuori Porta San Frediano: un testimone del cammino di Emancipazione', in Dora Liscia Bemporad & Giovanna Lambroni (eds), *L'arte dell'eternità: iconografia, storia e tradizione nei cimiteri ebraici dell'Emancipazione*, Florence, Edifir, 2018, p. 41.

7. See references in Levi D'Ancona Modena, 'Italian-Jewish Patrons of Modern Art in Nineteenth- and Twentieth-Century Italy', *Ars Judaica*, vol. 16, 2020, pp. 7–8.

8. Edoardo Cosentino, *L'opera di Cleomene Marini (1853–1917) e la cultura artistica italiana dei primi decenni postunitari*, Rome, Espera, 2018, pp. 121–30.

9. Paul Errera to Marie Oppenheim, 8 September 1897, in Bruxelles, Musée Juif de Belgique, Fond Errera, box 5, file 28, no. 57. Original in French.

10. Cotana, 'Giuseppe Boccini', p. 68.

11. Cosentino, *Marini*, p. 65. See also *Amministrazione della Fabbrica della Villa alla Montesca*, Archivio Opera Pia Regina Margherita di Roma, Fondazione Franchetti di Città di Castello (henceforth *Montesca* archive). On Leopoldo and Africa, see Guazzini Federica, 'Leopoldo Franchetti e la questione fondiaria nell'Africa Italiana: tra progetti e realizzazioni', in Sandro Rogari (ed.), *Leopoldo Franchetti: la nuova destra e il modello toscano*, Soveria Mannelli, Rubbettino 2019.

12. Laura Hamad, 'Giovanni Panti, pittore e decoratore negli anni della Firenze capitale', in Sandro Rogari (ed.), *Ricerche di storia dell'arte,* vol. 115, pp. 45–52.

13. On the varnisher Fanfani and the carpenter Cappelletti, see www.storiatifernate.it [accessed 14 September 2023].

14. Opera Pia Regina Margherita, *Inventario degli oggetti esistenti nella villa*, Roma, 1923.

15. Giuseppe Amicizia, *Guida artistico-commerciale di Città di Castello*, Città di Castello, S. Lapi, 1899, p. 19.

16. Vida Dutton Scudder to Anne Whitney, 30 August 1910, Wellesley College Archives, Whitney papers: repository.wellesley.edu/object/wellesley12485 [accessed 23 March 2022].

17. Rogari (ed.), *Leopoldo Franchetti*; Pace (ed.), *L'eredità di Leopoldo Franchetti*.

18. Leopoldo Franchetti, *Dell'ordinamento interno dei comuni rurali in Italia*, Florence, Pellas, 1872, p. 71.

19. Sandro Rogari, 'Il modello Toscano: Moderatismo e mezzadria', in Rogari (ed.), *Leopoldo Franchetti*, p. 34.

20. Moe Nelson, *The View from Vesuvius: Italian Culture and the Southern Question*, Berkeley, University of California Press, 2006, pp. 236–49.

21. Paolo Carusi, 'L'attività di Franchetti alla Camera dei Deputati', in Rogari (ed.), *Leopoldo Franchetti*, pp. 69–91.

22. *La Rivendicazione*, 8 November 1902, quoted in Alvaro Tacchini, 'Le vicende politiche di Leopoldo Franchetti', in Paolo Pezzino & Alvaro Tacchini (eds), *Leopoldo e Alice Franchetti e il loro tempo,* Città di Castello, Petruzzi, 2002, p. 89.

23. Ibid.

24. *La Rivendicazione,* 26 August 1904, quoted in Tacchini, 'Le vicende politiche', pp. 90–93.

25. Ibid.

26. Tacchini, 'Le vicende politiche', p. 81.

27. Danilo Breschi, 'Le masse e le élites', in Rogari (ed.), *Leopoldo Franchetti*, p. 237.

28. *History of Hallgarten & Co*: hallgartenco.com/history.asp [accessed 3 April 2022].

29. On Alice and the Hallgarten network, see Maria Luciana Buseghin, *Alice Hallgarten Franchetti: un modello di donna e di imprenditrice nell'Italia tra '800 e '900*, Perugia, Pliniana, 2013, pp. 1–9. The Nordheimers were known for their commitment to women's education and poor relief in Hamburg. Alice mentions visiting Marcus Nordheimer in Nice in a letter to Aby Warburg, 28 March 1895, Warburg Archives, London (WIA) GC/9998.

30. Luisa Levi D'Ancona Modena, 'Baronesses and Revolutionaries: The Activism of Foreign-Born Jewish Women in Liberal Italy', *Journal of Modern Jewish Studies*, vol. 21, 2022, pp. 148–71.

31. Luisa Levi D'Ancona Modena, 'The "Beautiful Enigma": A Case-Study of German-Jewish Women in Collector Networks in Rome (1880–1914)', *Journal of the History of Collections*, vol. 34, 2022, pp. 507–19. For Alice's correspondence with various Warburgs, see Warburg Archives, London.

32. Max Strack to Max Warburg, 7 July 1898, WIA GC/27742; Alice Hallgarten to Aby and Mary Warburg, 14 April 1898, WIA GC/335.

33. Alice Hallgarten to Mary Warburg, 20 November 1898. Several letters from Malwida von Meysenbug to Alice Hallgarten are in Detmold, Landesarchiv Nordrhein-Westfalen, D.72. On Meysenbug's position during the Dreyfus affair, see Gaby Vinant, *Un esprit cosmopolite au XIXe siècle: Malwida de Meysenbug (1816–1903). Sa vie et ses amis*, Geneva, Slatkine, 1976, pp. 328–9.

34. Alice Hallgarten to Mary Warburg, 27 March 1900, WIA GC/472.

35. Sandra Dab, 'La philanthropie laïque, facteur d'intégration des Juifs sous la IIIe République' in Colette Bec, Catherine Duprat, Jean-Noël Luc & Jacques-Guy Petit (eds), *Philanthropies et politiques sociales en Europe (XVIIIe–XXe siècles)*, Paris, Anthropos, 1994, pp. 105–12. On the Colonia, see Rome, ANIMI archive, Carte Franchetti, 32.

36. Roberta Fossati, 'Alice Hallgarten Franchetti e le sue iniziative alla Montesca', *Fonti e documenti*, nos. 16–17, 1987–8, pp. 269–347.

37. For Alice's visit to Adler's school in New York, see Giuseppe Lombardo Radice, *Athena fanciulla*, Florence, R. Bemporad, 1925, p. 36.

38. Maria Buseghin, 'Alice Hallgarten Franchetti: A Woman Beyond Barriers', in Elena Laurenzi & Manuela Mosca (eds), *A Female Activist Elite in Italy (1890–1920): Its International Network and Legacy*, London, Palgrave Macmillan, 2021, pp. 9–13, 59–92.

39. Alice Franchetti to Marietta Pasqui, 20 April 1911, in Maria Lucia Buseghin, *Cara Marietta: lettere di Alice Hallgarten Franchetti (1901–1911)*, Città di Castello, Tela Umbra, 2002, p. 422. For the *Schloßherrin von La Montesca* expression, see Charlotte to Mary Warburg, 11 November 1900, WIA GC/27260.

40. Montesca archive, Registro n.1. Rubrica sussidi.

41. Aurelia Josz, 'Fiammella francescana', *Nuova Antologia*, vol. 164, 1913, pp. 278–85; 'Alice to Marietta, 14 May 1909', in Buseghin, *Cara Marietta*, p. 350. On Italian-Jewish women philanthropists in the world of textiles, see Luisa Levi D'Ancona Modena, 'Donne ebree filantrope nel tessile: lavoro, arte e tradizione nell'Italia liberale e oltre', in Paola Vita Finzi & Elisa Bianchi (eds), *Donne ebree protagoniste: tra il XIX e il XX secolo*, Milan, Guerini, 2023, pp. 63–81.

42. *Album dei visitatori*. www.telaumbra.it/images/archivio-storico/album-visitatori-tela-umbra.pdf. [accessed 10 September 2023]. For details on the workshop and a bibliography, see Buseghin, *Cara Marietta*, pp. 365–6.

43. Dario De Salvo, 'Alice nel paese della miseria', *Pedagogia Oggi*, vol. 17, 2019, pp. 81–95.

44. Alice Franchetti to Mary Warburg, 18 January 1902, WIA GC/10148.

45. Buseghin, *Cara Marietta*, p. 471. Later, some classes moved to the ground floor.

46. Guglielmo Baldeschi, *Per ricordo della Baronessa Alice Hallgarten Franchetti*, Città di Castello, S. Lapi, 1912.

47. *Catalogo ragionato degli oggetti esposti dalle scuole a sgravio della Montesca e Rovigliano*, 1924, pp. 9–10.

48. Claudia Frattini, *Il primo congresso delle donne italiane, Roma 1908: opinione pubblica e femminismo*, Rome, Biblink, 2008.

49. Alice funded the Italian translation of Latter's book: Lucy Latter, *Il giardinaggio insegnato ai bambini*, trans. Bice Ravà, Rome, Dante Alighieri, 1908. On Latter and Alice, see also Buseghin, *Cara Marietta*, pp. 514–17.

50. Esperimento Montesca, Quaderni autografi di Alice Franchetti, Montesca archive, B.2.

51. See, for example, Alice to Marietta, 14 January 1907, in Buseghin, *Cara Marietta*, p. 248; or 20 September 1907, p. 274.

52. See letters from Alice to Marietta Pasqui in February 1906, in Buseghin, *Cara Marietta*,

pp. 219–22. On Josz, see Paola D'Annunzio, Simonetta Haeger, Eleonora Heger Vita & Carla Schiafelli, *Aurelia Josz*, Milan, Unicopli, 2016.

53. Alice to Marietta, 12 February 1910, Buseghin *Cara Marietta,* p. 384. On Alice and theosophist circles in Paris as mediators of the Montessori method in France, see Letterio Todaro, 'La circolazione della pedagogia montessoriana attraverso le reti internazionali della fratellanza teosofica nei primi decenni del Novecento: il caso francese', *Rivista di storia dell'educazione*, vol. 8, 2021, pp. 109–21.

54. Edith Bradley, 1 May 1906, *Registro*.

55. Mary to Charlotte Warburg, 5 May 1901.

56. On Ernst Ziller (1837–1923), see Friedbert Ficker, Gert Morinek, Barbara Mazurek & Peter Mazurek, *Ernst Ziller: Ein sächsischer Architekt und Bauforscher in Griechenland: Die Familie Ziller Taschenbuch*, Allgäu, Josef Fink, 2003.

57. For Fortunato, see www.animi.it/pdf/giustino-fortunato.pdf [accessed 26 March 2022]. For a recent bibliography on Nathan, see Marisa Patulli Trythall (ed.), *Ernesto Nathan: l'etica di un sindaco*, Rome, Nova Delphi Libri, 2019.

58. Hermann Mayer & Brigitte Salmen (eds), *James Loeb: Collector and Patron in Munich, Murnau and Beyond*, Munich, Herman Publishers, 2018. See also Andrea Olmstead, 'The Toll of Idealism: James Loeb—Musician, Classicist, Philanthropist', *The Journal of Musicology*, vol. 14, 1996, pp. 233–62.

59. Friedrich Wilhelm Forster, *Il Vangelo della vita: libro per i grandi e per i piccoli*, Turin, Società Tipografico – Editrice Nazionale, 1908; See also Buseghin, *Cara Marietta,* p. 524.

60. Kerr-Lawson wrote about the 'Influence of the Franciscan Legend on Italian Art', in Robert Goff & James Kerr-Lawson (eds), *Assisi of Saint Francis*, London, Chatto & Windus, 1908; On the Franchetti and Sabatier, see Buseghin, *Cara Marietta*, pp. 503–6. On Vida Dutton Scudder and Alice, ibid., pp. 508–14.

61. See letters from Alice to Marietta, 1 January 1907 and 25 October 1909 in Buseghin, *Cara Marietta*, pp. 247, 358; Vida Scudder, *On Journey*, New York, E.P. Dutton & Co, 1937, p. 314.

62. Ibid., pp. 313–14.

63. Ibid., p. 317.

64. Todaro, 'La circolazione della pedagogia montessoriana' (see note 53), p. 115.

65. Alice to Marietta, 8 September 1911, in Buseghin, *Cara Marietta*, p. 444.

Chapter 8
Kérylos: 'the Greek villa' (pp. 184–205)

1. On Pontremoli see Dominique Jarrassé, 'Emmanuel-Élisée Pontremoli, architecte, directeur de l'École supérieure des Beaux-Arts', *Archives juives*, vol. 30, 1997, pp. 125–7.

2. Pierre Birnbaum, *Les Fous de la République: histoire politique des Juifs d'État de Gambetta à Vichy*, Paris, Fayard, 1992, p. 123. On Reinach's engagement with Jewish culture, see André Lemaire, 'Les Reinach et les études sur la tradition juive', *Comptes rendus de l'Académie*

des Inscriptions et Belles-Lettres, vol. 151, 2007, pp. 1105–16. Reinach's *Histoire des Israélites depuis l'époque de leur dispersion jusqu'à nos jours*, Paris, Librairie Hachette et Cie, 1884, was reprinted five times in his lifetime.

3. On the Reinachs, see Sophie Basch, Michel Espagne & Jean Leclant (eds), 'Les frères Reinach', *Colloque de l'Académie des Inscriptions et Belles-Lettres*, Paris, Diffusion de Boccard, 2008.

4. Marc Doin, Jean Leclant & Régis Vian des Rives (eds), *Kérylos, la villa grecque: Beaulieu-sur-mer à la belle époque* [1934], Marseille, J. Laffitte, 1994.

5. Ibid., p. 12.

6. Alain Pasquier, 'La sculpture délienne et Kérylos: un rendez-vous manqué', in Jean Leclant & André Laronde (eds), *Un siècle d'architecture et d'humanisme sur les bords de la Méditerranée: la villa Kérylos, joyau d'inspiration grecque et lieu de mémoire de la culture antique. Actes du 19ème colloque de la Villa Kérylos à Beaulieu-sur-Mer les 10 et 11 octobre 2008*, Paris, Académie des Inscriptions et Belles-Lettres, 2009, pp. 119–53.

7. Here the title given by Fabrice Reinach (Théodore's grandson) in one of his reflections on the villa in which he lived is misleading, see Fabrice Reinach, 'Le rêve de Théodore Reinach: la vie à Kérylos de sa construction au Musée', *Architecture du rêve. Actes du 3ème colloque de la Villa Kérylos à Beaulieu-sur-Mer les 29 & 30 octobre 1992*, Paris, Académie des Inscriptions et Belles-Lettres, 1994, pp. 25–34.

8. Pierre Gros, 'De Vitruve à Pontremoli: l'invention de la maison grecque', *Architecture du rêve. Actes du 19ème colloque de la Villa Kérylos à Beaulieu-sur-Mer les 10 & 11 octobre 2008*, Paris, Académie des Inscriptions et Belles-Lettres, 2009, pp. 203–36.

9. Fabrice Reinach, 'Cent ans de la vie de la Villa Kérylos', in Leclant & Laronde, *Un siècle d'architecture et d'humanisme*, 2009, pp. 1–19, p. 12.

10. Jean Cassou, *Le pillage par les Allemands des oeuvres d'art et des bibliothèques appartenant à des Juifs en France*, Paris, Editions du Centre, 1947, p. 222; Pierre Assouline, *Le dernier des Camondo*, Paris, Folio, 1999, p. 315. See also Patricia Kennedy Grimsted, 'Livres et archives pillés en France par l'Einsatzstab Reichsleiter Rosenberg', *Bulletin des Bibliothèques de France*, vol. 10, 2016, pp. 90–110.

11. Anatole Stebouraka, 'Livres et archives des Reinach spoliés sous l'occupation et retrouvés à Minsk (Biélorussie)', *Comptes rendus de l'Académie des Inscriptions et Belles-Lettres*, vol. 159, 2015, pp. 1089–115.

12. Reinach, 'Cent ans de la vie de la villa Kérylos', pp. 25–34.

13. Régis Vian des Rives & Marc Doin, 'Beaulieu au temps de Théodore Reinach: la Belle Époque', in Doin, Leclant & Rives (eds), *Kérylos, la villa grecque*, pp. 101–7.

14. Thierry Maulnier, *Cette Grèce où nous sommes nés*, Paris, Flammarion, 1964.

15. Théodore Reinach, 'La Grèce retrouvée par les Grecs', in *La Grèce, recueil de conférences faites sous les auspices de la Ligue pour la défense des droits de l'hellénisme*, Paris, Société Française d'Imprimerie et de Librairie, 1908, pp. 338–94. See also the catalogue of the exhibition: Jean-Luc Martinez, *Paris-Athènes: naissance de la Grèce moderne, 1675–1919*, Paris, Hazan, 2021.

16. Pasquier, 'La sculpture délienne et Kérylos', pp. 119–53.

17. The upright piano Reinach commissioned had a very modern Manxman mechanism installed by Baillie Scott; Marcus Binney, 'Villa Kerylos, French Riviera: The Property of the Institut de France. Part II', *Country Life*, 21 July 1983, p. 142.

18. Henri Lavagne, 'Quelques mosaïques de la villa Kérylos: essai de lecture iconographique', *Un siècle d'architecture*, pp. 81–118.

19. We may think here of Fulgentius (*Mythologiae* 1 *praef.* 6), apparently the inspiration behind the couplet in the library cited previously: *ut … velut Alcyonei niduli placidam serenitatem villatica semotione tranquilior agitassem*, 'so that … like Alcyone I might enjoy the calm peace of my little nest, at rest in the seclusion of a country estate'. Thanks to Llewelyn Morgan for this translation from Latin into English, and careful reading of this text.

20. Eduard Norden, *Agnostos Theos: Untersuchungen zur Formengeschichte Religiöser Rede*, Leipzig & Berlin, Teubner, 1913. New edition with commentary: Chiara Ombretta & Tommasi Moreschini (eds), *Agostos Theos, Deo ignoto: ricerche sulla storia della forma del discorso religioso*, Brescia, Morcelliana, 2002.

21. See Marc Delage, 'Résonances grecques dans les discours de saint Paul à Athènes', *Bulletin de l'Association Guillaume Budé*, vol. 3, 1956, pp. 49–69; and Nathalie Siffer, 'L'annonce du vrai Dieu dans les discours missionnaires aux païens', *Revue des sciences religieuses*, vol. 81, 2007, pp. 523–44.

22. I would like to record my thanks to the late Ernst Kitzinger for drawing my attention to this similarity.

23. Personal conversation with the author at Villa Kérylos.

24. Gaston Bachelard, *La terre et les rêveries du repos: essai sur les images de l'intimité*, 8th edition, Paris, 1977, p. 183.

25. *Revue des études juives*, n. I, 1880, p. vii. A. Lemaire, 'Les Reinach et les études juives', n. II, notes that Théodore published more than fifty articles in this periodical, which he supported throughout his life.

Chapter 9
Schloss Freienwalde: the Jewish restoration of a Prussian legacy (pp. 206–27)

1. Theodor Fontane, *Wanderungen durch die Mark Brandenburg, zweiter Band: Das Oderland*, Munich, Nymphenburger Verlag, 1977, p. 59.

2. Walther Rathenau, 'Staat und Judentum. Eine Polemik', in Edgar Büttner, Alexander Jaser, Martin Sabrow & Ernst Schulin (eds) *Walter Rathenau: Schriften der Wilhelminischen Zeit, 1885–1914*, Düsseldorf, Droste Verlag, 2015, pp. 798–833, p. 809.

3. Ibid., p. 819ff.

4. Politisches Archiv des Auswärtigen Amts, Bonn, Presseabteilung, Deutschland 9, Akten Reichsminister Dr. Rathenau, Bd. 1.

5. Hellmut von Gerlach, *Von Rechts nach Links*, Zürich, Europa-Verlag, 1937, p. 259f; Walther Rathenau, *Hauptwerke und Gespräche*, Munich, Schneider, 1977, p. 854.

6. Walther Rathenau, 'Apologie', in *Ders., Schriften aus Kriegs- und Nachkriegszeit*, Berlin, S. Fischer, 1929, p. 411–55, p. 439f.

7. Hermann Schmitz, *Schloss Freienwalde: Herausgegeben vom Kreisausschuss des Kreises Oberbarnim* (Rathenau-Stift gmbH), Berlin, Wasmuth, p. 9.

8. Ibid., pp. 5, 9.

9. Ibid., p. 10.

10. Ulf Meyer, 'Baumeister ohne Bauten. Der vor 250 Jahren geborene Friedrich Gilly war Vordenker der Moderne und hat dadurch die Architekturgeschichte geprägt', *Frankfurter Allgemeine Zeitung*, 16 February 2022; Schmitz, *Schloss Freienwalde*, p. 10f.

11. Hermann Schmitz, 'Schloss und Park Freienwalde', *Berliner Tageblatt*, 15 December 1926.

12. Ibid.

13. Schmitz, *Schloss Freienwalde*, p. 32.

14. 'Walther Rathenau an Gerhart Hauptmann, 23.12 1911', in Alexander Jaser, Clemens Picht & Ernst Schulin (eds), *Walther Rathenau, Briefe 1871–1913*, Düsseldorf, Droste Verlag, 2006, p. 1034f.

15. Entry from 16 March 1911, in Hartmut Pogge von Strandmann (ed.), *Walther Rathenau, Tagebuch 1907–1922*, Düsseldorf, Droste Verlag, 1967, p. 133.

16. Walther Rathenau, 'Zur Kritik der Zeit', in *Ders., Gesammelte Schriften*, Berlin, S. Fischer, 1925, pp. 7–148.

17. Ernst Schulin, 'Zu Rathenaus Hauptwerken', in Walther Rathenau, *Hauptwerke und Gespräche*, pp. 499–595.

18. 'Hans von Seeckt an Dorothea von Seeckt, 31.3.1917', in Hans Meier-Welcker, *Seeckt*, Frankfurt am Main, Bernard & Graefe, 1967, p. 184.

19. Rathenau, 'Staat und Judentum', p. 826f.

20. 'Lili Deutsch an Paul Kahn, 13.12.1909', in Hans Dieter Hellige (ed.), *Walther Rathenau. Maximilian Harden. Briefwechsel 1897–1920*, Munich, G. Mueller Verlag, 1983, p. 592, note 2.

21. Hans Fürstenberg, *Carl Fürstenberg: Die Lebensgeschichte eines deutschen Bankiers*, Wiesbaden, Rheinische Verlags-Anstalt, 1961, p. 478.

22. Ibid.

23. Ibid., p. 479.

24. Gustav Hillard, *Herren und Narren der Welt*, Munich, List, 1954, p. 232.

25. Stefan Zweig, *Die Welt von gestern: Erinnerungen eines Europäers*, Gütersloh, Bertelsmann, 1960, p. 204.

26. 'Walther Rathenau an Maximilian Harden, 14.7.1910', in Hellige, *Walther Rathenau*, p. 616.

27. In Fürstenberg's memories, the royal even became the 'Imperial Schloss Freienwalde (he had attached importance to the continuation of this title when he acquired it)'. Hans Fürstenberg, *Lebenserinnerungen*, Wiesbaden, Rheinische Verlags-Anstalt, p. 477.

28. 'Fritz von Unruh, Die Krone über dem Schloß Freienwalde hatte er mitgekauft: Erinnerungen an Walther Rathenau', *Der Tagesspiegel*, 9 June 1963.

29. 'Maximilian Harden, Moritz und Rina', *Die Zukunft*, 11 October 1913, p. 38, quoted from Hellige, *Walther Rathenau*, p. 592. Here Harden refers to the enamelled snuff boxes decorated with portraits of Frederick II that James Simon gave Wilhelm II; see Wolfgang Büscher, 'Ein Leben für Berlin', *Die Zeit*, 6 April 2006.

30. Walther Lambach, *Diktator Rathenau*, Hamburg, Deutschnationale Verlagsanstalt Aktiengesellschaft, 1918, p. 52.

31. Martin Sabrow, *Der Rathenaumord und die deutsche Gegenrevolution*, Göttingen, Wallstein Verlag, 2022, p. 114f.

32. Ernst Norlind, *Gespräche und Briefe Walther Rathenaus*, Dresden, Carl Reissner Verlag, 1925, p. 57.

33. Rathenau, 'Apologie', p. 439f.

34. Rathenau, 'Staat und Judentum', p. 191.

35. Quoted after Martin Sabrow, 'Schloßherr und Zeitkritiker', in Martin Sabrow, *Die Macht der Mythen: Walther Rathenau im öffentlichen Gedächtnis*, Berlin, Verlag Das Arsenal, 1998, pp. 37–66.

36. Schmitz, *Schloss Freienwalde*, p. 42.

37. Sabrow, 'Schloßherr und Zeitkritiker', p. 65.

Chapter 10
Nymans: an English house and garden (pp. 228–47)

1. For the full Messel family history and all references, see John Hilary, *From Refugees to Royalty: The Remarkable Story of the Messel Family of Nymans*, London, Peter Owen, 2021.

2. Robert Habel, *Alfred Messels Wertheimbauten in Berlin: Der Beginn der modernen Architektur in Deutschland*, Berlin, Gebr. Mann, 2009; Elke Blauert (ed.), *Alfred Messel 1853–1909: Visionär der Großstadt*, Berlin, Minerva, 2009.

3. 'Die Architektur dieses Anbaues wurde auf besonderen Wunsch des Besitzers in kontinentalen Formen gehalten.' The designs were published as 'Anbau zum Landhaus Nymanns [sic] bei Crawley (England)', *Architektonische Rundschau,* vol. 12, 1896, figs. 17–18.

4. Familiar from German ecclesiastical architecture, a similar lantern appears in Alfred Messel's 1896 design drawing for the State Museum of Hesse in Darmstadt: Architekturmuseum, TU Berlin, inv. no. 13429.

5. See the discussion of these and many similar buildings in Roderick Gradidge, *Dream Houses: The Edwardian Ideal*, London, Constable, 1980.

6. Artur Gärtner, Robert Habel & Hans-Dieter Nägelke, *Alfred Messel: Ein Führer zu seinen Bauten*, Kiel, Verlag Ludwig, 2010, especially Chapters 16 & 20.

7. From Rudolph Messel's unpublished notes for an autobiography, copies of which are available in the Nymans archive, along with an annotated transcript.

8. David Dolan & Leigh O'Brien, 'Sir Walter Tapper and the Guildford Grammar School Chapel', *Early Days: Journal of the Royal Western Australian Historical Society*, vol. 12, 2006, pp. 616–33.

9. Rosalys Coope, 'The "Long Gallery": Its Origins, Development, Use and Decoration', *Architectural History*, vol. 29, 1986, pp. 43–84. Leonard and Maud Messel were familiar with the long gallery at nearby Parham, the ceiling of which would be so memorably redesigned by their son Oliver in the 1960s.

10. Christopher Hussey, 'Nymans', *Country Life*, 10 September 1932, p. 295; Ian Nairn & Nikolaus Pevsner, *The Buildings of England: Sussex*, London, Penguin, 1965, p. 479.

11. According to Maud's daughter Anne, Countess of Rosse; see John Cornforth, 'Nymans, Sussex', *Country Life*, 5 June 1997, p. 60.

12. *Burke's Landed Gentry*, London, Shaw, 1937, p. 1584.

13. Intriguingly, Leonard's son Oliver Messel would also use the Star of David as the central motif on Sarastro's costume in his 1956 Glyndebourne production of Mozart's Masonic opera *The Magic Flute*; see the design drawing in the Oliver Messel Collection at the Victoria and Albert Museum, accession no. S.161-2006.

14. Even more intriguingly, a broken brick bearing a six-pointed star was found in the kitchen block at Nymans during recent building works, suggesting further traces of Jewish heritage. The design has, however, been identified as a standard feature of brick manufacturers P & S Wood of West Bromwich, who used the hexagram with a W in its centre as their mark; information supplied by Michael Hammett of the British Brick Society, October 2021. I am most grateful to Caroline Ikin of the National Trust for sharing this with me.

15. Adrian Tinniswood, *The Long Weekend: Life in the English Country House Between the Wars*, London, Jonathan Cape, 2016, p. 29.

16. Hussey, 'Nymans', *Country Life*, 10 September 1932, pp. 292–97, and 17 September 1932, pp. 320–25; George Taylor, 'Nymans: The Gardens', *Country Life*, 24 September 1932, pp. 346–52.

17. Eleanour Sinclair Rohde, 'The Nymans Garden Library', *Journal of the Royal Horticultural Society*, vol. 58, 1933, pp. 329–43.

18. Muriel Messel, *A Garden Flora: Trees and Flowers Grown in the Garden at Nymans by L. Messel, 1890–1915*, London, Country Life, 1918.

19. Shirley Nicholson, *Nymans: The Story of a Sussex Garden*, Stroud, Alan Sutton, 1992.

20. *West Sussex Gazette*, 1 April 1954, p. 6.

21. Vivian Lipman, 'The Rise of Jewish Suburbia', *Transactions of the Jewish Historical Society of England*, vol. 21, 1962, p. 84.

22. For the dialectic between Jewish space and assimilation, see Jürgen Heyde, 'Making Sense of "the Ghetto": Conceptualizing a Jewish Space from Early Modern Times to the Present', in Alina Gromova, Felix Heinert & Sebastian Voigt (eds), *Jewish and Non-Jewish Spaces in the Urban Context*, Berlin, Neofelis, 2015, pp. 37–61.

23. For the 'spy mania' that gripped Britain in the years leading up to World War One, see Christopher Andrew, *The Defence of the Realm: The Authorized History of MI5*, London, Allen Lane, 2009, pp. 10–52; for the experience of Britain's German-born minority during the war, see Panikos Panayi, *The Enemy in Our Midst: Germans in Britain During the First World War*, London, Bloomsbury, 1991.

24. See Linley Messel's entry in *Burke's Landed Gentry*, vol. 1, London, Burke's Peerage, 1965, pp. 498–9.

25. Jay Geller, 'Of Mice and Mensa: Anti-Semitism and the Jewish Genius', *The Centennial Review*, vol. 38, 1994, pp. 361–85.

26. Obituary leaflet reprinted from the *Mid-Sussex Times* of 11 February 1953, held in the Nymans archive, National Trust; the phrase is picked out in capital letters.

27. For an introduction, see Miri Song, *Choosing Ethnic Identity*, Cambridge, Polity, 2003.

28. For the British context, see Bryan Cheyette, *Constructions of 'the Jew' in English Literature and Society: Racial Representations, 1875–1945*, Cambridge, Cambridge University Press, 1993.

29. Sander Gilman, *The Jew's Body*, New York, Routledge, 1991, p. 177.

30. Deborah Cohen, 'Who Was Who? Race and Jews in Turn-of-the-Century Britain', *Journal of British Studies*, vol. 41, 2002, pp. 460–83.

31. Walter Laqueur, *A History of Zionism*, New York, Holt, Rinehart & Winston, 1972, p. 39. For a rejection of the essentialist myth written from the British context, see Cecil Roth, 'Are the Jews Unassimilable?', *Jewish Social Studies*, vol. 3, 1941, pp. 3–14.

32. Todd Endelman, 'German-Jewish Settlement in Victorian England', in Werner Mosse (ed.), *Second Chance: Two Centuries of German-Speaking Jews in the United Kingdom*, Tübingen, Mohr, 1991, pp. 37–56.

33. *Western Morning News*, 27 May 1929, p. 4.

Chapter 11
Max Liebermann's villa at Lake Wannsee: a public retreat (pp. 248–69)

1. Cited by Alfred Lichtwar, letter to the administration of the Hamburger Kunsthalle,
19 October 1910, in Alfred Lichtwar, *Reisebriefe: Briefe an die Kommission für die Verwaltung der Kunsthalle*, vol. 2, Hamburg, Westermann, 1924, p. 333. All quotations provided in this chapter are the author's own translations from the original German texts.

2. Regarding Liebermann's view of the house as a retreat, see for example the letter from Max Liebermann to Hermann Müller, 3 May 1920, in Ernst Braun, *Max Liebermann: Briefe*, vol. 6, Baden-Baden, Deutscher Wissenschafts-Verlag, 2016, p. 360. 'Tomorrow we will go to Wannsee and I'm happy that I'll be able to work again in peace and without distractions.'

3. Information here regarding the history of the Liebermann family is taken from Regina Scheer, *'Wir sind die Liebermanns': Die Geschichte einer Familie*, Berlin, Propyläen Verlag, 2006; Marina Sandig: *Die Liebermanns: Ein biographisches Zeit- und Kulturbild der preußisch-jüdischen Familie und Verwandtschaft von Max Liebermann*, Neustadt/Aisch, Degener, 2005.

4. Max Liebermann, 'Aus meinem Leben', in Herman Simon (ed.)*, Was vom Leben übrig bleibt, sind Bilder und Geschichten. Max Liebermann zum 150. Geburtstag*, exhibition catalogue, Stiftung Neue Synagoge Berlin – Centrum Judaicum and Jüdisches Museum Berlin, 1997, p. 148.

5. Michael Haupt (ed.), *Villencolonie Alsen am Großen Wannsee, Begleitband zur Ausstellung in der Gedenk- und Bildungsstätte Haus der Wannsee-Konferenz*, Berlin, 2012; Nils Aschnbeck, *Villen in Berlin – Kleiner Wannsee: Mit der Colonie Alsen und dem Kleist-Greb*, Petersberg, M. Imhof, 2011.

6. Matthias Eberle, *Max Liebermann 1847–1935. Werkverzeichnis der Gemälde und Ölstudien*, 2 vols., Munich, Hirmer, 1995, no. 1901/1.

7. Max Liebermann to Alfred Lichtwark, 10 May 1903, in Ernst Braun, *Max Liebermann: Briefe*, vol. 3, Baden-Baden, Deutscher Wissenschafts-Verlag, 2013, pp. 116–17.

8. Nina Nedelykov & Pedro Moreira, 'Die Liebermann-Villa am Wannsee und ihr Architekt Paul Otto Baumgarten', in Lucy Wasensteiner (ed.), *Wir feiern Liebermann! Leihgaben aus deutschen Sammlungen zu 25 Jahren Max-Liebermann-Gesellschaft*, exhibition catalogue, Berlin, Liebermann-Villa am Wannsee, 2020, pp. 167–87; also Nina Nedelykov & Pedro Moreira, 'Eine kurze Baugeschichte der Liebermann-Villa', in Martin Faass (ed.), *Die Idee vom Haus im Grünen: Max Liebermann am Wannsee*, Berlin, G & H, 2010, pp. 31–4.

9. Max Liebermann to Alfred Lichtwark, 26 July 1909, in Ernst Braun, *Max Liebermann: Briefe*, vol. 4, Baden-Baden, Deutscher Wissenschafts-Verlag, 2014, p. 309.

10. Moreira, Nedelykov, 'Eine kurze Baugeschichte der Liebermann-Villa', p. 32.

11. See for example Stefan Schweizer, 'Die zweite Gartenrevolution: Die Reform der Gartenkunst um 1900 im Kontext ihrer Zeit', in Martin Faass & Stefan Schweizer (eds), *Neue Gärten! Gartenkunst zwischen Jugendstil und Moderne*, exhibition catalogue, Berlin, Stiftung Schloss & Park Benrath, 2017, pp. 13–37.

12. Erich Hancke, *Max Liebermann, sein Leben und seine Werke*, Berlin, B. Cassirer, 1914, pp. 476–82.

13. Erich Hancke, 'Der Meister im Atelier', *Vossische Zeitung*, 19 July 1927, no. 166.

14. Regarding Liebermann's art collection, see Martin Faass (ed.), *Verlorene Schätze: Die Kunstsammlung von Max Liebermann*, exhibition catalogue, Berlin, Liebermann-Villa am Wannsee, 2013.

15. Max Liebermann to Alfred Lichtwark, 18 March 1910, Braun, *Max Liebermann*, vol. 4, pp. 379–80.

16. Max Liebermann to Alfred Lichtwark, 31 July 1910, Braun, *Max Liebermann*, vol. 4, pp. 418–19.

17. Max Liebermann to Max Sauerlandt, 11 August 1910, Braun, *Max Liebermann*, vol. 4, pp. 420–21.

18. Max Liebermann to Fritz Wichert, 28 July 1910, Braun, *Max Liebermann*, vol. 4, pp. 417–18.

19. Max Liebermann to Harry Graf Kessler, 13 May 1911, Ernst Braun, *Max Liebermann*, vol. 5, Baden-Baden, Deutscher Wissenschafts-Verlag, 2015, p. 77; Max Liebermann to Franz Servaes, 28 December 1910, Braun, *Max Liebermann*, vol. 4, pp. 470–71.

20. Max Liebermann to Alfred Lichtwark, 31 July 1910, Braun, *Max Liebermann*, vol. 4, pp. 418–19. Tschudi left the National Gallery in 1908 following a scandal surrounding his purchase of modernist works from the Barbizon school.

21. Max Liebermann to Alfred Lichtwark, 27 May 1911, Braun, *Max Liebermann*, vol. 5, pp. 80–81.

22. For example, a double-page spread in the journal *Haus Hof Garten* on the occasion of Liebermann's eightieth birthday: Anon., with photos by S. Frank, 'Professor Max Liebermann und Sein Heim. Zum 80. Geburtstag des Meisters', in *Haus Hof Garten*, vol. 49, 23 July 1927, pp. 354–5; For example: Willy Lange, *Gartengestaltung der Neuzeit*, Leipzig, J. J. Weber, published in six editions between 1907 and 1928, Liebermann's garden appearing from at least 1919.

23. With thanks to Katja Bomhoff of the Ullstein Bild photographic archive.

24. For example Eberle 1916/17 *The Kitchen Garden Looking to the North East, Flower Beds* and 1916/18 *The Floral Terrace in the Wannsee Garden Looking North West*; Eberle 1916/20 *The Floral Terrace in the Wannsee Garden Looking North East*; Eberle 1929/21 *View from the Birch Pathway Looking North West*; Eberle 1916/22 *The Garden Bench*, acquired by the National Gallery as a gift in 1917; 1919/15 *Flower Beds by the Gardener's House Looking North East*, gifted to the National Gallery in 1919; Eberle 1918/18 *Beeches on the Banks of the Lake in the Wannsee Garden Looking North*.

25. Quoted in Bernd Schmalhausen, *'Ich bin doch nur ein Maler': Max und Martha Liebermann im 'Dritten Reich'*, Hildesheim, Georg Olms Verlag, 2018, p. 43. The detail provided here, when not otherwise referenced, is taken from this comprehensive overview of the Liebermann family in the context of Nazism.

26. Martin Faass (ed.), *Der Jesus-Skandal: Ein Liebermann-Bild im Kreuzfeuer der Kritik*, exhibition catalogue, Berlin, Liebermann-Villa am Wannsee, 2009.

27. Franz Landberger, 'Erinnerung an Max Liebermann', p. 6, in Schmalhausen, *'Ich bin doch nur ein Maler'*, p. 43.

28. 11 May 1933, published in the *Central-Vereins-Zeitung*, in Schmalhausen, *'Ich bin doch nur ein Maler'*, p. 54.

29. Schmalhausen, *'Ich bin doch nur ein Maler'*, pp. 79–80.

30. Günter Busch, *Max Liebermann 1847–1935*, exhibition catalogue, Bremen, Kunsthalle Bremen, 1954; *Max Liebermann in Hamburg*, exhibition catalogue, Hamburg, Hamburger Kunsthalle im BAT-Haus, 1968.

31. Sigrid Achenbach & Matthias Eberle, *Max Liebermann in seiner Zeit*, exhibition catalogue, Nationalgalerie Staatliche Museen Preußischer Kulturbesitz, Berlin, 1979.

32. Monika Tatzkow & Georg Graf zu Castell-Castell, 'Verlorene Schätze? Die Sammlung Liebermann ab 1933', in Martin Faass (ed.), *Verlorene Schätze. Die Kunstsammlung von Max Liebermann*, exhibition catalogue, Berlin, Liebermann-Villa am Wannsee, 2013, pp. 91–105; p. 93.

33. Julius Posener, 'Liebermann und die Froschmänner', *Der Tagesspiegel*, 5 December 1971.

34. For an overview of the history of the Max Lieberman Society, see Wasensteiner, *Wir feiern Liebermann!*

Chapter 12
From the palatial to the modern: industry and luxury in Habsburg Europe (pp. 270–97)

1. Alena Borovcová, *Kulturní dědictví dráhy císaře Ferdinanda* (*The Cultural Heritage of the Kaiser Ferdinands-Nordbahn*), Ostrava, Národní Památkový Ústav, 2021, p. 8.

2. Jan Županič, *Židovská šlechta podunajské monarchie* (*Jewish Nobility of the Danube Monarchy*), Prague, Lidové Noviny, 2012, p. 579.

3. Roman Sandgruber, *Rothschild: Glanz und Untergang des Wiener Welthauses*, Vienna, Molden Verlag in Verlagsgruppe Styria GmbH & Co., 2018, pp. 85–6.

4. Ibid., p. 350; Destailleur later designed Waddesdon for Ferdinand de Rothschild, and a palace in Vienna for Albert de Rothschild.

5. Županič, *Židovská šlechta*, p. 582.

6. Vilém Plaček & Magda Plačková, *Šilheřovice v historii a současnosti* (*Šilheřovice in History and Present*), Šilheřovice, Šilheřovice local council, 2006.

7. The sculpture in Schillersdorf is different from a sculpture with the same subject in Vienna; formal correspondences can be found with the works of Henri Chapu for the Château de Chantilly. However, the work is not included in the list of works by this sculptor (Octave Fidière, *Chapu, sa vie et son œuvre*, Paris, E. Plon, Nourrit et Cie, 1894).

8. For example, A. J. Downing, *Cottage Residences; or a Series of Designs for Rural Cottages and Cottage Villas and their Gardens and Grounds*, London, 1844; J. C. Loudon, *Encyclopedia of Cottage, Farm and Villa Architecture*, London, Longman, 1833.

9. Provincial Archives in Opava, Velkostatek Schillersdorf, box 22.

10. Provincial Archive in Opava, Schillersdorf Estate Fund: Collection of building plans of the former Rothschild estate Schillersdorf, inventory no. 387.

11. The Rothschild Archive, 'Evelina de Rothschild; September 9th, 1865', 000/23.

12. 1697–1728 (designed in 1697; construction completed in 1728); designed by Johann Lucas von Hildebrandt and Johann Bernhard Fischer von Erlach.

13. Županič, *Židovská šlechta* p. 306.

14. Ibid.

15. Antonín Ugwitz, *Z minulosti města Tovačova a okolí* ('From the Past of the Town of Tovačov and its Surroundings'), Prostějov, V. Horák, 1907, p. 160.

16. On the topic in detail, see Ivo Hlobil & Eduard Petrů, *Humanismus a raná renesance na Moravě* (*Humanism and the Early Renaissance in Moravia)*, Prague, Academia, 1992, pp. 107–15.

17. Recognising the importance of the commission, Fleischer published about it in detail, see Max Fleischer, 'Schloss Tobitschau in Mähren', *Zeitschrift des österreichischen Ingenieur – und Architekten – Vereins. LVII. Jahrgang*, vol. 35, Vienna, 1 September 1905, pp. 489–95.

18. Leoš Mlčák & Karel Žurek, *Stavebně historický průzkum zámku Tovačov* ('Architectural and Art-Historical Survey of the Chateau in Tovačov'), Olomouc, 2002.

19. Hana Holásková, 'Stavební a umělecká historie zámku v Tovačově' ('Architectural and Artistic History of the Chateau in Tovačov'), bachelor's thesis, Faculty of Arts, Masaryk University, Brno, 2009, p. 45.

20. Borovcová, *Kulturní dědictví dráhy císaře Ferdinanda*, pp. 11–12.

21. Michaela Ryšková, *Brno's Textile Heritage*, Ostrava, National Heritage Institute, 2018.

22. *Wohnungskultur* ('Housing Culture') was a magazine published in 1924–5 in both Czech and German. The editorial board was based in Brno and consisted of Jan Vaněk, Bohumil Markalous, Ernst Wiesner and Adolf Loos. The editors borrowed the name of this lecture series from the title of Le Corbusier's 1923 book, as they identified with his principles.

23. See especially Hermann Muthesius, *Das Englische Haus*, Berlin, Ernst Wasmuth, 1904.

24. This is an axonometric depiction from the period from 1927, which has been preserved in the archives of the Architecture Department of the Brno City Museum.

25. Iveta Černá, Kateřina Konečná, Veronika Lukešová, Jakub Pernes, Petr Svoboda, Petra Svobodová & Lucie Valdhansová (eds), *Exploring the History of the Textile Industrialists in Brno: Löw-Beer, Stiassni, Tugendhat*, Brno, Museum of the Brno Region, 2017, p. 20.

26. Iveta Černá & Dagmar Černoušková (eds), *Mies in Brno: Tugendhat House*, Brno, Brno City Museum, 2018, p. 28.

27. From a lecture by Grete Tugendhat in 1969 at Brno's House of Arts.

28. For more detail, see notes 23 & 24; most recently in Iveta Černá & Dagmar Černoušková (eds), *Tugendhat: Ludwig Mies van der Rohe, Realisation in Brünn*, Brno, Brno City Museum, 2018; Daniela Hammer-Tugendhat, Ivo Hammer & Wolf Tegethoff (eds), *Tugendhat House: Ludwig Mies van der Rohe*, Basel, Birkhäuser, 2015.

29. This company also supplied furniture to the Müller Villa in Prague, designed by Adolf Loos.

30. Karel Teige, *Nejmenší byt* ('The Minimal Dwelling'), Prague, Václav Petr, 1932, p. 20.

31. Justus Bier, 'Can One Live in the Tugendhat House?', *Die Form* 6, vol. 10, 1931, pp. 392–3; Walter Riezler, 'Commentary on the article by Justus Bier', *Die Form* 6, vol. 10, 1931, pp. 393–4; Grete & Fritz Tugendhat, 'The Residents of the Tugendhat House Speak Out', *Die Form* 6, vol. 11, 1931, pp. 437–8; Luwig Hilberseimer, 'Epilogue to the Discussion about the Tugendhat House', *Die Form* 6, vol. 11, 1931, pp. 438–9.

Chapter 13
Trent Park: a house under German occupation (pp. 298–311)

1. On the Sassoons, see Joseph Sassoon, *The Global Merchants: The Enterprise and Extravagance of the Sassoon Dynasty*, London, Allen Lane, 2022; also: Esther da Costa Meyer & Claudia Nahson, *The Sassoons*, New Haven, Yale University Press, 2023.

2. The history of Sassoon ownership of Trent Park given here follows Peter Stansky, *Sassoon: The Worlds of Philip and Sybil*, New Haven, Yale University Press, 2012, p. 63. For Park Lane, see Marc Fecker, 'Sir Philip Sassoon at 25 Park Lane: The Collection of an Early Twentieth-Century Connoisseur and Aesthete', *Journal of the History of Collections*, vol. 31, March 2019, pp. 151–70.

3. Cited after Robert Boothby, *I Fight to Live*, London, Victor Gollancz, 1947, p. 49.

4. 'Trent Park II', *Country Life*, 17 January 1931.

5. Robert Boothby, *Recollections of a Rebel*, London, Hutchinson, 1978, p. 72.

6. Cecil Roth, *The Sassoon Dynasty*, London, Robert Hale, 1941, p. 270.

7. Adrian Tinniswood, *The Long Weekend: Life in the English Country House Between the Wars*, London, Random House, 2016, p. 92.

8. For a detailed study, see J. G. P. Delaney, *Glyn Philpot: His Life and Art*, Farnham, Ashgate, 1999.

9. Cited after Tinniswood, *The Long Weekend,* p. 92.

10. Philip Sassoon, foreword to *Loan Exhibition of English Conversation Pieces; in Aid of the*

Royal Northern Hospital at 25 Park Lane, March 4th to 30th (inclusive), exhibition catalogue, London, 1930 [unpaginated].

11. Boothby, *I Fight to Live*, p. 50.

12. Ibid., p. 49.

13. Chris Bryant, *The Glamour Boys: The Secret Story of the Rebels who Fought for Britain to Defeat Hitler*, London, Bloomsbury Publishing, 2020.

14. Susan Ronald, *Hitler's Aristocrats: The Secret Power Players in Britain and America who Supported the Nazis, 1923–1941*, Stroud, St. Martin's Publishing Group, 2023.

15. Roth, *The Sassoon Dynasty*, p. 270.

16. Bryant, *The Glamour Boys*, p. 244.

17. Sandy Kidd, Principal Archaeology Advisor (London Planning Group), Historic England, to Mr. Andy Bates, 14 February 2017. For a complete history of its wartime role, see Helen Fry, *The Walls Have Ears: The Greatest Intelligence Operation of World War II*, New Haven, Yale University Press, 2019; Sönke Neitzel (ed.), *Tapping Hitler's Generals: Transcripts of Secret Conversations, 1942–45*, Barnsley, Frontline, 2007. Here and elsewhere, I draw on primary research and my interviews across fifteen years with surviving secret listeners.

18. For his biography, see Helen Fry, *Spymaster: The Man Who Saved MI6*, Newhaven, Yale University Press, 2021.

19. References to Trent Park as Camp 11 in WO 208/3504.

20. SRN 1, 23 December 1939, WO 208/4141.

21. Interrogation reports dated 8 January 1940 & 19 January 1940, WO 208/5158.

22. Interrogation report, 8 January 1940, WO 208/5158. For more detailed research on the case of Erich May and the relationship between Trent Park and Bletchley Park, see Fry, *The Walls Have Ears*, pp. 33–5.

23. *The History of Hut Eight*, p. 25, HW 25/2.

24. Godfrey to Davidson (DMI), 7 January 1941, WO 208/5621.

25. Lustig completed the manuscript of a memoir, *My Lucky Life*, shortly before his death in 2017. He did not serve in Trent Park but one of its sister sites. Yet he consciously spoke also for those who remained silent, writing his memoir only after he knew that the files had been declassified, as he had signed the Official Secrets Act. In the memoir he says that he reflected the experience of the secret listeners across all three sites.

26. 'Intelligence from Prisoners of War', section 122, AIR 40/2636.

27. Matthew Sullivan, *Thresholds of Peace: German Prisoners and the People of Britain, 1944–1948*, London, Hamish Hamilton 1979, pp. 51–2.

28. GRGG 130, 17–23 April 1944, WO 208/5016.

29. Chiefs of Staff memorandum, COS(43) 592 (O), entitled 'German Long Range Rockets', section 3: 'First Report of the Long range Rockets', 29 September 1943, CAB 80/75.

30. The conversation took place on 22 March 1943 and was reproduced in a Chiefs of Staff memorandum, COS(43) 592 (O), entitled 'German Long Range Rockets', section 4: 'Von Thoma's Evidence', 29 September 1943, CAB 80/75.

31. Ibid.

32. The photographs were analysed at RAF Medmenham at Danesfield House in Buckinghamshire.

33. For a more detailed argument and evidence that led to the bombing of Peenemünde, see Fry, *The Walls Have Ears*, pp. 50–171. The view that the bugged conversations acted as the final trigger for the bombing of Peenemünde is supported by historian Max Hastings in *The Secret War: Spies, Codes and Guerrillas 1939–1945*, London, 2016, p. 421.

34. Lieutenant Colonel Pryor to Rawlinson, 10 August 1944, WO 208/3437.

35. SRGG 209, 10 July 1943, WO 208/4165.

36. GRGG 189, 8–9 September 1944, WO 208/4364.

37. '"Eric Mark", Obituary', *The Times*, 21 November 2020.

38. Ibid.

39. GRGG 311, 7 June 1945, WO 208/4178; the belief that the photographs were faked was still circulating that summer. See GRGG 344, 21 August 1945, p.14, WO 208/4178.

40. GRGG 314 in WO 208/4178

41. 'Some of the prisoners held at Special Camp 11': www.specialcamp11.co.uk/Generalleutnant%20Curt%20Siewert.htm [accessed 25 September 2023].

42. For a discussion of these issues see Fry, *The Walls Have Ears*, pp. 253–8.

Chapter 14
An American postscript (pp. 312–23)

1. Our thanks to Tobias Brinkmann, Heather Ewing, Jaclyn Granick and Laura Leibman for their feedback on this chapter.

2. Theodore Rosengarten & Dale Rosengarten (eds), *A Portion of the People: Three Hundred Years of Southern Jewish Life*, Columbia, University of South Carolina Press, 2002, pp. 102–3.

3. Charles Monaco, *Moses Levy of Florida: Jewish Utopian and Antebellum Reformer*, Baton Rouge, Louisiana State University Press, 2005, Chapter 7.

4. Stanley Nadel, *Little Germany: Ethnicity, Religion, and Class in New York City*, Urbana, University of Illinois Press, 1990. On the problematic nature of these categories, see Tobias Brinkmann, '"German Jews"? Reassessing the History of Nineteenth-Century Jewish Immigrants in the United States', in Ava F. Kahn & Adam Mendelsohn (eds), *Transnational Traditions: New Perspectives on American Jewish History*, Detroit: Wayne State University Press, 2014, pp. 144–64.

5. Avraham Barkai, *Branching Out: German-Jewish Immigration to the United States 1820–1914*, New York, Holmes & Meier, 1994, pp. 22–4. See also Stephen Birmingham, *"Our Crowd": The Great Jewish Families of New York*, New York, Harper & Row, 1967.

6. See, above all, Clive Aslet, *The American Country House*, New Haven & London, Yale University Press, 1990, especially pp. v–vi on definitional differences; on the migration and translation of building and collecting styles from Europe to the US, see, for example, Michael Hall, '"Le Goût Rothschild": The Origins and Influences of a Collecting Style', in Inge Reist (ed.), *British Models of Art Collecting and the American Response: Reflections Across the Pond*, Farnham, Routledge, 2014, p. 113 for the Rothschild influence on J. Pierpont Morgan, and other essays in this book.

7. Emma Lazarus, 'In the Jewish Synagogue at Newport', written in 1871.

8. Eric Goldstein, *The Price of Whiteness: Jews, Race, and American Identity*, Princeton, Princeton University Press, 2006.

9. 'Mr Seligman Blackballed', *New York Times*, 15 April 1893.

10. Susie J. Pak, *Gentlemen Bankers: The World of J. P. Morgan*, Cambridge, Massachusetts, Harvard University Press, 2013, p. 91.

11. Aslet, *American Country House*, p. 24.

12. Ibid., p.148; citing also T. C. Turner, 'A Group of Farm Cottages', *American Homes and Gardens*, May 1914, p. 160.

13. For images and details of OHEKA, see Joan Cergold & Ellen Schaffer, with foreword by Nelson DeMille, *Oheka Castle* (in the 'Images of America' series), Charleston, South Carolina, Arcadia Publishing, 2012; for Otto Kahn, see Theresa M. Collins, *Otto Kahn: Art, Money, & Modern Time*, Chapel Hill & London, University of North Carolina Press, 2002.

14. For context, see Christina A. Ziegler-McPherson, *The Great Disappearing Act: Germans in New York City, 1880–1930*, New Brunswick, Rutgers University Press, 2021.

15. Peter Pennoyer & Anne Walker, *The Architecture of Delano & Aldrich*, New York, Norton Books, 2003.

16. Collins, *Otto Kahn*, p. 24. On *Bildung*, see above all Aleida Assmann, *Arbeit am nationalen Gedächtnis: Eine kurze Geschichte der deutschen Bildungsidee*, Frankfurt & New York, Campus, 1993.

17. Collins, *Otto Kahn*, pp. 96, 109–13.

18. This was Edgar Kaufmann jr's preferred spelling.

19. Edgar Kaufmann jr, with foreword by Mark Girouard, *Fallingwater: A Frank Lloyd Wright Country House*, New York & London, Abbeville Press, 1986, pp. 14–23, 172–4.

20. Ibid., p. 104.

21. Montefiore Mausoleum, Ramsgate; Eduardo Cahen d'Anvers Mausoleum, Torre Alfina; Morpurgo de Nilma Mausoleum, Villa Varda.

Biographies

Robert Bandy has worked as the custodian of Hughenden and the Disraeli collections for twelve years. He has an intimate understanding of Benjamin Disraeli and his life and appears regularly on television and radio to offer insight into this compelling character.

Hélène Binet is a Swiss–French photographer, who studied in Rome, is based in London and is internationally acclaimed for her photographs of both historic and contemporary architecture. She is a fervent advocate of analogue photography, working exclusively with film, and she believes that 'the soul of photography is its relationship with the instant'.

Juliet Carey is Senior Curator at Waddesdon Manor (National Trust / Rothschild Foundation), where she initiated the Jewish Country Houses project. She has curated exhibitions on subjects including Guercino, Jean-Siméon Chardin and Gustave Moreau, and has also published on subjects including Elizabethan portraits, eighteenth-century drawings, Sèvres porcelain and the history of collecting.

Silvia Davoli, a specialist in eighteenth- and nineteenth-century collections and patronage, is Head Curator at Strawberry Hill House and Garden, and Associate Researcher at the University of Oxford (Jewish Country Houses project).

Helen Fry has authored more than twenty-five books covering the social history of World War Two – and in particular British Intelligence and the secret war, espionage and spies – including *The Walls Have Ears* (2019), *Spymaster: The Man who Saved MI6* (2021) and *Women in Intelligence* (2023), all for Yale University Press. She appears frequently on TV and in documentaries, is the foremost authority on the secret listeners and the wartime eavesdropping programme at Trent Park and its sister sites, and the official biographer of MI6 spymaster Thomas Kendrick.

Jaclyn Granick is Senior Lecturer in Modern Jewish History at Cardiff University and Co-Investigator of the Jewish Country Houses project. She wrote the National Jewish Book Award-winning *International Jewish Humanitarianism in the Age of the Great War* (Cambridge University Press, 2021) and co-edited the 'Gendering Jewish Inter/Nationalism' issue of the *Journal of Modern Jewish Studies* (2022).

Abigail Green is Professor of Modern European History at the University of Oxford, a Fellow of Brasenose College and has led the Jewish Country Houses project since its inception. She is the author of the award-winning *Moses Montefiore: Jewish Liberator, Imperial Hero* (Belknap Press, 2010), and of *Fatherlands: State-Building and Nationhood in Nineteenth-Century Germany* (Cambridge University Press, 2001), as well as numerous edited collections, articles and book reviews.

John Hilary is an Honorary Professor at the School of Politics and International Relations at the University of Nottingham. His book, *From Refugees to Royalty: The Remarkable Story of the Messel Family of Nymans*, was published by Peter Owen Publishers in 2021.

Henri Lavagne, born in Paris in 1939, is an archaeologist and historian of art, specialising in the Roman period. He was a professor at the Sorbonne from 1977 to 2005, teaching the history of Roman Gaul. He is now a member of the Académie des Inscriptions et Belles-Lettres (Institut de France).

Dr Alice S. Legé, born in 1992, is Chief Curator at the Montmartre Museum and a member of the Society for the History of Collecting's steering committee. She curated the exhibition *The Jews, the Medici, and the Ghetto of Florence* at Palazzo Pitti (2023); has collaborated with the Louvre, UNESCO and the Royal Palace of Caserta; and is the author of *Gustave Dreyfus* (Officina Libraria, 2019), *Les Cahen d'Anvers en France et en Italie* (IFJD, 2022) and *La villa Altoviti ai Prati di Castello* (Officina Libraria, 2024).

Luisa Levi D'Ancona Modena (PhD, Cambridge University, 2004) is an Italian historian, living in Jerusalem, affiliated with the Jewish Country Houses project at the University of Oxford. Her publications include *La nostra vita con Ezio e Ricordi di guerra* (Florence University Press, 2021), *Jane Oulman Bensaude: Memorie* (Florence University Press, 2016), and numerous articles relating to Jewish philanthropy, women and civil society in Italy and southern Europe.

Pauline Prevost-Marcilhacy is an Associate Professor at the Université de Lille. A specialist on architecture, patronage and collections, she is the author of *Les Rothschild: bâtisseurs et mécènes* (Flammarion, 1995) and *Les Rothschild: une dynastie de mécènes en France* (3 volumes, Somogy, 2016).

Martin Sabrow was Director of the Leibniz Centre for Contemporary History in Potsdam (ZZF) between 2004 and 2021, and Professor of Modern and Cultural History at the Humboldt Universität Berlin. Currently a Senior Fellow at the ZZF and the spokesman for the Leibniz Research Alliance 'Value of the Past', he is the author of *Erich Honecker: Das Leben davor, 1912–1945* (C. H. Beck, 2016) and *Der Rathenaumord und die deutsche Gegenrevolution* (Wallstein, 2022).

Tom Stammers is Associate Professor of Modern European Cultural History at the University of Durham and Co-Investigator of the Jewish Country Houses project. He is the author of *The Purchase of the Past: Collecting Culture in Post-Revolutionary Paris, c.1790–1890* (Cambridge University Press, 2020), which won the 2021 RHS Gladstone Prize; has co-edited two volumes on Jewish dealers and Jewish collectors in Europe; and is finishing a new book on the Jewish cultural revival in early twentieth-century London.

Nino Strachey is a writer and historian, formerly Head of Research for the National Trust, and a relative of Frances, Countess of Waldegrave, who celebrated her Jewish heritage at Strawberry Hill. Nino is the author of *Rooms of Their Own* (Pavilion Books, 2018) and *Young Bloomsbury* (John Murray, 2022), which examine the creative environments formed by the Bloomsbury Group.

Petr Svoboda (CZ) is Branch Manager of the Methodological Centre of Modern Architecture in Brno, which is part of the Czech National Heritage Institute. He is involved in research projects focused on technology and twentieth-century architecture, and the co-editor of *Exploring the History of the Textile Industrialists in Brno* (Muzeum Brněnska, 2017).

Lucy Wasensteiner is Junior Professor of Art History and Provenance Research at the University of Bonn. From 2020 to 2024 she was Director of the Liebermann Villa in Berlin. Her research explores modern German art, National Socialist cultural policy and UK–German cultural relations and provenance research, notably with *Sites of Interchange: Modernism, Politics and Culture between Britain and Germany 1919–1955* (Peter Lang, 2021).

Index

Aberconway, Lord 237
Abrahamson, August 19, 329
Acerbi, Giovanni 149
Adele, Villa 327
Adler, Felix 174, 183
All Saints' Church, Tudeley 28, 29, 330
Ancona, Villa d' 32
Ancona, Viviano Levi d' 32
Andersen, Hans Christian 20–1, 329
Angeli, Heinrich von 69
Antonini-Brunner, Villa 35
Arendt, Hannah 32, 59
Arnhold, Eduard 253, 263
Arnhold, Johanna 263
Arnim, General Hans-Jürgen von 307, 308
Arnold, Matthew 199
Arons, Barthold 253
Ascott 22
Ashley Park 21
Ashton Wold 33
Aslet, Clive 316
Aston Clinton 126
Aumale, duc d' 85, 109, 116, 117, 142
Avigdor-Goldsmid, Sir Henry d' 28, 29, 330
Avigdor-Goldsmid, Lady d' 28, 29, 330

Bachelard, Gaston 205
Bad Ischl 20
Badeau, Adam 117
Baglioni, Dianira 152
Bailiffscourt 236
Baillie, Lady 237
Baker, Herbert 301
Barraud, Henry 19
Barth, Erwin 327
Bassani, Giorgio 37
Bassenge, Generalmajor 309
Baumgarten, Paul Otto 249, 258
Bearsted, Lady 20
Bearsted, Marcus Samuel, 1st Viscount 21
Bearsted, Sir Walter Samuel, 2nd Viscount 20, 21, 22, 27, 33, 329
Beauregard, Château de 35
Beazley, Samuel 102
The Beeches 315, 316
Beerbohm, Max 304
Behrens, Peter 215
Belcourt 315, 316
Belmont, August 315
Belmont, Caroline (née Perry) 315

Belmont, Oliver 315, 316
Belsen 311
Belvedere House 17
Bembo, Pietro 72
Bentinck, Lord George 66
Bentinck, Lord Henry 66
Bentley, Richard 97
Bérain, Jean 89
Berlin Secession 211, 249, 252
Bernhard, Karl 215
Bernhardt, Sarah 199
Bertaux, Émile 55
Berthelin, Armand 82
Bethlenfalva, Elisabeth de (née Gutmann) 276
Bethlenfalva, Géza Erös de 276
Bettenfeld, Louis-François 193
Bevans 299
Bevis Marks Synagogue 9
Binet, Hélène 37, 38–41
Birnbaum, Pierre 191
Bismarck, Otto von 91
Bleichröder, Gerson von 91
Bletchley Park 28, 36, 306
Boccini, Giuseppe 162
Boffrand, Germain 153
Bonnat, Léon 157
Boothby, Robert 301, 303, 304
Bossi, Pietro 69
Boucher, François 131
Boulle, André-Charles 157
Boulogne-Billancourt, Château de 82, 85, 92, 193
Bourvallais, Paul Poisson de 155
Bradenham church 28
Bradenham Manor 60, 66, 68, 72, 73
Bradford, Lady 72
Bradley, Edith 180
Braham, Charles 117
Braham, Frances see Waldegrave, Lady Frances (née Braham)
Braham, John 100, 101–2, 101, 109, 110
Braham, John Hamilton 109, 110
Brandström, Elsa 327
Breguet, Abraham-Louis 54, 57
Brno 27, 35, 272, 274, 279–97, 279–96, 328
Brodersen, Alfred 249
Broomhill 21, 42–57, 42, 45–6, 48–9, 53
Brzezie 27
Budík, Miloš 285
Bullet, Jean-Baptiste 155
Bullet, Pierre 155

Bunce Court 33
Burton, Decimus 50
By-the-Sea 315
Byron, Lord 67–8, 73

Cahen d'Anvers 28, 144–59
Cahen d'Anvers, Albert 145
Cahen d'Anvers, Alice 144
Cahen d'Anvers, Charles 23, 156–7
Cahen d'Anvers, Christina (née Spartali) 146, 148, 149
Cahen d'Anvers, Clara (née Bischoffsheim) 145
Cahen d'Anvers, Édouard 145, 146, 147, 149, 152, 157, 159
Cahen d'Anvers, Elisabeth 144
Cahen d'Anvers, Hugo 149
Cahen d'Anvers, Louis 23, 145, 146, 147, 153, 155–7, 159
Cahen d'Anvers, Louise (née de Morpurgo) 146, 155, 157
Cahen d'Anvers, Meyer Joseph 145–7
Cahen d'Anvers, Raphaël 145
Cahen d'Anvers, Rodolfo 149, 152, 157
Cahen, Meyer Joseph 145
Cannadine, David 33
Cardoso, Isaac 70
Carew, John Edward 46, 51
Carlo Alberto of Piedmont 145
Carolus-Duran 157
Carrobio, Helene Countess di 277
Caruso, Enrico 320
Casson, Sir Hugh 57
Catholics 16, 28, 35, 50, 82, 327
Cavalieri, Enea 168
Cellini Bell 142, 143
Chagall, Marc 28, 29, 330
Chamonard, Joseph 193
Champs-sur-Marne, Château de 23, 144–59, 153–4, 158, 324
Chapman, P. 116
Chapu, Henri 274
Charsley, Frederick 136
Chirac, Auguste 155
Choltitz, General von 309
Chute, John 97
Clarke, Colonel Stephenson 244
Clement VII, Pope 72
Cobb, Edward 103
Cohen, Albert 36–7
Cohen, Robert Waley 33
Collins, Theresa 319
Colonia Agricola 174, 180

Colonie Alsen 249, 253, 258
Colyer-Fergusson, Sir Thomas 329
Comber, James 244
Conrad, Wilhelm 253
Conway, David 101
Cordier, Charles 89
Corsini, Tito 157
Courances, Château de 22–3, 130, 324
The Cousinhood 45, 329
Crawford, Lord 34
Crédit Mobilier 83
Croft Castle 330
Croft, Fred 330
Crüwell, General Ludwig 307
Cuypers, Pierre 26, 324

Dairnvaell, Mathieu Georges 83, 83
Damer, Anne 100
Damrosch, Frank 180
Daudet, Léon 199
Davillier, Jean Charles 82
Delamotte, Philip Henry 108, 111, 117
Delano and Aldrich 319
Denniston, Alastair 306
Desanges, Louis 116, 117
Desart, Lady (née Bischoffsheim) 19
Desgots, Claude 155
Destailleur, Gabriel-Hippolyte 23, 130–1, 153, 155, 274, 324
Destailleur, Walter-André 23, 147, 155, 157
Deutsch, Lili 219
Devey, George 22, 126
Devis, Arthur 303
Devonshire House 301
Dighton, Robert 101
Disraeli, Benjamin 28, 58–79, 58, 103
D'Israeli, Isaac 28, 60, 67–8, 69, 72, 73
D'Israeli, James 60, 67
D'Israeli, Maria 60
Disraeli, Mary Anne (née Viney) 66, 67, 73, 73, 79
D'Israeli, Sarah 60, 72
Dittmar, Generalleutnant 311
Doornburgh 16, 192
Downton Abbey 37
Drage, Sir Benjamin 33–4
Dreyfus, Captain Alfred 155, 174, 191, 191
Dreyfus, Auguste 21
Drummond, William 72
Drumont, Édouard 29, 89, 155, 159

Duban, Félix 85
Duchêne, Achille 147, *154*
Duchêne, Henri 147, *154*, 155–6
Dumas, Alexandre 155
Duncan, Isadora 199

East Cliff Lodge 9, 14–15, *14*
East Tytherley Manor 17
Eckert, Reinhold 269
Edward VII, King 29, 138, *138*
Efrons 18
Eichhorn (Veveří) Castle 328
Eiffel, Gustave 199
Einsteinhaus 327
Eisler brothers 284
Elkan, Sophie 329
Engel, Joseph 51
Engels, Friedrich 83
Ephrussi de Rothschild, Villa
    324–5
Errera, Isabella Goldschmidt 162
Erreras 27
Esher, Lord 34
Esslinger, Anna 33
Evill, Norman 234, 235
Exner, Karel 274

Falcieri, Tita 68, *68*
Falkenhausen, General Alexander
    von 32, *33*, 324
Falkensee Museum 327
Fallières, Armand 199
Fallingwater 28, 320–3, *321–3*
Fauré, Gabriel 204
Favre, Jules 91
Ferrières, Château de 23, 27, 29,
    80–95, *80*, *85–9*, *91*, *94–5*,
    126, 324
Fitz-James, Count Robert Charles
    Henri de 276
Fitz-James, Rosalie de (née
    Gutmann) 276
Fleischer, Max 277, 278
Flohr, Friedrich 275
Fontane, Theodor 207
Forster, Friedrich 180, 183
Fortescue, Chichester 111, *116*, 117
Fortunato, Giustino 180
Fouché, Joseph 82
Fould, Achille 83
Fould, Benoît 83
Fraenkel, Dr Max 327
Franchetti, Alice (née Hallgarten)
    161, *168*, 169, 174–5, *175*, 180, 183
Franchetti, Giulio 161, 162, 163
Franchetti, Baron Isaac 161, 162
Franchetti, Leopoldo 19, 161, 163,
    168–9, *168*, 174, 180, 183
Franchettis 19
Francis I, Emperor 273
Franco-Prussian War 91
Franks, Naphtali 17
Franz Josef, Emperor 18, 138
Freeze, ChaeRan 33
Freienwalde, Schloss 26, 206–27,
    206, *208–9*, *212–13*, *216*, *218*,
    220, *222–3*, *225–6*, 327
French Revolution 18, 81, 131, 136
Friedlaender-Fuld, Fritz von 221
Fuchs, Bohuslav 280
Fuchs, Eduard 283
Fürstenberg, Carl 219–20

Gainsborough, 138
Gambetta, Léon 185

Garibaldi, Giuseppe 145, 149, 175
Garnier, Charles 193
Gartenberg, Villa 328–9
Gartner, Jakob 277
Gascq, Paul Jean-Baptiste 193
George, Sir Ernest 233
Gerlach, Hellmut von 210
Gestetner, Henny 34
Gestetner, Sigmund 34
Giacometti, Alberto 322
Gideon, Samson 17
Gilbert, Arthur (né Abraham
    Bernstein) 313
Gilbert, Rosalinde 313
Gilly, David 207, 214
Girouard, Mark 320
Gissey, Henri *131*
Gladstone, William 79
Godfrey, Admiral John 306
Godman, Frederick DuCane 244
Goebbels, Joseph 32
Goering, Hermann 305
Goethe, Johann Wolfgang von *71*
Goldberger, Alice 34
Goldman sisters 180, 183
Goldmid, Asher 17
Goldsmid, Benjamin 17
Goldsmid, Isaac Lyon 17
Goldsmids 101
Gompertz, Benjamin 53
Goncourt brothers 15, 155, 159
Goncourt, Edmond de 85
Goodman, Paul 9
Goudstikker, Jacques 32
Grant, Charles Jameson *50*
Grant, Francis *21*, 67, 109
Grant, W. J. 55
Grassalkovich-kastély 328
Grondona, Lieutenant Colonel St
    Clare 309
Gros, Pierre 198
Grüneburg 126
Grünewald, Isaac 329
Grünewaldvillan 329
Guardi, Francesco 122, 127
Guette, Château de la 33
Gunnersbury 126
Gunzburgs 33
Gutergötz 27
Gutmann, David 32, 276–8
Gutmann, Wilhelm 276–7, 279,
    280
Gutmanns 35, 275

Haar, Kasteel de 26, *26*, 324
Haber, Samuel de 22, 130, 324
Habsburg railway 271
HaCohen, Michal *52*
Hahn, Hermann *31*
Hahn-Warburg, Lola 33
Hallgarten, Adolph 169
Hallgarten, Constanze 180
Hallgartens 315
Halton Hall 27, 36, 126
Hancke, Erich 263
Handyside, Andrew 111
Harcourt, George Granville 102, 117
Harden, Maximilian 221
Hart, Moses 17
Hart, Solomon Alexander 14, *51*, 55
Hatvany-Deutschs 20
Hauptmann, Gerhart 217, 225
Hayward, Abraham 101
Hendersons 244
Hesse, Lucien 192

Highclere Castle 37
Highdown 244, 330
Hiller-Steinbömer, Gustav *220*
Hindley, Charles 103, 116
Hirsch, Maurice de 35, 328
Hirschsprung, Heinrich 329
Hittorff, Jacques Ignace 146
Hittorff, Jakob 84
Hochried 27
Hölderlin, Friedrich 205
Holste, Generalleutnant 311
Holy Thorn Reliquary 142, *142*
Homolle, Théophile 204
Hönigsberg, Israel Hönig von 273
Houghton Hall 23, 330
Huet, Christophe 157
Hughenden Manor 58–79, *60*,
    62–6, *70*, *73–7*, 329
Hunt, Leigh 101
Hunt, Richard Morris 315, *316*
Hussey, Christopher 236, 302
Hutton, Kurt (né Hübschmann) *34*

Ibels, Henri-Gabriel *191*
Ightham Mote 329
International Style 27
Isleworth 17

Jacoby, Johann 79
Janner, Lord 57
Janssen, Benno 320
Jaulmes, Gustave 192, 193
Jebb, Sir Richard 299
Jewish Naturalisation Act 17, *17*
Jødeland 20
Johnson, Frances Benjamin *190*
Johnson, John 111
Joseph II, Emperor 18
Josephus 72
Josz, Aurelia 174, 180
Judith Lady Montefiore College
    14, *14*

Kahlo, Frida 321
Kahn, Addie 317
Kahn, Otto *312*, 317–20
Kaiser Ferdinand Northern Railway
    271, *272*, 276, 278, 279, 297
Karbowsky, Adrien 193
Kaufmann, Edgar Jonas 320–2,
    323
Kaufmann, Edgar Jr 322
Kaufmann, Liliane 320–2, *323*
Kaufmanns 28
Kelk, John 111
Kendrick, Thomas Joseph 305–8,
    311
Kent, William 23
Kerr-Lawson, James 183
Kérylos, Villa *24*, 184–205, *184*,
    186–90, *194–7*, *200–3*, 324,
    325
Kessler, Harry Graf 263
Kindertransport 33
Kitzinger, Ernst 205
Kolmar, Gertrud 327
Koszyłowce 15, 28, *28*, 35, 37
Kraaz, Johannes 214, *215*
Kronenberg, Jan 329
Kronenberg, Leopold 27
Küenburg, Franz Count 277
Kuenen, Abraham 72
Kullrich, Franz *220*
Kurska, Anna (née Modzelewska) 37
Kurski, Jarosław 28, 37

Lagerlöf, Selma 329
Lamb, Charles 101
Lamb, Edward Buckton 67, 73, *73*
Lami, Eugène *80*, 81, 85, *86–9*,
    89, 90
Lamm, Carl Robert 26, 329
Landhausgarten Dr Max Fraenkel
    327
Latham, Sir Paul 304
Latter, Lucy 175, 180
Lattes, Bruno 327
Lattes, Villa 327
Lazarus, Emma 315, *316*
Lazarus, Moses 315
Lear, Edward 110, *110*
Lederer, Ernst 306, 309, *310*
Leeds Castle 237
Leo XIII, Pope 149
Leon, Sir Herbert 28, 33
Leopoldskron, Schloss 328
Levy, Moses 314
Libeskind, Daniel 37
Lichtwark, Alfred 249, 253, 258,
    259, 263
Liebermann, Joseph 253
Liebermann, Käthe 252, 259, 264,
    265
Liebermann, Louis 252
Liebermann, Martha (née
    Marckwald) *251*, 252, 264, 265
Liebermann, Max 21, 35, 249–69,
    250–1, *262*
Liebermann Villa 248–69, *248*,
    252, *254–62*, *265–8*, *326*, 327
Lietz, Hermann 175, 180
Lightfoot, John 72
Lind, Jenny 110
Lindo, E. H. 72
Lingfield children 34
Lion, Hilde 33
Lloyd Wright, Frank 27, 320–1
Löb, Jakob 18
Loder, Sir Edmund 244
Loder, Wilfred 244
Loeb, James 27, 180
Loewe, Louis 49
Loos, Adolf 280
Lopes, Manasseh Masseh 17–18
Lousada, Emanuel Baruh 17, 18
Löw-Beer, Alfred 283, 284
Lustig, Fritz 306, 311
Lutyens, Edwin 233, 234
Lyon, Myer 101

Macaulay, Thomas Babington 97
Maclise, Daniel 67, 68, *68*
Magni, Pietro 117
Malleson, Hope 180
Mariette, Jean *154*
Marini, Cleomone 163
Maristow House 17
Mark, Eric 306, 309, *310*
Massarani, Tullo 29
Massé, Victor 90
Maulnier, Thierry 199
Maurras, Charles 199
May, Erich 306
Mayer, Astorre 33
Mayer, Leo Ary 57
Melchett, Villa 22, *23*
Melchiors 20–1, 329
Mentmore 34–5, *36*, 84, 126
Merton 17

Messel, Alfred 28, *31*, 232–3, *233*, 247, 258
Messel, Anne 245
Messel, Leonard 234, 236–7, 244–5
Messel, Lina *241*
Messel, Ludwig 229, 232, 237, 244, 245, 247
Messel, Maud 234, 236–7
Messel, Muriel 244
Messel, Oliver 245, 247
Messel, Rudolph 234, 247
Messiah, Aaron 324
Metsu, Gabriel 126
Mewès, Charles 325
Mewès and Davis 27
Meysenbug, Malwida von 169
Middleton, James 67
Mies van der Rohe, Ludwig 283–4, 297
Mocatta, David 9
Moïse, Theodore Sidney *314*
Monaldeschi della Cervara, Sforza 149, 152
Mond, Alfred 22, *23*
Mond, Ludwig 20, 29
Monds 22, 27
Monk's House 330
Montefiore, Sir Francis 276, 330
Montefiore, Lady Judith 9, 14
Montefiore, Marianne (née Gutmann) 276
Montefiore, Sir Moses 9, 14, *52*
Montefiore synagogue *8, 9, 10–14,* 14, 330
Montefiores 27, 28, 36
Monteforte, Alexander Wielemans von 277
'La Montesca', Villa 22, *25,* 160–83, *160, 162, 164–7, 170–3, 175–9, 181–2,* 327
Montessori, Maria *176,* 180, 183
Mora 19, *20,* 329
Morgan, J. P. 316
Morgenthau, Henry Sr 316
Morpurgo de Nilma, Baron Carlo 327
Mortlake 17
Moses, Isaiah 314, *314–15*
Moses, Rebecca Isaiah (née Phillips) 314, *314*
Mosse, George 19
Mosse, Rudolf 19
Mosses 35
The Mote 21
Mottisfont Abbey 26, 330
Mouchy-le-Châtel 130
Moyne, Lord 236
Müller, Leopold *272*
Munch, Edvard *211*
Munk, Salomon 72
Munro, Ian Thomson 308

Nääs estate 19, 329
Namier, Lewis (né Ludwik Bernstein) 19, 35–6, 37
Napoléon III 81, 82, 83, 84, 90, 93, 101, 123, 130, 145
Näsby 26, 329
Nathan, Ernesto *162,* 180
National Trust 34, 57, 143, 244–5, 329
Nazis 27, 32–5, 225, 247, 269, 280, 297, 304–11, 321, 324–5, 327–8

Nebbia, Cesare 152
Nedelykov Moreira Architekten 269
Nemours, duc de 85
Neuffer, Generalleutnant 309
Neumark, Walter 279
Neutra, Richard 320
Nicoli, Carlo 155
Niemirowski, Józef (né Bernstein) 28
Niemirowski/Bernsteins 15
Noble, Matthew 110
Norden, Eduard 204
Nordheimer, Julia 169, 180
Norlind, Ernst 224
Norris, John 66, 67
Norwich, Viscount 34–5
Nosotti, Charles 103, 117
Nüll, Eduard van der 278
Nuttall, John 84
Nyenrode Castle 32
Nymans 26, 228–47, *228, 230–5, 237–43, 246,* 329

The Oaks 314
Oberschöneweide 28, *30–1*
OHEKA Castle 317–20, *317–19*
Ohmann, Friedrich 280
Olmsted Brothers 318
Oppenheim, Moritz Daniel 127
Oppenheims 253
Ottolenghi, Villa 327

Panama Scandal 155, *156*
Panti, Giovanni 163
Pariser Platz 252, *252,* 263–4, 269
Park Lane 299, *301*
Partini, Giuseppe 147, 149, 152, 157
Pasquier, Alain 198
Passaglia, Augusto 163
Paul IV, Pope 156
Paulus, Generalfeldmarschall 308
Paxton, Joseph 34, 81, 84, 85, 126
Peak House 17, 18
Pennell, Lieutenant 306
Penshurst Place 236
Pereire brothers 83, 84
Peter, Wenceslaus 204
Petzolt, Hans *142*
Pevsner, Nikolaus 236
Philippson, Franz 23, *23,* 32, 33, 324
Philippson, Mathilde (née Mayer) *23,* 32, 33, 324
Philips, Clara *42,* 55
Phillips, Henry Wyndham *111,* 116–17
Phillips, Sir Lionel 21
Philpot, Glyn 302
Pignatelli, Villa 327
Pius II, Pope 72
Pius IX, Pope 149
plutocrats 29, 32
Poggi, Giuseppe 162
Pointe des Fourmis *190,* 193, 199
Poliakov, Lazar 27
Poliakovs 18, 33
Pompadour, Madame de (Jeanne Antoinette Poisson) 155, 157
Pontchartrain 21
Pontremoli, Emmanuel 185, *190,* 193, 198, 205
Porgès de Rochefort-en-Yvelines, Château 325

Porgès, Jules 21, 325
Port Lympne 27, 36, 301–2, *302,* 330
Posener, Julius 269
Pressburg Cup 142, *142*
Proust, Marcel 36, 192
Pryor, Lieutenant Colonel 309

Rabinowitz, Moritz 20, *23*
Radstock coalfields 102, 109
Randlords 21
Rathenau, Emil 30–1, 207
Rathenau, Walther 26, 28, 207–27, *211, 218, 224*
La règle du jeu 37, *37*
Reich, Lilly 283, 297
Reinach, Béatrice (née Camondo) 28
Reinach, Baron Jacques de 185
Reinach, Joseph 185
Reinach, Léon 198
Reinach, Salomon 185, 191, 205
Reinach, Théodore 19, 185–205, *191*
Reinhardt, Max 328
Renner, Franz 278
Renoir, Jean 37, *37*
Renoir, Pierre-Auguste *144,* 157
Repton, Sir Humphrey 299
Reynolds, Joshua 101, 117, *137,* 138
Ridolfi, Pietro 157
Riepl, Professor Franz 271
Riezler, Kurt 263
Riou, Édouard *91*
Rivera, Diego 321
Roberts, David 49
Roehampton 17
Rolighed 20–1, 329
Rosebery, Lord 34
Rothschild, Albert von 18, 274
Rothschild, Alfred de 27, 37
Rothschild, Aline de 299
Rothschild, Almina de 37
Rothschild, Alphonse de 92
Rothschild, Amschel 273
Rothschild, Anselm von 18, 274–5
Rothschild, Anthony 126
Rothschild, Béatrice Ephrussi de 199, 325
Rothschild, Betty de 81, *82*
Rothschild, Carl von 327
Rothschild, Dorothy de 34
Rothschild, Édouard de 92
Rothschild, Evelina de 90, 123, 275
Rothschild, Ferdinand de 122–43, *123, 139,* 275
Rothschild, Baroness Germaine de 33
Rothschild, Guy de 92–3
Rothschild, Hélène de 26, *26*
Rothschild, James de 34
Rothschild, James Mayer de 81–95, *82*
Rothschild, Leonora de 92
Rothschild, Lionel de *19,* 50, 244, 330
Rothschild, Marie-Hélène de 93
Rothschild, Baron Mayer de 84, 126
Rothschild, Miriam 33
Rothschild, Nathan de 81
Rothschild, Nathaniel von 274, *274*
Rothschild, Salomon Mayer von 18, 27, 123, 271, 273–4, 275

Rothschild, Schloss 328
Rothschild, Yvonne de 33
Rothschilds 18–19, 20, *21,* 29, 33, 34–5, 101, 315
Ruskin, John 109, 234
Russell, Maud (née Nelke) 26, 330

Sabatier, Paul 183
St James's Theatre 102, 109
Saint-Aubin, Charles Germain de 131, *131*
Saint-Simon, Henri de 83
Salomon, Otto 19
Salomon, Yoel Moshe *52*
Salomons, Sir David 44, 45, 47, 50–1, *50–1,* 53, 55, 57
Salomons, David Lionel 21, 43, 44, 45, *45,* 47, 49, 51, *52,* 53–7, *54*
Salomons, David Reginald 44, 49, 51
Salomons, Emma *42,* 51, 55
Salomons Estate *see* Broomhill
Salomons, Jeannette *42,* 51, 55
Salomons, Laura (née de Stern) 47, 54
Salomons, Philip 47, 49, 51
Salomons, Vera 43–5, *44,* 47, 49, 51, 54, 55, 57
Sampson, Noel *22*
Sans Souci 21
Sant, James *108,* 109
Sargent, John Singer *298*
Sassoon, Albert Abdallah *300*
Sassoon, David 21, *300*
Sassoon, Sir Edward 299
Sassoon, Elias David *300*
Sassoon, Sir Philip 27, *298,* 299, 301–5, *304*
Sassoon, Reuben 47
Sassoon, Sybil 23, 28, 330
Sassoons 21, 22
Sauerlandt, Max 263
Sazbó, István 37
Scalza, Ippolito 152
Schenkendorf 19, 35
Schiff, Jacob 316, 317
Schillersdorf 18, 126, 130, *273–5,* 274–5, 297, 328
Schinkel, Karl Friedrich 214, 216
Schmidt, Friedrich von 277
Schmitz, Hermann 214, 216–17
Schok, Hans 278
Schossberger, Baron Sigmund 328
Schossberger-Kastély 27, 328
Scott Fitzgerald, F. 320
Scudder, Vida 163, 183
Sea Marge 330
Seeckt, General Hans von 219
Seelow, Schweizerhaus 327
Seligman, Isaac *241*
Seligman, Jesse 316
Seligman, Joseph 315
Seligman, Theodore 316
Seligmans 315
Seneffe, Château de 23, *23,* 32, *33,* 324
'La Serena', Villa *22*
Sert, José María 302
Servaes, Franz 263
Shiprut, Esther 60
shoshonata 52
Sicardsburg, August Sicard von 278
Sichulski, Kazimierz 28, *28*

Siemens, Charles William 54
Siewert, Generalleutnant 311
Simon, Hugo 327
Simon, James 221
Skraenten 329
slavery 17–18
Solomon, Abraham *42*, 55
Solomon, Rebecca 55
Solomon, Simeon 55
Somerhill *29*, 36
Sonnino, Sidney 168
A Souvenir of Broomhill, Kent 46, *47, 49, 51, 53, 53*
Spence, William Blundell 109, 117
Speyer, Edgar 330
Splendid Paupers 29, 32, 32
Springer, Julius 253
Starling, J. P. *70*
Stead, W. T. 29, *32*
Stern, Ernesta 192
Stern, Sir Frederick 244, 330
Stern, Louis Antoine *190*
Stiassni, Alfred 279, 281–2
Stiassni Brothers 279–80, *280*
Stiassni, Gebrüder 279
Stiassni, Hermine 279, 280–2, 283, 297
Stiassni, Villa 279–82, *281–2*, 284, 297
Stiassnis 35, 328
Stoatley Rough 33
Stokes, George Henry 126
Stokes, Leonard 232
Strawberry Hill 28, 36, 96–117, *96*, *98–9, 104–8, 111–17*, 329
Strugach, Abraham *35*
Strugach, Leiba *35*, 328

Stüler Palace 252
Svanemøllen 20
Svyatoi Dukh 328

Talbot's Inch 19
Talleyrand, Hôtel de 82
Tapper, Walter 234–6
Tedeschi, Elena 162
Teige, Karel 297
Tela Umbra 174, *176*, 183
Tenniel, John *78*
Thiel, Ernest 329
Thoma, General Wilhelm Ritter von *307*, 308, 309
Tietz, Carl 277
Tilden, Philip 301–2
Titchfield, Lord 66
Tobitschau 32, 277–9, *277–8*, 297, 328
La Torelle 320
Torre Alfina 144–59, *150–1*, 327
Torre Clementina, Villa *190*, 192
Toscanini, Arturo 320
Toussenel, Alphonse 83
Townhill Park 36
Trench, Lieutenant Colonel Bernard 306
Trent Park 27, 298–311, *303, 307, 310*, 329
Tring 126
Triqueti, Henri de 89
Tschudi, Hugo von 263
Tugendhat, Fritz 283
Tugendhat, Grete (née Löw-Beer) 283–4, 297
Tugendhat, Villa 283–97, *283–96*, 297

Tugendhats 35, 328
Tuker, Mildred 180
Turing, Alan 306
Turner, J. M. W. *14*
Twyman, John C. *14*
Tylney Hall 36, 330

Uhl, C. W. *314*
Uhlman, Diana 330
Unruh, Fritz von 221
Upton House 21, *22*, 329

Varda, Villa 327
Velázquez, Diego 237
Veronese, Bonifazio 237, *237*
Victoria, Queen 68–9, *70–1*, 72, 79, 138–9
Viel, Jean-Marie Victor 85
Viollet-le-Duc, Eugène 156
Vittorio Emanuele II 145, 152
Vivier d'Oie, Château du 27
Voysey, Charles 233

Waddesdon Manor 27, 34, 118–43, *118, 120–5, 128–35, 137–8, 140–3*, 329
Waldegrave, Lady Frances (née Braham) 28, 100–17, *100, 116–17*
Waldegrave, George, 7th Earl 100
Waldegrave, Admiral William 101
Wallace, Lady 142
Walls, G. L. *235*
Walpole, Horace 97, 100–3, 117, 142
Wannsee 20, 21, 35, 248–69, *248, 252, 254–62, 265–8*
Warburg, Aby *162*, 180
Warburg, Mary 174

Warburgs 33, 314–15, 327
Weinmann, Jakob Eduard 279
Weissenhof development 283
Welles, Orson 320
Wells, H. G. 29
Whistler, James Abbott McNeill *148*
Whistler, Rex 26, 301, 302, 304
Whiston, William 72
White House 33, 327
Wichert, Fritz 263
Wieniec 27, 329
Wiesner, Ernst 280–1, 283, 297
Wilfert, Franz 282
Wilhelm II 217
Willyams, Mrs Brydges 72, 73, 79
Winnington Hall 20
Wolff, Abraham 317
Woolf, Leonard 330
Woolf, Virginia 330
Worth Park 36, 330
Wren, Christopher 126
Wright, John Buckland *234*

Young England trilogy 61

Ziller, Ernst 180
Zoffany, Johann 303
Zorn, Anders 19, *20*, 329
Zorn, Emma (née Lamm) 19, *20*, 329
Zornsamlingarna 329
Zuylen, Baron Étienne van 324
Zuylen, Hélène (née de Rothschild) 324
Zweig, Stefan 221

Picture credits

The Tauber Institute Series for the Study of European Jewry

First published in The United States of America
in 2024 by Brandeis University Press
415 South Street, Waltham MA 02453,
brandeisuniversitypress.com

First published in Great Britain in 2024
by Profile Editions, an imprint of Profile Books Ltd,
29 Cloth Fair, London EC1A 7JQ
www.profileeditions.com

Printed and bound in Italy by LEGO SRL

1 3 5 7 9 10 8 6 4 2

Text design and layout: Eleanor Ridsdale
Project management: Angela Koo

Library of Congress Cataloging-in-Publication
Data available at https://catalog.loc.gov/

9781684582204

Jehuda Reinharz, General Editor
ChaeRan Y. Freeze, Associate Editor
Sylvia Fuks Fried, Associate Editor
Eugene R. Sheppard, Associate Editor

The Tauber Institute Series is dedicated to publishing compelling and
innovative approaches to the study of modern European Jewish history,
thought, culture, and society. The series features scholarly works
related to the Enlightenment, modern Judaism and the struggle for
emancipation, the rise of nationalism and the spread of antisemitism,
the Holocaust and its aftermath, as well as the contemporary Jewish
experience. The series is published under the auspices of the Tauber
Institute for the Study of European Jewry—established by a gift to
Brandeis University from Dr. Laszlo N. Tauber—and is supported, in part,
by the Tauber Foundation and the Valya and Robert Shapiro Endowment.

Jewish Country Houses is a designated Sarnat Library Book, published
in part with the support of the Sarnat Center, Brandeis University.

For the complete list of books that are available in this series, please see
https://brandeisuniversitypress.com/series/tauber